Also by Leigh Montville

The Mysterious Montague

The Big Bam

Ted Williams

At the Altar of Speed

Manute: At the Center of Two Worlds

Evel

The High-Flying Life of Evel Knievel:

American Showman, Daredevil, and Legend

LEIGH MONTVILLE

DOUBLEDAY

New York   London   Toronto   Sydney   Auckland

www.doubleday.com

DOUBLEDAY and the portrayal of an anchor with a
dolphin are registered trademarks of Random House, Inc.

Grateful acknowledgment is made to the following for
permission to reprint previously published material:

Dick Cavett: Interview from *The Dick Cavett Show,*
copyright © 1971, reprinted by permission of Dick Cavett.

FeelingRetro.com: Toy collectors' comments, reprinted by
permission of FeelingRetro.com.

The Montana Standard: "Citizens of Butte" letter, reprinted
by permission of *The Montana Standard,* Butte, Montana.

Rolling Stone: Excerpt from "King of the Goons"
by Joe Eszterhas from *Rolling Stone,* November 7, 1974,
copyright © 1974 by Rolling Stone LLC. Reprinted
by permission of *Rolling Stone* magazine.

Jacket design by Michael J. Windsor

Library of Congress Cataloging-in-Publication Data has
been applied for.

ISBN 978-0-385-52745-3

PRINTED IN THE UNITED STATES OF AMERICA

10 9 8 7 6 5 4 3 2 1

First Edition

For Colin Andrew Moleux
Born September 8, 2008

I had his action figure!! Mom picked it up for me at Amvets because she was too poor to buy me one new. My Evel came with broken parts . . . JUST LIKE THE REAL THING!

—Special Ed V, October 6, 2008,
WTOP message board

You can waste your time on the other rides
This is the nearest to being alive

—Richard Thompson, "Wall of Death"

Contents

Introduction

The first biography of Evel Knievel was written in the winter of 1970–71 in three days, maybe four, maybe five, hard to remember, in a house in Palm Springs, California, that was owned or borrowed or maybe just rented by George Hamilton, the actor. The sound of the typing—yes, an actual typewriter was used to do the job—was drowned out by the high-fidelity, 33⅓ vinyl majesty of a series of Strauss waltzes that were played constantly from the latest in stereophonic equipment, each note bouncing off the white walls and white ceilings and white furniture and out the open windows to the swimming pool, where assorted women sunbathed without the stifling confinement of clothes.

The first biography of Evel Knievel, of course, was a screenplay.

The writer was twenty-seven-year-old John Milius. He had been hired on the cheap, a flat fee of $5,000, and asked to pound out a script about a thirty-one-year-old motorcycle daredevil from Butte, Montana, who had begun—but only begun—to capture the attention of assorted pockets of the American public. The deal was enhanced by the delivery of some fine Cuban cigars, secured from Colonel Tom Parker, best known as the manager of singer Elvis Presley, and the promise that upon completion of his duties Milius would be treated to an afternoon of what he called "commercial affection" with one of the undressed women at the pool.

He tore into his work. A macho, firearm-loving graduate of the University of Southern California School of Film, frustrated by the fact that his asthma had kept him out of the Vietnam War, which he saw as the great historic moment of his time, Milius was part of a group of young writers, directors, and producers like Francis Ford Coppola, Steven Spielberg, and George Lucas who were in the first throes of success in the film industry. They were all grabbing ideas out of the air, slamming them down on paper, hurrying, hurrying, trying to get things done in a rush because they didn't know how long their good fortune would last.

Milius was in the midst of that hurry-hurry stretch of creativity. He had written part of the script for the movie *Dirty Harry*, starring Clint Eastwood, which soon would be released . . .

("I know what you're thinking—'Did he fire six shots or only five?' " Clint/Harry said in the most memorable monologue. "Well, to tell you the truth, in all this excitement, I've kind of lost track myself. But, being this is a .44 Magnum, the most powerful handgun in the world and would blow your head clean off, you've got to ask yourself one question, 'Do I feel lucky?' Well do ya, punk?")

. . . Work on *Jeremiah Johnson*, which would star Robert Redford, was pretty much finished, and Milius's next project was *The Life and Times of Judge Roy Bean*, which would star Paul Newman. The pieces of dialogue for *Apocalypse Now* ("I love the smell of napalm in the morning") already were floating around in his busy head. Evel Knievel fit in there quite well too.

The idea of a guy, some crazy son of a bitch, jumping over an ever-growing string of parked cars on a motorcycle was revolutionary, different, funky, extreme. The story offered a combination of noise, smoke, crashes, broken bones, white motorcycle leathers, American individualism, and a long middle finger lifted directly at all forms of authority. This was a definite plus in a time of long middle fingers everywhere pointed at all forms of authority. Add a dash of romance, maybe a warning about trying any of these stunts at home. Shake well. Pour.

This was fun.

"The whole thing was modern and absurd," Milius said years later. "This character going over trucks on his motorcycle, riding through flaming hoops and all that. I just settled down and did it. I played that one record of Strauss waltzes over and over again. (I love Strauss waltzes.) I wandered around the white furniture, white walls, felt I soiled anything I touched. There was a bumper pool table in the house. I took breaks. I learned how to play bumper pool."

This was a lot of fun.

Facts were not a problem. Milius had never met Evel Knievel and had never been to the copper-mining splendor/grime of Butte, Montana, but that didn't matter much. First of all, the foundation of Knievel's life story was filled with half-truths, semi-truths, and flat-out whoppers anyway, a collection of tall tales designed by the man himself to make people perk up and pay attention. He would say anything to make himself more marketable. Second, the task was not so much to write an actual portrayal of Evel Knievel's life, but to write a vehicle for George Hamilton to look very good on a motorcycle in the leading role. Hamilton had put the production together, hoping to energize a career that had grown fuzzy in the wilds of network television with a couple of canceled series. He wanted to add a little hair and grit to his perceived image as a well-tanned playboy.

Milius was handed a first script, written by someone else, but hated it and threw it into the swimming pool. (Hamilton eventually made him retrieve the soggy pages.) The basis for a new script was a long magazine article, a few interviews on first-generation videotape, and Milius's active imagination.

A disclaimer ("based on incidents in Evel Knievel's life"), tagged on the end of the story, allowed Milius to do just about anything. He invented characters, invented dialogue, invented scenes that never had happened in Knievel's life. He had a car disappear, swallowed into the hollowed-out, heavily tunneled ground of Butte, directly at an adolescent Knievel's feet (never happened). He had an aging rodeo cowboy die, thrown from a bull, right before Knievel's first jump (never happened). He took single sentences from Knievel's résumé and inflated them into fat, pop-art events, quite different from what actually happened.

The Milius version of the character had tongue planted well into cheek, wry and funny most of the time. A chase with the Butte police, Knievel on motorcycle, police in a too-slow patrol car, was played completely for laughs. The same was true for Knievel's courtship with his wife as he rode his cycle straight into a sorority house, past the stammering housemother, up the stairs to the second floor, through squealing, pajama-clad residents, and back down the stairs and out the front door with his bride-to-be holding on to him for dear imperiled life. A dwarf with a cowboy hat was written into the script as a friend of Knievel's. Knievel was written as a hypochondriac, a comic contrast to all of his experience with doctors and hospitals. The language often was outrageous. The paying customers all wanted to see Knievel "splatter," a comic-strip word that Milius used over and over again.

The story was told in a series of flashbacks as the hypochondriac, madcap risk-taker prepared for his longest jump of all, nineteen cars, all American cars, "not a Volkswagen or Datsun in the row," at the Ontario Motor Speedway. The ending, after Knievel successfully cleared the nineteen American cars, not a Volkswagen or Datsun in the row, showed him continuing to ride, flying through the air to the edge of the Grand Canyon, his biggest proposed jump of all, the ultimate challenge that he always promoted. Milius gave him these self-inflated words to say in closing:

> Important people in this country . . . celebrities like myself, Elvis, Frank Sinatra, John Wayne, we have a responsibility. There are millions of people that look at our lives and it gives theirs some meaning. People come out from their jobs, most of which are meaningless to them, and they watch me jump twenty cars, maybe get splattered. It means something to them. They jump right alongside of me . . . they take the bars in their hands and for one split second they're all daredevils. I am the last gladiator in the new Rome. I go into the arena and compete against destruction and I win. And next week I go out there and do it again. At this time, civilization, being what it is and all, we have very little choice about our life. The only thing really left to us is a choice about our death. And mine will be glorious.

Fade to credits.

Milius shoveled his work to Hamilton, who was staying at the Plaza Hotel in New York, in long daily telegrams. Hamilton pinned the telegrams to the hotel walls, delighted with each arrival. This was his exact vision of the movie. Milius was delighted that Hamilton was delighted. They thought they had put together a suitable motorcycle extension of *Easy Rider*, the movie that had been a recent cultural and box office hit and made stars out of Peter Fonda, Dennis Hopper, and Jack Nicholson.

Hamilton, as soon as he returned to Los Angeles, wanted to show the finished script to Knievel. He found him at the low-rent Hollywood Land Motel on Ventura Boulevard, holed up in a room with a Kotex pad wrapped around an injured leg and a bottle of Wild Turkey in close proximity. Hamilton later described the meeting in his autobiography *I Don't Mind if I Do*. The meeting did not start well. He said that Knievel told him to read the script out loud.

"I declined," Hamilton said in the book. "[I said,] 'I don't read scripts. I act them.'

"Read," Evel demanded and literally put a gun to my head. And cocked it. Read, he said. And so I read. For more than two hours. I gave the performance of a lifetime, as if it might be my last, which was clearly the case. Evel liked what he heard. He liked it so much that he began adopting John's fictionalized dialogue and style as his own, life imitating art this time. Thank my lucky stars. Problem was that Evel got so into it that he became as grandiose as a Roman emperor.

Fade to credits.

The movie was not a great hit. It was shot in Butte and Los Angeles, released in the summer of 1971. Critics didn't swallow Hamilton's change from pretty guy to tough guy. The public was diverted to films like *The French Connection, Billy Jack, Fiddler on the Roof, Summer of '42*, and *The Last Picture Show. Evel Knievel* mostly came and went, made a few bucks for everyone concerned, and was consigned to that long video afterlife that now exists for movies everywhere.

The big winner in the operation was the subject. He received only a reported $25,000 for his rights, but the value of the publicity that came from the movie was incalculable. He was splattered—nice word—across America. His name was spread everywhere in ads, on theater marquees, in casual conversation. The made-up story, added to his own story, pushed his exploits further into the main stage spotlight that he always had craved.

Milius, the screenwriter, finally met Knievel on the set in Los Angeles. He liked him well enough, but really didn't get to know him. Knievel showed him the scars from his assorted crashes, which Milius thought looked like so many zippers on a human body, strange to behold. Knievel tried to explain the sequence of surgeries, doctors going back through the same openings to readjust bent pins and bones after each calamity, but Milius got lost somewhere in the explanations.

More memorable was a story he heard about Knievel rather than from Knievel. This came from that promised afternoon of "commercial affection" that was the reward for finishing the script on time.

The woman in question was lovely, professional, and probably quite skilled, but Milius never really could be a judge of that. He was young, impetuous, and very fast in his affection. Left with a lot of time on the clock, the couple sat around and talked, covering a bunch of subjects. One of the subjects was Evel Knievel. The woman in question said she previously had been a gift to Knievel for a similar afternoon of commercial affection. She said it had been remarkable mostly for the client's instructions.

"You don't have to do anything special for me just because of who I am," the woman said Evel Knievel said. "I want to be treated like a normal, mortal man."

Milius was astounded by the words.

The real-life character was even more grandiose, more outrageous, more preposterous, had a larger ego, than the cartoon-style character in the movie. Wow. *You don't have to do anything special for me because of who I am.* That would be something a caliph, a count, okay, a Roman emperor or some other libidinous head of state might say. *It's okay. I want to be treated like a normal, mortal man.* Maybe the pope would say this to a member of the faithful, maybe a general to a private on KP. A man who rides motorcycles for a living?

Wow.

Who was this guy?

Almost forty years have passed since this first cockeyed tale of Evel Knievel played on the screen of the local movie theater, which no doubt has long since closed and now is a full-service pharmacy or purveyor of designer coffee drinks. The man himself died on November 30, 2007, succumbed to pulmonary fibrosis, a quite different death, at age sixty-nine, than anyone envisioned, and he now lies in a plot at the Mountain View Cemetery in Butte close to the fence, across busy Harrison Avenue from the Wal-Mart where his ex-wife Linda worked not so long ago.

Who was this guy?

Cue the Strauss waltzes. Tell those assorted women—they'd probably be in their sixties now—to put down their grandchildren and get back out by the pool. Clothing is optional.

Maybe we can figure it all out.

The typing begins. Again.

1 Video

He walks onto the black-and-white screen a few minutes after midnight wearing a zebra-striped leisure suit. There is a quick thought that something might be wrong with the television this late at night. Static of some kind in the neighborhood. An electrical malfunction. No, the stripes only move when Evel Knievel moves. This is his outfit.

He is a one-man test pattern. The collar on the leisure suit is exaggerated, Edwardian, huge. The pants flare out at the end, bell-bottoms. His white leather kick-ass boots, which stick out from the edges of the bell-bottoms, would be suitable for either a well-dressed gang fight or an open-ended night in a Las Vegas cocktail lounge. The stripes on the leisure suit—back to the stripes—are random, run every which way, as if somebody had splashed white paint across a black background. The effect is dramatic. He is a work of modern art, certainly a piece of work, a cat on the prowl.

He is here to be on *The Dick Cavett Show*. He has dressed for the occasion.

"My next guest is an incredible character," Cavett tells the studio audience at the Elysee Theater on West Fifty-eighth Street in New York City.

He's a motorcycle daredevil driver. All his life he's been doing death-defying feats. Death has nearly defied *him* several times. His longest jump was fifty yards, a fifty-yard jump over the fountains of Caesars Palace in Las Vegas. This jump did not go well. You may have read about it. Or seen some still photos of it. He has some film with him of what happened. He seems to spend his life, or what he has left of it, it sometimes seems to me, seeing what he can do to shorten it. Incredible things he does . . . Will you welcome the legendary Evel Knievel.

The Bob Rosengarden Orchestra plays "Daisy Bell" in the background, better known as "Bicycle Built for Two," a family standard written in 1892. The audience applauds. The "incredible character," the "motorcycle daredevil driver," walks across the stage with a slight limp in his left leisure-suited leg.

First impression: he is pool-hall handsome, good chin, prominent nose, steady eyes, sandy hair combed back, semi-serious sideburns. Self-confidence is not a problem. Second impression: if he came to the front door to pick up your daughter, left the engine running in the flashy car outside, he would make you nervous. Third impression: your daughter would be thrilled.

He shakes hands with the shorter Cavett, then turns and shakes hands with a middle-aged black man who wears glasses under a modest Afro. The middle-aged black man is jazz trumpet player Dizzy Gillespie, already finished, the first guest of the night. Dizzy Gillespie! Dizzy is smoking a cigarette.

Everyone sits down.

"How are you?" Cavett asks from behind his desk, then immediately laughs at the absurdity of his own first question.

How are you? How *are* you? Evel Knievel? How do you ask Evel Knievel, "*How are you?*" Significant stretches of his life have been spent in intensive care units. He has been in more hospitals than Dr. Christian Barnard or Marcus Welby, MD. He has more stitches in him than a Raggedy Ann doll, enough metal for a full Erector Set. How are you? His X-rays are his calling cards.

"Have you ever been hurt?" Cavett says, flummoxed.

"Yes, several times," Evel Knievel replies. "Several times."

The year is 1971. The month is August.

The interview has begun.

The Dick Cavett Show is the ABC entry in a three-network talk show race for the attention of the insomniacs of America at 11:30 p.m. Johnny

Carson talks behind a desk at NBC. Merv Griffin does the same at CBS. The Cavett show is third in the late-night ratings, but seen as the intellectual alternative. Cavett attracts the most interesting guests, the newsmakers, the provocative people of the day. The talkers actually talk rather than wink, blink, sing a song, tell a joke as they promote their next endeavor.

Groucho Marx previously sat in the brown leather chair at the side of this desk. Jimi Hendrix. Alfred Hitchcock. Kirk Douglas. Sonny and/ or Cher. Orson Welles. Satchel Paige. Bill Russell. Marlon Brando. Lester Maddox. John Kerry, the young Vietnam War resister. Jim Brown. Ingmar Bergman. Woody Allen. Joni Mitchell. Ann Landers. Truman Capote. Little Richard. Janis Joplin. Ralph Nader. Art Garfunkel. Dick Clark. Bette Davis. The list continues. John Lennon and Yoko Ono will be here within a month.

The thirty-two-year-old man in the zebra-striped leisure suit (who has been hurt several times) fits the chair as well as any of them. He is another emerging oversized figure of the moment. The movie about his life, starring George Hamilton, is in theaters across the country. He has played Madison Square Garden, the Astrodome, the Los Angeles Coliseum, a long list of arenas and stadiums and state fairs. He has talked, soared, flipped, bounced, skidded, and crashed his way into the public conversation.

CAVETT: Gee, I've heard so much about you . . . do I detect a slight
    hesitation in your walk?
KNIEVEL: When I got hurt in Las Vegas, I pushed my hips through
    my pelvis. That's what's known as a central protrusion fracture.
    And my left leg was pulled out. They put you in traction, pull
    you. That left hip did not come out. However, I've missed a
    jump like the Caesars Palace jump nine times in five years. And
    as a result of that, I've been operated on some twelve times . . .
CAVETT: When they say you've broken every bone in your body,
    they actually don't mean every bone . . . in your ear and every-
    where . . . but have you broken over a dozen?
KNIEVEL: Oh, yes. I imagine all the major bones except my
    neck . . .
CAVETT: All the major bones . . .
KNIEVEL: Both legs. Both arms. My back twice last year.
CAVETT: Where's the fun?

No one ever has done exactly what Evel Knievel does for a living. Trapeze artists and tightrope walkers and human cannonballs have made good money forever by challenging fate, by putting themselves in peril, Man versus the Grim Reaper, but he has brought the battle to modern dimensions, motorized it, wrapped it in a 1971 weird modern mix of sport and gasoline, showbiz and derring-do.

He drives his motorcycle at a high speed off a ramp, over assorted objects, mostly lines of cars, but also buses or trucks or the fountains at Caesars Palace, and he attempts to land on a ramp on the other side. The foundation of his success is failure. The more times he lands in an ambulance instead of on the specified ramp, the more times he is carted away for more reconstructive surgery, the more captivating his show becomes. There are no Harry Houdini tricks, no false bottoms or optical illusions. He makes the jump. Or doesn't. The times he doesn't make headlines.

> CAVETT: I know you're sick of being asked, "Why do you do it?" But why do you do it?
>
> KNIEVEL: That's a standard question everybody asks anyone, is why they do what they do . . .
>
> CAVETT: There are a lot of nice office jobs available . . .
>
> KNIEVEL: There are three mysteries to life: where we came from, why we do what we do, and where we're going to go. You don't know the answer to any of those questions, and I don't know the answer to any of them. So I never try to answer that. I do it because I'm Evel Knievel and there's something within me that makes me do it, and I don't try to figure it out, I just try to do it the best I can.
>
> CAVETT: Are you curious, would you ever like a psychiatrist to tell you why you . . .
>
> KNIEVEL: I've had a couple of them talk to me. They wound up talking to themselves.
>
> CAVETT: Do they come up with fancy theories, like you show your contempt for death by defying it and by tempting it and . . .
>
> KNIEVEL: They like to get me in a corner and look at me . . . I don't care what they want to talk about: the Vietnam situation, the financial situation in the United States of America, the . . . anything . . . the educational system. I talk to them about the stunt work and the life and death of it and how I feel about God, being religious or not, and they don't know what to think.

CAVETT: They're more likely to say that you have some hidden
   loathing of yourself . . .
KNIEVEL: A death wish maybe. I don't know. To me, life is a bore.
   Just doing nothing. I saw a guy working in that tunnel I came
   through here today. Why would a guy want to stand around in
   a tunnel for? Could you imagine wanting to work in a tunnel?
   He should get a motorcycle. Jump through the air. Breathe a
   little.

It is hard to say why Knievel has attracted America's attention. His
notoriety is a curious fit into a curious time. He is a young Elvis dropped
from a previous generation of pegged-pants, duck's-ass rebellion into the
Age of Aquarius, more about trouble and excitement than peace and love.
He even dresses like Elvis when he goes to work: white leather jumpsuits,
red-white-and-blue stars and bars on the chest, flashy belt buckle with
his initials on the front. He wears a cape. He carries a cane. Everything
he does is counter to the counterculture. He is showing off, not dropping
out, burning hydrocarbons instead of any kind of incense. There is not a
mellow bone, broken or unbroken, in his body.
   Maybe he fills a need. The Vietnam War is shit, has gone on forever.
The politicians, led by Richard M. "Tricky Dick" Nixon in the White
House, are shit. Authority of all kinds is shit. Society is shit. A dust of
negativity has settled over everything familiar. Cynicism rules. Maybe
there is a need for some muscle in the room, some noise, some unvar-
nished order. Move over, Maharishi. Get that sitar out of the way. Coming through. If the traditional heroes have disappeared, the soldiers and
policemen and buttoned-down business leaders, then maybe a vacancy
was opened on the pedestal. Maybe this self-invented hero with his
self-invented name and his self-invented challenges has taken the spot.
Someone was bound to get the job.

CAVETT: Is there one moment where the big kick comes? Do you
   crave applause, for example?
KNIEVEL: No . . . I've tried to figure myself out. I think when I
   was a youngster, I tried to impress people, and I got a big kick
   out of it. Not now. Playing with your life is really not much of a
   game . . .
CAVETT: So you don't need the mob approval.
KNIEVEL: No, I have to be right with myself.

CAVETT: So why don't you just jump in the desert where nobody's around? Could you do it and still get the same kick?

KNIEVEL: Oh, I doubt that very much. To be a performer and to be the only one in the world and to take pride in doing what I do, which I do, drives me, keeps me going. I'm certain of that.

He is a one-man ethical dilemma. That is what he is. The romance in his message is to take a chance, to get off your butt, to put down your nine-to-five chains and go for it, whatever it might be. These are solid motivational thoughts perhaps, but the possible consequences in his execution of them are large. He has chosen a career in professional Russian roulette, twirling the chamber and pulling the trigger for public consumption. The choice just about leaves you breathless.

How much reward is worth how much risk? How much do you hate that job at the factory, the office, slicing cold cuts behind the delicatessen counter? Could you ever hate it as much as this man? The price he has paid so far—the injuries, the time in the hospital—might actually work on a balance sheet compiled by a sympathetic accountant. The possible price he could pay, though, would be out of the question.

Then again, that is what he wants you to think. He is selling fear and worry. Fear and worry are good. Marketable.

KNIEVEL: I'd like to get serious for a second, if it's all right. When you talk about the jumping, I know I've been called a lot of things by a lot of people. A crazy man. A con man. But when you head down that long white line, you'd better have made your peace with God or know what you're doing, because a con man ain't going to get there.

CAVETT: I was going to ask you—do you think about God?

KNIEVEL: Well, of course I do. I flirt with my life so much, every month, two or three times a month, of course I'm a lot more aware of life and what it involves, I think, than a lot of people are who get in a car and go down and have an accident happen, and it's something you're not planning on or suspecting.

The interview goes well. Cavett is a perfect fit with Knievel: the classroom smarty-pants, the mama's boy A student who will go to Yale, talking with the wiseguy from the back of the room, the future dropout who is still the resident idol and heartthrob in the school. Cavett has the energy of an anthropologist studying an odd primeval culture. Knievel has the patience to explain.

He is not flamboyant in the least with his tone or actions. He lets the words bring the adventure. The simple recitation of the injuries and the dire possibilities, the matter-of-fact mention of the word "death," do the job. He does not seem at all like a crazy man. Only the things he does are crazy.

The footage he shows of the crash at Caesars Palace on New Year's Eve 1967, short and blunt and brutal, less than a minute in length, is as mesmerizing as any filmed carnage that has been shipped back from Vietnam. The images are new, different, startling, a real man really being hurt. The viewer has not seen much, if any, of this.

As Knievel's body flies off the handlebars at impact, as it bounces and rolls, bounces again and rolls, bounces and rolls, he delivers a voice-over play-by-play. He has done this many times now on television and in press conferences, in restaurants and function rooms. This . . . this film . . . is what made him famous. He describes his thoughts, his feelings, his pain, as his body continues to travel across the pavement in slow motion.

"That's pavement?" Cavett asks.

"If you look close, you can see the chrome being scraped off the motorcycle," Knievel says.

He moves into the plans for his next extravaganza, jumping across the Snake River Canyon in Idaho. No date has been set, but he is going to do it. He wanted to jump the Grand Canyon, but says he was denied access by the federal government, so now it is Snake River. One mile wide. He is going to use a "jet-powered, streamlined motorcycle." He is going to land with a "ballistically employed parachute." He rattles off figures about thrust (two thousand pounds) and speed (over three hundred miles per hour). The landing will be upside down. On the rocks. On the other side. This will be his masterpiece. This will be the scariest thing he ever has done.

"That sounds exciting," Dick Cavett says. "Can I go with you?"

"If you lose a little weight," Evel Knievel says.

The jokes are nervous jokes.

A canyon. Holy sweet Jesus. An imaginary toe scuffs an imaginary rock over the side. The rock falls and falls, goes out of sight. Still hasn't landed. Holy Mary, Mother of God. Who is this guy? What is he thinking? A canyon? On a motorcycle? The presentation makes this stunt sound like a climb up the Matterhorn in bad weather, another NASA trip to the moon, this time by slingshot. The enterprise seems totally foolhardy. The sense of doom is bigger than it ever has been.

Which is the way Evel Knievel likes it. Tickets will be available.

"Well . . . ," Dick Cavett says. Pause.

"All right . . . ," Dick Cavett says. Pause.

"Good luck," Dick Cavett says.

He goes to commercial.

The final guest of the night is Averill Harriman, the governor of New York. The governor does not wear a zebra-striped leisure suit.

2 Words

He was from Butte, Montana, and the voices in his head seemed to work differently from most other people's voices in most other people's heads. The voices worked differently, for sure, when he was Evel Knievel, intrepid daredevil, riding that motorcycle over some perilous void, some made-up challenge that could suck him down in an instant, maim or hurt him or snuff him out, just like that, but they also worked differently when he was Bob Knievel, Bobby Knievel, or Robert Craig Knievel, private citizen, putting one foot in front of another on an ordinary summer's day.

That was because there were no ordinary summer's days. Not for him. Never. He always lived as if his pants were on fire.

"Go ahead," the voices said.

"Don't be shy."

"Do it," the voices said. "Do it. Do it, do it, do it. *Do it*."

He proceeded in everything he did without reservations, without qualms or second thoughts. The mechanism for internal debate did not exist. He was a man without filters. The same permission, no, encouragement that allowed him to kick that fat bike into gear at the top of a ramp and shoot off into the unknown allowed him to have a daily breakfast belt of Wild Turkey bourbon, make it a double, to lie, to cheat, to boast about his various sexual conquests after describing family life with his wife and kids, to gamble, to preen, to piss away every last cent he ever earned on cars and boats and planes and, sure, buy another round for the boys . . . and a little something for that woman at the end of the bar.

"Do it," the voices always said.

"Sure," he always said.

No matter what it was.

He followed his inclinations, his wants, his desires, as if they were instructions on how to rearrange the Red Sea. Adventure and misadventure were wrapped in the same daily package under the heading of "action." He lived for action, lived for danger, for conflict. If there was no action, he made it happen.

Drive with him on an idle afternoon in his hometown or in any of his adopted way stations, L.A. or Las Vegas or Fort Lauderdale, Florida, or anywhere else, and chances were good that the speedometer would go past 100 and the trip would end up somewhere strange. Play golf with him and the bets would become larger and larger until you stood over a putt that could cost you $1,000 or $5,000 or whatever figure made you really nervous. Drink with him and the night would never end. He established the pace, the tone, no argument allowed. You had to keep up or float away. Work for him and there was about a 100 percent chance that you would be fired at some point. (There was also a 75 percent chance you would be rehired.) Work out a deal with him and there was a good chance . . . well, cash all checks in a hurry.

"He told me I'd done a great job," a welder in Butte who fixed the hitch on Knievel's trailer once said, words that began a fairly common refrain. "He said the work was so good that he wanted to buy me dinner. He'd take me to dinner and pay me at the same time. I should go back to the hotel, take a good shower, and meet him in the lobby at seven o'clock that night. So I went back to the hotel, took a shower . . ."

Uh-oh.

"I suppose I still could be waiting. Except that was thirty years ago."

His relationship with money was curious. He not only stole when he had no money, but he sometimes stole from friends. When he had money, he not only would squander it, but sometimes squander it on the same friends. Money was everything to him. Money was nothing. Money somehow was both of the above. He was a one-man tornado when it came to money. His own. Or anybody else's.

He eventually reached a level of success where he bought Italian sports cars on whims, nothing more than that, bought an eighty-foot boat because he needed a place to stay for a night. He leased jet airplanes. He had a bulletproof golf cart built, armor-plated, because he kept making holes in the fiberglass body of the previous golf cart when he hit a bad shot, then swung his club at the cart in anger. He built a house on the sixteenth fairway of the Butte Country Club, stables and horses in the back. He bought jewels and fur coats, carried his magic cane that would unscrew at the top and reveal three ready-to-drink vials of whiskey.

He would take a $20 bill, crumple it into a ball, and throw it out the window of the moving car. Just like that. Money was nothing. Money was everything. Money somehow was both of the above.

"Bobby robbed me," the owner of the Acoma Lounge, a Butte bar, once said, back at the beginning. "That hurt because we were friends. The place was broken into during the night. I just figured it was Bob."

A few weeks later, someone broke into the Acoma Lounge again. This time the robbery happened in reverse. The robber left the amount that had been robbed the first time, plus $100. The owner, in Knievel's presence, remarked on his good fortune. Just to see what Knievel would say.

"Aren't you going to buy a round?" was what Knievel said.

His personal relationships depended on his moods. His moods could change in a moment. Smart as he was—and everybody pretty much admitted he worked from a well-disguised intellect—he still could be profane and stupid. He could be incredibly rude. He also could be canny, clever, shrewd. He could be thoughtful, but seldom quiet. Never shy. Never reserved. A friend from his early motorcycle time in California, Skip Van Leeuwen, told him years later that money had not changed him a bit: he was just as arrogant rich as he was when he was poor.

Arrogance made him an expert at everything, even things he didn't know. He always figured that the best advice came from his gut, not from someone on or off his payroll. This got him into assorted stretches of hot water, eventually landed him in jail and killed his career. He seldom apologized for anything he did or said to anyone. He seldom backed away or backed down from a challenge.

He lived for the challenges.

"I have a proposition," he would say to a stranger, a new listener, when a lull came to conversations. "I bet you . . ."

There always would be another proposition, another bet. There usually would be a twist somewhere in the outcome, a trick. The football game on the television might be shown on a tape delay. Something like that. The trick would make Bob Knievel, Bobby Knievel, Robert Craig Knievel, eventually the famous Evel Knievel, the winner. The loser would not be happy with the twist.

"I'll bet you that my penis is soft longer than your penis is hard," he suggested more than once, an example of a proposition handed to a new listener.

The words might be a little rushed, slightly garbled, the emphasis on some parts of the proposition, not on the others. The new listener would hear what he wanted to hear, usually a slightly dyslexic arrangement of the sentence. Sure, he would bet on that. His penis, hard, had to be longer than this guy's penis was soft. The new listener would conjure up an erection by some means, show the bulge in his pants to Knievel, and prepare to collect the bet.

"Not so fast," Knievel would point out. "My penis will be soft longer than yours is hard. That was the bet. You can't keep that erection all day. You thought the bet was supposed to be that your penis would be longer hard than mine was soft? Why would I bet on something like that? You must have heard wrong. Pay me."

The new listener would have a choice: pay or fight. There would be no big *ha-ha-ha, fooled you, don't give me any money, just a joke*. Pay up and shut up. That was the rule. The moment, the tension, would arise out of nowhere, totally driven by Knievel. He created the situation. He controlled the outcome. He would not budge. What would this guy do in response? What next? This was the action, the challenge. This was the reason for the bet in the first place. Anything could happen.

The daredevil life was a full-time occupation. At least it was for this daredevil.

Always had been.

A story. The two cousins played together so often, they thought they were brothers. Bobby Knievel was five years old, and Pat Williams was six, and on this day they were in the kitchen of Bobby Knievel's grand-mother, Emma, in the house on Parrot Street in Butte. The linoleum floor had been shined, and the two cousins were in their stocking feet, sliding across the high gloss the way kids do. Maybe they were whooping a little bit, bouncing off each other, in the process.

Pat Williams was in awe of his younger cousin, a tough fact to admit when the year's difference in their ages was a sixth of his life, but true. The kid not only had an easy athleticism about him, but also had a quirky mind and boundless energy. He would and could do anything. Five years old. He was a brass band all by himself.

One of his less attractive attributes, alas, was a tendency to pinch other people. He not only liked to pinch, he liked to pinch as hard as he could for as long as he could, simply to see the reaction from his subject. The reaction from Pat Williams, whom he had pinched often, was anger. Pat Williams had told his cousin, again and again, how much he didn't like to be pinched. Bobby Knievel continued to do it.

In fact, he did it again in his grandmother's kitchen. As the two boys slid on the floor, he came up from behind and pinched Pat Williams as hard as he could and held on. Pat Williams turned around and hit him with one punch, hard as he could, to the stomach.

Knocked him out.

It was an amazing punch, really, probably went straight to the solar plexus. Bobby Knievel made the sound a balloon makes when the air suddenly is released, *pffffft*, then went straight down. His head hit the linoleum, *blam*, and then his eyes rolled backward, and then they closed and he didn't move. A trickle of blood came from one ear. Pat Williams yelled at him to wake up, wake up, at the same time fearing the worst. One cousin was convinced he had killed the other cousin. He would spend his life behind bars.

Wait.

Bobby Knievel started to move.

Yes.

He came back in stages, the way knocked-out people did in the movies. He twitched a little, moaned a little, seemed to tip a big toe back into consciousness, then wade forward. A curious smile appeared on his face as his eyes finally opened, thank God. He said nothing, even as Pat Williams kept asking if he was all right. He pulled himself upward, still smiling, and assumed something that looked very much like a football lineman's stance. He stared straight ahead.

A pantry door had been left open, just a bit, on the other side of the room. Bobby Knievel suddenly sprang from the stance, ran as absolutely fast as he could across the linoleum floor, socks or no socks, put his head down, and, *ka-pow*, hit the pantry door headfirst and was knocked out again. Same sequence. He fell backward, hit his head again on the floor, eyes rolled back and closed. He was out again.

Pat Williams didn't know what to think. Was his cousin dead this time? No, the recovery process was also repeated. Bobby Knievel had the same small smile, same stare when he opened his eyes. Except this time it was directed straight at his cousin.

"You see, Pat," he said, "nobody can hurt me."

Five years old.

Where did that come from?

"Jesus Christ," the six-year-old Pat Williams said to himself as he looked at the five-year-old Bobby Knievel. "There's something wrong with this guy."

This guy was different.

He was from Butte, Montana, and television made him a star. Once he ducked under the rabbit ears and climbed into the living rooms of the United States through that open twenty-one-inch window in the final hours of 1967, the first hours of 1968, he pretty much made himself at home for the next decade. People never had seen anyone quite like him. Not up close.

He was a character straight from the dusty back roads of self-promotion, from the land of carnival shows and fast talk, three-headed goats and cotton-candy excitement. He didn't have a talent, really, couldn't sing or dance or juggle pie plates, but his fearlessness, his courage or craziness, depending on the point of view, was certainly different. The size of his guts, his nuts, his stones, agates, crokies, testicles, family jewels, balls—the balls of a giant, biggest balls on the planet, etc., etc.—attracted instant attention. The size of his mouth kept that attention.

He could talk. Yes, he could.

"He always was talking," Jack Kusler, who grew up in Knievel's neighborhood in Butte, said. "You couldn't shut him up. He was always the best, the best in everything. He was the best motorcycle rider. He was the best skier, the best skater, the best athlete. He wasn't the best in any of them. He was the best bullshitter. That was the only thing he was best at."

"He could talk to anyone," Rodney Friedman, his onetime boss at Combined Insurance, a door-to-door operation, said. "He wasn't afraid to talk to lawyers, doctors. A lot of guys are intimidated by education. Not Bob. He went right in there. And women just loved him. He'd go inside a beauty salon, and he'd sell everyone in the place. They'd all be laughing. He had that charm. Good-looking guy. They'd all buy policies for their husbands too."

"He knew how to get attention," Doug Wilson, a producer at ABC's *Wide World of Sports*, said. "He was the world's greatest barnstormer.

Everyone always would compare him to Muhammad Ali, the two athletes who got all the attention at the time. The difference was that Ali had the mythology and tradition of the heavyweight championship to help bring attention. Evel Knievel had nothing. He generated every bit of attention that ever came to him.

"These were the two athletes who dominated their time. Ali succeeded in an established sport. Evel invented his sport."

He landed in front of the cameras at exactly the right time. Ten years earlier, 1958, he would have been stranded on the county fair circuit, his voice gone hoarse, his body battered, as he tried to gather a live crowd each night and sell tickets all over again. In its grainy infancy in 1958, television, black and white and limited in all it could do, never could have captured the danger in his performances. If he had arrived ten years later than he did, in 1978, he would have had to fight his way through a crowd to find attention as technology opened the field to more channels, more sports, more attractions. Color! Instant replay! UHF! Choices! Daredevils were everywhere.

In 1968 he was a revelation. The viewers of America still watched the three networks with happy dedication. There was no cable, no satellite, no pooh-bah on the couch with a clicker. There was no clicker. The shows that were successful were giants, huge, a weeklong parade that went from *Bonanza*, *The Ed Sullivan Show*, and the controversial *Smothers Brothers Comedy Hour* on Sunday night through *Gunsmoke* and *The Andy Griffith Show* (Monday), *The Red Skelton Hour* (Tuesday), *The Beverly Hillbillies* (Wednesday), *The Dean Martin Show* (Thursday), *Gomer Pyle, U.S.M.C.* (Friday), all the way to *The Jackie Gleason Show* and *The Lawrence Welk Show* on Saturday.

If a man could force his way onto the screen, on any network, he was assured of a good audience. If he could force himself onto the right show, the numbers were staggering. Knievel never had his own show, but with frequent appearances on *Wide World*, mixed with talk shows like the one with Dick Cavett, with news reports, sports reports, with comedy walk-ons, with whatever came along, he was able to deliver his life story to the American public in well-watched installments.

He was reality television before reality television was invented, an outrageous and outspoken personality who became prime water-cooler conversation on a Monday morning. *An American Family*, a twelve-part series in 1973 on PBS about Bill and Pat Loud of Santa Barbara, California, their disintegrating marriage, and their five kids, especially their gay son, Lance, would be seen as the start of the reality trend, but Knievel certainly was in the territory before these people arrived. The costs were low to televise what he did, the ratings were high, the story dramatic and intimate.

"It's hard to imagine now how big he became, how he was such a cult figure," said Dennis Lewin, former senior vice president of production for *Wide World of Sports*. "Evel, Ali, *Monday Night Football*, Howard Cosell. They were all huge. Everything was anti-establishment at the time. Evel was a reaction to that. He really did believe in America . . . He always was a real package. He always delivered. He always did it."

"He was part of seven of the ten highest-rated shows in *Wide World* history," Doug Wilson said. "People loved him."

There was no competition. He was a strobe light brought into a darkroom. There were no home computers. There was no Internet. There was no Facebook, no Twitter, no YouTube, no sports sites, no porn sites, no MapQuest to tell a person where to go, no Google to answer all other questions, no dark hole to capture time and attention. The home computer would not start to appear until 1978. Watch Evel Knievel or, oh, read a good book.

There were no video games. There were no Mario Brothers, no Ms., no Mr. Pac-Man, no space aliens to be handled, no Grand Theft Auto, no Wii, no joystick, no Xbox, not even Atari. The video game Pong would not be introduced until 1972. Watch Evel Knievel or play a good board game of Chutes and Ladders.

There was no ESPN, so there was no *SportsCenter*, no *Baseball Tonight*, no highlights package featuring great athletic plays in a twenty-four-hour cycle. The replay camera had been invented but was costly, primitive, and used sparingly. ESPN did not begin operation until 1978. Watch Evel Knievel or watch, oh, *American Fisherman*.

There were no extreme sports. Surfing had been around forever, and the Beach Boys sang about it every day on the radio, and the 1966 movie *The Endless Summer* had made it even more appealing, but most American kids did not live next to an ocean. The skateboard was around, but very low priority. The polyurethane wheel, the basis for all good tricks, would not be invented until 1972. The first national snowboard race would not be held until 1982. Even motorcycles were in a low evolutionary stage. The first U.S. motocross event was held only in 1966. If you wanted to see someone flipping and flopping, flying through the air like a largemouth bass on the end of some fifteen-pound test line, you pretty much had to, yes, watch Knievel.

He was different. America always has loved different.

A story. The two cousins went in separate directions through the succeeding years. They lived at different ends of Butte as kids, made different friends in different neighborhoods, went to Butte's two different high schools, then to different career paths. Bobby Knievel, of course, became what he became, storied in word and song and Saturday afternoon television. Pat Williams went to the University of Montana and the University of Denver and eventually became a nine-time congressman from Montana, which was pretty good because Montana only had two congressmen for much of his time, then only one.

The cousins did remain in touch, linked by age and familiarity, by common knowledge. Family stuff. When they would bump into each other somewhere in Butte, somewhere in the rest of America, they would pick up the easy and natural dialogue from those childhood mornings and afternoons on Parrot Street.

"You're sure good on those takeoffs," Pat Williams would say about his cousin's new occupation. "You're not so good sometimes with those landings."

"And you're still an asshole," Bobby Knievel would declare.

Williams always saw his cousin as an engaging rascal. There was nothing hidden about his deviousness. He had an attitude that should have made any buyer beware, tied to his track record of sometimes shady dealings. What saved him was a twinkle in his eyes, a little stage laugh, a sort of "heh-heh-heh" that made all sins smaller, got him off a succession of hooks. Trouble that he was, he was fun to be around. He lit up people's dull lives.

"I came back to Butte after college with a little MGB sports car," Pat Williams said. "That was really different in those days. I think I might have been the first person with an MGB in Butte, maybe all of Montana . . ."

Williams was getting into the car when Knievel drove past, braked fast, and double-parked. What kind of car was this that his cousin had? Very sharp. Let me drive it. Williams said the last thing he would ever do in this world was let his daredevil cousin drive his good-looking sports car, oh, no, never, and of course they were taking off in a moment, Knievel at the wheel.

The speedometer and the tachometer were spun to numbers never seen previously in this particular car. The speeds were two, then three times and maybe more above the limit. The cornering, while terrifying, seemed to be very good. Three minutes into the test drive, coming down the original street, Knievel spotted three men standing around his double-parked car. They clearly could not move their own car because it was boxed in by Knievel's car.

"Hey, what are those guys doing with my car?" Knievel asked.

He hit the brakes on the MGB. He turned the wheel hard left. The sports car went into a 180-degree turn, accompanied by 180-degree squeals and the 180-degree smell of burning rubber. The car skidded, squealed, sent the smell through the air as it flew sideways at Knievel's car—Pat Williams braced for the grand crash and demolition of both cousins' cars in one accident—and stopped, yes, a foot short. Perfect.

"What's the problem?" Knievel asked the three strangers.

Just like that.

"Are you scared before you do this stuff you're doing?" Williams asked once.

"I'd better be," his cousin said. "Yeah, I'm scared every time. That shows that I'm not crazy. If I was crazy, I wouldn't be scared."

The cousins would run into each other, say, at Stapleton International Airport in Denver, headed in their different directions. Pat Williams would laugh as the rods and plates inside Knievel's body sent the metal detector into high dudgeon. ("It's okay, Mr. Knievel," the attendant would say. "Come right through.") They would run into each other at the 5-Mile Bar in Butte, Knievel surrounded by people, buying them drinks. They would meet anywhere, and Pat Williams would want more attention, more time, because he liked his cousin, still was fascinated, but more time wasn't possible because now the world was fascinated.

"I was somewhere, and I clipped out a story about Bob," Williams said. "He was having trouble with the people who ran the Astrodome. I forget what it was about. He was threatening not to jump. The wording made it sound like he was going to jump over the Astrodome, not in the Astrodome. I put the clipping in my wallet. Saved it."

At one of those occasional extemporaneous meetings with Knievel, Pat Williams took out his wallet and took out the clipping and read it aloud and said, "What kind of shit is this? You're going to jump over the Astrodome?" They both laughed. The conversation continued for a while, and as the cousins said good-bye again, Knievel took out his own wallet and also unfolded a newspaper clipping. This was a story about Pat Williams, a state assemblyman in Montana, running for Congress.

"What kind of shit is this?" Bobby Knievel asked. "You're going to run for Congress?"

Pat Williams was flabbergasted again.

This guy always could surprise you.

He was from Butte, Montana, and his life was a grand, sloppy American saga. It was one of those morality tales filled with immorality, lust, a certain amount of violence, greed, fame (and the loss of fame), twists, hairpin turns, and more than an occasional "I told you so." It could have been written long ago by Theodore Dreiser, by Frank J. Norris, by John Steinbeck, then brought up to date with golf and motorcycles, with go-go dancers and Playboy bunnies, pinball machines, bars and lounges, private jets and press conferences, toys that went *whirrrrr* and shot off into the night. A substantial dollop of religion was available to be added or skipped at the end by the writer.

"There is no king, no prince, no president, no athlete, nobody that has ever lived a better life than I have," the famous daredevil said often, one of the many stock quotes he would repeat in interviews and speeches.

Was he right?

He was from Butte, Montana, and he traveled a long way, met a lot of famous people, made and spent a lot of money, kissed a lot of girls. That was for sure. He was from Butte, Montana, and he never left, no matter where he went, his horizons constructed by his point of view. That also was for sure. He was from Butte, Montana, a different kind of man from a different kind of place, a skyrocket of a character who flew across the sky, bright and dazzling, spectacular for a moment, then fell apart in full public view and dropped back to the ground, his life following the same arc as one of his many jumps.

He was from Butte, Montana, and that was the most important fact of all in understanding how everything worked. He was from Butte, Montana.

3 Butte, MT (I)

The public face of Butte, Montana, in the middle third of the twentieth century belonged to a woman named Jean Sorenson. She was called "Dirty Mouth Jean" by people who knew her well and also by people who had spent but a few minutes in her company. There was little argument about whether the name was appropriate.

Born in 1907, matronly in appearance as she moved into her fifties, sixties, yes, her seventies, Jean Sorenson turned swearing, cursing, into a personal art form. She not only cursed like a U.S. Marine drill sergeant, she cursed like the entire platoon on a ten-mile hike in inclement weather. Foul words fought each other to come out of her lips first.

She was the proprietor of the Stockman Bar at the corner of Wyoming and Galena, a low-rent drinking establishment in a city that prided itself on the number and history of its low-rent drinking establishments. A former prostitute, former madam, she was a link to Butte's rip-roaring past, a one-woman tourist attraction. She kept a petrified walrus penis, three feet long, behind the bar for protection.

"This here is a genuine walrus dick," she would tell patrons. "Got it from a fucking Eskimo. He was hung fucking near as good as the walrus."

That was Dirty Mouth Jean.

She charmed even the most earnest churchgoers with her consistent vulgarity, did a great business as she filled her bar with businessmen, day laborers, visiting firemen, neckties and blue jeans, anyone and everyone in a noisy mix. She often boasted that she had had sexual relations with every miner from Alaska to Mexico during her time as a prostitute. She used other words for "sexual relations."

Her reputation was enhanced by the rumor that she had shot her first husband dead in the long ago and the known fact that she had drilled her second, common-law husband, Ted Record, with the same result on July 1, 1959, then successfully pleaded self-defense. She was not a woman who was afraid of violence. She pretty much was not a woman who was afraid of anything. She kept a loaded, hammerless Smith and Wesson .32 behind the bar, next to the walrus penis, in case problems too large for the penis to handle might arise.

On November 8, 1978, after more than thirty years at the Stockman, that kind of problem landed. Three young men, released from the Army in Fort Lewis, Washington, were forced to spend a night in Butte in the middle of their bus trip home. They decided to spend that night drinking, a decision that eventually led them to the Stockman and Jean after a number of stops. They ordered three Lowenbrau beers. Jean said she didn't serve Lowenbrau beer. They ordered three Miller beers. Jean said she did serve Miller beer, but wouldn't serve a Miller to them, wouldn't serve any beer, in fact, wouldn't serve the three men.

One of them was black.

It should be noted that Jean's off-color language often contained unflattering words to describe African Americans. Though Butte traditionally had been a great beef stew of races and nationalities, men drawn from all over the world to work in its copper mines, the sight of a black man walking the streets was still a curiosity. Few black men lived in Butte because black men historically were not hired for the mines.

"Are you refusing to serve me because I'm black?" the young man asked.

"If you're looking for a reason," Jean replied, "that's as good as any."

The men became agitated. Jean bypassed the walrus penis and pulled out the hammerless Smith and Wesson .32. Accounts varied on what happened next, about who pushed the issue, who was the aggressor, but the results were not debated. Jean shot one young man dead, wounded a second, and the third escaped out the door.

She eventually would be sentenced to ten years for manslaughter, would serve two, but the very next night she was out on bail and back at the Stockman, running the show her way. A drunken patron, talking about the trouble, advised her to purchase a larger gun, said she needed a .45, maybe something larger than that. Maybe a shotgun. The drunk persisted with his advice.

Jean knocked back her favorite drink, sloe gin mixed with Squirt in a small glass. She always called the process "taking a douche." She slammed the glass on the bar.

"When they put that motherfucker in the hearse," the public face of Butte, Montana, said, "he wasn't wiggling, was he?"

This was the city where Robert Craig Knievel was born on October 17, 1938.

The charm of Butte always was the fact that there was no charm. This was never one of those traditional western destinations like Cheyenne, Wyoming, or Santa Fe, New Mexico, like most of the places on the far left side of the forty-eight-state map that were wrapped up in cowboy culture with the long-ago gunfights at some old corral, with cattlemen and sheepherders, solid folk who called each other "partner." No, Butte was more like a gritty piece of Pittsburgh, Pennsylvania, or Youngstown or Toledo, Ohio, maybe even a borough of New York City, maybe Queens lopped off its urban roots and transported to one of the highest points in the Rocky Mountains and left to try to survive in a largely inhospitable environment.

"An island entirely surrounded by land" was one oft-quoted description.

Born in greed with the discovery in 1864 of assorted mineral deposits along the Continental Divide, then called "the Richest Hill on Earth" when massive amounts of copper ore were found three hundred feet under the ground in 1882, Butte became a gathering place for young and hard men who worked hard and dangerous jobs. They came from all over the world, these young and hard men, desperation and daydreams sending them to the coldest spot in the continental United States (an average 223 days below freezing every year) to live a mile above sea level and to work as much as a mile below the ground.

The daily job, from the beginning, was an eight-hour descent into a reasonable facsimile of hell. The bulky clothes worn up on "the sheets," the outside, the jackets and scarves suitable for the frozen streets and sidewalks of normal Butte living, were replaced underground by minimal clothing in "90 by 90 conditions"—90-degree temperatures, 90 percent humidity, a wet, nasty, tropical depression far from any white sand beaches.

Perils were everywhere. A rock could fall at any time and kill a man, just like that. Or maybe leave him a quadriplegic. So perilous were the rocks, they were called "Duggans," named after Larry Duggan, a prominent Butte mortician on North Main Street. They also were called "widow-makers," a noncommercial term that nevertheless brought Mr. Duggan to mind.

Floods could happen in an instant, everybody doomed. Fire was a constant possibility. Dynamite, used often, had obvious dire potential, especially when a stick or three or five would not ignite with the rest of the package and lay buried and dangerous to whoever might work in the area. These unexploded dynamite sticks were called "requiem masses," another grim term. Normal workplace accidents brought about by a trip or fall, or perhaps the misuse of a hammer or chisel or other tool, were a worry. Especially in a confined area, dank and dark, a claustrophobic hole. A constant drip of sulfuric acid off the walls added to the discomfort, burning holes in clothing and skin. The smells underground also could be staggering, the disposal of human waste always a problem.

No area of the United States ever was mined as extensively as the seven square miles directly under Butte. In 1916, the time of peak production, 14,500 men, one-fifth of the city population, worked in the mines, harvesting minerals from over 2,700 miles of excavations. The ground constantly shifted from all of this activity. The shifts brought the constant fear of cave-ins. The fear brought the name Duggan to mind again.

Every day started with a question for the miner headed to work. Every return home was a relief.

"Once you got on that cage [to be lowered into the ground], you never knew you'd come out of there," Victor Segna, who started working in the mines in 1922, said. "You never knew it. You got on there and you got down there, you may come up and you may not."

The mines, it was claimed, averaged one injury or one death per day in their early operation. Statistics were unreliable, downplayed because the city and mines and everything that touched them were pretty much controlled by the Anaconda Copper Mining Company, a monopoly, but 559 men were listed in state records as dead from fire or accident in the mines between 1914 and 1920. A substantial part of that mortality figure came from one of the worst mining accidents in U.S. history, on June 8, 1917. The spark from a miner's carbide lamp onto a piece of insulation started a fire 2,400 feet belowground that killed 163 men at the Speculator mine. Virtually all of them suffocated.

Accidents happened all the time. One study by the Bureau of Mines predicted that if a man worked ten years in the mines he had a one-in-three chance of being seriously injured. He had a one-in-eight chance of being killed. A poignant accident happened on September 3, 1911, at the Black Rock mine when eight children, "nippers," whose job was to bring damaged tools to the surface, were killed when their cage went out of control and they were crushed to death.

"When the mine whistles blew in chorus," an old-timer said, "every woman in Butte whose old man was down in the holes would throw a shawl over her head, grab a couple of kids, and hit out lickety-split for the mine he was workin' in—dead certain that he was being buried alive."

The long-term prospects for the miners were even worse than the treacherous short term. The average miner never lived much past fifty years of age. Many never reached fifty, dead from silicosis, a lung disease sometimes called "miner's consumption." The advent of the pneumatic drill brought constant clouds of heavy dust that filled the mines and began to scar lungs as early as two years on the job. Statistics were obscured for death by silicosis, often recorded as death by tuberculosis, but families knew the truth.

"Nobody had a father," Muzzy Faroni, son of a miner, remembered at the bar of the Butte Country Club. "Everybody's father was dead, sometime in his forties. My father was dead. His father . . . his father . . . his . . . I think back on my neighborhood . . . nobody had a father."

None of these perils stopped the line of ready replacements. The next surge of young and hard men always arrived to take the place of the previous surge. Living somewhere on the other side of an ocean, any ocean, thousands of miles away, the newcomers had heard the tales of jobs, money, opportunity, in the mines of Butte. They purchased a one-way boat ticket and they came. The economics was what mattered, not the danger.

Mostly single men, they were stuffed close together in the vertical, tight city that was so different from other cities in the West. Homes and rooming houses were built as close as possible to the mines to keep the cold return from work in wet clothes—subzero temperatures after a day of 90 degrees underground—as short as possible. (Pneumonia and other cold-related diseases were also perils.) Businesses were built close to the houses. A fire in 1895 had destroyed most of the business district, and wood-framed buildings had been banned, so the replacements were large and formidable, built of brick and stone.

The Irish and Cornish settled in Corktown, Dublin Gulch, and Centreville, local neighborhoods. The Italians settled in Meaderville, the Finns in Finntown, the Germans in Dogtown, the Croats and Serbs in the Boulevard and Parrot Flats, the Chinese in Chinatown, and the slums of the Cabbage Patch were open to just about anyone. A survey in 1918 found that Butte residents had been born in thirty-eight different countries, merchants from merchant nations following the great rush of miners, the population estimated now at close to 100,000 people, more than Houston or Dallas or Phoenix, a major stop for the five different railroads, which sent thirty-eight trains per day through the city. The foreign smells from foreign foods, the foreign words from foreign languages, the little eccentricities of different races from different places, were woven into daily living.

Not much planning had been involved in any of this. The city almost grew by itself, built to service the needs of the young and hard men who lived day to day, taking that long trip into the ground at the start of every shift, one misstep away from a visit to Mr. Duggan. Risk-takers every one of them. Butte was a city built for risk-takers from the beginning. Yes, it was.

This was the city where Robert Craig Knievel was born on October 17, 1938.

The life outside the mines in Butte was fast, as fast as any fast life in any big city in the country. Faster. If the population was tilted heavily toward young single men, and if young single men were the people with money, well, the services offered were services that young single men might enjoy. Whoopee.

Butte not only was a wide-open place—212 drinking establishments were already listed in the 1893 city directory—but reveled in being that way. Prostitution was legal, the sites ranging from plush parlors to Spartan, anonymous rooms called "cribs," often located in basements. Gambling was illegal, but tolerated everywhere without repercussion. The drink of choice after a day in the mines was a Sean O'Farrell, a shot of whiskey backed by a beer chaser. The fun proceeded from there. If tomorrow should be the bad day in the mines, well, tonight would be a wonder.

Novelist Gertrude Atherton, who wrote a 1919 best-seller about Butte called *The Perch of the Devil*, said that an hour was only forty minutes long in the city. That was how fast life seemed to fly. When the mines employed three shifts, work around the clock, the parties also never stopped. The owner of a new bar would throw the keys down the toilet or into the street in celebration of the grand opening. There was no need for keys, no need for locks. The bars also were open twenty-four hours.

"I have never seen a town as wide open as Butte!" famed reformer Carrie A. Nation declared when she arrived on January 23, 1910. "I have never seen so many broken hearts! I have never seen so many homes consumed to keep up the saloon! If I could touch a button and blow all the saloons in Butte to hell, I would do it in a minute."

She and members of her Women's Christian Temperance Union had taken hatchets to bars and houses of ill repute across the country. If she planned on doing that in Butte, she was mistaken. Two days after her arrival, as she tried to convince bartenders, half-dressed working girls, and patrons at the Irish World, a saloon, brothel, and dance hall, to give up their lives of sin, she tangled with owner May Maloy. Carrie said some Jesus words and wondered how May could not have some compassion for those young girls whose lives she was ruining. May said a bunch of those Dirty Mouth Jean words and said that Carrie had to leave. There was some pushing. Carrie A. Nation's bonnet was askew as she left.

"It's a shame you should attack an old woman," the sixty-one-year-old reformer shouted.

She never took the ax to another establishment. Butte was known forever as her Waterloo, sending her to retirement. Bigger and more well-known sinful districts might have existed in bigger and more well-known cities—in San Francisco, say, with the Barbary Coast, or on Bourbon Street in New Orleans—but Butte was tough to top, "an island of easy money surrounded by a sea of whiskey," in the words of Jere "The Wise" Murphy, the police chief from 1893 until 1935.

The whiskey was poured in places named the Bucket of Blood, the Graveyard, the Cesspool, the Good Old Summer Time, the Pick and Shovel, the Alley Cat, the Beer Can, the Open All Night, and on and on. The Atlantic, which was huge, ran for a city block from Park to Galena Street and boasted that it possessed the longest bar in the country. Fifteen bartenders worked that longest bar at the same time. Stanley Ketchel, who became middleweight champion of the world, started his boxing career at the Casino. That was how big the Casino was.

The bars offered food, entertainment, conversation, and definitely games of chance, starting with keno, a game invented within the city limits. A man could play cards, bet on the ball games back east, bet on the ball games at the high school, bet on what color horse or car might come up the street next. The get-rich-quick mentality that had founded the town in the first place took a walk every night.

The Butte bar scene was memorably described by Jack Kerouac in his novel *On the Road*, written in 1951. He expanded on that description in "The Great Western Bus Ride," an article published in the March 1970 edition of *Esquire* magazine five months after his death at age forty-seven in St. Petersburg, Florida, from cirrhosis of the liver. This was a night in Butte:

> Arriving, I stored my bag in a locker while some young Indian cat asked me to go drinking with him; he looked too crazy. I walked the sloping streets in super below-zero weather with my handkerchief tied tight around my leather collar and saw that everybody in Butte was drunk. It was Saturday night. I had hoped the saloons would stay open long enough for me to see them. They never even closed! In a great old-time saloon, I had a giant beer. On the wall was a big electric signboard flashing gambling numbers. The bartender gave me the honor of selecting a number for him on the chance of beginner's luck. No soap. "Arrived here twenty-two years ago and stayed. Montanans drink too much, fight too much, love too much." What characters in there: old prospectors, gamblers, whores, miners, Indians, cowboys, tobacco-chewing businessmen! Groups of sullen Indians drank red rotgut in the john. Hundreds of men played cards in an atmosphere of smoke and spittoons. It was the end of my quest for an ideal bar. An old blackjack dealer tore my heart out, he reminded me so much of W. C. Fields and my father, fat, with a bulbous nose, great rugged pockmarked angelic face, wiping himself with a back-pocket handkerchief, green eyeshade, wheezing with big asthmatic laborious sadness in the Butte winter night games till he finally packed off for home and a snort to sleep another day. I also saw a ninety-year-old man called Old John who coolly played cards till dawn and had been doing so since 1880 in Montana . . . since the days of the winter cattle drive to Texas, and the days of Sitting Bull. There was another old man with an aged, loving, shaggy sheepdog who ambled off in the cold mountain night after satisfy-

ing his soul at cards. There were Greeks and Chinamen. The bus didn't leave Butte till dawn. I promised myself I'd come back. The bus roared down the slope and looking back I saw Butte on her fabled Gold Hill still lit like jewelry and sparkling on the mountainside in the blue northern dawn.

The sporting houses, congregated around Mercury Street, the area called Venus Alley, were treated as local industry. Two blocks from Butte High School, on the edge of the business district, they were a part of the community, passed every day as if they were so many exotic hardware stores. They were more memorable to visitors from out of town than to locals, visitors like comedian Charlie Chaplin, who first stopped in the city in 1910 and came back more than once. "The red-light district of Butte, Montana, consisted of a long street and several side streets containing a hundred cribs, in which young girls were installed ranging in age from sixteen up—for one dollar," Chaplin recalled in his 1964 book *My Autobiography*. "Butte boasted of having the prettiest women of any red-light district in the West, and it was true. If one saw a pretty girl smartly dressed, one could rest assured she was from the red-light quarter, doing her shopping. Off duty, they looked neither right nor left and were most acceptable."

Butte was a man's city, an all-night city, a city where money meant good times and a lack of money meant getting your hands dirty. Butte was a city where women painted their faces and sold their evening's attention on an open market. Butte was a city where con men conned, where policemen and politicians often accepted sealed envelopes for services rendered or not rendered. Butte was a city of fistfights and braggadocio, tall tales and sporting propositions. Butte was a city where alcohol made the wheels go round.

This was the city where Robert Craig Knievel was born on October 17, 1938.

A story. A nineteen-year-old Irishman, Patrick Keough, from the copper-mining town of Avoca, County Wicklow, arrived in town in 1906 with the same idea as everyone else: to see what small part of the riches in the ground might stick to his hands. He had followed the up-to-date advice from home: "Don't stop in America. Go straight to Butte, Montana." Fifteen-year-old Elizabeth Hagan, accompanied by her father, arrived at approximately the same time, clutching a lace shawl wrapped around her shoulders by her tearful mother at the docks in Belfast. She was part of the tradition that the eldest daughter leaves first with the father when the family decides to emigrate.

Patrick Keough went to work in the mines, taking his chances, and Elizabeth Hagan got a job cleaning houses, and eventually they met and one thing led to another, as often happens, and they were married in 1912. They built a family consisting of four girls, Mary, Elizabeth, Ann, and Katherine, and a late-arriving boy at the end, John Patrick, also called Charlie. Life was fine until the Depression hit in 1929 and copper prices fell through the floor and Patrick's job disappeared with them.

Forced to find an alternative way to support their kids, Patrick and Elizabeth tapped into the prosperous, but illegal, field of bootlegging. Prohibition, now a decade old, had done little to slow the fast Butte pace. Bars like the M&M were simply renamed "cigar stores," and nothing changed as they did their same solid business. Laws were laws, though, and the revenue agents did catch a few traffickers in forbidden fluids. Patrick eventually was one of them.

Facing both federal and state charges, he was kept in the local jail. Elizabeth, called Lizzy, felt bad for him. To improve his sagging spirits, she decided to provide him with a taste of the family product. She painted the insides of a baby bottle white, let the paint dry. She then poured in some spirits to improve her husband's spirits.

On visiting day, she brought baby Charles and the baby bottle to the jail. While Patrick held Charles, she handed him the bottle. He started to feed the baby.

"No," Elizabeth said. "You should test the bottle before you ever give it to the baby."

"Aw, I hate milk," Patrick said. "You know I hate milk."

"Well, you should test this milk," Elizabeth said, staring straight at him. "You should test it now. Do it right now."

Patrick took a pull on the bottle. His eyes registered great surprise. He spit the whiskey onto the ground.

"Jesus Christ, Lizzy," he said in Irish brogue, "are ya trying to get me sent to San Quentin?"

In 1937 Ann Keough, the third of Patrick and Lizzy's four daughters, married Bob Knievel, the second of Butte businessman Ignatius Knievel's two sons. Bob Knievel was twenty-one years old and she was seventeen, and the plan was to start a family and live in Butte.

This was the city where Robert Craig Knievel was born on October 17, 1938.

The Knievel name was well known in Butte. Originally from Halle Westfalen, Prussia, Knievels had settled in Antelope, Nebraska, as farmers in the 1880s, and spread out in succeeding years. One of the landing spots was Butte. Anton Knievel became one of the city's leading businessmen, the owner of the Butte Potato and Produce Company, which had a five-story warehouse on the corner of Iron and Utah Streets. He was a charter member of the Rotary Club, the Chamber of Commerce, and the YMCA, and a stout parishioner of St. Patrick's Church.

Ignatius, his younger brother, who followed him to Butte, was decidedly less successful. Drummed out of the family produce business for some shady dealings, he became a tire salesman, then a car salesman. He focused on foreign cars in later life, with Knievel Imports, and eventually became the first Volkswagen dealer in the United States on the far side of the Mississippi River. He was called "Iggy" in Butte. Iggy Knievel.

Iggy Knievel was married to Emma Brown, an Iowa girl, and they begat Robert, called Bob, in 1917 . . .

Robert Knievel, called Bob, grew up and married Ann Keough, and in 1938 they begat the second Robert, also called Bob, later to be called Evel . . .

And that was the short version of the family tree . . .

Tidy . . .

Except the newest branch was shaky.

Bob Knievel, Iggy's son, was not ready to become a husband or a father in 1938 at age twenty-one. And he definitely was not ready to become a father a second time, which pretty much was a certainty when Ann became pregnant within a month after she had delivered the first baby. Responsibility and then more responsibility loomed as a lifelong straitjacket. Bob reacted.

Ann worked during the second pregnancy at the American Candy Shop in uptown Butte with her mother and sisters. The family-run establishment was huge, three stories that included a dance hall, a restaurant, and an ice cream and soda shop. The ice cream and soda shop was a gathering spot for young people, especially young women, jukebox music in the background, a place where gossip ran free.

A lot of the gossip concerned Bob Knievel and girls. Reports came back

about this girl, that girl, a succession of girls, a succession of embarrassments for Ann. Bob was a hound. No doubt there were confrontations.
No doubt there were tears. Ann waited out the end of the pregnancy,
delivered Nic, a second healthy baby boy, then stepped away from the
embarrassments. She filed for a divorce as soon as possible.

It was a familiar story, two people married too young, at least one
partner not ready to settle down, but this time the words were backed
by fast and irreversible action. Bob Knievel soon took off for California,
settled in the Sacramento area, drove a bus and raced cars. Ann Keough/
Knievel took off for Reno, Nevada, a place where Butte residents tended
to relocate to escape the cold. She eventually lived on the edge of show
business in Reno, sang a bit, sang sometimes with the Mills Brothers,
appeared in some local plays, did impressions. Each partner married
again in the new locations, new lives. Each started a new family. Bob
had three daughters. Ann had two. Neither had another son.

The sons they did have together, oh yes, Bob and Nic, wound up with
the dinner check for everyone else's liberation. They were left in Butte
to be raised by Ignatius and Emma, their paternal grandparents. This
did not go well. Ignatius was forty-eight years old when he suddenly had
two babies under the age of two in the house again. Emma was forty-six.
They were overmatched from the beginning.

Ignatius was bipolar, people later decided, sometimes open to long
conversation, but sometimes silent for months. He didn't have the temperament for the job. Emma tried, everyone said she tried, and everyone
said she was very nice, smart, a reader of books—but she was no match
for two restless, nonstop boys, especially the older one. Bob Knievel,
Bobby Knievel, needed action. The house, Ignatius and Emma's house
at 2511 Parrot Street, was too quiet, too controlled, too cuckoo-clock
cautious and dull. Maybe if the young Bob lived in some wilderness
somewhere, some Great Plains outpost of the immigrant Knievels in
Nebraska, it would have been okay, boredom on the outside matched
against boredom on the inside, but that was not where he lived. He lived
in Butte, Montana.

He became a classic semi-orphan Butte kid, same as all of those
semi-orphan kids whose fathers had perished from working in the mines.
He was different, perhaps, because his father had gone to Sacramento,
not some place described in the Bible, different because his mother also
had disappeared, but he was the same because he did what all of these
other fatherless kids did in Butte. He went to the streets for his education,

for his concepts of right and wrong, good and bad, winning and losing. In this manliest town in America, he learned the manly life in a hurry, with heavy emphasis on the vices as opposed to the virtues, the physical over the cerebral, the importance of gambling, drinking, stealing, cursing, talking all talk, walking any walk, standing as tall as possible at all times and finding a compliant if not necessarily good woman for a good roll in the hay. He was a true child of Butte, Montana.

This was the city where Robert Craig Knievel was born on October 17, 1938. There was no wonder in his hometown about why he was the way he was, or why he became what he became.

4 Butte, MT (II)

The request was for Clyde Kelley's belt. Clyde Kelley had to be convinced to give it up, a strange bit of business before the bell even rang to start another day at Butte High School, but if anyone could convince him, Bob Knievel would be the one to do the job. Bob Knievel had the charm, the style, to convince people to do things that didn't fit into their normal plans. He was a fine adolescent con man.

"Just give me your belt," Knievel said.

"What do you need it for?" Kelley asked.

"Just give it to me."

There was a ticking inside this Knievel kid's head, a faster syncopation, that kept him one step ahead of just about anyone else in the school. He wasn't a star athlete—didn't play football for Swede Dahlberg, or basketball for Bob Rae—and he certainly wasn't a star student, but he was a presence. He was good-looking enough, cocky as could be, boastful, devious. Mischief ran through him, crackled out of his pores. Mischief had its allure.

"Okay," Kelley said, undoing his belt. "But why do you need it?"

"You'll find out," Knievel said.

He was one of those kids who could have been book-smart if he wanted to be book-smart, but couldn't care less about that. Life was a lot more interesting than any book, especially life in Butte. He probably would be diagnosed with ADD or ADHD, some kind of attention disorder, in another time, but now he was seen as a fidget of a kid, always looking for new action. Plots and schemes abounded.

"Give me a hand with this," Knievel said one day to Kelley and a group of football players.

"Sure," they said, not exactly certain why they did.

A girl from the West Side, the more affluent part of Butte, had been handed a Nash Metropolitan by her father. The Nash Metropolitan was a tiny American car, undersized in all respects, perfect for a rich girl's commute to school. Knievel had his group of football players surround the Metropolitan, bend down, and lift at the count of three. They carried the little car (1,823 pounds) up the school steps and parked it in front of the front door and went away. Perfect.

That had happened a few weeks earlier. Now Knievel collected belts.

His plan soon was unfolded. He had a problem, it seemed, with the school librarian. She had turned him in for some infraction, made his life miserable in some way. He decided to make her life miserable. While she worked alone in the library, getting ready for the school day, he used the five or six belts he had collected to tie the doors to the library shut. He then pulled two wastebaskets, large and full, to the front of those doors. He lit the contents of the wastebaskets on fire.

The smoke from the fire quickly went under the doors and into the library. The librarian just as quickly responded to the problem and tried to get out of the room. The doors wouldn't open. Panic ensued. Fire trucks were called.

"He smoked her out," Clyde Kelley said. "Except she couldn't get out."

Score another one for Bob Knievel. The hell with the consequences. The hell with the school librarian. If there was punishment, hell, he could take it. Bring it on.

The time-lapse photography version of his run through the Butte streets from childhood to adulthood was filled with these types of moments. Some were more benign. Some were worse, much worse, featuring acts like thievery and fraud. Always, there was action.

Knievel was a loner, no real close friends, but seldom was alone. Everyone knew him or knew of him. He was someone who couldn't be overlooked, couldn't be missed. He brought his own spotlight with him wherever he went, focused it directly on himself.

"We'd sit in delinquency, which was detention at Butte High School, staying after school," Jim Blankenship, a classmate, said. "He was the kid, the teacher would say, 'One more peep out of anyone and you will all stay another half-hour,' and he would say, 'Peep.' He'd drive every-one crazy. Delinquency was supposed to last for an hour, but when he was there, it would stretch to two hours, three. It would be six o'clock at night when you'd get out of there. Kids would want to kick his ass. I would want to kick his ass."

The other kids would be sent to delinquency on rare afternoons after getting caught talking in class, arriving late, some minor infraction. Knievel was there every day. He would serve forty straight days of delin-quency, miss a day, then serve twenty more. He couldn't shut up. He couldn't sit still. He needed to dominate any situation.

That was how he always had been. That was how he always would be. His word was the last word.

"We were seven years old," his cousin Pat Williams said. "There was a bunch of us. We were playing down by the railroad tracks. We had a contest: who could balance himself and walk the furthest on one of the tracks. Nobody lasted very long. We all fell off, one after another. Bob went last. I can still see this . . . he bent over and pushed himself into the air and walked along the track on his hands! He walked further on his hands than anybody else did with their feet. He never really fell off. He could still be walking on his hands, if it hadn't become boring."

His brother Nic, younger and smaller, was the normal kid, a member of the clubs in school, someone who looked for good grades. Bob was the one collecting the belts. Nic pretty much followed the rules. Bob fol-lowed his passions. He was the one who walked on his hands.

He was always attacking something. He always was moving, moving, moving.

"You know how kids, when they start something new, they kind of go from onesies to twosies?" Nic said. "Bob never did that. He always skipped the beginning stuff. He didn't go into anything in onesies and twosies. He jumped right in. He went straight to threesies and foursies."

Raised by Iggy and Emma, the two boys were comfortable enough, never had economic worries. Bob was so well dressed all the time, never in jeans, always so clean, that Dan Killoy's mother down the street would look at her son on those odd moments when he too was well dressed and clean and say, "Oh, my gosh, it's you! I thought you were Bobby Knievel!" There was love and good cooking in the little house at 2511 Parrot Street, but not a lot of understanding. That was the problem. The generation gap with Iggy and Emma skipped an important genera-tion in the middle.

The boys saw their parents separately on vacations, special visits, but that was it. There would be trips to Sacramento, then El Sobrante, California, to see their father, trips to Reno to see their mother. Both parents expressed hope that someday they could fold in their older boys with their younger girls to make one family, but that didn't happen. After a while, it became an impossibility.

"My mother always had the thought that she would get the boys back," half-sister Loretta Young said. "Then one Christmas Nic came to visit, but Bob stayed in Butte. I remember my mother took Nic to see one of those department store Santas. The Santa told Nic he could have anything in the world, any toy, any bike, what did he want? Nic said all he wanted was to be with his brother, Bob, in Butte. Broke my mother's heart. She knew right then that she would never have the boys."

In 1954 their father returned to Butte. Bob was sixteen and Nic was fifteen and their father went into the family car business with Iggy, Knievel Imports. If the move was to give guidance, structure, to the boys, it was too late. The boys were gone. Things happened fast in Butte. The driving age was twelve or thirteen, whenever your feet could reach the pedals, no need even for a license. The drinking age was the same as the driving age, except your arms had to reach over the bar in this case. Gambling was everywhere. Sex? The age of consent for a young boy was whenever he could collect enough money for the experience. The houses of prostitution on Mercury Street awaited.

"Two bucks to get laid, three bucks for half-and-half, five bucks for around the world," Sandy Keith, Butte High grad, said. "I was twelve years old when I lost my virginity."

The boomtown glow had begun to dim in Butte after World War I when vast amounts of copper were discovered in Chuquicamata, Chile, a new Richest Hill on Earth for the Anaconda Company to tackle, but even at half-speed the pace was faster than the rest of the country. The bars were still open twenty-four hours per day. The mines still put a lot of money in local pockets. The Korean War had brought an added demand for copper, a measured rebirth. The operating theory was that when the country had trouble—and the price of copper rose—Butte did well.

"It was just the best place to grow up back then," Jim Lynch, who grew up at the same time as Knievel, said. "There was a freedom to do anything. Your house might not have been the greatest, but when you went outside . . . I lived right on the Continental Divide. There was a million-acre playground right behind my house."

Lynch did a lot of skiing with Knievel at the old Beef Trail Ski Area when they were both in junior high school. His mother would drive the two of them to the area, and they would ski and explore. One day when the temperature was 45 degrees below zero they were the only skiers on the property. They were the only skiers on the ski jump on another day. It was one of those real ski jumps, just like the Olympics, a man-made hill that shot you off the platform at the end to an uncertain fate at the end of a long, long drop.

"It was the first time we'd ever gone up to the top," Jim Lynch said. "The jump wasn't even open. We were examining it when we could hear the ski patrol coming. We knew they'd check the jump. They didn't want kids to kill themselves. Bob said we had to hurry."

Hurry? Hurry for what?

Knievel was gone, down the ramp, *swoosh*, off the end, gone. Lynch, flustered, figured he better follow. He shoved off, went down the ramp, *swoosh*, went off the end, spotted Knievel from midair in a clump at the bottom, and soon joined him in another clump. Alone, Lynch never would have gone down that jump. With Knievel, here he was.

The kid made you do crazy things.

Somewhere after his junior year, presumably with the Butte High School record for successive delinquency sessions established, with the librarian convinced of her mistaken ways, Knievel retired or was forced to retire from his forced march toward a diploma. He was off to the mines, a familiar path for early retirees from the Butte school system.

The joke was that, with technological improvements, the mines had become Montana's answer to collecting unemployment checks, filled with men who did little except sit next to a machine, hide underground, and take a paycheck. Knievel fit well into this idea.

"He worked there," one former miner said. "He punched in and punched out, but you never really saw him."

Knievel told a story in later years, could have been true, could have been half-true, could have been fiction, that he did a wheelie on the job with a payloader, hit a power cable, and put out half the lights in Butte. The most important thing that happened for him in the mines was that he learned, for sure, that he didn't want to work in the mines. They were an extension of high school, someone else telling you what to do, except they were dirtier than high school.

He also joined the U.S. Army Reserve, the 592nd Ordnance Company, after he left Butte High to head off the possibility of being drafted. He did his six months of active duty at Fort Lewis, Washington, hated it, then came back for the five and a half years of weekend and summer camp reserve commitments, which he also hated. There was no surprise in the fact that he was not a very good soldier.

"He was the shits," Sandy Keith, who was his commanding officer in the Reserves, but also the owner of the Acoma Lounge, said. "I always gave him one order—stay the fuck away from me. I liked him in the bar. I didn't like him in the Army. We went on summer camp once to Fort Lewis, he fell out of the jeep on the first day, said he hurt his ankle, couldn't do anything for the rest of camp. I told him that was fine . . . just stay the fuck away from me."

His passion now was his motorcycle. He had ridden his first cycle on a visit to his dad in El Sobrante when he was fifteen, almost killed himself, and soon after that bought a used Triumph TR5000 with trophy gears from Rob Slack in Great Falls. There were weekend races in Great Falls, which he joined, but the way he rode, fast and fearless, there pretty much were races every night, even if he was simply racing against himself. He tore around the streets of Butte, went off-road, up around the mines, came back down, engine screaming. He liked to do things fast.

"He picked me up once," Jim Blankenship said. "He had a motorcycle that could go 150 miles an hour. We went 150 miles an hour. I was never so scared in my life. I was really mad."

He would roar by the high school during the day, popping a wheelie, showing off. He would make the circuit of the bars at night. He would go to the Freeway Tavern to see Muzzy Faroni, to the Met Tavern to see Bob Pavlovich, to see Joe Dosen at Joe's Mirror Bar, to the Yellowstone, to a half-dozen places. He was mobile, young, fearless, into the action. If the action was on the other side of some law, well, action was action.

"He had a deal with some girl who owned a Volkswagen," Pavlovich said. "He would have her park it outside the bar. He would find somebody and bet that he could drive his motorcycle up and over the car. The guy thought Knievel would worry about damaging a stranger's car. Except Knievel already had a deal. He'd drive his motorcycle over the Volkswagen and collect the money."

Need a fast deal? He had fast deals.

"He sold a guy in the bar four tires," Muzzy Faroni said. "The guy went out to my parking lot at the end of the night. His car was on blocks. Knievel had sold him his own tires."

The stories accumulated in a fat pile. Moving, moving, moving. He always was doing something. He took some friends to Reno—here's one—to see his mother for Thanksgiving. He said he and his friends would supply the entrée for dinner. They went hunting. No more than an hour later they were back with a pillowcase filled with dead ducks.

"You did very well," Bob's mother said. "You must be great hunters."

"It was easy," Bob replied. "There were all these ducks in that nice park down the street."

He made deals that sometimes were too good to be true . . .

"His father brought in the first go-karts to the showroom in Butte," Jack Kusler said. "Bob drove one of them to my house. I think they cost $250. He said it was his and he would sell it to me for $100. I bought it. I had the first go-kart in Butte. Then his father came around the next day and took it back. Bob Knievel sold me a go-kart he didn't own. His father was not happy."

He took things that did not belong to him . . .

"A guy told me he went duck hunting in Whitehall with Knievel," Mike Byrnes, a Butte contemporary, said. "They ran out of ammunition. They went to the nearest sporting goods store to buy some more. They were still wearing all of their gear because they were going back to hunt some more. The guy buys the shells, and Knievel starts motioning to him to get going, they have to leave. Knievel is hurrying, but walking with a big limp. When they get to the car, he pulls out a 30.06 Springfield rifle he had stuffed into his waders."

Moving. Moving. Moving. Knievel and another guy learned about a ring of hubcap thieves, football players at the high school. Hubcaps, especially specialty hubcaps, spinners, were a prized item during the custom-car fifties. Knievel and the other guy learned where the thieves kept the stolen hubcaps, then raided the spot, stole the hubcaps for themselves. Thieves stealing from thieves.

"There must have been five hundred hubcaps," the other guy said. "We sold them off by bits to some character on the East Side for a buck, maybe two bucks a hubcap. The thing with Knievel, though, was that he was lippy. He liked to tell people, 'Hey, we stole all these hubcaps.' He liked the attention. I was worried that the police would find out, more worried that the football players would find out."

The picture that caught Knievel's style best at this time of his life—free and flying, lippy, single, not worried about anything—probably came from a spot behind the A&W Root Beer stand at the bottom of Woodville Hill in Meaderville, one of the Butte neighborhoods. The A&W parking lot was the place to be seen on a summer night. Kids and young adults would hang around, buy some food, see some friends, hang around, see some more friends, buy some more food, waste the night. And watch Bob Knievel ride his motorcycle.

The old smelting plant was up the hill, and piled on the ground nearby were the tailings, which were the remnants from the smelting process, the leftover rocks. The biggest pile went four hundred, maybe five hundred feet high, a mountain of tailings, ugly and foreboding, a Mount Everest of refuse, so steep and loose that no one could possibly walk up the side. This was where Bob Knievel rode his motorcycle. Or tried to ride his motorcycle.

He would begin at the bottom, perched over his little 250 Tiger Cub or whatever he was riding, get moving as fast as he could before he hit the mountain, then try to fight gravity and common sense and reach the top. He usually was the only one who tried this, a one-man show. The diners in the A&W parking lot had a perfect view as he charged so hard at first, then started to slow, then slipped somewhere in the middle or the last third of the climb and slid and went back to the beginning, short of his goal again.

He was entertainment. Up he went, down he came. Up he went, closer, down he came. Up, down, up down, closer, closer, still closer. Up . . . up . . . there. Every now and then he would finish the entire climb. Made it. Did it. He would finish high above the city with a big bounce, breathing hard, still upright, still astride the bike, looking at the spread-out lights on top of the many gallows from the mines.

The diners in the parking lot at the A&W would blow their horns in appreciation. Magic. Management—Jim Lynch's grandmother owned the place—gave him a standing offer of free food any time he performed.

A story. The felon's given name was William C. Knofel, but he sometimes was known as Clarence William Knofel and also sometimes was known as Clarence Junior Richards. He made a lot of work for the Butte justice system throughout the fifties. His record included time in the city jail, the county jail, and the Montana State Prison on charges ranging from murder to carrying a concealed weapon to grand larceny. He also spent some time at the state mental hospital in Warm Springs.

The biggest headlines came from the murder charge in 1954. He was accused of killing eighty-year-old Quong On, also known as Old Charlie, ransacking his house on East Mercury Street in search of money, then dumping the body near the Butte Gun Club. Knofel also was famous for his jail escapes. He escaped the county jail by sawing through the bars with a hacksaw blade, escaped the city jail by sawing through a hinge on the door, escaped once simply by running away from his guards after a court appearance.

He was recaptured each time, and the murder charge was dismissed when a key witness disappeared, but that did little to change the local perception that he was a pretty bad actor. The Butte police, kept busy with his many alleged infractions, gave him a nickname. They called him "Awful Knofel." He did his best to live up to the name.

A deal was struck in July of 1960 that finally ended his one-man crime spree. Promising to relocate to California, he pled guilty to a grand larceny charge and was given a five-year suspended sentence. The stipulation was that he leave immediately for California, a move that was in everyone's best interests.

"I hope you can get from here to the bus station without breaking any laws," Judge John B. McClernan advised from the bench.

The anonymous court reporter for the *Montana Standard* pointed out in his story that the bus station was about two blocks from the courthouse. He added that there was a crosscut shortcut that reduced the distance to one block.

Awful Knofel apparently made the trip without incident. He was gone.

His place in Butte history was not assured until years later. One of the many stories about how Bob Knievel became Evel Knievel involved a night in a Butte jail cell and an officer named Mulcahy declaring, "Look at this, we've got an Awful Knofel and now we've got an Evil Knievel." Mulcahy claimed it was true, and Knievel sometimes claimed it was true, sometimes gave the words to someone else, sometimes said his Little League manager first called him "Evil."

Whoever used it first, the name did not stick in Butte. Everybody called him "Bob."

* * *

Hockey was his next occupation. Hockey? His high school football career, people said, had lasted no more than a couple of freshman practices because he tried to step on other kids with his cleats, tried to break arms, leave marks, and was sent home. He was a skier, of course, and rode his motorcycle, and he was an ad hoc pole vaulter, even owned his own bamboo pole, practiced, but never went out for the school track team. Hockey?

It didn't seem to fit his personality, a team sport, a collective approach to anything, but he always had played hockey. Every empty lot in the neighborhood around Parrot Street—and there were a lot of empty lots—became a skating rink in the winter. Skating was part of growing up in Butte. Hockey was the next step.

The organized version of the game was played at the rink at Clark Park, the prime recreational area in Butte. Knievel became a rink rat as a kid, showed up by himself, skates and stick, watched from the periphery as the older kids played. One of the regulars was Tubie Johnson, whose father coached the local youth teams.

"Knievel was small, this little punk kid who kept hanging around the rink," Johnson said. "My father noticed him. I think he took pity on him, because he let him start practicing, showed him the things you had to do to be a hockey player."

Johnson went into the Army for two years, and when he came back in the winter of 1956 he found a different Knievel. The little punk kid had grown into a six-foot, 175-pound hockey player. Knievel's father, back in the picture, had sent him to a couple of hockey schools, one in Canada, and he had improved. He now was a physical center-ice man, good size, shot every time he had the chance, probably could have passed a little bit more, but scored enough to be effective. He talked a far better game than he ever played, but he could play. Not afraid to fight.

"He was decent," Tom McManus, another Butte hockey player, said. "On a scale of one to ten, he was a seven. But I'd trust him about as far as I could throw him. He was a real show-off, had to be the life of the party all the time."

"He was a good athlete, but he always was in a lot of trouble," Tubie Johnson said. "He was the biggest bullshitter in the world. I couldn't believe a thing he'd say. He could sell an Eskimo a refrigerator."

In September of 1958, nineteen years old, Knievel suddenly became the most important figure in Butte hockey. He started his own semiprofessional team, the Butte Bombers. He was the owner, the coach, the starting center. Nineteen years old. It was a remarkable string of titles.

The start-up money, not much, came from his father and Ignatius and the car dealership. Local sporting goods dealer Phil Judd provided a bunch of uniforms and equipment on credit. Butte had a five-year-old civic center with dates to fill, so the move made some economic sense. Knievel offered players $50 per game, recruited some Canadian talent out of the Montana School of Mines in Missoula, put together an ambitious schedule that included other semipro teams from the United States and Canada, a few minor league juggernauts, and some big-name colleges like Minnesota and Michigan.

There was no chance that anyone would wind up in the National Hockey League—the NHL contained only six teams and virtually 100 percent of the players came from Canada—but this was good local theater.

Knievel put himself on the ice for power plays, penalty killing, and all big moments as center for the first line. He set himself up to be the star. Little self-placed stories soon appeared in the *Montana Standard* about how different minor league teams coveted his services, but the final paragraph always noted that he had decided to stay with the Bombers.

The other players soon learned that the $50 a game was a mirage. Knievel was tough to pin down for money, but hockey was hockey. This was the only team around if a player wanted to play.

"We never got paid too often, but I remember a couple of good meals," Tubie Johnson said. "God bless Phil Judd. He kept the thing afloat, giving credit for sticks, uniforms, equipment. I don't think he ever got paid either."

The Bombers survived a first year, came back for a second in 1959–60. Knievel scheduled games with U.S. teams from Great Falls, Salt Lake, Spokane, and Denver, plus Canadian teams like Medicine Hat, Calgary, Lethbridge, Trail, and Rossland. He also secured an exhibition with the Czechoslovakian Olympic team at the Butte Civic Center on February 7, 1960. The Olympics would begin eleven days later in Squaw Valley, California, and the Czechs, two-time world champions, would stop on the way.

The game was a coup. A coup? It was the coup of coups. The two-time world champions? In Butte? Against the Bombers? Knievel had tried first to attract the Russians, the defending Olympic champions, but was turned down when he couldn't guarantee certain financial considerations. The Czechs were a suitable substitute, another hockey power from the dark side of the Iron Curtain, grim and foreboding and very good. The finances were shaky here also—Knievel said in the newspaper two weeks before the contest that it would be called off if attendance at a pair of games with Salt Lake didn't bring in enough revenue—but all parties pushed forward.

On February 7, 1960, the largest crowd in Butte hockey history, over two thousand fans, packed the civic center. Tickets were $2 for reserved seats, $1 for general admission. The pregame festivities featured both national anthems, all the appropriate pomp and circumstance. The Czechs then proceeded to pulverize the Butte Bombers, 22–3. The game was the rout of routs. Butte goalie Jerry Sinclair made sixty-nine saves.

"The score could have been 105–0 if the Czechs wanted," Tubie Johnson said. "They were kind to us. They did things we never had seen before. A guy flipped the puck on end, picked it up with his stick, and just skated through everyone with the puck on his stick, three feet in the air. That's how good these guys were."

"They cleaned the ice with us," McManus said.

The postgame results, however, were entirely different. The home team allegedly fared much better. Knievel himself allegedly fared much better. He had come onto the ice between the first and second periods and pleaded for financial help from a microphone as assorted buckets were passed around the arena. He repeated the plea between the second and third periods, mentioned that the Czechoslovakian Olympic delegation was much bigger than expected, filled with officials, and the expenses were much larger than expected. The money was collected again . . . and allegedly none of it ever reached the Czechs or any of the creditors.

The legend of the larceny that ensued took many forms. One story said that the Czech locker room also was burglarized during the rout. Another story said that Knievel had worked out a deal with a national hotel chain that included not only the rooms for the Czechs but their air travel on a chartered company plane. The national hotel chain never saw a dime. The all-encompassing story was that money from the gate receipts and the buckets disappeared and the Czechs paid dearly for their visit and their big win in Butte, and that the U.S. Olympic Committee had to help defray costs in the end.

One fact was sure: this was the end of the Butte Bombers. They played one last game a week later, half the roster missing, a fourteen-year-old boy in the starting lineup, lost to the Montana School of Mines, 11–8, and folded operations. The first lawsuit against Knievel and the Bombers was filed a week later by the Greenfield Paper Company for $247.35 for unpaid printing costs.

One other fact also was sure: the Czechs went straight off the map when they left Butte. They lost an upset to the spunky United States, 7–5, to open their visit to Squaw Valley on February 19, 1960, and closed with another loss to the United States, 9–6, when they gave up six goals in the third period on February 28. The surprising United States team won the gold medal. The Czechs finished fourth.

Knievel never played on a hockey team again. He was twenty-one years old, retired from the sport, off to other interests, other pursuits. There was no money to be made in hockey. Why stick around? He had been doing a bunch of other things while he was running the team. His ski-jumping career had gained some form with a first-place finish at Beef Trail in the class B Northern Rocky Mountain Ski Association championships. He played a sport at Walsh Field in Butte called motorcycle polo, roaring around and trying to kick a basketball at sixty miles per hour. He raced motorcycles at the new dirt track on Continental Avenue, a winner in three different categories. He won an organized hill climb at the old slag heap near Timber Butte. He tried rodeo riding.

Oh, yes, and he also was married.

5 Married

He had been married on September 5, 1959, in Dillon, Montana, at the residence of the Beaverhead County justice of the peace. Two pictures in the *Montana Standard* on the day of the game against the Czechs ran under the headline "Greater Love Hath No Woman . . . Than to Stand in Direct Line with the Hockey Puck That Can Travel as Fast as 100 Miles per Hour." Both pictures showed the former Linda Bork, dressed in a Bombers goalie uniform, ready to take shots from her husband of six months. The caption said she was his target when no one else was around.

The caption was not wrong.

She was the daughter of John Bork, who owned the company that owned and serviced most of the billboards in Butte. She was from the West Side, another girl from the affluent side of town. She was a cheerleader, pretty, smart. She had long dark hair, beautiful eyes. College certainly was in her future. Or could have been before now. There were some people who wondered what she was doing with Bob Knievel of Parrot Street, fast talker, fast mover, but not a lot of people.

"I can honestly say that in Butte there was not much class consciousness," Alec Hansen, former reporter for the *Montana Standard*, classmate of Linda Bork, said. "People just took you as you came along in Butte. I know that isn't true in most other places, but it was there."

The one person who didn't like the way Knievel came along was John Bork. He was like most of the fathers in the city. He knew trouble when he saw it. A guy who entertains people by driving up a slag heap behind the A&W Root Beer stand on a motorcycle was not a great catch.

"I had a date with Bob Knievel once," Patty Sturis, another student at Butte High, said. "Or at least I thought I did. He pulled up in front of my house, and my father saw him and said, 'No.' My father was six-foot-ten. He was known as the tallest man in Butte. He went out on the porch and told Bob to go home. Bob went. That was the end of my date."

The truth was that Knievel didn't have a lot of dates. He would become a celebrated womanizer, boast about his staggering total of one-night stands, but he was awkward around girls before he met Linda Bork, holes showing through his self-confidence. Before he met Linda, he trailed another girl everywhere she went, tried to convince her of his virtues. She would have none of it. Her friends would gather around her in a circle at school dances so he couldn't find her.

"All she wanted," one of the friends said, "was for him to go away."

That was not a problem when he settled on Linda Bork. They became a couple. He was four years older, doing his best to run wild, and she was known as quiet and sensible, but he made her laugh and certainly had big plans and . . . who knows why people fall for other people? She fell for Bob Knievel. No matter what her father said.

"She sat next to me in English class," George Markovich, a classmate, said. "I kind of liked her. And I thought she kind of liked me. Then one day I saw Bob, he was driving a 1948 Oldsmobile, and she was sitting next to him, and that was that. She was his girlfriend."

The story that Knievel always told was how he eventually had to kidnap her to marry her. This was one of the assorted basic legends that he attached to himself. The story had different permutations, sometimes sounded suspiciously like the scene John Milius later created for the movie, sometimes not. There even might have been two kidnappings. Knievel sometimes said that happened.

One kidnap story was that he dragged her off the ice rink by her hair, maybe from an ice rink in her backyard, maybe at Clark Park, and they drove away in the Olds, headed toward Idaho and marriage. The trip was ended by a snowstorm, and they found shelter in a highway maintenance shed in Whitehall. Her father called the state police, and when they found the shivering couple, she was still wearing her ice skates. All was well. All charges were dropped.

The second kidnap story was that she went to college in the fall after the first kidnap story. Her father had gotten a restraining order against Knievel to keep him away from her. The restraining order was no more threatening to this restrained party, of course, than most laws were at the time. He showed up at the college, swooped her up, and away they went to see that Beaverhead County justice of the peace in Dillon, Montana. She was seventeen years old. He was a month short of his twenty-first birthday. This was more like a traditional story of the time than kidnapping. Kids decided to marry young. Parents objected. Kids eloped.

"I hope you didn't do anything silly like get married," John Bork supposedly said to his daughter when she called him on the phone.

"Daddy, I am married," she supposedly replied.

No woman knows, especially at seventeen, what kind of trouble she might have bought by saying "I do" to a freewheeling young man ("He'll settle down" is the eternal hope), but Linda had signed on for a bunch. She had married a high school dropout, a con man, a thief, a motorcycle rider, a hockey player, a daydreamer, a fast talker, and a full-blown egomaniac, all in one package. Bob was all about Bob. That was the basic truth about Bob.

His idea of marriage was that the woman should serve the man. The man should be in charge, and the woman should do what he said she should do. That would never change. Maybe these were ideas he had collected from his grandparents. Or from some long-ago generation. He should be able to do whatever he wanted, whenever he wanted. The woman, his wife, should do what he told her to do.

"Bob, I don't think, ever understood women," George Markovich said. "I know he developed a reputation, all those women, but those were one-night stands, whatever. A relationship with a woman, I don't think he ever understood them."

The couple came back to live in a double-wide next door to Iggy and Emma's house on Parrot Street. Linda had signed on for a hard road.

A story. One of the jobs he concocted after the end of the hockey project was the Sur-Kill Guide Service. He was the president, chief financial officer, and leading tracker of animals that hunters might want to hunt. He was the entire company, a one-man corporation.

The job did not last long—he apparently had a tendency to take his customers onto posted land to fulfill that sur-kill promise—but was notable for one celebrated event. He went to the White House, trying to track down President John F. Kennedy.

The trip began when the U.S. Park Service announced that the elk population had grown to ten thousand head inside Yellowstone Park, an unsustainable figure, and it was going to send sharpshooters into the park to slaughter half of the herd, five thousand elk. Knievel had become active within various sportsmen's groups that opposed the kill. The sportsmen's groups wanted either permits for hunters issued for the parkland or the capture and transportation of the excess elk to other areas, many of them in Montana. Either move would benefit an operation like the Sur-Kill Guide Service.

Knievel went to a public meeting on the subject at the Elks Lodge in Livingston, Montana, where he reported that ninety elk had been killed by park rangers on Monday, sixty more on Tuesday. Something had to be done. He organized a petition to save the elk, collected three thousand names, and said that he would hitchhike to Washington to personally deliver them to Washington.

And he did.

He killed a six-point buck elk himself, maybe on parkland, maybe not, and removed the antlers. He then hitchhiked to Washington to present the antlers and the petition to JFK.

Or so he said.

The cynics in Butte suggested that maybe Knievel had a friend, maybe someone like Jack Ferriter, drive the route, Knievel stepping into different press conferences in different towns with his hitchhiking story and his appeal to save the elk. Ferriter denied this happened, but stories persisted. Knievel said he had twenty-seven rides between Butte and Washington, which would have been a lot of times putting those antlers, which were fifty-four inches wide, in and out of cars. Someone might have helped.

Anyway, he left Butte on December 1, 1961, and reached Washington on December 9, 1961. On December 10, his picture with Montana congressman Mickey Boryan, antlers in the foreground, U.S. Capitol dome in the background, was shipped across the country by the wire service Unifax. Knievel wore a jacket and tie, had a buzz cut, and looked incredibly young and incredibly earnest, a charter member of JFK's New Frontier.

On December 11, 1961, he had a fifteen-minute visit with Secretary of the Interior Stewart Udall. "He was very interested in the situation,"

Knievel told United Press International. "He said that we've got a lot of room to kick about what they're doing in Yellowstone."

On December 12, 1961, he visited the White House and presented the antlers to JFK assistant Mike Manatos.

"I'm sure he will call the situation to the president's attention," Knievel told United Press International.

On the same day, his picture and a story were on the fourth page of the B section of the *Washington Post*. He told the reporter that people had been nice to him on the trip. When they found they couldn't fit the antlers into the car, they put them in the trunk or tied them on the top. No mention was made of a hitchhiking return.

The slaughter supposedly was curtailed after this grand trip. The immediate effects on Knievel's business were minimal because the business soon died. The long-term effects were more important.

He had discovered an important truth about self-promotion: if you talk to reporters, they will write down your words and put them into the newspaper. Nothing will be checked. The more interesting the story, the faster the words will appear.

And a good prop does not hurt.

His main, listed occupation during this time was merchant policeman. The job was mentioned in the article in the *Washington Post*. His unlisted occupation, besides policeman and hunting guide, was burglar. The listed and the unlisted occupations complemented each other, strange as that sounded.

A merchant policeman was not a Butte policeman but a private contractor, what was called a "door-knocker." He offered his clients protection from robbery and vandalism. Every night he would check their businesses, make sure the locks were locked, the windows unbroken. He would have his eye open for suspicious characters, for strange doings. Signing a contract with him—Knievel was the only private policeman in Butte—was insurance against bad news.

The major cause of that bad news, of course, was him.

Decide not to sign that contract and maybe there would be a robbery, maybe a broken plate-glass window, maybe a small fire. See? Bad news could arrive as fast as that. Decide to sign the contract and the robberies, the broken windows, the small fires, would cease. See? Bad news could disappear as fast as that. Life would resume at its normal pace.

The door-knocker business was nothing more than an extortion scheme, the old protection business, a staple of illicit income around the world, and it worked. Knievel put together a client list that even included many of his friends in the bar business. He was able to rob with a purpose, have one business help the other. The robbery would show the problem. The service would stop the problem.

"He robbed *me*," Bob Pavlovich at the Met Tavern said, still incredulous years later. "He robbed me more than once."

"I made sure he did his job," Muzzy Faroni at the Freeway Tavern said. "I stayed up all night after I hired him. I made sure he checked the locks, and I made sure he didn't come in. I was sitting there with a shotgun in the dark. Just in case."

"I'd do some of the robberies for him," one friend said. "He would stand guard in the parking lot. I'd go inside. It worked out fine."

Knievel did make his rounds, did make the job look official. He would leave a piece of paper under the door for the store owner as proof that he had visited, and sometimes he'd have his name in the *Montana Standard* for some chase of some suspicious character. He and the Butte police would be in pursuit. Shots would be fired. Knievel invariably would be the one who fired.

He carried a gun on a regular basis and was not afraid to show it. One of his stops on social nights was the Yellowstone, one of the tougher bars in Butte. He was in there one night, talking, yapping, fooling around with some other young guys. Normal stuff. One of the older regulars took offense. He said that the young guys were too noisy. He asked the bartender to throw them out. Maybe he placed a hand on Knievel while he spoke. Knievel took offense. He tapped the regular on the shoulder.

"Open your mouth," he said.

"What?"

"Open your mouth."

The regular opened his mouth. Knievel, in one fluid motion, pulled a pistol from his boot and shoved it into the man's open mouth.

"What do you say now?" he asked. "Is it still too noisy?"

This was where he lived now. The dark side. The dark side, the easy money, was attractive. He and Linda had a son, Kelly, born on August 21, 1960, who was followed by Robbie, born on May 7, 1962, and would be followed by a daughter, Tracey, born on October 22, 1963. The double-wide on Parrot Street became full and noisy in a hurry. Knievel rented other, larger places around Butte to live. There was a string of these places, low rents, linoleum on the floor, basic living. The one constant was that he wasn't in these places a lot. He was always gone, out of the house, moving.

"I lived down on Idaho Street, the low-rent side of town, in this little apartment," Jim Blankenship said. "They lived near me. I remember I'd see Linda, all the time, outside with three little kids. They'd all be in their snowsuits, buttoned up. She'd be running around after them. They'd be giving her a workout. I never saw Bob. He was off. Gone. Doing whatever he was doing."

The expenses of family life, Linda and the three kids, added to the expense of the fast, every-night social life, created a demand for more and more money. The dark side was an answer to the demand.

"We were looking for a place to rob one night," a man said. "We stopped to buy gas. The attendant was in the garage, didn't see me when I went in to pay. I tried to open the register, take the money, but the register was locked. I unplugged it, lifted it up, and carried it to the car. We drove away, broke the thing open someplace else.

"The next day Bob saw a story in the paper. He started laughing. He said, 'Hey, you got that guy fired.' The owner heard about the robbery and fired the guy for not being at the register."

The robberies took place everywhere, many of them more serious than a cash register taken from a gas station. Butte was in the midst of a crime wave—a perpetual crime wave, some residents said—that even included members of the Butte police force. Knievel was operating at the same time. He described the excitement of entering a building with bad intentions, boasted about his prowess at opening safes. He brought a safe into the Freeway Tavern one night, showed how he could open it, just to win a bet.

He later admitted being involved in a lot of robberies, apologized for the inconvenience. He robbed pharmacies, sporting goods stores, grocery stores, any place that could be robbed. One robbery that he admitted was left as unfinished business was an attempt to break into the vault when the Prudential Bank switched headquarters, moved from one side of the street to the other. Knievel and his robbery associates tried to cut through the wall next door, then through the vault, but moved too slowly and had to quit before they reached the money because sunrise had arrived.

Another robbery, which he never admitted, happened at the court-house. The safe was filled with money, silver dollars. Someone came in through the roof, broke open the safe, and stole the silver dollars. The prime suspect was the local door-knocker, former hockey executive.

"It was the weekend of Lincoln's Birthday," Jack Kusler said. "A bunch of us were going down to Las Vegas for go-kart races. On Friday I talked to Knievel. He said he really wanted to go, but he was flat broke. He told us to have fun. The rest of us put our karts on a trailer and went. On Saturday night in Las Vegas, there's Knievel. He has all kinds of money. He's got $4,000 spread out on the dice table. He said he got lucky.

"I heard he was stopped by the police on the way back. He had thousands of dollars in silver dollars. He said the same thing, he got lucky. What could they do? Bets are paid off in Vegas in silver dollars. The cops knew he did it, but they couldn't prove anything."

Knievel did admit later that he was headed in the worst directions. Most of his accomplices ultimately would have bad fates ranging from death to drug addiction to long stretches in prison. The Butte policemen would be sent away after a celebrated trial. For the moment, though, everybody was young and bulletproof. The people on the dark side in Butte could do anything. They might have had suspicions that bad things could happen, but the bad things hadn't happened yet.

Every day was exciting.

"I'd see him in a bar," Clyde Kelley, the grown-up kid who had surrendered his belt to Knievel in the plot against the Butte High librarian, said. "I'd watch him. He'd be looking at the jukebox or the cigarette machine, trying to figure out if it was full of money or not. If he thought it was full, well, he was going to try to figure a way to get that money. That was just the way he was.

"A hustler."

6 Insurance

He settled down in the summer of 1962, found his first actual suit-and-tie job, selling insurance for the Combined Insurance Company of Chicago, Illinois. The legend later became that he had broken his collarbone riding in a motorcycle race and was forced to take a job in the dull everyday world to pay the rent, but he mentioned at the time that he had a feeling that his illegal activities were catching up with him. He was scared.

"He told me he thought the police were waiting for him to make a mistake," Matt Tonning, another salesman at Combined, said. "They knew that he had robbed the courthouse. Everybody knew he had robbed the courthouse. They just couldn't prove it."

If that was the case—or even if a broken collarbone from a racing crash was the reason—he substituted the excitement of insurance sales for his previous excitement. The excitement of insurance sales was a surprise. He was hired by Alex Smith, the district manager for the western Montana territory, and sent to Combined's headquarters in Chicago for a two-week sales course that appealed to him in ways that high school or the United States Army never could.

The head of the company was W. Clement Stone, an energetic multimillionaire who had turned business success into a sort of capitalistic religion. With a tidy aristocratic mustache and a partiality to bow ties, he was a living representation of the pint-sized millionaire pictured on the box for the board game Monopoly. He had lived a true up-from-nowhere story, a high school dropout, former newspaper boy, his path to success laid out by the Horatio Alger books he read in the Chicago tenements. He was sixty-two years old now, more convinced than ever that if he could succeed, anyone and everyone could follow.

To work for Combined was to be immersed in an ocean of Stone's aphorisms:

- Aim for the moon. If you miss, you may hit a star.
- All personal achievement starts in the mind of the individual. Your personal achievement starts in your mind. The first step is to know exactly what your problem, goal, or desire is.
- Big doors swing on little hinges.
- Like success, failure is many things to many people. With Positive Mental Attitude, failure is a learning experience, a rung on the ladder, a plateau at which to get your thoughts in order and prepare to try again.
- Sales are contingent on the attitude of the salesman—not the attitude of the prospect.
- Thinking will not overcome fear, but action will.
- Try, try, try, and keep on trying is the rule that must be followed to become an expert in anything.
- Regardless of who you are or what you have been, you can still become what you may want to be.

The first duty for all recruits at the training sessions was to read a book that contained all of these thoughts and more, *Success Through a Positive Mental Attitude*, written by Stone and Napoleon Hill. (When Stone eventually died in 2002 at the age of one hundred, the *New York Times* headline on his obituary read "Clement Stone Dies at 100; Built Empire on Optimism.") The second duty was to take the information in the book and use it to sell a hell of a lot of insurance.

Which was what Bob Knievel did. He followed this program in ways he never had followed any program in his life.

"A lot of guys shut themselves off from all of that rah-rah stuff, thought it was corny," Matt Tonning said. "Not Bob. He followed what you were supposed to do. I did too. I believed it. That stuff worked. It could make you a lot of money."

The policies were for accident coverage, three dollars for six months' coverage that would pay the customer a modest benefit if he was disabled. The salesman would earn sixty cents on each three dollars, so he had to move policies in bulk to make money. The company provided all of the essentials for sales, right down to a Five-Part Rebuttal System to customer objections. What the mind can conceive, the mind can achieve! There were contests, rewards, constant memos, a sequence of honors for salesmen that went from Pearl to Ruby, Sapphire, and then Grand Diamond. The big contest every year was held to celebrate Mr. Stone's birthday on May 4. On every salesman's birthday, Mr. Stone would send him a book, perhaps *Think and Grow Rich* by Napoleon Hill, perhaps *The Power of Positive Thinking* by Norman Vincent Peale, perhaps some other manual for success.

"You took these principles into your personal life," Jay Tamburina, another salesman at Combined, said. "Of course you did. The importance of eye contact. The Socratic method, teaching by questions. You realized how you can control people's minds just sticking to the goddamned script."

Playing with people's heads. Bob Knievel loved it all. This was what he had been doing for all of his life.

The sales week would begin on Sunday night, a trip to some town somewhere on the Montana map, registration at some bad motel, a bright start on Monday morning. Salesmen would travel through the state on a six-month cycle, renewing past clients, but also armed with a list of referrals. They would work their lists, also make some dreaded cold calls, which W. Clement Stone called "gold calls."

Initiative was part of the operation.

"Bob would rent a booth in a bar for a week," Matt Tonning said. "He'd go to a place like Eureka, Montana, find a place that he liked, and ask the bartender how much it would be to rent a booth. That would be his office. It was all cattle country, and those ranchers would come into town and line up, and Bob would write 'em up. They all would have money, those ranchers. Shit on their boots maybe, but they had money. There would be lines out the door."

The self-confidence and aggressiveness and fast talk that had made some people walk away from Knievel in Butte were assets in this job as he made deals, shook hands, moved along to the next customer. He was Harold Hill, the Music Man, discovering trouble right here in River City. The trouble could be averted by a fine insurance policy, three dollars for six months.

Part of his initiative was making deals even if cash was not involved.

He would barter insurance for goods or services as well as for money. A rancher offered him a horse in exchange for a big policy in Eureka. Knievel jumped at the chance. The rancher took the horse out of a trailer and left it outside the bar. Knievel tried to sell the horse to ranchers who followed.

"That horse is Sweeneyed," a rancher said after inspection.

"What's that?" Knievel asked.

"It means his shoulder is gone," the rancher replied. "He's worthless."

Not every deal was a triumph.

A better result came at the roundhouse in Lewistown, Montana, where trains were serviced and turned around, sent back on different tracks. Knievel convinced the foreman to let him talk to the workers and sell policies during lunch breaks. All was proceeding nicely until the big boss arrived and saw this commercial activity and ordered it to stop. Knievel argued that this was lunch break. The big boss argued that this was a place for railroad business, not insurance business. Knievel said he would take this to the president of the company and would be back. He did indeed write a letter to the president, who, it turned out, was a good friend of W. Clement Stone's and quickly dispatched a telegram to his man in Lewistown.

Policies were sold.

"He was an absolute bullshitter," Jay Tamburina said. "He had bigger cojones than anyone I ever met. There were things about him that were great. There were some that were not great. We had a lot of fun."

Any approach could be tried. Faced with a disinterested business owner one afternoon, Knievel threw his insurance book at the man, hitting him in the chest. The book weighed about five pounds.

"I'm offering you the best God damned insurance in the world," Knievel shouted. "You better pay attention, by God."

Sold.

The salesmen sometimes would invade a Montana town in pairs. Tamburina would work with Knievel. They looked a little bit alike, short hair, same coloring, same eyes. They would follow their leads, compare notes. Drinking would be involved at the end of the day, Montana Marys in a long line. They would argue about who was better-looking.

The fifteen or so salesmen in the western Montana district all were around the same age, late twenties, early thirties, most of them married. They were road warriors, partners sometimes, competitors more times, always restless, working on the same daily dose of W. Clement Stone adrenaline. They would gather on Friday nights at Alex Smith's house in Helena on their way home to cheer their successes, bemoan their plights, report their sales results.

Smith, older, forty-five, was the charismatic model of what the salesmen wanted to be. He wore custom-tailored suits and sports jackets, all of them with a signature red lining. He wore alligator boots. He drove a white Lincoln Continental, expensive, long as a city block. He had a bar and a pool table in the basement of his home. He was a gracious host, a good talker, a big drinker. Work long enough for the company, hell, this is what you could be. Alex Smith.

"I thought the sun rose and set on Alex Smith," Jay Tamburina said. "I wanted to be exactly like him. Everybody did."

The salesmen sometimes would gather for parties, sometimes with wives, sometimes without wives. At one affair, Knievel stunned everyone with his agility. A sort of logrolling competition was held in the host's backyard, using part of a kids' play set. One after another, salesmen fell off the log hanging from two chains. Knievel stepped up, and not only could he walk on the log, he started spinning it with his feet. No one came close to what he did.

At another affair, a Christmas party, wives involved, drink involved, Knievel stood up late in the proceedings to propose a toast "to the woman I love." Everyone anticipated and looked at Linda . . . and he said some other woman's name. Linda started crying. Another woman, backed by her husband, stood up and began to chew him out for making Linda feel bad. Knievel reacted.

"You just shut up," he said to the woman. "Because I fucked you too."

The room became very quiet. People soon started to gather their coats and leave. This was not exactly a power of positive thinking moment, although W. Clement Stone had an aphorism that seemed to apply:

"You always do what you want to do. This is true with every act. You may say that you had to do something, or that you were forced to, but actually, whatever you do, you do by choice. Only you have the power to choose for yourself."

True enough.

A story. The two salesmen finished the sales day at the Capri Bar in Helena, Montana. They sat next to each other, Tamburina and Knievel, joined by the county attorney, a Helena lawyer whom they both knew.

There was a crowd in the place, most seats filled around the large circular bar, one of those arrangements where the bartenders work in the middle of the circle, serving customers on all sides.

Knievel seemed preoccupied.

"What are you doing?" Tamburina asked.

His fellow worker in the Combined Insurance empire seemed to be figuring out some kind of calibration at the edge of the bar. The distance between the edge and his glass seemed important. The measurement now was perhaps a foot.

"No," Knievel said, moving the glass a half-inch, maybe an inch.

"No," he said again, moving the glass another half-inch, maybe another inch.

This continued for a while. The glass was moved, half-inch by half-inch, inch by inch until it was two feet from the edge of the bar. Maybe more. Maybe two feet, six inches. Both Tamburina and the county attorney, who also had become interested, repeated the question. What was Knievel doing? He finally answered as he moved the glass a final half-inch, maybe an inch.

"I think that's it," he declared.

"That's what?"

"I've been trying to figure, if I stood at the edge of the bar, if my dick could still reach the glass. How far away would the glass have to be to be as far as I could reach? I think this is it."

He was serious. The county attorney and Tamburina stared at the distance. The idea seemed preposterous. Seabiscuit, the racehorse, didn't have a member that could stretch that far. Bob Knievel? Either he was a biological freak or he was self-delusional. All evidence pointed toward self-delusional. The men had been drinking for a while.

"Nobody's dick is that long," the county attorney said. "You're out of your mind."

"Do you want to bet?"

"Sure."

"Five hundred bucks."

The county attorney knew a sucker when he saw one. This was easy tax-free money. He shook Bob Knievel's hand. Knievel quickly got out of his chair, stood. He moved close to the bar and put his hand on his zipper.

"What are you doing?' the attorney asked.

"I'm going to show you," Knievel said. "There's only one way to do that."

The fact should be mentioned that the circular bar at the Capri was not a flat circular bar. One side was higher than the other, so the patrons on the higher side could look down on the patrons on the lower side and see every single thing that they might be doing. Knievel, Tamburina, and the county attorney were on the lower side. If Knievel unfurled his member, his dick, and tried to reach the glass, the people on the high side would see the entire show. The fact also should be mentioned that other lawyers, maybe a judge or two, maybe a couple of newspapermen, and certainly a fair share of gossipy voters sat on the higher side. A reputation could be destroyed in a moment.

"You can't do that," the county attorney said.

"Sure I can," Knievel said, starting to unzip.

"No, you can't."

"Then I win the five hundred dollars. If I can't show you, then you have to take my word. Give me the money."

The county attorney, after a substantial amount of grousing, eventually paid. Knievel received $500 for not exposing himself in the Capri Bar.

Tamburina wondered forever if his fellow salesman had plotted out the whole scene in his head, if he knew the attorney would bite and then would have to back off. Was Knievel such a student of human nature that he could predict all that? Could he play a game that far ahead? Apparently so. Tamburina couldn't figure out any other explanation to the story.

"The guy," Tamburina said, "was sharp as a tack."

His biggest moment in the insurance business came when he visited the state mental hospital in Warm Springs, Montana. He tore through the hospital during a competition called "I Dare You Week," sold 110 three-dollar policies in a day, 271 three-dollar policies in the week. These were both record numbers in his district. He sold policies to doctors, nurses, clerical staff, everyone except the residents, though later in life he would not mind leaving the impression that, yes, well, maybe he sold to a couple of residents too. Hey, it was I Dare You Week.

His efforts made him a Grand Diamond winner, highest honor in the company, and were extolled in a mailing distributed to all Combined salesmen in the region. Under the headline "Bob Knievel Sets Record" and a shirt-and-tie head shot that could have been any corporate young man on the move, he handed out advice on how to do exactly what he did.

"You asked me to tell you how I broke the records last week in daily and weekly sales . . . Well, to tell you the truth, it wasn't very hard . . . after I conceived in my own mind that I could do it," he said. "I enjoyed it and had a lot of fun . . . All it takes is accepting the challenge to do it . . . I'll admit I worked long hours during that one day and all through the week, but I had a lot of fun.

"I've got a wallet full of money, and that helps me to realize what a great System and a great product that we have to sell . . . it's easy."

He had been inspired when he saw awards handed out to successful salesmen at a subregional sales meeting in Casper, Wyoming. Why wasn't he winning those awards? He had made up his mind to move into the game! That was half the battle right there! Everything else was easy! You could do it too!

"First of all, have a lot of fun," he advised. "Be serious in your selling, but at the same time laugh and have fun . . . Know everything you can about the Policy . . . Know the Sales Talks, the Rebuttals, how to get permission . . . Know what is really meant by working Systematically.

"All I was doing was what I've been told to do . . .

"I'LL MAKE YOU ANOTHER PROMISE," he finalized in capital letters. "AT OUR NEXT REGIONAL SALES MEETING, YOU'LL HAVE ANOTHER LETTER TELLING YOU HOW I BROKE BOTH OF MY OWN RECORDS ALONG WITH THE 1964 NATIONAL SALES RECORD.

"THAT'S A PROMISE.

"BOB KNIEVEL."

The triumph did not last. He didn't take his own advice to put his head down, work harder, and good things might come. He was the rookie who hits a big homer, the actor who scores an Oscar nomination the first time out, flush with success, who immediately looks for a new contract to replace the previous contract. He wanted to talk to W. Clement Stone himself but settled for Matt Walsh, the international sales manager. He asked to be named a vice president.

"I'll break every sales record in the history of this company," he promised.

Walsh came back with a negative answer. Protocols had to be followed.

There were other people who had worked longer with the company who already were in line for that kind of job. Nobody was promoted from sales right to vice president. Stay with the program. Do well. Promotions will come soon enough.

Knievel quit.

The lack of logic to his decision stunned his contemporaries. He was built for selling insurance. A lot of aspiring salesmen went through Combined's payroll, sent home because they were tongue-tied, shy, couldn't close the deal. This guy closed every deal. He was a master at this business, already making good money, sure to make more. How could he quit?

"Mr. Stone would talk about a thing called the 'Mastodonian Instinct,' " Matt Tonning said. "You reach a certain pinnacle in what you do, then you can't stop yourself from just screwing up, losing it all. Some people are like that. They can't help themselves. That was Bob. That was how he operated. He didn't have a backup in his personality."

Maybe that explanation was a little complicated. Maybe Knievel simply had learned what he had to learn. Maybe the excitement of the insurance business wasn't exciting enough. Maybe he didn't give a shit.

The lessons of Combined and W. Clement Stone did stay with him for the rest of his life. They could be heard in his words, could be seen in his actions. Conceive and achieve. He could sell. He would come back a couple of times to the company when he needed fast money, desperation trumping pride, but never with ambition or commitment. The important lessons from Combined already had been learned. He had the method for success. He knew what to do when he found what he wanted to do. He had to find what he wanted to do.

His next job was selling motorcycles.

7 Moses Lake, WA

He was a mess when he showed up at Barry Queen's house on this particular morning in the summer of 1964 in Moses Lake, Washington. He had so many bumps, scabs, abrasions, that it seemed as if he had bumps, scabs, and abrasions on his bumps, scabs, and abrasions. He was a cartoon version of a cartoon version of a character that has undergone a physical mishap. There may have been a cast on at least one extremity. Perhaps two casts on two extremities.

"What happened to you?" Barry Queen asked.

Bob Knievel explained:

1. He had been riding his Honda Scrambler 250 last night . . .
2. He had a logging chain with him . . .
3. He wanted to see what kind of sparks the logging chain could generate off the road if he dragged it behind his Honda Scrambler 250 . . .
4. He especially wanted to see if more sparks came off the chain if he drove faster and faster . . .
5. It all was true. The sparks came off the chain. More speed meant more sparks. He came down the streets of Moses Lake like a noisy, fiery vision from hell. He was roaring, outrageous. Everything was perfect . . .
6. Alas, the end of the chain bounced under the back wheel of a parked car . . .

7. The chain immediately became taut . . .
8. Well, hell, this was the result . . .

"I was lying in the street," Bob Knievel said. "All broken and bloody. It wasn't pretty."

One of the most successful campaigns in American advertising history was being waged in the summer of 1964. "You Meet the Nicest People on a Honda" was the slogan. Those eight words, eleven syllables, had revolutionized the motorcycle business.

Devised by the Grey Advertising Agency, the campaign centered on pictures of housewives and businessmen, postmen and preachers, college kids, ordinary-looking people riding Honda's clean and ordinary-looking motorcycles. Everybody laughed, everybody smiled, everybody looked as if he or she lived off a diet of sunshine and Jesus. The image of the motorcycle rider had been taken from the Hells Angels and Marlon Brando and *The Wild Ones* and planted in the middle of Main Street, U.S.A. The effects of the ads were phenomenal. U.S. sales of Honda motorcycles now were in the midst of a jump from 40,000 in a year to 200,000 in a year. That was a 500 percent increase. Americans wanted to buy a Honda.

Barry Queen, an enlisted man in the Air Force, had bought a Honda. The first "nicest person" he had met was Bob Knievel, who didn't look like any of those people in the advertising pictures. Bob Knievel had sold him the Honda.

Then he went riding with him.

"He'd just show up at the house and say, 'Let's go,' and I went," Queen said. "My wife wouldn't want me to go because I wasn't too smart. I'd do whatever he did. I'd crash and bleed. We'd just roar around. Go out to the sand dunes. He crashed one time and had a cut on his leg that went so deep I could see his shinbone. I'd never seen anything like that."

The nicest people in Moses Lake drove fast.

Knievel had ridden bikes for years in weekend races just outside Spokane, made friends with some of the locals, and when one of the better riders, Darrell Triber, offered him a job selling Hondas at the Triber family's Spokane dealership, he had moved his family out of Butte. Three kids in four years made this a substantial undertaking, but when Triber offered a better job after a few months, manager of a new dealership in Moses Lake, Knievel moved everyone again. Linda found a job at a hardware store on Monroe Street.

He latched right on to the "You Meet the Nicest People on a Honda" approach. He tried to sell to everyone he met, motorcycles replacing insurance in importance in a potential customer's daily life. He tried to whip up interest, enthusiasm, get known in town. He hired a local high school English teacher and wrestling coach, Gary Frey, to help.

"I went in the dealership in Moses Lake when it had been open about two weeks," Gary Frey said. "I had an old Harley 125, where you had to mix in kerosene and oil with the gas, and I wanted to move up. I'd also had five kids in six years, so I didn't have any money. I just went down there to see if I could work a deal with this new guy."

Knievel saw the bike. Knievel laughed at him.

"Well, what can I do to get something I'd be proud to drive?" Frey asked.

"You can work for me," Knievel said.

Frey had never met anyone like Knievel. The guy was charming and devious and crazy. All at once. He not only would say anything, but do anything. He could sell like nobody's business, close a deal on most customers who wavered, but you couldn't trust him for a moment. He was danger and fun and full of himself. Every day around him was a day at a strange circus.

An example. He had a standing offer for arm-wrestling matches: he would put up a Honda 50 motorcycle against $100, winner take all. News about this deal filtered around the bars and restaurants, high schools and college campuses, in the state of Washington. The starting price for a Honda 50 was $245, so the bet was more than two-to-one. A succession of beefy young men showed up at the dealership, $100 in hand. Knievel whipped them, one after another.

A report that he was going to take on yet another challenger would run through the neighborhood, and a small crowd would assemble to see if the streak would be broken. Maybe a hundred people, maybe more, would slide inside the shop, stuffing the place. Frey suggested selling seats.

"He had a strong right forearm," Frey said. "Maybe from hockey, I don't know. He just wore out those kids. After a while, they didn't come around as often, because he'd beaten them all."

Frey had a next-door neighbor who was a sheet-metal worker. The sheet-metal worker was a big guy. He never had been interested in the bet because he was not a motorcycle rider. He was, however, a boat enthusiast. Frey told him that Knievel had taken a boat in trade for a motorcycle.

The sheet-metal worker, the big guy, appeared at the dealership with $200 to bet because the boat was more expensive than the motorcycle. Ten minutes later, he walked out, still with his $200, plus a boat.

"There were only three people in the shop," Frey said. "I was the third one. I'll give this to Bob: he didn't complain, didn't try to get out of the bet. The only thing he did was get my neighbor and me to swear that we would never tell what happened."

Knievel's big promotional idea was to build a racetrack. He figured it would stimulate sales of both bikes and accessories, give kids a place to ride. Everyone would win with a racetrack, especially Moses Lake Honda. Where can we build it? Well, Frey told him, there were a lot of farms around, vacant areas left fallow as farmers rotated crops. What farm would be a good choice? Well, we could check out the farms where the Moses Lake wrestlers lived. Well, what are we waiting for?

The site turned out to be a corner of the farm owned by the father of Moses Lake wrestler Billy Richardson. Billy Richardson's father saw no harm, the field just sitting there for a couple of years. The equipment to lay out the track came from the Moses Lakes public works department, although the public works department really didn't know about the project. Frey was also the track coach at the high school, so he had access to a roller, a grader, a backhoe. The work took place on weekends and summer nights, as Knievel recruited local motorcyclists to help. The eventual result was a good-looking but very dusty quarter-mile track.

"We need to oil it down," Knievel decided.

A truck from Standard Oil somehow appeared, another quiet Knievel deal, spread oil on the track. Billy Richardson's father wondered out loud about the effects on future crops, but Knievel assured him that all would be fine. The oil, he said, would just wash away. Maybe it even would help the crops.

After all of this hard work, the track was ready to open for business and shenanigans. All it needed was an opening day attraction. There would be opening races, of course, but there should be something more for spectators.

"I was driving in my car," Gary Frey said. "The announcer on the radio started describing the races and a big show at the new Moses Lake track. The feature event, he said, was Moses Lake English teacher and wrestling coach Gary Frey driving through some flaming boards. I couldn't believe it. I said, 'Oh, no, that's never going to happen.' "

Frey was firm. This was too dangerous, too stupid. He had never done anything like this. He had five kids. His wife would kill him. Flaming boards were regulation pieces of particleboard, four feet by eight feet, set up like so many freestanding closed doors at intervals on the racetrack. The pieces of particleboard would be set on fire. An adventurous motorcycle rider (supposedly him) would crash through the burning obstacles at a high rate of speed. (Maybe.) There was no way in the world he would do this.

Knievel presented a list of reasons why going through flaming boards would be fun, safe, profitable. Frey said no. Knievel said he would do it himself, except he had to run the races, run the show. No. Knievel said Frey had to do it because he had the local big name. No. Knievel challenged his manhood. No, no, no.

Then L. V. Shaw, the district superintendent of schools for Moses Lake, called. He told Frey that he had heard the ads on the radio and he was calling to forbid him to take part in this escapade. Forbid? Frey heard the word, became angry. Who was this guy to forbid? This was the summer. Forbid? He called Knievel.

Yes.

They picked out a bike from the trade-ins that would have the best chance of success, a big battering ram of a Harley. The bike had a hand shift, and Frey drove it for days, working out the gears. Knievel told him he should be doing forty miles per hour to blast through the board, but the bike was so big that he might get away with going a little slower.

On the grand opening day of races at the Moses Lake track, wearing Bob Knievel's helmet and leathers, Frey nervously tried to get the Harley up to speed. The races had broken down the oiled topsoil, made the dirt loose and the motorcycle slow, and the best he could do was twenty-five miles per hour. Knievel told him that was fine. Fine? The teacher-coach looked into the small crowd and saw his wife and children, many of his wrestlers, all with "a look of consternation and worry" on their faces. He sighed deeply, rolled down the track, speedometer still under twenty-five, flaming boards in front of him . . . and pulled away at the last second. The people began to boo.

Boo?

He came around again, gave the Harley as much gas as possible, sort of hung down to one side to protect himself from the big collision, hit the first flaming board at twenty-five miles per hour, *crash*, then the second and third, *crash* and *crash*, and came out the other side. Knievel was right. The bike was big enough to do the job. Frey was alive and whole. The Moses Lake track was open in style. The people now cheered.

Frey told Knievel he was happy that this craziness was finished at last. Knievel told Frey he had booked the show in coming weeks in Yakima and Sunnyside. Frey said, "Bullshit."

In coming weeks, he blasted through flaming boards in Yakima and Sunnyside. The people cheered again.

Saturday mornings soon became a prime time for racing on the new track. There was nothing formal to the proceedings, just show up and ride. Fool around. Slide and get dirty. When the track became worn down again, soft and slow and dusty, needed to be rolled one more time, the riders moved to the Corral Tavern, a bar on Broadway, Moses Lake, to drink away the effects of that dust.

Four or five riders were left at the Corral on a Saturday not too long after the grand opening at the track. They had been there for a while. Knievel was not a particularly big drinker, but already was known to do strange things in Moses Lake when the beers piled up. (Example: riding with the logging chain, making sparks.) On this Saturday, the beers had piled up.

Part of the entertainment had been watching a couple of workers unload a flatbed trailer across the street, bringing appliances into Swartz's Electric store. The job was almost finished now, maybe one or two boxes left on the truck, the ramp still attached.

Knievel excused himself from the table. He went outside, put on his helmet, kicked his motorcycle into action, put it into gear, stepped hard on the gas, hurtled across Broadway, up the ramp, and onto the back of the flatbed. Ta-da.

His fellow drinkers applauded the show.

This was impressive.

He then proceeded to do stationary wheelies on the flatbed, holding the bike steady. This was also impressive, more impressive . . . except he didn't hold the bike steady enough.

The back wheel caught traction somewhere on the flatbed. Maybe it hit a piece of tape. Maybe it hit the tops of a couple of screws. Something happened. The motorcycle shot forward, Knievel on top, and flew through the plate-glass window of Swartz's Electric.

Flew through the plate-glass window of Swartz's Electric!

The fellow drinkers ran out from the restaurant and across the street. Knievel was inside the store, stretched out on the showroom floor. Glass was everywhere. He stood up, checked the exposed parts of his body. He didn't have a scratch on him.

Didn't have a scratch on him! Magic.

This was another moment. This was another escape. He could do anything and somehow land on his feet. He was invincible. This was further proof that he was bulletproof.

"I seriously think it was right here that he got the idea that he lived a charmed life," Gary Frey said. "He went through Swartz's window and nothing happened. I think this opened him up to everything that came afterward."

He did apologize to Mr. Swartz. Mr. Swartz said he had insurance.

A charmed life, it was.

On Monday morning, Knievel started building a ramp. He told Frey he was going to jump over some rattlesnakes.

"I'm going to jump over some mountain lions and some rattlesnakes" was what he said.

"Where are you going to get mountain lions and rattlesnakes?" was what Frey said.

"There's a guy up in Coulee City," Knievel said. "He has a roadside zoo. I want you to go up there. Get him to bring the mountain lions and the snakes down to Moses Lake."

Knievel had hinted that he was going to perform at the second set of races at Moses Lake. He saw the reception Frey received for going through the flaming boards. Frey became a local hero. Knievel wanted that kind of attention for himself. No flaming boards, this was his trick.

Frey, relieved to be free from the Harley and the flaming boards, still wasn't happy about the trip to Coulee City. He didn't like going on the road for Knievel, because he knew as soon as he left Moses Lake, Knievel would show up at his house and try to romance his wife, Rita.

Frey had seen it happen again and again. There was a pathological streak to Knievel's womanizing. Friendships meant nothing. He pursued all women all day, every day, twenty-four hours per day. The schoolteacher was astounded at how many women Knievel caught. Good-looking women. Married women. He knew that Knievel didn't worry about consequences. He was surprised that the women also didn't worry.

"We were coming back from the races somewhere, and he had me stop at this woman's house," Frey said. "It was a farm that she and her husband ran. They had kids. This was five o'clock in the morning. He wanted me to let him off. He said she'd give him a ride to work.

"I said, 'Well, what if her husband's there?' He said, 'The husband's gone. She told me he was gone.' I said, 'But what if he returned?' Bob pulled out his penis right there in the front yard. He said, 'If the husband's home, I'll tell him I'm the milkman and he hasn't paid his bills and I'll piss on his shoes.' Then he went up and rang the doorbell."

The one fistfight Frey fought with Knievel was about Knievel sweet-talking Rita. Frey didn't like it. Rita hated it. Knievel always would say that he wanted to make a trade, Linda for Rita, funny if someone else might say it, but creepy when he said it because he meant it. Frey and his wife not only had the five kids, but they also had a big Chesapeake Bay retriever that they mostly kept in the basement. On the days Knievel sent Frey on the road, Rita let the dog out of the basement for protection.

Frey finally told Knievel to cut it out one day at the shop. Knievel took issue with Frey's words and asked what he was going to do about it. While he said that, he grabbed a chain to use as a weapon, which he swung.

Frey, the wrestling coach, dodged the chain, got inside, and threw Knievel to the floor. He proceeded to put him into a submission hold. That ended the fight and curtailed the romantic proposals. Then again, Knievel was Knievel.

"You had to know two things about him," Frey said. "You had to know that he would steal from anybody and that he would chase all women. It didn't matter how good a friend you were. If he saw something you had that he liked, he'd try to take it. If you understood this from the beginning—and it was a lot to understand—you could get along with him. You just had to watch him."

So while the Chesapeake Bay retriever prowled the lawn at Frey's house and while Rita worried about any strange car that might appear in the driveway, he negotiated with the old-timer in Coulee who owned the mountain lions and the rattlesnakes. The old-timer agreed to bring two mountain lions and an unspecified number of rattlesnakes to the event. Frey agreed that Knievel would pay the old-timer $50.

The death-defying stunt had its main ingredients.

Knievel practiced for the stunt in an alleyway next to the store. The ramp, built out of plywood and two-by-fours, was modest in size. The jump was modest in size. There was little worry that he could cover the distance required. His performance would come after a day of racing at the quarter-mile track on Billy Richardson's father's farm. Knievel distributed flyers, bought radio advertising.

A crowd of maybe three hundred people, laced with friends and relatives of the racers, gathered at the track on Billy Richardson's father's farm for the big event. It was a hot day, the dust stirred up in a hurry, covering everybody and everything. The man from Coulee City appeared as scheduled with the two mountain lions and maybe a dozen rattlesnakes, maybe fourteen or fifteen, maybe twenty, hard to count.

The mountain lions were small, no more than seventy pounds apiece, and not threatening at all. They seemed exhausted by the heat. The owner didn't want them put in any danger, so they were chained to the sides of the jump ramp. The two of them immediately crawled under the ramp for the shade. The snakes were put in a large cardboard box that previously had contained a refrigerator. The snakes, unlike the mountain lions, were energized by all of this activity. They rattled and moved inside that cardboard box, made that *sssssss* sound, angry at the heat, angry at being confined.

Knievel roared around on a Honda 350, built the suspense for the big jump. The mountain lions were prodded to come into the sun and at least watch. The snakes continued to sputter. Knievel started into the run-up for this jump that he had done at least a hundred times, no problem, in the alley next to the store. If he could make that jump, he certainly could make this one. There was far more room to operate here.

Ah, but there also was that dirt track. The same problem that had confronted Gary Frey and his tangle with the flaming boards now confronted Knievel. The races had loosened up the track. He could not get any speed, could not get any speed, could not . . . could not clear the simple forty-foot jump over the cardboard box filled with angry rattlesnakes.

His back wheel hit the box . . .

The box flipped over and opened . . .

Knievel landed, shaky, sprained his ankle . . .

The rattlesnakes started slithering and rattling toward the crowd . . .

"Get my snakes," the man from Coulee City said. "Get 'em . . ."

"Fuck you," Knievel said.

"Fuck you," Gary Frey said.

Who wants to pick up an angry rattlesnake? The crowd moved away in a hurry. The snakes split up in a jailbreak attempt to find freedom. Billy Richardson's father worried about his livestock, about his cattle, his chickens. What if the rattlesnakes got near them? Knievel assured him it would be all right. The man from Coulee City worried about his $50. At least he should get his $50. Knievel assured him that the check would be in the mail. (Which, of course, it wasn't.)

This was the beginning. This was the first professional daredevil show in Knievel's daredevil career. It was a small disaster, if you were looking at it on a performance basis. Nothing really happened the way it was supposed to happen. If you looked at it on an entertainment basis, though, it was a hoot. What would those three hundred people be talking about when they went back to work on Monday? Wouldn't they mention the rattlesnakes?

When Knievel went back to work on Monday, he began to experiment with other, larger jumps. He started to jump whatever objects he could find in back of the store. He started with boats. There were a couple of boats, taken in trade, and he would start his run-up across Third Avenue, next to the plumber's store, shoot across the street, up the driveway, through the alleyway, and over the boats. After jumping boats, he started to jump a car. Two cars. He would add to his totals as the days went past. Not a lot of room in that alleyway to build up speed, but enough to jump a couple of boats, a couple of cars.

This was the beginning.

A story. Frey arrived one morning to open the shop and found Knievel already was there. This happened every now and then, the boss first to work, usually connected to some leftover nocturnal wanderings for romance, but this was different. Knievel had a safe in the middle of the floor. He pounded at it, drilled at it, swore at it, tried to get it open.

"Triber's coming this week," he offered in explanation.

Frey knew immediately what he meant.

The Knievel accounting system at the dealership had some inherent flaws. He basically went to the cash drawer whenever he needed money. Almost every day around noon, for instance, he would say to whoever was in the shop, "Come on, boys, we're going to lunch," and dig into the till to pay for the entire check.

To cover these and other excursions, he sometimes took parts from the showroom motorcycles to replace outworn parts on customers' motorcycles. This worked out pretty well in the short term. The customer was happy with a new part. Knievel was happy with the money he was able to make from the part, refilling the cash drawer. Those new bikes, missing parts, couldn't be sold, of course, but the short-term problems were handled. The only loser in the exchange, perhaps, was Darrell Triber in Spokane, but he seldom came to Moses Lake.

Except he was coming this week. Coming to take a look at the books.

To secure an influx of cash to clean up the accounting mess, Knievel had returned to his safe-breaking career. In the middle of the night, he had entered the Aero Mechanic building through the skylight. He had been able to pull the safe back through the skylight with a winch on an old wrecker the shop used to pick up disabled motorcycles. He had brought the safe back to the shop to open it.

Except it wouldn't open. A couple of hours' work had accomplished nothing.

With the workday starting, with the threat of visitors or customers arriving at any moment, Knievel walked across the street and bought a couple of sticks of dynamite from a plumber. The plumber kept dynamite in his shop because the area was filled with caliche, a hardened sediment that sometimes obstructed his work. Knievel bought the two sticks, loaded the safe back on the wrecker, and went to the sand dunes on the edge of town. Frey stayed to mind the store.

A couple of hours later, Knievel returned. He didn't have the safe. He didn't have the money. Unable to drill even a hole in the side of the safe to insert a stick of dynamite, he had become frustrated again. He simply slid the sticks of dynamite under the safe, lit the fuse, ran, and hid. The dynamite blew the safe two hundred feet in the air, he figured, something to see.

Except the safe had landed in one of the many sinkholes in the area. The safe was gone, down a sinkhole. There was nothing he could do to get it out.

"Once again he danced out of everything, though," Frey said. "He figured out something to say to Triber. And he made a deal with the police.

He called and said he had confidential information from the person or persons who robbed the safe. He would tell the location of the safe if the police would promise not to press their investigation of the robbery. They promised, and he told and he was all right."

Except, of course, he still needed the money to replace the money in the cash drawer. That was an ongoing problem.

Frey left after his second summer with Knievel to get a master's degree in California. Knievel tried to work a deal to buy the dealership, offered half of the deal to Ray Gunn, another young rider at the track and on late-night runs through the streets of Moses Lake. Gunn turned the offer down. His fearlessness didn't extend to his checkbook.

"It didn't sound like a bad deal," Gunn said. "Not a lot of money was involved. But I knew how it all would work. I'd do all the work. He'd spend all the money. I knew Knievel well enough to stay out of it."

Money was an ever-present problem. One Moses Lake resident remembered when Knievel was "so poor he didn't have a cracker in the cupboard for his kids." The creative accounting grew worse. The Internal Revenue Service began to look at the dealings at the dealership. The first nicest person you met on a Honda in Moses Lake increased time in his after-hours career as a burglar, a one-man local crime spree. He was the first suspect, only suspect, in assorted robberies, but the police never could catch him. He was an everyday exhibition of self-destruction.

"He was always doing these little criminal extracurricular activities," Ray Gunn said. "He robbed a lot of places. Burglarized. Whatever you want to call it."

Darrell Triber finally ended the arrangement at the dealership. The numbers never added correctly when matched with the numbers at other locations. He still liked Knievel, thought he was a wonderful salesman and an engaging character, but the numbers were the numbers. Something was fishy. He didn't pursue the problem, but wanted it to end.

Knievel took the family back to Butte and Parrot Street. He tried to sell again with Combined Insurance, but the motivation was gone. When another rider from Washington, Don Pomeroy, offered a chance to sell Yamaha motorcycles in Sunnyside, Washington, which was about one hundred miles south of Moses Lake, Knievel accepted in a hurry.

This put the family on the road again. The important quality in the dynamic always was what Bob wanted. Wife came second. Kids came third. Home was another trailer, this time in Sunnyside. Linda took a job picking asparagus at Pomeroy's seven-acre farm. She worked with teenagers, dressed every day as if she were heading to a church social instead of hard labor. Babysitters took care of the kids. Knievel was at the dealership on Thirteenth Street and Highway 12.

He also was back on his self-made tightrope.

"One of my first memories is the police coming to the shop and escorting him out in handcuffs," Ron Pomeroy, one of Don Pomeroy's sons, remembered years later. "I'd never seen anything like that. It made quite an impression on me. I still don't know what he did. I know he missed a few days' work."

"He'd cashed a bad check," Ron Hazzard, a friend, said. "I bailed him out. He was in jail a couple of times."

The craziness at the end in Moses Lake was even crazier here. The Sunnyside police department, like the Moses Lake police department, formed the idea that he had committed a bunch of robberies but couldn't prove he had. He had also dusted off the Butte idea of the protective private police agency. Once again, it sold best after businesses had been victimized. A rock through the window was still the best reason to buy protection from rocks being thrown through the window.

The police looked for reasons to arrest him. They thought they eventually would catch him. They never did.

"He wasn't much of a drinker," Hazzard, who owned a bar, said in a bartender's appraisal of his friend. "He wasn't much of a pool player either, though he'd play. He'd play shuffleboard too. He wasn't afraid to fight. I'll say that. He had more than one fight. And you didn't have to push him real hard."

His motorcycle skills improved working for Pomeroy, who was a terrific rider. (Pomeroy's son Jim would become the first American to win an FIM international race, the 250cc Spanish Motocross Grand Prix in 1973.) At one race, Knievel saw Pomeroy wheel-walk—doing a wheelie and standing up on the seat. He wanted to add that to his repertoire. He practiced and practiced, came back to the next race to show what he had learned.

The day was warm. He was wearing only a T-shirt, not his racing leathers. The track was asphalt. He crashed and peeled the skin off much of his body. He went to the hospital, came back in bandages to race.

"I'll never forget all that blood oozing through," Pomeroy said. "He was a crazy bastard."

The time in Sunnyside ended much the same way the time in Moses Lake ended, the police on the lookout for transgressions, money a problem, assorted relationships with women becoming another problem, especially with their boyfriends and husbands. Knievel formulated a new plan. Professional motorcycle racing had begun to take hold in southern California. He would go down there and see what he could do. The land of opportunity. Los Angeles. Hollywood. Maybe he could be a stunt man in the movies. Maybe anything could happen.

He made a stop in Spokane before he left, checked in with Darrell Triber, who had brought him into the motorcycle business. They talked about good times. In an amazing coincidence, Triber's dealership was robbed later that same night. The take was roughly $350. The robbery was the only robbery at Triber's before or after that night.

"Bob did it," Archie Triber, Darrell's brother, said years later. "We all knew he did it. There were things . . . things that only someone who'd been around the store would know . . . that made us sure. Darrell never said anything to him. Darrell never went after him. Darrell still liked him. If he needed the money that bad to go to California, okay, he had the money."

In Sunnyside, Knievel stopped at Ray Gunn's house on the way south. He had his motorcycle in a trailer hitched to his car. He told Gunn he was heading to Los Angeles to be a motorcycle racer. Gunn was not exactly a bundle of good wishes and confidence.

"They'll eat you alive down there," he said.

8 Orange, CA

The idea was taken for a walk in the early evenings at a bar called Marty's in Orange, California. This was a neighborhood place, located in a strip mall on North Tustin Avenue, a dark and air-conditioned refuge for drivers from the nearby Costa Mesa Freeway, known by its highway number, the 55. The door opened and closed as regulars and irregulars stopped at the end of their workdays for a little fortitude before they joined or rejoined the full-bore evening commute on the 55.

Bob Knievel talked through the commotion. He was going nowhere. He lived around the corner.

The words tumbled out of his mouth, descriptions of some kind of motorized circus that would take place, thrills and chills, family entertainment with a bite. He would put it all together, sign all the acts, book all the dates at racetracks and state fairs, anyplace available. This would be a daredevil show, understand, that topped all daredevil shows, the first daredevil show that featured motorcycles. He would be the head daredevil.

There was money to be made in this business. He had seen how excited people could become when watching a man risk his life by driving a motorcycle off a ramp and into the fresh air, consequences be damned. What you saw in front of you, sir, ma'am, was the man who had taken that risk. Lived to talk about it. Promoted right, and he could do that job too; this could be an attraction that would have people knocking down doors and climbing through windows to catch a look. This could be Elvis

Presley and the New York Yankees and, oh, maybe the pope and Francis Albert Sinatra coming to your town.

That one wacky afternoon in Moses Lake, his singular experiment in the professional daredevil business, as opposed to his lifetime as an amateur daredevil, became as exciting in Knievel's recitation of the story as any matchups in the Coliseum in Rome ever could have been. He was a Christian, and those were mountain lions in Moses Lake, weren't they? Did the Romans have rattlesnakes? People were terrified when those rattlesnakes got loose, ran for their lives. The scene, when he described it, slightly resembled the streets of downtown Tokyo as Godzilla approached. The people in attendance still were talking about that day in Moses Lake. They would be talking about it forever.

A daredevil show.

This was the future.

This was his future.

He had come to that decision quickly in his new life in California. The realization that he wasn't going to be a great motorcycle racer had arrived as fast and hard as Ray Gunn had predicted it would. Los Angeles was a step ahead of the rest of the country in the sport. Most of the riders back in Washington and Montana, good as they were, would have trouble keeping up with the professional stunt men, the surf-bum stoners, the forever golden adult-children of L.A. Knievel hadn't won a thing, hadn't even climbed out of the novice division to race once against the headliners. He was a good rider, unafraid, but the novice division was restricted to 250cc bikes and he was simply too big physically to compete with the smaller, more nimble racers who moved to the front.

"My brother paid the racers, so he knew exactly how much every racer had won," J. C. Agajanian Jr., whose father promoted the races at Ascot Park in Gardena, said. "Knievel never got more than the minimum. If he got that."

Broke, he called Alex Smith for a recommendation and returned yet one more time to knock on doors for Combined Insurance. Linda worked in the fields in Westminster, stoop labor, picking strawberries, green beans, whatever was in season. Finances were so tight that Knievel convinced his neighbor to allow him to run an extension cord from one tiny apartment to another tiny apartment to siphon off electricity. He couldn't pay the bills.

Ah, but he still could sell. His new boss at Combined, Rodney Friedman, called him "the best salesman I ever came across."

The game was still tough, even tougher in California than in Montana. Friedman would meet his salesmen for breakfast in a designated restaurant in a different designated area every day. The men would fan out from there, hit every business in the neighborhood, cold calls, reconvene for lunch to boast or lick wounds, then return to the streets for the afternoon. It was a daily routine that left feet tired, minds numb. The sale of one introductory six-month policy now returned $1.20 to the salesman. He had to sell 100 policies to make $120.

"Bob understood what you had to do," Friedman said. "He was a believer in the W. Clement Stone approach. I ran sales meetings on Monday nights, and I'd put up these different quotations from Mr. Stone on the walls around the room. A lot of guys just laughed at them, thought they were hokey. Not Bob. He got it. The company would run these sales contests, and he would drive himself. He'd be out there till midnight, working on his numbers.

"He was trying to get his show set up. That's why he was doing everything."

The idea of the daredevil show, stewing in Knievel's head since Moses Lake, was his new grand passion. He threw himself into it the same way he did with his other passions. The need, of course, was for working capital. That was why he talked about his plan everywhere he went, why he talked about it with the other salesmen, why he talked in Marty's with the regulars and irregulars, with anyone who would listen. He was fishing for wallets.

Rod Friedman's wife, Joyce, volunteered to type letters for him. She wasn't excited about Knievel, didn't like him, the way he let Linda work so hard while he pursued a half-ass dream, but she was a good typist and made her contribution to the cause. The letters, punchy and positive, were sent to petroleum companies, tire companies, motorcycle companies, any operation that might want to sponsor a bold man doing bold and dangerous motorcycle feats.

The lessons of W. Clement Stone and Napoleon Hill were woven through everything Knievel did. The true believer sold himself as much as he sold his product. The difference was that this time the product and the person were pretty much the same thing. He sold himself to sell himself.

"Your mind is your invisible talisman," Stone and Hill advised in *Success Through a Positive Mental Attitude*.

The letters PMA (Positive Mental Attitude) are emblazoned on one side, and NMA (Negative Mental Attitude) on the other. These are powerful forces. PMA is the right mental attitude for each specific occasion. It has the power to attract the good and the beautiful. NMA repels them. It is a negative mental attitude that robs you of all that makes life worth living.

Knievel had PMA coming out of his ears. The NMA was stuffed clear out of sight as he talked about the glories of motorcycle jumping, the size of the potential crowds, the giant financial return that surely would arrive from any investment.

"To become enthusiastic, act enthusiastically!" the book advised. "To speak enthusiastically and overcome timidity and fear: (a) talk loudly; (b) talk rapidly; (c) emphasize important words; (d) hesitate when there is a period, comma, or other punctuation in the written word; (e) keep a smile in your voice so that it isn't gruff; and (f) use modulation."

Without timidity or fear, he talked loudly and rapidly in the bar, a smile and modulation in his voice, emphasizing the important words and hesitating in the right punctuated places. Alas, the other patrons listened or half-listened, eventually paid their tabs, and left, back on the 55, but one other character in the every-night cast did not leave. He was paid to listen to tales of lost love, disappearing dreams, asshole bosses, cold fronts approaching from the west, and sports teams that couldn't fucking hit. A proposal to stage a daredevil show was downright exciting stuff compared to all of that, no matter how many times he heard it.

The bartender turned out to be Bob Knievel's customer.

"I was just out of the Army, back from thirteen months in Korea," Tim Perior said years later. "There was nothing imminent in my life. I was looking for something to do."

Bartending was a pit stop on the way to this indeterminate future. He had lied to get the job at Marty's, said he'd been a bartender back in Michigan, where he grew up, but the truth was that he'd never worked in a bar in his life. He didn't know how to make a scotch-and-water. On the night of his debut, a Friday night at that, owner watching from the end of the bar, he'd written the ingredients for various drinks on the palms of his hands and kept a "Guide to Cocktails" at his side. Somehow he had survived. He was still there when Knievel appeared.

Perior's fuzzy career plan was to become a commercial artist. He had taken art in high school back in Detroit, liked it, had painted supermarket signs in an after-school job. He had a steady hand and a good eye. He already was enrolled in courses at the Los Angeles Art Center. In the Army he had purchased a Nikon 35mm camera at the PX and then won a photography contest on his first roll of film. Perhaps a photography shop would be a business.

Knievel, the more he talked, offered a chance for experience in both of those potential fields. Perior could paint the signs for the shows. He could paint the trucks. He could take the photographs, handle all publicity. He could be the manager, a 50 percent partner in the fat, grand adventure. Wouldn't that be the best part? The adventure? All he had to do was come up with some money to get the project started.

"When I got out of high school, I just took off for Europe," Perior said, describing his free-form approach to life at the time. "I had a friend, each of us had enough money for a one-way ticket to Europe plus $25 to get started when we got there. We just went. My mother was really mad . . . we stayed for two years. Then I came back for a couple of months and took off for California."

He met Knievel one afternoon before work, and Knievel showed him how well he could ride a motorcycle, doing wheelies up and down the streets of Orange. Perior decided Knievel hadn't been lying. He could ride that bike, definitely was fearless. The idea grew muscle, noise, belched fumes. The conversations at the bar became more about details than possibilities. Perior was on the team.

He wasn't a rich man, fresh from the Army, certainly no big numbers in the bank, but he did have something that Knievel did not have: perfect credit. He also had a brother-in-law, his sister's husband, who also had perfect credit and was looking to make an investment. That was enough.

Perior and Knievel went shopping. Using the two lines of perfect credit, plus a few bucks down, they bought:

- two Matchless motorcycles
- a large trailer
- two Ford pickup trucks
- enough lumber and steel to build two ramps
- incidentals

The Ford dealer in Anaheim, where they bought the trucks, made unlimited after-hours access to the open back parking lot part of the deal. This was where Knievel and Perior and anyone else who was available built the ramps. This was where they put together Bob Knievel's rolling circus.

The first trial jumps, small, were done by Knievel in the parking lot. Ramp to ramp, the separation was maybe a few feet, the height no more than two feet at the start. Okay, the separation grew larger, the height grew higher, as the practices continued. The plan was to jump high enough and far enough to clear the two pickups, parked lengthwise, tail to tail.

Knievel also worked out a parasail routine, a tow rope attached to the back of a car, a parachute strapped to his back. The speed of the car, combined with the lift from the parachute, pulled him ten feet, twenty feet, a hundred feet, more, off the ground, as if he were some out-of-control water skier. He would run behind the car to get started, then *whoosh*, go up in the air.

Also, the first four-by-eight sheets of particleboard were doused with gasoline, then set on fire in the parking lot. Knievel crashed through them at seventy miles per hour on his Matchless bike, like Gary Frey did in Spokane. A small cast was assembled in the parking lot: a couple of guys from Butte, "Jumping Jack" Stroh from Sunnyside and Butch Wilhelm, a four-foot-four midget Knievel had befriended.

Wilhelm, riding a pocket bike, a motorcycle in miniature, practiced the same stunts Knievel did, but on a miniature scale. He jumped across toy trucks on the pocket bike. He crashed into a wall of foam rubber bricks instead of blasting through the burning particleboards. He crashed, period. He crashed a lot, crashed every time he attempted a jump. The smallest imperfections, a rock in the parking lot, a dip in the ground, could make his miniature bike fly out of control. He became discouraged, wanted to quit.

"Bob gave him this big pep talk," Perior said. "He told him that crashing was nothing, part of the game. He said, 'Look at me, I crash all the time.' (And he did.)"

Knievel booked three shows around southern California for the first two months of 1966. The first was in Indio on January 23, 1966, a Sunday, at the Indio Date Festival fairgrounds. Knievel promoted the show, put flyers on poles, went to Indio schools to talk about helmet safety. The crowd that appeared was small, notable mostly for the fact that it included actor Lee Marvin. Marvin and Steve McQueen were the two noted cycle enthusiasts among the local Hollywood movie stars.

McQueen competed in races under the alias Harvey Mushman. Marvin was a hard-core motorcycle rider, straight from the Marlin Brando image.

The show he saw on this first day went as perfectly as possible. Perior was the announcer. The tricks went as planned. Knievel cleared the two trucks, end to end. It all worked. The pay, to be split among the people involved, was $500. Professional show business life for Evel Knievel and the Motorcycle Daredevils officially had begun.

The name had been formulated on the advice of Bob Blair, the owner of ZDS Motors in Glendale, part of the Berliner Motor Corporation, which distributed Norton, Matchless, and Ducati motorcycles in the United States. Blair had become a sponsor of the daredevils and suggested that "Bob Knievel and the Motorcycle Daredevils" sounded a bit dull. The unused nickname from long ago, "Evil Knievel," was a suggestion to improve the sound of the name, to make it more memorable. Knievel switched an "e" for an "i" to stay away from a dark, hulking image. Evel Knievel it was. Perfect.

"I painted the name on the pickups, on the black tarp for the trailer, on the doors of the cab, on everything," Perior said. " 'Evel Knievel and the Motorcycle Daredevils.' There was a feeling that this was going to be something special."

A show in Hemet, California, was rained out, so the next appearance for the troupe was at the San Bernardino County Fairgrounds in Barstow. In the warm-ups before the show, Perior and Jumping Jack Stroh started racing each other around the dirt track. They hit one particular turn on the edge of control, started sliding, and went out of control. Crashed. Perior was uninjured, but Jumping Jack was a mess. He had scraped a bunch of skin off the right side of his body. His racing leathers had been ripped, and blood was leaking from various locations.

Jumping Jack's major job in the show was an act where he stood in the middle of the track and Knievel drove straight at him at sixty, maybe seventy miles an hour. Knievel would dip low, flatten himself against the body of the motorcycle. Jumping Jack would jump, spread-eagled, at the appropriate moment, and clear Knievel and the bike. The act was a definite crowd-pleaser.

Unfortunately, Jumping Jack's injuries now precluded him from jumping. He was in pain simply walking. The act would have to be taken out of the show unless, fuck it, sure, the roles were reversed. Knievel decided he would be the jumper. Stroh was healthy enough to ride the bike.

Knievel waited at the prescribed spot. Stroh came from the prescribed direction at the prescribed speed. Knievel jumped, but not high enough, not fast enough. The motorcycle hit him, straight on, at sixty or seventy miles per hour. He always described the point of impact as "the handlebars hit me right in the balls." His legs caved the wrong way. He flipped high into the air. He fell to the dirt.

That was the end of the performance for Evel Knievel and the Motorcycle Daredevils. The star was taken to the hospital, where he was treated for cracked ribs and heavy bruises and sprains to his lower body.

"He was really hurt bad," Tim Perior, who followed him to the hospital, said. "In fact, I don't think he ever was healthy again. This was the start. I think he always was hurt after this."

A film surfaced later that supposedly showed Knievel being knocked into the air by Jumping Jack and the motorcycle. Jumping Jack claimed that the film in actuality was from another show and that he, Jumping Jack, was the one being clipped. The figure, whoever it was, wore a crash helmet and did get hit hard. If using the film of Jumping Jack allowed Knievel to show the perils of his profession, then it was one of his lesser sins. He did get hit by the motorcycle in Barstow. He did get hurt.

The nimble kid who walked on his hands at a moment's notice, the fast-moving center-ice man, the athlete, was no more. A lifetime of convalescence and pain had begun. He was twenty-seven years old. The next show didn't take place for almost four months. He never would attempt the jump over a moving motorcycle again.

The return of Evel Knievel and the Motorcycle Daredevils, the first booking outside southern California, was scheduled for Post Falls, Idaho, on June 1, 1966, at the State Line Speedway. The state line mentioned in the name was between Idaho and Washington, the track close to Spokane. Knievel was headed back to familiar territory.

The cast of characters traveled north. One important change had occurred. Tim Perior, the partner, had begun to have doubts about the entire enterprise. He wondered where he fit. The more he saw the way Knievel operated, the more he became convinced that his own role did not extend much past his financial assistance. Knievel made all decisions, ordered him around the same way he ordered everyone else around. Knievel was in charge of everything. This was not the partnership Perior had in mind.

"Everything was about him," Perior said. "He was convinced he was going to be famous. We'd go into a bar and he would have himself paged. He would go outside and call the bar from a phone booth, just to have his name spoken over the loudspeaker."

A small incident, six months earlier, just before Christmas, still stuck in Perior's mind. He had heard Knievel's lament that he didn't have any ornaments for the tree. Perior owned a box of ornaments that had hung from his family's Christmas trees in Michigan. Touched by Knievel's problem, he brought the box to practice and gave it to Knievel. Somehow the box wound up tied to Knievel's roof rack. Somehow Perior was in the car. Somehow the box hadn't been tied tight enough and went flying off the car and onto the road.

Perior mentioned the fact. Knievel said the heck with it. Perior mentioned the fact again. They could stop and get the ornaments. Knievel said the heck with it. Perior was struck by how oblivious Knievel was to everybody else's feelings except his own. Didn't the guy know that the ornaments meant something to Perior, that this was an important gift? Apparently not. Didn't he want to bring the ornaments home for his kids? Apparently not.

In Spokane, before the Stateline Speedway show on June 1, 1966, even took place, two things happened that reinforced Perior's unease. The first was that he discovered Knievel had spent twice, maybe three times as much money for publicity and advertising as they had agreed to spend. Knievel never had consulted Perior, he simply spent the money. In fact, he had lied to Perior about it.

The second thing happened in a strip club. Perior, Knievel, and a couple of the daredevils went to the club. They drank a bit, had some fun. One of the dancers, pleasant, decided she liked Perior. She paid extra attention to him, said those things that women say when they might be attracted to someone. Flirted. That was what she did.

Knievel, who had flirted with her most of the night without any positive response, became madder by the moment. The idea that she would select someone else, Perior, instead of him seemed to be an affront. As Perior talked with her, flirted back, Knievel kicked him under the table. This was not one of those conspiratorial kicks, *pssst*, to gain attention. This was a hard kick that hurt. Perior was astounded. He stifled his first inclination to punch Knievel in the face and sat at the table and steamed. Knievel steamed on the other side.

"I couldn't figure it out," Perior said. "I was single. He was a married guy. I was just talking to the girl, and he was upset that she wasn't interested in him."

This was the end of the partnership. Perior was mad about the money that had been spent without his knowledge, mad about his place in the operation, mad about the kick in the strip club. The next morning he told Knievel that he was done. He already had bought a ticket on a Greyhound bus back to Los Angeles.

He figured he was $36,000 in debt and couldn't see any way the number wouldn't grow larger. Maybe he would stay if he had a partner he could trust, but he didn't think he had that. Knievel could keep all the stuff, good luck, but now the payments belonged to him.

"I took my chance," Perior explained years later. "It wasn't as crazy as it sounds now. This was Hollywood, where people mortgage their houses to make a movie. It took me a long time to pay off that money, $36,000, but I can't complain.

"I was young. I learned a lesson—never go into business with someone you can't trust. That was a good lesson to learn."

Knievel tried to convince him to change his mind, took him to the bus station, talked all the way. The departure was emotional. Knievel cried. Perior fought back second thoughts about staying with the show, somehow felt sorry for Knievel in the end. He still left. The bus pulled out into a steady rain. The scene was something out of a movie.

"The show should have worked," Perior said. "Bob had a great idea, had a lot of things going for him. Everything was there . . . except it was just a click off. Bob did things where he couldn't help himself. It was all about Bob Knievel. He wanted to get ahead, and if someone was in his way, he'd just kick 'em down the side of the mountain. That was the way he was."

The Stateline jump was his first jump over a string of cars. There were eleven of them, and he cleared them all to great applause. He claimed a world record, most cars jumped at one time, and since no one else was in this newly invented sport of jumping cars in a line he had to be right. It wasn't exactly like breaking the record for the 100-yard dash.

In his next jump, on June 19 at the Missoula Auto Race Track out on Miller Creek Road, part of a daylong schedule of motorcycle races, Knievel tried to break his three-week-old world record. He lined up twelve cars this time, plus a cargo van at the end.

He had learned through trial and error that the most important component for making these jumps was reaching a proper speed at liftoff from the ramp. Too much speed and he could overshoot his target. Too little speed and, sure, he would undershoot. When he came onto the ramp this time he thought his speed was perfect.

He was mistaken. His speedometer said he was traveling fast enough, but not too fast. His speedometer was wrong. He figured out later that the wheel must have spun in some gravel on the way to the takeoff, delivering a faster number on the speedometer than he was traveling. Not a big discrepancy, but enough to make him fail.

He cleared the twelve cars, but the back wheel of his motorcycle clipped the cargo van at the end. The motorcycle and Knievel went flying. He wound up in St. Patrick's Hospital in Missoula with a severely broken arm, lacerations, and broken ribs. A lesson that he learned here was not to look at the speedometer. He would jump in the future strictly on feel. He would let his senses tell him how fast he was going.

"I'm sorry that we didn't give the folks a better show," he told a reporter from the *Daily Missoulan* newspaper at the hospital. "I promise that we'll come back and jump again in Missoula."

He showed his wounds to any reporter who asked. One of them said his arm was "stitched together like a baseball."

A story. He stayed at "Good Time Charlie" Shelton's house in Kalispell, Montana, after he was released from the hospital. Charlie was originally from Butte, ten years older, a friend who had worked for a radio station. Knievel had another show scheduled in a couple of days at Doran's Family Campground in Kalispell, a modest affair (an RV park!), performing for campers watching from a grandstand that seated no more than fifty people. The show would have to go on without him, because his arm was in a cast and his body ached in at least a dozen places. He would appear, but he certainly couldn't jump.

The entire daredevil enterprise seemed in jeopardy. He was busted, broke. He told Good Time Charlie that he'd cleared $400 from the Missoula jump, then paid over $300 in hospital costs. He had put on four shows now and had been seriously injured in two of them. This was not an encouraging statistic. None of the statistics were encouraging. Most of the other daredevils already had left.

The whole deal seemed dead almost before it started.

"You know what you have to do?" Good Time Charlie said over cocktails in his living room. "You have to jump something big. Nobody gives a shit if you jump thirteen Volkswagens or whatever it was you jumped in Missoula. If you're going to take the risk, you have to jump something that will get people's attention, something big."

Big?

"You have to jump Soldier Field in Chicago," Good Time Charlie said. "You have to jump the Washington Monument. You have to jump the Grand Canyon . . ."

Knievel considered the idea. He didn't consider long. He shouted to his wife in the kitchen.

"Linda," he said, "I'm going to jump the Grand Canyon."

The words sounded natural the first time he said them.

A focus was added to the operation. Just like that. He had a goal, a subject for easy conversation in all promotions. He was not some carnival act coming through your town, another clown trying to take a local dollar, he was a Man on a Mission, building up to the death-defying stunt of stunts that would captivate the world. He was going to jump the Grand Canyon.

There was no hesitation, not even the glimmer of a second thought. He and Good Time Charlie went that afternoon to Moose's Saloon, a peanuts-on-the-floor place in Kalispell run by former University of Montana football player Moose Miller. Almost as soon as they sat at the bar, Knievel pointed at a picture on the wall with his good arm and said to anyone within hearing range, "That's the Grand Canyon, and I'm going to jump over it on my motorcycle." No matter that the picture showed nearby Flathead Lake, not the canyon, the message was what mattered.

(Knievel in later years would say that he had the idea to jump the canyon while drinking a number of Montana Marys and staring at a picture of the Grand Canyon at Moose's Saloon in Kalispell. Reporters would call and ask if the picture of the Grand Canyon still was there. Moose Miller, a nice man who did not want anyone to be mad, would diplomatically say, "No, it's not.")

After the stop at Moose's Saloon, Knievel went on local television that night to promote the appearance at the RV park. He talked more about the jump over the Grand Canyon than he did about the upcoming show. He already had invented all the details about how the jump was supposed to work.

"He said that Robert F. Kennedy was going to be there," Good Time Charlie said. "He said Kennedy had promised to be part of the rescue team."

The canyon was part of the show.

The jump at Doran's Family Campground on August 7, 1966, went fine. Knievel tried to recruit Darrell Triber's younger brother, Archie, a high school kid, to come down from Spokane as a replacement, but after Archie agreed, Archie's mother disagreed. A young guy named Chuck Burt from Mossyrock, Washington, came down and cleared the ten cars. He also jumped ten cars four weeks later in Helena, Montana, as Knievel's body continued to heal.

There was nothing wrong during that time, however, with Knievel's mouth or his imagination. In between the two jumps by Burt, an Associated Press story came out of Butte about a local daredevil who said he was going to jump the Grand Canyon. The daredevil said he would be traveling to Arizona that very weekend to search for a proper spot for the attempt. Three weeks after Good Time Charlie made his off-the-wall suggestion, hell, plans were being unfolded in the newspaper about how it would be done. They sounded wonderful, well researched, and almost official, but they were total nonsense.

"I won't say definitely that I will be able to jump it until I get a look at it, but I will say I'm going to try it," Knievel told the AP. "I'm determined to drive off the edge at 140 miles per hour."

He said he envisioned a paraglide landing, the speed of his motorcycle shooting him into the air, the parachute opening to carry him the rest of the way. He sounded as if he had been planning the jump for a long time, said the Arizona Chamber of Commerce, and "television networks" had asked about becoming involved. Included in the story were mentions of the accident in Barstow and the crash in Missoula. The implications were obvious: the unwritten headline was "Crazy Son of a Bitch Soon to Kill Himself."

He finished out the year with a successful ten-car jump at Naranche Stadium, the high school football field in Butte, plus similarly successful ten-car jumps at drag strips in Tucson, Arizona, and Deming, New Mexico. He was pretty much a solo act for these shows, but his entire approach was different. He sold his product, the jump over the canyon, everywhere, rattled long-term interest in the future with his appearances in the short-term present. He was that Crazy Son of a Bitch.

He announced at his appearance in Butte that he hoped to jump the Grand Canyon in a year, in November of 1967. He now said he was exploring a spot on the northern rim that was three thousand feet high. His scenario for success had changed. He had added two imaginary jet engines to the sides of the imaginary motorcycle he would use. The first jet engine would shoot him off the takeoff ramp at 130 miles per hour. The second jet would cut in almost immediately to increase the speed to 300 miles per hour and lift him a thousand feet higher than the take-off point. As he approached the opposite side of the canyon, he would parachute off the motorcycle and flutter safely to the ground. A second parachute, radio-controlled by his crew, would drop the motorcycle to the same stretch of real estate, where heroic man and heroic steed would be reunited.

This was perfect. Made a potential customer tear up a bit, just thinking about it all.

9 Gardena, CA

The best motorcycle racetrack in the country in 1967 was Ascot Park in Gardena, California, the place where Bob Knievel had tried and failed as a rider. Sitting at the confluence of three major roads ("Ascot Park—Where the San Diego, Harbor, and Riverside Freeways collide!" ads on half the radio stations in Los Angeles shouted all day, every day), the half-mile clay oval was the home to flat-track racing and motocross racing and sprint car racing and demolition derbies and figure-eight racing, and just about any event that involved the burning of hydrocarbons for spectator pleasure.

The proprietor, forty-four-year-old J. C. Agajanian, was a definite motor-sports character. He wore a cowboy hat all day every day, had a cigar tucked under his mustache at most times, and every May took up residence in Indianapolis, Indiana, where he sponsored the 98 car in the Indy 500. Troy Ruttman in 1952 and Parnelli Jones in 1963 had won the race in the 98 car.

The son of an Armenian immigrant who had made big money in the combination businesses of trash hauling and pig farming—the refuse of people was feed for the pigs, the pigs were feed for the people who created the refuse, a never-ending ecological cycle—Agajanian wanted to be a driver of race cars when he was eighteen years old. His father told him that an occupation that dangerous would be fine; however, he should kiss his mother and pack his bags because he no longer would be living at home, and he also probably should change his name since he no longer would be a part of the family. This advice had sent him into the business side of the sport.

Ascot, his home base, was a dusty, noisy wonder. The noise and smells filtered through the surrounding neighborhoods, a strict 11:00 p.m. curfew in effect. The cramped stands held 7,500 cramped bodies, always a cheap night of live entertainment. The prime motorcycle times were Friday nights and Sunday afternoons.

Knievel saw an opportunity here. No longer a part of the racing, he returned to Ascot with his new idea. He set up a business meeting with Agajanian, delivered a proposal.

"ABC television is going to be here to film your motocross race for *Wide World of Sports*," he said. "I'd like to be a part of that. I'd like to jump fifteen cars in a line with my motorcycle, which would be a world record."

"What do I need you for?" Agajanian asked. "I already have *Wide World of Sports* coming. I'll get a good crowd. I don't have to pay a jumper."

"You're right, you don't have to pay me," Knievel said. "Unless I bring in more people. Look at your attendance for last year. Just give me a dollar per person for everybody over the figure for last year. If the number is the same or lower, you don't owe me anything."

Agajanian was receptive to the idea. He was intrigued by Knievel's personality and guts. He would do this deal. Sure. No risk really was involved. The date for the Ascot Park show was set for March 5, 1967. This was Knievel's first appearance of the new year. He was gone from the apartment in Orange, the family often back in Butte as he lived in his car, in low-rent Hollywood motel rooms, in the spare rooms of friends and acquaintances.

"He'd stay at my house sometimes," Skip Van Leeuwen, one of the Ascot racers Knievel had befriended, said. "Neither of us had any money. We'd go to restaurants on Sunset Strip where we'd work the dine-and-dash. We'd each try to finish faster than the other so we could get out the door first. That way the other guy would have the check, and he would take the risk bolting out the door."

Van Leeuwen was fascinated with Knievel's promotional skills. He came home one day and Knievel was writing a letter to the president of Sun Oil asking for $250,000 in a sponsorship deal. Van Leeuwen was astounded. He said Knievel didn't need money like that. Hell, $2,500 was more like what he needed, not $250,000.

"Skip," Knievel said. "I want the president of Sun Oil to read this. Do you think his secretary is going to show him a letter from some guy looking for $2,500? She'll show him this one, though, for $250,000."

The canyon jump definitely was now his prime promotional tool. The motorcycle daredevils of the past year pretty much were disassembled. He was a one-man canyon-jumping show. This was how he presented himself when he was interviewed by Jim Murray, the sports columnist for the *Los Angeles Times*, before the March 5 jump at Ascot.

"Evel proposes to jump over the Grand Canyon in a motorcycle," Jim Murray wrote. "You heard me, *over* it, not across it, or through it . . . "

Murray, nationally syndicated, at the front end of a thirty-seven-year career at the *Times* that would land a Pulitzer Prize for commentary, had the perfect ear to hear what Knievel was selling. Death! Craziness! Sick fun! This was the best column that ever had been written about the man and his ideas, capturing their base-level appeal. Murray quoted Knievel's promise to jump the canyon—"You can bet your life I'll do it"—near the end of the column.

" 'Correction,' I told him," Murray then wrote. "You bet *your* life. I wouldn't fly over the Grand Canyon in anything that doesn't have stewardesses."

The Murray column and other publicity brought a crowd to Ascot Park. Knievel made the jump—the fifteen-car world record—without problems. Agajanian, after the show was finished, tossed him an envelope full of money back in the office. Knievel counted the bills, saw there was $3,000, put the money back in the envelope, tossed the envelope back onto Agajanian's desk. The promoter was on the phone to someone else and said, "I'll have to call you back. I think I have a problem here."

The problem, Knievel said, was that too much money was in the envelope. By his count, 2,300 more people had come to the races this year, so he was owed only $2,300. Agajanian had given him $700 too much. Agajanian said that his turnstile count was the same. The extra $700 was a bonus. He liked Knievel's work, thought maybe this could be the start of a longer business relationship.

He wanted to see more of this car-jumping act.

A story. The first famous car-jumping daredevil in the United States was a Noblesville, Indiana, farm boy named Earl M. "Lucky" Teter. Automobile thrill shows had been part of the state fair circuit almost since the invention of the automobile itself, but the Depression caused a jump in the business as an estimated 250 different shows filled with desperate but brave men rolled back and forth across the country in search of the vanishing entertainment dollar. Lucky Teter came out of that group.

His big trick was to drive an automobile off a ramp at high speed to create a parabolic curve that he hoped would clear a designated car or cars, maybe a bus or some other object, then land on another ramp on the other side. He was a showman, one who "marched out like the American Legion," one observer said. He wore dust goggles, jodhpurs, and a scarf around his neck and looked every night as if he were off to find that pesky Baron von Richtofen.

In the summer of 1942, he decided that the real daredevil business had switched to Europe and World War II, so he announced that he was going to shut down his show. The last appearance of Lucky Teter and his Hell Drivers would be on Sunday night, July 5, 1942, at the Indianapolis State Fair.

"I'm ready to join the armed forces when my number comes up," he said in lead-up publicity. "That day may come any time now, so I'll be shooting the works next Sunday to give my friends enough thrills to hold them until war's end."

A crowd of twelve thousand people that included his mother, father, and sister arrived to watch his attempt to clear a semi-trailer transport truck in his Plymouth sedan. His wife gave him a customary pre-jump kiss before he entered the car. He then drove off that ramp and killed himself.

He landed short. The car never reached the proper speed to get the height, 20 feet, and clear the distance, 150 feet, that he needed. He crashed into the second ramp. The wooden boards on the ramp, in a fatal mistake, had been nailed lengthwise instead of sideways. They became spears sticking into the car. The car was crushed. Lucky Teter was crushed inside. He was dead before he reached the hospital, thirty-nine years old.

His widow, disconsolate about seeing her husband die on his last jump on the last night of his career, soon asked a friend, Joie Chitwood, an auto racer, to see if he could sell Teter's equipment. Chitwood, who was 4F, still at home, looked for buyers, but auto racing pretty much had been shut down for the war and no one was buying much of anything, and after a bunch of thinking he decided to buy the equipment himself.

This was the birth of the Joie Chitwood Thrill Show, which began on July 4, 1943, one day short of the first anniversary of Lucky Teter's death, and ran for the rest of the twentieth century. The thrill show was so successful after the war that as many as five separate editions traveled the country, crashing cars and scaring the local populations in small towns and large, becoming a basic part of corn dog and Ferris wheel summers.

One impressionable eight-year-old who was fascinated lived in Butte, Montana. Or so he always said. He said that his grandmother took him to the Chitwood show and he always remembered it, especially the rider who did tricks on a motorcycle. Knievel always was quick to say that the earliest notions of doing what he did were inspired by Joie Chitwood's heroics.

Which, of course, made Evel Knievel a direct descendant of Lucky Teter.

The *Wide World of Sports* segment was run three weeks after the Ascot jump, on March 25, 1967. The show, which started in 1961 as a summer replacement on ABC, had become a staple of Saturday afternoon television in the 5:00–6:30 time slot, offering coverage of a smorgasbord of sports that existed outside the familiar choices of football, baseball, and basketball. Technology dictated that many of the events were taped and often shown on an exaggerated delay.

The Knievel jump was shown in the middle of the 100-lap motocross race, which was won by Van Leeuwen, a first prize of $1,750. Bill Fleming was the announcer, a classic baritone boomer, a man who projected a definite excitement in his voice. He interviewed Knievel in one segment, then came back for the jump in another.

The Knievel in the interview was the young man on the rise, the insurance salesman, white shirt and sedate brown tie, quiet tan sports coat, boy's regular haircut, pleasant smile, slight squint into the sun. One hand held on to the other, the way someone would stand in the back of a church or in front of the class giving a book report. Fleming proclaimed him "a most unusual young man" and said that his "specialty in sports" would be to jump fifteen automobiles on his motorcycle.

"Have you ever jumped fifteen before, Evel?" Fleming asked.

"Bill, I never have," the clean-cut daredevil said. "I missed a jump in the northwest part of the United States over thirteen, and I was hospitalized and laid up for over five months. And I sure hope that doesn't happen today."

"How many cars were you attempting at that time?"

"Thirteen."

"Thirteen and you missed it?"

"I did."

"You're trying fifteen today?"

"The parachute's ready, the motorcycle's ready, and I'm ready. And I'm not going to miss today."

The jump segment went perfectly. Knievel changed into the black-and-yellow leathers he had worn with the Daredevils. The words "Evel Knievel Motorcycle Daredevils" and "Hollywood" were sewn in black on the back of his yellow leather vest. A line of black stars went down the sides of each of his yellow pants legs. He looked good.

After the usual false start, part for safety, part for drama, he hit the ramp at the proper speed, stood up, held the front wheel high, landed at the proper spot, kept riding. Fifteen cars were gone. The record. ABC showed the jump again, and Fleming, at the end, boomed that this was "a wild way to ride a motorcycle."

In households across the United States, any memories from the jump no doubt were consigned to the same mental wastebasket that contained *Wide World* pictures of lumberjack competitions, Ping-Pong matches, and perhaps pairs figure skating or bull riding, but for Knievel this was another line for the résumé. He was legitimate. How legitimate? He was on *Wide World of Sports*.

He also was signed to a string of shows at Ascot Park. Part of the ABC picture of the jump showed J. C. Agajanian walking around on the sidelines in his cowboy hat, then standing by the side of the landing ramp to watch the jump as closely as he could. He obviously liked what Knievel did, and especially liked the jump in attendance.

There are people who have an inherent knack for grabbing attention. This kid certainly had it, had it as much as anyone J. C. Agajanian ever had seen in the most attention-grabbing city in the United States. Knievel was in the *Long Beach Independent* only a week after the jump, talking about the proposed canyon jump. He made it sound like a historic and newsworthy undertaking.

"I feel that the thing has significant value to people right now and in the future," he told columnist Rich Roberts. "It's just like Lindbergh when he flew across the ocean. People said, 'Why does he want to fly across the ocean, and if he does, so what?' Well, now we're all going across the ocean, although we didn't know then that there was any significant value to it."

Roberts, unable to stop himself, did mention that Lindbergh was flying an airplane. Knievel would be trying to fly a motorcycle.

"That's the only way to fly, baby!" Knievel replied, Roberts wrote, in "a moment of exuberance."

In the next two months, the daredevil would do at least three shows at Ascot. He would jump fifteen cars, fourteen cars, finally sixteen cars, all jumps successful. He also put together a reconstituted daredevil show called "The Evel Knievel Stunt Show of Stars" just for Ascot and a motorcycle convention in Sacramento. The only holdover from the Motorcycle Daredevils was Butch Wilhelm, the midget. The other stars were the best riders from the Tourist Trophy steeplechase races, the first generation of motocross at the track. Van Leeuwen, Eddie Mulder, Gene Romero, Rod Pack, Bryan Farnsworth (who had to race under the name "Clutch Cargo" because he was employed in the motorcycle industry), and Swede Savage were familiar Ascot names.

The shows were slapstick hilarious. Everybody buzzed around, did wheelies, busted through flaming boards, made a lot of noise. Clutch Cargo dressed up like a woman, riding a motorcycle out of control. It was a circus.

"One night the flaming boards didn't burn like they were supposed to burn," Van Leeuwen said. "Everybody looked at everybody else. Nobody wanted to hit those boards. Knievel, he just said, 'Fuck it,' and took off and went through 'em, one after another, *blam, blam, blam*. He bruised his knuckles. He was woozy at the end."

Rod Pack had an act where he climbed to the top of a very tall telephone pole. After appropriate dramatics, he dove off the pole. A pit had been dug, filled with a number of large inflated air mattresses, and Pack landed fine, but the effect from the stands was that he had landed on the ground and was seriously injured. He milked the moment, then bounded up, happy and healthy.

Wilhelm, the midget, still had problems riding his miniature motorcycle. One skit involved a pickup truck hitting a collapsible outhouse. The walls fall down. Wilhelm comes flying out on the miniature motorcycle. The pickup truck chases him. He collides with a fake brick wall, falls down. The men in the pickup truck grab him, throw him in the back of the truck, appear to beat him up, then throw a dummy from the truck that looks like him. All of this worked fine on one given night . . . outhouse, chase, fake brick wall, into truck . . . except for the ending.

"I was driving the truck," Van Leeuwen said. "I can hear the midget just screaming in the back. I said to myself, 'This guy's a great actor, making a lot of noise.' Then they threw the dummy out and the guy still was screaming. Turned out he'd broken his collarbone when he hit the fake brick wall. I could see the bone just sticking out.

"He was in a lot of pain. He still was supposed to jump the toy cars with his miniature motorcycle. Said he couldn't do it. Knievel comes out of his trailer and says, 'Get back out there. You don't do that fucking jump, you don't get paid.' He did the jump."

Knievel fit into the group with the motorcycle racers, everybody young and fearless. They drank hard, partied hard, chased the Hollywood night. Van Leeuwen, Mulder, and Farnsworth were early TT champions, traveled around the country to race. ("I found a life right there," Eddie Mulder said years later. "Motorcycles, beer, all those pretty women. What was wrong with that? I never had to grow up and get a job. I just raced.") Savage would switch to Indy cars and die from injuries suffered at the 1973 Indianapolis 500. Pack already had a certain amount of fame. He was the first man to make a recorded jump from an airplane without wearing a parachute. The stunt on January 1, 1965, was captured in a photo spread for *Life* magazine. Pack jumped out of the plane without the chute. Bob Allen, his friend, jumped from another plane 1,500 feet away with an extra chute. Pack and Allen met in midair. Allen handed Pack the second chute. Pack slipped into the chute, pulled the rip cord, and landed safely. He now did a lot of stunt work in movies. Mulder also was a stunt man. He said Knievel was not.

"Stunt work is very precise," Mulder said. "You have to take a lot of orders, follow orders, for everything to go right. Knievel was not very good at taking orders from anyone."

Knievel was the last arrival to the motorcycle group, but was the fastest talker, the self-promoter. He was the same commanding presence he was everywhere else, with one exception. The unspoken truth was that he couldn't ride a motorcycle nearly as well as these other guys.

"Between you and me and the skeletons in the closet, Evel Knievel was not a very good motorcycle rider," Eddie Mulder said. "He just didn't have the natural talent. Plus, he wasn't in good physical shape. Never was."

He did have one quality in abundance that nobody else in the group had.

"He was crazy," Mulder said. "Just crazy. He was a character, man."

The final Ascot show was on May 30, 1967, and Knievel soon was back in Butte. He scheduled a string of jumps in the state of Washington. More than any place, even Los Angeles, the Pacific Northwest was where he performed in his early career. The area was dotted with little racetracks and fairgrounds, and he knew most of the proprietors—or at least knew their names—from his racing days and motorcycle sales time in Moses Lake and Sunnyside.

A couple of lists eventually would evolve, dates and records of his jumps, looking as official as a major league baseball schedule and results, but some of the earliest jumps would be missing. Any number of jumps happened in a publicity vacuum, never reported in any newspaper, remembered or only half-remembered by the people who were there.

An example was a jump Knievel performed for Ted Pollock, the promoter and owner of the Yakima (Washington) Speedway. Maybe it happened around this time. Maybe earlier. Maybe later. Pollock was sure that it was one of Knievel's first jumps in the state. He had never met Knievel before he scheduled this event.

"He showed up one day, asked if I would promote a jump here," Pollock said. "We talked, and he said he'd want $3,500. I agreed and asked if he wanted $1,000 in advance. That floored him. He said no one ever had offered him an advance like that before."

The two men agreed on a date—whatever it was—and a promotion. He would jump ten Pepsi trucks. Not the big ones, the smaller Pepsi trucks. Pickups. The show was scheduled for a weekend night, and Knievel appeared that day to set up his equipment. He was alone, traveling with a little house trailer that he parked in the middle of the infield. The Pepsi people somehow had made a mistake and sent thirteen trucks instead of ten. Knievel, as he put up his ramps, said that the extra three trucks might as well be added to the line. He thought he could clear thirteen trucks.

Except a couple of hours later, he thought he couldn't. He called Pollock and expressed his fear.

"Come down and have a drink with me in my trailer," Knievel said to the promoter. "Talk with me."

Pollock was taking care of his ten-year-old son, Tommy, for the day, so he went to the trailer with his son. They sat around a cramped table with the daredevil. The daredevil said they should have whiskey. He pulled out three glasses, poured a shot of Wild Turkey bourbon in each. The two men and the boy all drank, just like that. The boy's eyes were opened very wide.

"It was okay," Ted Pollock said later about his son's debut with hard liquor. "There's worse things to say than you had your first drink of whiskey when you were ten years old with Evel Knievel."

Knievel kept drinking.

He outlined his concerns. He never had jumped thirteen Pepsi trucks, never had gone that far. There was a finite limit to the power and possibilities of one man and one motorcycle. This well could be it. He still would jump, mind you, because he had said he would, but he did not think he would land safely. The news was both a relief and a burden to Pollock, a relief because he would not have to refund any ticket money from a good house, a burden because he didn't want the death of this stranger on his soul.

The afternoon moved into the evening, and the evening moved into showtime, and the promoter noticed that the bottle of Wild Turkey was pretty much empty and no one else had joined the party. Knievel was shattered, drunk. He still said he had misgivings about the jump, but he left the trailer to cheers, staggered to the bike, kicked her into action, and went down the ramp. The takeoff was perfect. The flight was uneventful. The landing was perfect.

"The guy couldn't walk," Ted Pollock said. "But he could jump thirteen Pepsi trucks."

Pollock would wind up promoting seventeen Knievel jumps in the Northwest.

The summer trip through the region—not promoted by Ted Pollock—was not a great success. The crowds were fine, four thousand people the number quoted at most stops, but he crashed in three of his four jumps. He cleared thirteen automobiles from Centralia Dodge at the Lewis County Fairgrounds in Centralia, Washington, on June 9, 1967, then appeared the next day to speak at the Seattle Cycle Show at Exhibition Hall in Seattle on a bill that included actor Nick Adams and Miss Cycle, Linda Humble, but his next three stops all ended with hospital visits.

In Graham, Washington, he tried to jump sixteen Volkswagens at the Graham Speedway on July 28, 1967. He was supposed to be moving at seventy miles per hour when he went off the ramp, but was only at sixty. He came up short. The front wheel hit the sixteenth car, and he bounced and rolled, bounced and rolled, for nearly seventy feet. He wound up with a concussion.

"I don't feel too bad," he said from the hospital. "They haven't taken any X-rays yet, though. I guess I'll be here for another four or five days."

What did he remember from the crash?

"I can't remember anything after hitting the car," he said.

He promised from his bed that he would return in three weeks and complete what he started out to do. He returned on August 18, 1967, faced the same sixteen Volkswagens, and crashed again. He completed the jump but couldn't hold on to the handlebars. He broke his left wrist, his right knee, and a couple of ribs. He was back in the hospital again.

On September 24, 1967, five weeks later, still in recovery from the broken left wrist, right knee, and assorted ribs, he tried to clear sixteen Allen Green Chevrolets at Evergreen Speedway in Monroe, Washington. His failures were spelled out in the ad for the event: "Two months ago he tried to clear 16 Volkswagens and wound up in the hospital twice." Again he completed the Evergreen jump, cleared all sixteen Chevys, but landed hard enough to compress his spine. Back in the hospital.

"A motorcycle coming down thirty feet at seventy miles per hour gives you a terrible jolt," he said.

A losing streak in this business had consequences.

10 Caesars (I)

Finances had become a problem. The publicity was nice, but the payoff certainly had not arrived. The future always was delayed by the latest crashes in the present. Not only did hospital bills eat up the profits, time in the hospital ate up time on the job. If he couldn't perform, he had no income. The most daring part of the daredevil business, once again, was trying to sustain a workable bottom line.

Knievel had three days of jumps lined up at the San Francisco Civic Center in the last week of November and four days at the Long Beach Sports Arena in the first week of December, but he was floundering for capital. Even his backup, his grandmother, had told him that funding from Parrot Street was no longer an option. That was why he was pretty much broke when he arrived in Las Vegas to join the tavern regulars of Butte on their vacation.

The trip was almost mandatory for the tavern regulars. One of their own was boxing for the world light heavyweight title on November 17, 1967, at the Las Vegas Convention Center. A story would evolve later that Knievel liked boxing and traveled to Las Vegas to see Dick Tiger, the famed champion from Nigeria, at work. The truth was that he went to see Roger Rouse kick the famed Dick Tiger's ass. Everybody from Butte did.

Rouse was a thirty-two-year-old divorced father of two from Opportunity, Montana, which was an afterthought extension of Anaconda, Montana, which was a town built at the turn of the century twenty-five miles outside of Butte around the toxic smelting facility that handled all of the copper from the mines. ("Why did they name your town 'Opportunity'?" Rouse was asked. "Somebody was trying to be funny, I guess," he replied.) A solid workman who could knock people down and out, he had reached the quarterfinals as a middleweight in the 1956 Olympics in Melbourne, Australia. He then slowly put together a 30-5-3 record as a professional in the next ten years, a record that established him as the number-one contender for Tiger's crown but brought little other recognition. Most of his fights were in Montana and the state of Washington. Five were in the Butte Civic Center, five more in Memorial Auditorium in Anaconda.

The promoters brought him to New York for introductions at other televised title fights, dressed him in newly purchased boots, hat, and string tie from a Manhattan western wear store in an attempt to sell him to the American public as a Montana cowboy, but he was not exactly Roy Rogers or Tom Mix. He was another tough guy from a tough Montana town. He was the same as Knievel, same values, same background, same as the other Butte tough guys. Some of his best boxing work had been done for free, back to back with his three brothers, punching against other angry drinkers.

"When we were young, drinking was a matter of dissipating our aggression," Rouse's older brother, Don, said. "Now Roger's drinking is incidental to getting women."

"I don't train for the fight," Roger said. "I train for the party after the fight."

He and his brothers were friendly with Knievel. Anaconda had arguably the highest tavern-to-population ratio in the country—thirty-seven establishments to serve 12,054 men, women, and census-counted children—but the brothers often took the road to Butte for added evening excitement. That was how they knew Knievel.

"We used to hang out together, drink and raise hell," Jim Rouse, another brother, younger, another boxer, said. "He always used to say, 'You guys are crazy, going in that ring and letting someone hit you in the head.' We always said, 'If we're crazy, what are you?' "

A story. One night, as part of the drinking and raising hell, Knievel left a bar, maybe it was the Yellowstone, maybe not, with a prostitute. A short while later, the phone at the bar rang, a call for the Rouse brothers. This, remember, was before the time of cell phones and instant communication. Knievel was on the line from a phone booth at a gas station on

Harrison Avenue. There had been a problem with the prostitute, a bigger problem with her pimp. Knievel needed a ride from the Rouse brothers, needed it now.

En route to the gas station, right in the middle of Main Street, right in front of the M&M, right at the stoplight, the Rouse brothers passed Knievel's car. The doors on both the driver's and passenger's sides were open. The car was still running. No one was in the car. No one was around.

"The pimp pulled up beside me in his car, pointed a gun out the window right at me," Knievel reported when rescued at the gas station. "I got the hell out of there. He wanted to kill me."

Knievel never did explain why the pimp was mad.

Now Roger Rouse was matched against Dick Tiger for the title, and the fight felt like the greatest international moment in Butte athletic history, not only up there with that hockey meeting between the Butte Bombers and the Czech Olympic team but bigger, bigger, bigger. Roger Rouse actually had a chance to win. Or at least Knievel and the rest of the Butte tavern regulars thought so.

They arrived days early for the Friday night fight, checked into a succession of $6 per night, fleabag Vegas motels, began to party extensively, and looked for the best price to make underdog bets on their man. Knievel, with his troubled finances, drove into town in a used Volkswagen off his father's lot with $300 in his pocket. He checked into one of the $6 motels and joined the crowd.

Somewhere in the next few days, he answered a knock at his motel door. He was surprised to see Rouse, the man of the moment. The fighter had brought someone with him.

"I was writing a long story on Roger," Gil Rogin, a longtime writer and editor at Sports Illustrated, one of the magazine's earliest employees, said years later. "I'd been up to Montana, met his family, learned a lot about him. He said one day in Las Vegas, 'You want a story? I'll introduce you to a guy you won't believe. He wants to jump the Grand Canyon on a motorcycle.' "

The first thing the thirty-seven-year-old Rogin noticed about the guy who wanted to jump the Grand Canyon on a motorcycle was how small his motel room was. The writer never had seen a room this small. Knievel had been forced to put his suitcase underneath his bed because that was the only place it fit.

The second thing Rogin noticed was how talkative Knievel was. The man was a quote machine. He didn't seem to realize that his room was so small he had to keep his suitcase under the bed. He talked with a confidence that sounded like he was the one who was fighting for the world championship.

"I always liked to do stories about underdogs," Rogin said. "And I always liked to do stories about people who could talk. That made everything so much easier."

Evel Knievel? The *Sports Illustrated* writer was interested.

The biggest attraction in Vegas in November 1967 was Caesars Palace, the $25 million, fourteen-story casino and hotel that had opened fifteen months earlier. Built with a $10.6 million loan from the Teamsters' Central States Pension Fund and Teamster president Jimmy Hoffa's blessing, the casino was unlike any of its eleven competitors on Las Vegas Boulevard, "the Strip." With its seven hundred rooms, mirrors over the beds, waitresses and keno girls dressed as Roman goddesses, with its Circus Maximus showroom featuring top entertainment, with its daily celebration of hedonism and decadence, Caesars was a double-down bet on the Vegas future, an opulent operation that never had been seen anywhere. A first. It *was* the Vegas future.

"I dreamed up the plans for this whole place, and I designed or supervised everything," Caesars president Jay Sarno told reporter Jane Wilson. "I'm a builder, and I've always been very impressed by Roman architecture. It's very romantic. You ever been in Rome? What do you think about the fountains out front of the hotel? Fantastic, eh?"

Sarno claimed that a million dollars had been spent on the casino opening on August 5, 1966. Andy Williams, backed by a full orchestra, sang in the Circus Maximus. Harry and Jimmy, the two surviving Ritz Brothers, played in the Nero's Nook lounge. A well-comped planeload of eighty-two writers was flown in from the East Coast. The guest list was cut down from 20,000 to 1,800 lucky high-rollers who consumed, among other things, 30,000 fresh eggs, 50,000 glasses of champagne, and the world's largest Alaskan king crab. Lorne Greene, Al Hirt, Eva Gabor, Steve Lawrence, Eydie Gorme, and 550 Vietnam veterans were among the people in attendance. Robert Cummings, the actor, flew his own plane to Vegas to join the fun. A blond woman dressed as Cleopatra welcomed everyone at the front door. Her vital statistics were noted in newspaper accounts as 40-20-37.

This was overkill, of course, the Vegas party to top all Vegas parties. The first wedding at Caesars, sixty-six-year-old bandleader Xavier Cugat and his teenage singer, Charo, was held two days later. All the appropriate ribbons were cut. Performers ranging from Woody Allen to Jack Benny to Johnny Mathis to Victor Borge and Petula Clark headlined the Circus Maximus in the first year, but the main attraction still was the place itself.

The fountains, as Jay Sarno pointed out, were the most extravagant feature of the architecture. Unlike the other Vegas casinos, Caesars was set back from the Strip. A 135-foot circular driveway led to the front doors and easy entry to the low-ceilinged casino, which featured "the world's largest chandelier." In the middle of the circular driveway were eighteen fountains, forming "the world's largest private fountain display," that pumped out 350,000 gallons of water per minute, 10,000 gallons per second. A series of cypress trees, new to the Nevada desert environment, imported from Italy, provided a stately guard for the rushing waters.

"I don't worry if the trees die off," Jay Sarno said. "I'll just keep replacing them. People say to me, 'So why not have palm trees?' But I say they just don't have the character we want here."

The visitors from Butte were as entranced as everyone else by the spectacle. They checked out the goddesses, the blackjack tables, and, of course, the bars. Knievel sneaked away at times to call himself from a pay phone, his familiar routine. Since he couldn't be connected to himself, he was paged.

"Paging Mr. Evel Knievel. Mr. Knievel."

Knievel was Knievel.

"He says, at Caesars, 'Give all these guys a drink,' " Dick Pickett, a bartender at the Freeway, one of the guys from Butte, said. "The bill comes. He signs for it. The waitress can't read his writing. There's a reason for that. He was signing it to someone else's room."

Somewhere during the time at Caesars, another one of the guys, Billy Yganatowicz, a Butte fireman, made a suggestion. It was a moment that should have been recorded with more precision.

"Hey, Bob," Billy Yganatowicz said. "You should get a motorcycle and jump those fountains."

What?

"That would be good."

Once more an idea was laid out, a throwaway line, simple conversation, much more than half in jest, that sounded so good that Knievel adopted it immediately. Good Time Charlie Shelton in Kalispell had given him the Grand Canyon as an ultimate goal. Billy Yganatowicz, the Butte fireman, gave him the fountains at Caesars Palace, 350,000 gallons of water per minute, 10,000 gallons per second, the largest private fountain display in the world, as an immediate goal.

Knievel went to work. Immediately.

"He called me up," Dennis Lewin at *Wide World of Sports* said. "He said he was going to jump the fountains at Caesars Palace and we should do the broadcast. I really didn't remember him at the time. I wasn't interested, but I told him he could send me some film after he did it and we would take a look. That's the best we could do. I forgot all about it. I guess from there, he used my name as if we had a deal. That's the story that I heard."

The story had many versions, the names and organizations and details tweaked by Knievel, exaggerated with each rendition, but the basic tale always stayed the same: he proceeded to bombard Caesars president Sarno with hoax phone calls. He drove Sarno crazy. All of the calls involved Knievel and his attempt to jump the fountains with a motorcycle. Sarno was romanced as if he was the last customer in the world and Knievel was at his door with the last W. Clement Stone $3 policy in the world. Urgency was part of the sales presentation.

"Dennis Lewin of ABC Sports calling for Mr. Sarno . . ."

"Gil Rogin of *Sports Illustrated* for Mr. Sarno . . ."

"Fred Blumenstein from NBC in Los Angeles . . ."

Knievel changed his voice with each call. He used some real names, but mostly fictitious substitutes, mostly Jewish lawyer–sounding business names. The queries all were about this daredevil guy, this Eagle Beagle, Deevil Spleevil, Evel Knievel, whatever his name was, and this crazy plan to jump over the fountains at Caesars Palace. When was this happening? We might want to get a crew out there to cover something like this. We might want to be involved. What is the date? What is the time? What do you mean you don't know? Everyone is talking about this.

The final call—well, the next-to-final call—was brilliant. Knievel again impersonated a lawyer. Say the name was Epstein. Say it was Rothfarb. Whatever. Attorney Epstein/Rothfarb/Whatever represented Mr.

Evel Knievel of Evel Knievel Enterprises, Butte, Montana. Mr. Knievel, a nationally known daredevil, had been fielding a bunch of telephone calls about a supposed jump over the fountains at Caesars Palace. He didn't know a thing about this. He had no contracts. His inclination was to sue the hotel for using his name without his permission.

"But I have a problem," Epstein/Rothfarb/Whatever admitted. "I am also the attorney for Lawrence Welk, the bandleader. Perhaps you have seen his show on television? I am supposed to leave tomorrow with Mr. Welk and his band for a European tour. If I weren't leaving, I would be filing a lawsuit in the morning, but as it is, I am going to have my client call your office. Hopefully you can meet with him and come to some accommodation. If not, I will file suit when I return."

The forty-five-year-old Sarno was not a pushover. He stood only five-foot-six, had one of those roly-poly bodies, but he already was a large Vegas presence, a gruff gambling man in a gambling town. A University of Missouri graduate who had built successful businesses in Miami and Atlanta and other stops, mostly on loans from good friend Jimmy Hoffa's union, he had headed west for the action. He ate big, partied big, already was involved in the construction of a second casino to be called Circus Circus. He was known for his nightly trips up and down the Strip with his chauffeur, Little Jimmy. Sarno would start out each night with $10,000 in gambling money. That was his budget. Every casino was instructed to refuse him credit, no matter how much he begged. He either would come home with a lot of money or come home broke. The odds always favored broke. The next night he would start out with Little Jimmy and another $10,000. He was a one-man boost for the local economy.

Making deals was a basic part of his job. He and his entertainment director had completed a much larger, much messier transaction a month earlier when he signed Frank Sinatra to a multimillion-dollar, three-year contract to appear at Caesars, beginning in 1968. Sinatra's final confrontation, in early September, with the management of the rival Sands Hotel, which ended his sixteen-year association with the hotel, had included a crash-filled ride through the casino in a golf cart, followed by a punch in the nose from Sands president Carl Cohen. The indignant singer promised to bring Dean Martin, Sammy Davis, and Joey Bishop, the rest of his "Rat Pack," to Caesars with him. Sarno, of course, would be happy to oblige.

He also was happy to deal with Knievel.

"I arrived at Sarno's executive suites and was greeted by his secretary,"

Knievel later said in the book *Evel Ways: The Attitude of Evel Knievel.* "She ran behind a door and I overheard 'Mr. Sarno, it's him, it's him.' Sarno comes running out of his office and says 'Where the hell have you been? We've been looking all over for you.' "

Knievel signed a contract that day to jump the fountains at Caesars at two-thirty on the afternoon of December 31, 1967. If he was successful, he would jump the fountains again on January 3 and January 6, 1968. The fee for the three jumps would be $4,500. He also would receive a complimentary room and meals at Caesars, plus drinks. He would not receive complimentary gambling privileges. This was not a Sinatra-sized contract perhaps, but it was the biggest contract for Knievel in his short daredevil career.

This was the stage he always wanted. Someone was going to pay attention to what he did. A lot of someones.

Roger Rouse, alas, did not become the light heavyweight champion of the world on November 17, 1967. He was knocked down for the mandatory eight counts in both the ninth and tenth rounds, and when he was dropped again fifty-two seconds into the twelfth round, referee Jimmy Oliva simply stopped the fight. The thirty-eight-year-old Tiger, worried father of seven children back home, his country embroiled in civil war, retained his crown.

A first-generation computer that filled an entire room somewhere had been fed assorted pre-fight information and along with the boys from Butte had predicted a Rouse upset. Tiger sounded as happy to beat the computer as he was to beat the boxer from Anaconda.

"A computer is just handmade," Tiger said. "I call him a liar and prove it tonight."

The boys from Butte went back to the Freeway, the Met, the Acoma Lounge, the assorted haunts. Knievel, who supposedly lost $1,000 on the fight, went back to work. He jumped one hundred feet, ramp to ramp, for three straight days, November 23 to 26, at the San Francisco Civic Center as part of a sports cycle exhibition. He was at the other end of California four days later, seated behind a table at Long Beach Honda from three to six on the afternoon of November 30 to sign autographs, talk motorcycles, talk danger, the first of four appearances to promote his jump on December 2 at the Long Beach Sports Arena.

The motorcycle talk now involved a different motorcycle. In San Francisco he had switched from his Norton 750 to a 650cc Triumph T-120. The switch came at just the right time. Norton had determined that the motorcycle it gave Knievel was worth more as a motorcycle, even used, than any publicity he might give the company in return. One of his financial woes in Las Vegas was being a motorcycle daredevil without a motorcycle. Bob Blair wanted the Norton back.

Triumph came up with a replacement partly because of the Caesars Palace deal, partly because Knievel had worked his contacts in the motorcycle business in the state of Washington. The contacts had convinced management at the Triumph/BSA distribution and racing facility in Duarte, California, to give Knievel a bike. This was a big deal.

"Companies didn't give away anything in those days," Bryan Farnsworth, part of the Hollywood Motorcycle Daredevils shows and also a mechanic for Triumph, said. "I raced the bikes, and the company gave me $30 off dealer cost, plus a break on parts, and I thought I was in heaven. It was a big thing to give away a bike."

Knievel drove to the Duarte garage to finalize the agreement in a Chevrolet El Camino pickup truck with his Norton motorcycle in the back. This was considered bad form. Motorcycle brand rivalries were huge, such a big deal that a plywood wall had been built directly down the middle of the garage, because although Triumph and BSA motorcycles had merged business operations, they had not merged racing teams. There were so many animosities between the mechanics on the two teams that the wall had been built to keep the peace.

And now this guy with a Norton in his truck bed wanted a new Triumph motorcycle? Pat Owens, the chief racing mechanic, wouldn't even touch the box that contained the new bike. He said Evel Knievel was "a carnival act," not a racer, and refused to assemble the bike. The job had no dignity.

Farnsworth, who always had been charmed by Knievel, did the job. He set the bike up the way he would set up a bike for desert races at the time, a heavy, four-hundred-pound monster with no real springs, no shocks, none of the basics for big jumps that light, bouncy bikes would have in the future. There were no light, bouncy bikes for big jumps in 1967.

This was the T-120—which had been advertised as "the world's fastest motorcycle" since Detroit Triumph dealer Bob Lipper set a speed record of 245.66 miles per hour at the Bonneville Salt Flats in 1966—that Knievel would use at Caesars. This was the bike he used at San Francisco and Long Beach.

"There's a publicity picture of him making one of the jumps at San Francisco," Farnsworth said. "He's in the middle of the air, and you can see a black dot in the middle of the picture. You think it's some ink that was left there by the printer or some imperfection. No, it's the rubber guard from the foot peg flying off. There was a cotter pin that I forgot to fasten. We got it for the next jump."

The Long Beach jump on December 2, 1967, advertised as an attempt at an indoor record, was supposed to cover ten cars. The hard part was a short run-up of only 90 yards to get up to speed. The distance Knievel really needed was 125 yards, but just to get 90 he had to start in the lobby. Even then, he was backed up against a flight of stairs.

Everything would happen in an explosive hurry.

"You just got to grab and go," he explained. "You got to gas that motorcycle and don't let go. Speed doesn't necessarily get distance. You got to get up right on top of the power curve, right at the peak so that the rear wheel is driving fast off that chain. It's just like a person crouching and springing up. You got to get up on the foot pegs on the balls of your feet, hang on and guide it through the air. If you're going to miss, just grit your teeth . . ."

The explanation was given to Gil Rogin, the *Sports Illustrated* writer. Unable to shake the image of the suitcase under the bed in the tiny Vegas hotel room, he had returned to New York and convinced his bosses that Knievel would be a good subject. Now Rogin was on the job again, collecting the varied pieces of Knievel's life, trying to separate the truths from the exaggerations, watching his subject, yes, jump over the ten cars successfully and afterward drink stingers, straight up, in a hotel bar in celebration. This was scheduled to be the long story in the back of the magazine, known every week as "The Bonus." Knievel was on the job too, spinning his tales, trying to put as many exclamation points in "The Bonus" as he could.

"I really came bursting through that door," he said about the Long Beach jump. "The tach was 7,500 rpm and the speedometer was bouncing between 60 and 70. I saw those white lines heading up that ramp and I said I got to do it!"

Rogin hung around Los Angeles, wrote down all the specifics of what seemed to be absurd undertakings. Knievel lived in his own bus in L.A. this time. Rogin would meet him at the bus, then follow him around. When Knievel went to Las Vegas to get ready for the Caesars jump, Rogin went with him. Knievel drove.

The car was a 1937 purple Rolls-Royce, which he said he had picked up a day earlier. (Just another fact for the story that wrote itself.) The pace was moderate, conservative. (The guy is driving to Las Vegas to jump the fountains at Caesars Palace on a motorcycle and he drives at fifty miles per hour, seat belt fastened, like an old man in a station wagon bringing his Social Security check to the craps tables.) Knievel sang a happy song over and over.

> *Never worry,*
> *Never fuss,*
> *When Evel Knievel drives the bus.*

The talk was constant. Rogin had decided that he liked the daredevil even though the daredevil seemed decidedly anti-Semitic. Rogin, Jewish, wore a Star of David from a chain on his neck, but that didn't stop the idle remarks, the jokes about Jews. Rogin surprised himself by letting it slide. Knievel's youthful exuberance, his ambition, maybe where he was from . . . there were other parts of this guy that seemed to mute the unfortunate words he said here or there.

"He wasn't really a roughneck, which I had thought he might be," Rogin said. "He was good company. I enjoyed being around him."

The trip, L.A. to Las Vegas, always boring, was not boring at all. Knievel prattled along, talked about swindling, arm wrestling, blowing safes, jumping the Grand Canyon, assorted subjects. When Vegas came into view, the lights in the middle of the desert, a burst of color, electricity, megawatt magic, Knievel became philosophical. He knew the importance of what awaited.

"If I keep making these jumps," he said, "I'm going to wind up dead. And I just don't want to wind up dead."

Caesars Palace. The fountains.

What had he done?

Whatever it was, it belonged to him. He had created the moment from nothing. This would be a self-imposed fate.

"I haven't come down this road by accident," he also said to Gil Rogin. "I'm here."

A writer never can go wrong with a quotable man.

11 Caesars (II)

The best indication that this was more than just another jump over a string of cars or panel trucks at some dusty drag strip or fairgrounds was that it was going to be the starting point for an Evel Knievel movie. The working title was "Why?" and the producer-director-cinematographer was actor John Derek. Knievel and Derek had met at the Tiger-Rouse fight, and Derek had watched the show in Long Beach, and the two men had made a deal to do a documentary on Knievel's life.

The actor and the daredevil were a natural pair. The most famous line the actor ever had spoken was "I want to live fast, die young, and make a good-looking corpse" as a murderous juvenile delinquent in the 1949 film *Knock on Any Door*, starring Humphrey Bogart. Knievel, of course, pretty much had embraced that philosophy.

Now forty-one years old, Derek had moved beyond those delinquent roles, had appeared in epics like *The Ten Commandments* and *Exodus*, but probably was best known for his relationships with beautiful women. His first wife was starlet Patti Behrs, his second actress Ursula Andress, and now he was about to be married to Linda Evans, the star of *The Big Valley*. (He later would be married a fourth time to eighteen-year-old Mary Louise Collins, who became known by her nickname, Bo, and married second name, Bo Derek.) Knievel obviously shared this appreciation for beautiful women.

"John was an exceptionally creative man," Linda Evans said years later, trying to describe Derek's charm. "He could get interested in many things, things that were off the beaten path. An example, he made me my boots. He started talking one day with a bootmaker on the set of *Big Valley* about how boots were made. Then one day, out of nowhere, John brought home a last, the form you use to make a pair of boots. The first boot took him a year to finish, the second one half of a year. That was John. He could do anything. He was very intelligent, very creative. The films he shot, they were just gorgeous."

Derek had rented two enormous cameras—at least they looked enormous to Evans—to film the jump. One had a normal lens, which would be used from long range. Derek would use this camera to capture the crowd, the atmosphere, the panorama. The second camera with a long lens was for a close-up. This would be trained at the landing ramp, catching the flight of Knievel and motorcycle as they became larger and larger, directly into the camera. Evans never had worked a camera like this in her life. She was nervous about the idea. Derek told her not to worry. Then Derek himself became nervous the night before the jump.

"We went out to dinner at Caesars, the three of us, John and Evel and myself," Evans said. "It was supposed to be low-key. Except John and Evel got into a terrible fight."

The fight was about the jump. Knievel solemnly informed Derek that the jump was not going to be a success. He had calculated all there was to calculate, and he could not make this jump. He would land short. He would crash. This was the pessimism that eventually surfaced prior to most appearances for Knievel, the whistle-past-the-graveyard moment that seemed to be a necessary part of his preparation, but it sounded awful to Derek. He was horrified. He didn't want to film a tragedy.

"Cancel the show," he said.

"I can't do that," Knievel said.

"You could kill yourself . . ."

"It'll be all right . . ."

Around and around the two men went, variations on that argument. Derek was angry. This was the stupidest thing he ever had heard, a man putting himself in a situation that he knew would cause him bodily harm, perhaps even death. Knievel repeated that a promise was a promise, this was what he did for a living. Derek repeated that this was the stupidest thing he ever had heard.

Finally, he quit. The partnership was done. He was Evel Knievel's friend, and he didn't want to be a partner in any production that could take his friend's life. Nothing could be that important. He would film the jump, yes, he and Linda would do that because it was too late now for Knievel to find someone else, but he didn't want the film, didn't want the rights, didn't want any part of this deadly enterprise. There would be no movie.

"If you're going to kill yourself," John Derek said, "I don't want to be one of the reasons. You're on your own."

Knievel went off to take care of his jitters in whatever ways he could find. Derek and Evans went outside to the parking lot to set up their cameras and to practice for most of the night. Evans was terrified. She not only didn't know if she could operate the camera, now she didn't know if she could look at what might happen in front of her.

"I never liked violence in movies," she said. "I never watched. My mother always talked about taking my sister and me to the movies. I'd be the one with my head between my knees, my hands over my ears, at the scary parts. I never even liked the dramatic parts. I'd walk outside to get popcorn. I liked the frothy movies."

The froth had disappeared from this production.

The final day of 1967 was cool in Las Vegas. The temperatures, high of 48 degrees, low of 29, were nothing compared to the reading of –13 degrees (with windchill of –48 degrees) in Green Bay, Wisconsin, where the nation was captivated as the Packers outlasted the Dallas Cowboys, 21–17, in the NFL playoff game that would soon be called "the Ice Bowl," but still, the numbers were cool for Vegas. Sunny, but brisk.

The marquee at Caesars Palace advertised *Fiddler on the Roof*, the Broadway production starring Theodore Bikel, which would have performances at 8:30 p.m. and 2:00 a.m. at Circus Maximus to celebrate the New Year. No mention was made of Knievel. The other attractions in town ranged from Phil Foster and Joe Flynn at the Aladdin to Louis Armstrong and His All-Stars at the Tropicana to comedian Jan Murray at the Thunderbird to Arturo Romero and His Magic Violins at the Dunes and Psychedelic Topless at the Nevada Club. A reveler had choices.

The crowd, determined by guesstimate since there were no tickets, was somewhere around ten thousand people, everyone bundled a bit against the cold, the underdressed Roman slave girl waitresses from Caesars working with goose bumps in their cleavage. The magic word was "free." People took a break from the gambling tables, killed time while waiting for the celebratory night to arrive. They would hold a beer, a cocktail, in their hands and watch some knucklehead try to kill himself.

The knucklehead in question had spent a lot of time around Sarno's offices during the weeklong buildup to the event. He was a bundle of pleasant energy, didn't seem terribly involved in the planning. Sarno's secretary, Evelyn Cappadona, asked him one day why he wasn't outside, practicing, making sure everything was just right.

"You don't understand, Evelyn," Knievel said. "This is a one-shot deal. You do it or you don't."

Jim Dunbar, stationed near the jump site as a valet parking attendant, talked with Knievel daily as the ramps were built on either side of the fountains. He found the daredevil to be "cool, calm and collected, personable." Kim Kimball, a salesman for Montesa motorcycles from Spain, part of the Ascot crowd, did most of the work on the ramps. Dunbar also talked to him.

"Kimball was frustrated," Dunbar said. "He couldn't get Knievel to go out and see if he could get going fast enough to clear the fountains."

Technology was not part of the production. Knievel never had brought mathematics or physics into his plans and surely did not now. He felt like he didn't need experts. He was his own expert. His research was his performances, the feeling he took away from each success or each failure. He didn't even use the speedometer anymore, relying on touch, feel, sound, to determine if he was traveling fast enough or slow enough to complete the jump. The ramps were basic backyard construction, nothing special. The angle was again determined by the naked eye. There was no formula for jumping cars. There was no micrometer precision. All of this might be added by other people in a far more bulletproof future, much of the danger removed, but this was the primordial stage of motorcycle jumping. There was no need for slide rules, calculators, or even practice.

Suck in your breath and go. That was the game.

Standing on the front steps of Caesars, looking out toward Las Vegas Boulevard, the jump would travel from left to right, the opposite direction most people later would assume it went. Knievel would jump directly into the low, setting sun. The fountains, as dramatic as they looked, were not the challenge. They were no taller than the average line of cars. The challenge was the distance.

The takeoff and landing ramps each were 40 feet long, 10 feet wide, plywood and two-by-fours. An elevated 200-foot runway would lead Knievel into the jump. He would have to clear 140 feet, almost half of a football field, the longest distance he ever had jumped. A van, a panel truck, again was parked in front of the landing ramp for safety, a steel plate stretched on top of the roof. This was where he hoped to land if he came up short. He would have to be traveling somewhere between eighty and ninety miles per hour when he left the takeoff ramp to travel ramp to ramp. No one—it didn't have to be pointed out—had ever tried something exactly like this.

The parking lot, filled with cars, came right up to the landing area. On the morning of the jump, Dunbar noticed how close the cars were. He moved a bunch of them to give Knievel a larger landing zone, basically a free area that went to the retaining wall at the edge of the Caesars property. On the other side of the wall, the property for the Dunes casino began.

Knievel had become more and more nervous as the jump approached. John Derek and Linda Evans were not the only people who heard his doubts about success. A number of the boys from the bars in Butte had arrived. Linda and the kids had arrived. His father. His mother even had come up from Reno. There were also representatives from Moses Lake, from Los Angeles, all the pit stops.

"I've got to admit, I'm getting a little edgy," Knievel told Al Guzman, a sportswriter for the *Las Vegas Sun* the day before the jump. "I'm still confident I can make it, but my nervous system doesn't seem to agree. I'll be glad when it's over."

Dressed now in the white-red-and-blue leathers that left no doubt that he was a purely American exhibitionist, he knocked back a shot of Wild Turkey, maybe two, in his suite to calm his nerves. ("He was shaking," Skip Van Leeuwen said, describing Knievel's pre-jump condition.) He stopped once in the casino on the way to the parking lot, according to his self-remembered legend, placed a $100 bet on red at the roulette wheel, saw the white ball land on black, and plodded forward to his self-appointed task.

The ultimate moment, as always, happened in an instant. After the requisite false starts to get a feel for the situation, he gunned down the elevated runway and up the forty-foot ramp and into the air—crossed over the fountains, freeze-frame perfect—and landed short. Crashed. He hit the final safety van. He went from healthy and free, perfect, to a man in need of a doctor and an intensive care ward.

Blink once. Blink twice.

That was how long it took.

The crash was a furious blur. Knievel flew off the bike—didn't he fly off the bike?—hands wrenched from the handlebars, and landed and bounced and rolled and bounced, and it was an instant mess. The crowd reaction was a gasp. People started running, moving everywhere, tried to help, maybe just moved to move. Knievel could be heard to complain about a pain in his back as he was carried one hundred feet to an ambulance, then taken with appropriate speed and solemnity to Southern Nevada Memorial Hospital.

What happened?

He clearly had lost control of the four-hundred-pound motorcycle. He clearly had gone flying. The motorcycle . . . half the people screamed because they thought the riderless motorcycle might come their way. Was there mechanical error? Someone suggested the throttle had fallen off. Was there driver error? What?

John Derek asked Linda Evans what kind of pictures she had shot. She still was shaking from the experience. She had no idea. She wasn't sure she had been looking at the right place. Fast. The motorcycle was coming straight at her, out of control. She saw everything. Did the camera capture it all? Proper lighting? In focus? No idea.

Jim Dunbar, the parking valet, looked at where Knievel landed. If those cars hadn't been moved the morning of the jump, he would have landed in the middle of them. Did Knievel realize how close he came? He probably would have been dead.

"I thought he was dead," more than one observer remarked. "He had to be dead the way he landed."

The jump, in the end, was no different from a pileup on Interstate 15 coming into the city, blunt and unsettling. Everyone had a personal perspective. Everyone had a different accident report to file.

Jay Sarno watched the proceedings from the roof of Caesars with his two sons, Jay Jr. and Freddie. Jay Jr. was nine. Freddie was six. They were wrapped in the same buzz as everyone else, the pageant unfolding in what was a piece of their everyday life, the parking lot. The kids had what amounted to box seats as Knievel came up the ramp, not fast enough, no, and landed short and started flipping.

The key mistake in the crash, Jay Jr. would remember for forty years and more, was in the way the safety van was set up. No one had thought to put blocks under the tires. When Knievel landed short, the truck underneath the metal plate had no resistance. The truck settled down on its springs and shock absorbers from the force, moved a little bit, then sprung back upward. The upward spring was what sent Knievel flying out of control.

While the daredevil was being loaded into the ambulance for the ride to Southern Nevada Memorial, the Sarno family cut through the chaos to the family Cadillac, where Little Jimmy, the driver, awaited. The Sarnos then followed the ambulance to Southern Nevada Memorial.

"There was all kinds of activity outside," Jay Jr. remembered. "Reporters, television crews. It was like one of those alerts for a nuclear disaster."

Jay Sr. left the kids in the car. He was gone for a long time, more than an hour. The kids, watching the activity, grew edgy, worried. When Jay Sr. returned, they wanted to know everything, starting with the basic question: was Mr. Knievel all right?

Their father gave them a quick and memorable lesson in promotion. The first thing he did was smile. Yes, Mr. Knievel was all right. He and Mr. Knievel had just been laughing together in the emergency room about the crash. There were some broken bones, of course, and Mr. Knievel's leg had been pushed back into his pelvis, so there might be an operation, but the only real worry was whether or not he would be able to walk without a limp. He was a lucky, lucky man. There were no other worries.

The father cautioned, however, that this was not what his sons would hear on television or read in the newspaper in coming days. The injuries would be much more serious when they were detailed for the general public. There would be questions about whether or not he ever would walk again, questions about whether he ever would perform. This was to keep the story alive, to keep Mr. Knievel's name in the paper, to keep Caesars' name in the paper. This was good business for everyone concerned.

Sarno Sr. and Knievel had cooked up the plan right there in the emergency room. That was the major cause of the great laughter. Sarno was late getting back to the car, he said, because he had been sprinkling some $100 bills throughout the hospital to selected orderlies and nurses to be sure that they, as unnamed sources, would report to the press that the daredevil was in a dire state.

"It was all a fabrication, all horseshit," Jay Sarno Jr. said years later. "My father and Knievel were like two giggling, sneaky teenagers. They were putting something over on everybody. They were a couple of promoters."

Sarno told other people in the following days that he had visited Knievel and given him the $4,500 for the three jumps, even though the last two never would be performed. He felt sorry for the kid. He said he agreed to pay the hospital costs. He also picked up the hotel room, plus meals, plus bar bill, part of the contract, and added on the gambling debts. They were not part of the contract, but, as he said, he felt sorry for the kid.

"Now get the fuck out of my life," Sarno said he had told Knievel in the hospital after detailing his largesse. "I never want to see you again."

He now said he was a little presumptuous with his words. At that good-bye moment, he thought the promotion was a disaster, beginning to end. Then he stopped back at Caesars that night. He couldn't find a parking space, not even his own. The carryover attention from the afternoon had made Caesars the hottest place in town.

Happy New Year's.

The story that came out the following day did indeed portray a man in serious trouble. Doctors supposedly were deciding whether or not to fuse his pelvis. If the pelvis was fused, he would be unable to walk and his career certainly would be finished. The Associated Press sent out a two-picture photo spread that was used across the country. The first showed Knievel in full flight on the Triumph T-120, high above the fountains, framed in the air by two of those Italian cypress trees. The second showed the separated bike and man rolling along the parking lot in a single ball of dust. The title for the two pictures was "End of a Stunt Driver's Career."

"Evel Knievel, 29-year-old Hollywood stunt driver, is pictured here in what probably will be the last such feat of his career," the caption read. "Flying high at left, Knievel fell short of the mark—the 150-foot flight over Las Vegas casino fountains—and crashed. Knievel was thrown against a retaining wall and suffered a badly fractured pelvis, probably ending his career."

The *Las Vegas Sun* ran a front-page story headlined "Injured Stuntman Fair; Medics Hold Up Big Decision" on January 2, 1968. Tom Diskin, the paper's sports columnist, wrote that he had been refused entry to Knievel's hospital room, "as expected." The columnist still was dizzy over what he had seen, thinking how easily Knievel "could have been decapitated" if he had landed a few feet shorter than he did.

"I once knew a veteran sportswriter who, after losing several friends in auto racing, refused to get acquainted with other drivers because of the way he felt when they were killed," Diskin wrote. "Now I think I know some of the feeling he had."

Three days later, doctors at the hospital announced that fusion surgery would not be necessary, but that Knievel probably still would be in the hospital "for months." The inference was that he still had some serious problems.

"The treatment originally diagnosed for Mr. Knievel is going to be continued," an unnamed doctor said at Southern Nevada Memorial. "No surgery is considered needed. Fifteen years ago surgery was felt necessary for a smashed pelvis, but now improved techniques allow it to be treated with traction."

Friends expected the worst when they went to visit, then were surprised when they found the patient up to his old ways. Bryan Farnsworth, who had set up the bike in the first place, had missed the jump, but showed up two days later from L.A. to see if there was anything he could do to help. He found that Knievel didn't need any help.

"They told me at the front desk he couldn't have visitors except for family," Farnsworth said. "I told them I was family. I was his cousin from Butte. They let me in.

"Evel was a little groggy from the drugs, but was sitting up. His leg was wrapped in plastic, otherwise he was fine. He spent the whole visit showing me newspaper clippings about the crash, magazine articles. I think he showed me something from *Time* magazine."

The crash was a publicity miracle. Knievel didn't have to be told twice about that. People always paid attention after he crashed, then came back to talk about his injuries, his fate. Voyeurs always perked up when he described his crashes . . . and who wasn't a voyeur? This clearly was the best crash of them all. The stories and attention multiplied and became even better when John Derek and Linda Evans came to the hospital a week later. They brought along the pictures from the big day.

After the crash, the two movie stars had sent the film to Los Angeles to be developed at a Hollywood laboratory. The process took four or five days, so they went camping. They drove around the wilderness, stopped when they had the urge to stop, slept under the open sky, reveled in being normal and anonymous. When they finally went to L.A. to pick up the finished product at the laboratory, they also received the first review.

"That's the most extraordinary film I've ever seen," the technician said.

Linda Evans was stunned. The technician said he had developed moving pictures for a long, long time. He had developed Academy Award winners. He had never developed anything as graphic as this one crash. He was amazed. Everybody who saw the film was amazed.

"You could see everything," Linda Evans said. "It was just so stunning to me. The camera captured every twist and turn of his body. Arms. Legs. Hips. Everything disconnecting."

Beginner's luck perhaps. Mind over matter. Whatever it was that she used in her filmmaking debut with the long lens, it worked. The entire edited clip of the jump was no more than a minute long. Her contribution was less than half of that, maybe twenty-five seconds, even that number inflated because the action from her camera was shown in slow motion. The twenty-five slow-motion seconds, though, were absolutely spectacular.

The film . . .

John Derek, with the other camera, pans the crowd at the beginning of the clip, a background noise of Roman trumpets and unruliness, people waiting for a show to get rolling. The action continues, still John Derek's camera, through the first warm-up ride to the edge of the ramp, yes, and then the real ride, everything done in a hurry, in front of your eyes before you are ready. Well into the jump, maybe two-thirds of the way, John Derek's shot from the side of the action disappears. Here is Linda's camera, straight on, different speed. Knievel is in the air, ready to land. Slow motion, everything happens in slow motion.

He hits, back wheel first, on the safety van . . .

Boom . . .

The metal panel lifts off the van. The front wheel of the motorcycle is turned, hard right, by the impact. His hands come off the handlebars. He starts to fly off the bike, straight up, propelled, then turning, turning . . .

He does a complete flip, perfect, as if he had come off the ten-meter board in an Olympic diving competition, a violent, unplanned somersault. His arms go out in front of him to break the fall, but are of little use because, yes, he lands hard on his back . . .

Boom . . .

He bounces, then rolls to one side, tries to cover up, but his momentum is in control and he does another complete turn, this time sideways . . .

Boom . . .

Another complete turn sideways . . .

Boom . . .

He rolls straight ahead one more time now, another complete turn, helmeted head over flame-resistant heels, helmeted head bouncing off the pavement, arms, legs, flying. "Like a ragdoll," most people will say . . .

Boom . . .

A final sideways flip puts him at rest, pretty much at Linda Evans's feet. The Triumph T-120, a secondary character in the production, has taken an eerie course, following Knievel's bouncing path, threatening to run him down. It finally clatters out of the picture, moving past Evans's camera and somewhere behind her.

Derek's camera takes control again, the return to normal, fast time—people running to the injured Knievel, post-crash chaos that looks like a scene from a Central American revolution—oddly enough is a relief. The man has stopped bouncing. Done. The painful part is finished.

"It's your film, do what you want with it," John Derek said when he presented the finished product to Knievel at Southern Nevada Memorial. "Linda and I just hope you never do something like this again. We don't want to see you get hurt."

"I'm glad that he got something he could use out of it all, but, wow, at what a price," Linda Evans said. "How do you do something like that? How could you ever get on a motorcycle again?"

Retirement never entered Knievel's mind. Retire? This was the beginning.

The film was everything. The film was instant credibility. (How dangerous, how scary, are the things I do? This is exhibit A.) The film was a passport, a not-so-secret word that opened the toughest doors in television, made its owner a desired guest. (I can bring along the clip from Caesars Palace. People love that.) The film was what made most of America first remember the name of Evel Knievel. (Did you see what happened to this guy? Lucky he's still alive.) The film was the foundation for a business, a career, found at last. The talking person from Butte now had a grand talking point. He crashed at Caesars Palace, and now he wanted to jump the Grand Canyon! Stay tuned.

Everything that followed came from the film.

Knievel always gave great credit to John Derek for following through and giving him the film. He also admitted, gladly, that the crash was the foundation of his entire career, the moment he was delivered to the American public. No one can say what would have happened if he had completed the jump, then completed the next two fountain jumps, but a pretty good guess is that the news would not have moved outside of Las Vegas.

A story. The first time the film was shown on national television, Matt Tonning was one of the more interested viewers. This was a Saturday or Sunday afternoon, *Wide World of Sports* on the TV as background noise, everything quiet in his Montana recreation room until this daredevil came onto the screen from Caesars Palace in Las Vegas. The announcer in the background noise mentioned the name "Evel Knievel."

Evel Knievel?

That had to be Bob Knievel, his friend, Bob Knievel from Butte. The crazy salesman for Combined Insurance. The one who worked with Jay. The one who sold the mental hospital. The one who conned the lawyer in the bar about betting on the size of his penis. The same Bob Knievel. Nobody ever called him Evel, not back then, but this had to be the same guy.

Sure was.

The filmed action from Las Vegas now became totally compelling. There was good reason. Tonning had been contacted in the intervening years a few times by Bob. There had been some genial conversation, more than a few laughs, then Bob had asked to buy some insurance. He no longer was employed by Combined, he said, but was still a true believer. He had bought a policy, then another and another, bought ten policies in all. The company had rules that a salesman should sell only two policies, maximum, to a single customer, but Bob was a friend and he really wanted to be protected and he was insistent, and so maybe a few rules had been broken. Tonning had entered other salesmen's names to sell the extra policies to Bob.

Now Bob was a daredevil? This was his new job?

Tonning watched the proceedings with an immediate sense of dread. He knew the ending before it happened.

"There I was," he said, "sitting at home and watching my career skid and crash across the Dunes parking lot. I knew right then I was going to be fired."

There would be rumors that Knievel had bought as many as fifty policies, maybe more, from different Combined agents, that he was very well covered by Combined Insurance when he crashed in Las Vegas, but the rumors didn't matter to Tonning. No clever little W. Clement Stone saying could get him out of this jam. He was called to the home office in Chicago during the next business week.

"What the hell were you thinking?" his boss asked.

He had no good reply.

He was fired.

A printed burst of publicity for Knievel arrived when Rogin's story appeared in the February 4 issue of *Sports Illustrated*. Entitled "He's Not a Bird, Not a Plane," the story ran for nine pages in the biggest sports magazine in the country, more than seven thousand words. A single picture of Knievel standing up on his Triumph halfway across the fountains, hanging in the middle of the air as if he were some Disney cartoon character, some product of a wild imagination, Caesars Palace in the background, the faces in the crowd waiting with mouths open to see what came next, was stretched across the first two pages. The caption read "He is Evel Knievel, self-styled conservative Wildman—here soaring over the fountains at a Las Vegas hotel—who intends to jump the Grand Canyon on a motorcycle."

Rogin had gone home, missed the jump and the crash, but that was all right. The event was stitched into the narrative nicely, the story more about the wacky character and his wacky plan to jump the canyon. The safecracking, the kidnapping of Linda, the hitchhiking to Washington to stop the elk kill, the hockey against the Czechs, the insurance career, all of that was included. This was the basic background tale of Evel Knievel that would be saved in a pile of old *Sports Illustrated*s, Olympic skiers Billy Kidd and Jimmy Huega on the cover of the issue, and brought out to fill up countless newspaper columns.

"Everybody expects Evel Knievel to be a long-haired guy, but I'm a conservative Wildman," Knievel told Rogin. "I am a guy who is first of all a businessman. I present myself to the public as an athlete and an average human being. I look like a pole vaulter."

The likeability that the writer had found in his subject came through in the story. Knievel was a bold scamp, a charming entrepreneur selling the possibilities of his own demise. He was cast in that grand role of An

American Original, talented in the whacked-out game he had invented for himself. He certainly was a stranger no more to the American public. Between *Sports Illustrated* and *Wide World* he had hit the two major sports media outlets. The film would bring him to the nonsports outlets, the talk shows that clogged the daily television schedules.

There was no doubt that he seemed to have a future when he checked out of Southern Nevada Memorial in a wheelchair on February 6, 1968, thirty-seven days after he had been delivered in an ambulance. He only needed time in Butte to heal before he stepped back onto that motorcycle, got back into the game.

The Caesars jump was his life-changing moment, the catapult into public view. He took the post-jump deceit he manufactured with Sarno and refined it, multiplied it many times, in the future. The more he would show the film, the worse his injuries would become. Knievel biographer and historian Steve Mandich noted in his SteveMandich.com blog that within two years a story appeared in the September 1969 issue of *Science and Mechanics* claiming that Knievel "suffered a severe brain concussion." The statement quickly grew from there to an almost routine Knievel response that he had been in a coma for twenty-nine days after the Caesars Palace crash. A basic part of his story, totally bogus, was that he landed in Southern Nevada Memorial in a coma and woke up twenty-nine days later and was famous.

("What's it like to be in a coma for twenty-nine days?" Richard Deitsch of *Sports Illustrated* once asked him. "How the fuck do I know?" Knievel replied. "I was in a coma for twenty-nine days.")

One of the people Knievel met during the buildup to the jump was Joe Louis, the former heavyweight boxing champion. Louis, one of Knievel's idols as a kid, worked at Caesars as greeter now, part of the operation. One of Knievel's friends said he heard that the champ, on the eve of the jump, had advised Knievel, "You know, it might work out a lot better for you if you don't make it," which ultimately turned out to be true.

The event became the most famous part of Caesars lore. ("It's still the most asked question I get," valet parking attendant Jim Dunbar, still on the job in 2010, said. "Where did Evel Knievel crash?") The film, despite all the photographic advances that have evolved, the computer simulations that can make anything and everything explode, still has remained startling, memorable. Linda Evans, living in the state of Washington, forty-three years after the event, was asked one day by the manager of her local supermarket if she would meet with one of his young employees who apparently was a big fan. She was flattered, prepared to talk about her career on the hit television series *Dynasty*. This was not what the young fan wanted to talk about.

"Did you really shoot that film of Evel Knievel at Caesars Palace?" he asked.

A final word came from Evelyn Cappadona, Jay Sarno's secretary. She continued to hear rumors that Knievel had not been injured as badly as the papers said. She didn't think they were right. Mr. Sarno always had said on television that Knievel was injured. He was quoted in the newspapers. He wouldn't lie about something like this, would he?

"You wouldn't lie about something like this," Evelyn said one day to Mr. Sarno. "Would you?"

The boss laughed out loud.

"Sure I would," he replied. "This was all about publicity. That was why it happened. That was why it was great. The publicity."

12 Movie

The return to action was scheduled for May 25, 1968, a Saturday night. The plan was to jump thirteen Bill Watkins Fords at Bee Line Dragway in Scottsdale, Arizona. The Bill Watkins dealership, at the corner of Scottsdale and Camelback, made a weeklong production of the event, with ads that announced thirteen new Fords, thirteen demonstrators, and thirteen used cars were for sale at "Evel-ly Low Prices!" Buyers not only were invited to look at the cars on the lot, but also could see "Evel Knievel's fantastic equipment" on display before it was moved to the drag strip for the jump.

The new notoriety obviously was in effect. Knievel was at a new venue, new city, but wasn't a stranger. The clip had been shown on *Wide World*; readers had read the stories and not only knew about the crash but knew about the plan to jump the canyon. For the first time he didn't have to beat a bass drum to announce his arrival. The noise already existed.

One of the people intrigued by what he heard was a twenty-eight-year-old engineer named Doug Malewicki, who was the chief rocket design manager at Centuri Engineering in Phoenix. He was intrigued by the idea of a rocket-powered motorcycle flying off a ramp and out over the Grand Canyon, also intrigued by the man who would ride it. On a lunch hour, early in the week, he convinced Centuri's head artist, Tom Cameron, to come along for a ride to Watkins Ford to look at this fantastic Evel Knievel equipment.

Part of the presentation, along with the forty-foot flatbed and the trucks and motorcycles, was a prototype jet cycle for the canyon jump.

The prototype was nonsense, partly slapped together in Moses Lake by Ray Gunn, who had been hired as Knievel's mechanic, truck driver, and general handyman. ("He'd been asking me to go with him from the beginning, but I couldn't see any financial sense in it," Gunn said. "Then, when he crashed at Caesars Palace and got all that publicity, I thought it might be worthwhile after all.") Gunn had attached a pair of ominous-looking wings and a pair of bottle-shaped thrust units to an ordinary motorcycle to create a contraption Knievel could use when he talked about the jump on television or in front of crowds. Knievel had wheeled it onto the set of *The Joey Bishop Show* two months earlier, sat down with Jerry Vale, Leslie Gore, and Charlie Callas and talked about doing the jump on July 4, 1968. The thing looked like a science-fiction version of a deranged mechanical housefly.

Malewicki, the engineer, as he looked at it during his lunch hour, was aghast at what he saw. The deranged mechanical housefly was worthless, a piece of garbage, a hoax. Look at this! Look at that! Wow! He had the outrage of a basic slide-rule, book-smart nerd, finding something so obviously wrong that the general public assumed was legitimate. Holy cow! Where were the general public's brains? His buddy Cameron, part of the 99 percent of Americans who knew little about rockets and mostly didn't care, listened and said, "Hey, if you feel so strongly about it, leave him a letter."

Malewicki borrowed three pieces of stationery and a pen from the Bill Watkins Ford receptionist. He not only detailed how worthless and foolish the prototype was, but outlined how a proper rocket/cycle actually could clear the canyon and land with Knievel still alive. All of this filled the three pages, which he presented to the receptionist along with his business card. She placed everything in an envelope with Knievel's name on the front.

Knievel called Malewicki the next afternoon. The call was noisy.

"What kind of bullshit is this?" the daredevil wanted to know. "Who are you to tell me what I should be doing?"

"He was antagonistic," Malewicki said. "He was mad. I could never figure that out. He knew what he had was bogus. Why would he start out antagonistic? He was mad at me. For what?"

The conversation did become reasonable after that first flurry. Knievel had read the letter. He was interested in Malewicki's ideas. How would the engineer prove some of his theories could work? Well, the engineer said he could build a model rocket in a couple of days, a different kind of prototype. He could fire off that rocket as part of the show at the Bee Line Dragway on Saturday night. Would that do the job? Knievel said he'd like to see that rocket.

Malewicki, it turned out, made model rockets for a living. His employer, Centuri Engineering, was a leading manufacturer of miniature rockets for science classes, for enthusiasts, for smart kids on Saturday afternoons. He recruited four other engineers, all Centuri employees who had heard about Evel Knievel and the canyon, to come to his house and work on the prototype. They quickly built a rocket that had wheels.

"That was what Evel talked about," Malewicki said, "so that was what we built."

On Saturday evening they turned up at the drag strip with ten thousand other people for the show. One of those people was not Knievel. In the afternoon, practicing after such a long layoff, he did the opposite of what he did in Las Vegas, got up too much speed (not too little) and overshot (not undershot) the landing ramp. He shattered his right leg and right foot when he landed. He was now at the Mesa Lutheran Hospital instead of the Bee Line Dragway.

News of his absence was held off until the crowd had come through the gates. The people then were told that Jumping Jack Stroh, back with Knievel to jump over that seventy-miles-per-hour motorcycle as part of the show, now would do Evel's jump. Three of the Bill Watkins Fords, all Mustangs, would be removed, so Jumping Jack would jump ten cars. The captive audience would still see a show.

Malewicki and company performed first. They sent off their rocket with precision and suitable applause. Perfect. Jumping Jack then tried Evel's act. Not perfect.

He made the same mistake Knievel made in the afternoon, too much speed, overshot the ramp. The announcer, in a surreal shout, said, "And he's made it," which technically was true, but Jumping Jack had hit the handlebars with his chin when he landed and was knocked out. The motorcycle wobbled, wobbled some more as it slowed, then fell down. Jumping Jack fell with it. A good-sized gash on his chin added a lot of blood to the picture. Jumping Jack was taken to Mesa Lutheran to join his boss.

A day or two later, Knievel called Malewicki, invited *him* to the hospital. The reports of the rocket firing had been good. Knievel was still interested. Malewicki went to Mesa Lutheran.

"Sitting in a chair outside Evel's room was his wife, Linda," the engineer said. "I introduced myself. She was very nice. She told me to go inside, and, well, it was classic Evel Knievel. He was in the room with a blond go-go dancer. His wife is outside in the chair, he's in there with this blonde. They seemed very friendly. His leg was in a big cast. It was the absolute perfect introduction to the man."

Malewicki convinced Knievel, and maybe the go-go dancer, that he could build a rocket/motorcycle that could take the daredevil across the canyon of his choice. This not only could be done, it could be done easily. Hell, NASA was getting ready to send a man to the moon in the next calendar year. A canyon should be easy. Knievel liked the idea, wanted to make a deal. He convinced Malewicki that this could be a financial bonanza. He offered 30 percent of any canyon-jumping profits, plus expenses. The two men shook hands. There was no contract.

"I was twenty-eight years old," Malewicki said. "What did I know?"

The canyon project had switched from daydream and nonsense to strong possibility. There was an actual chance this might actually happen.

Malewicki went to work in Arizona. He had to make the jump from model rocket to man-sized rocket, not only build the thing powerful enough to carry that man a significant distance and somehow deposit him safely on the other side, but build it under the restrictions of a tight, small budget. He also had to make it look a little bit like a motorcycle. That was a challenge. Knievel went back on the road in July, returned to his motorcycle-jumping career. That was another challenge.

He rolled off a string of successes to start, surprise, surprise, and seemed to have the process figured out at last. He jumped at least eight times, probably more, because records weren't kept anywhere, each show a local event, and landed safely every time. He went back to Missoula, jumped those thirteen cars just to show he could do it. He jumped at least three times at the fairgrounds in Salt Lake City, rattled through the Northwest, stopped at places like Blackfoot and Meridian, Idaho, Walla Walla and Spokane, Washington.

His success was mostly an illusion. The truth was that he had nothing figured out. Ray Gunn set up the ramps now and watched him every night he jumped. Every night was a quiet terror.

"I could look in his eyes and see he was afraid on most of the jumps," Ray Gunn said. "I knew he was afraid. I could even see it when he practiced. He was in a panic."

The ramp was never right. The bike was never right. Something was never right. The daredevil was never right . . . and yet he never backed down. There was something that kept him moving every night, one step after another, moving toward what came next, no matter what the cost. His brother, Nic Knievel, always said that the only competition for Evel Knievel was Bob Knievel and Bob Knievel was the one who would get them both killed. Bob Knievel was the source of all ambition, the one with the hundred-pound testicles, the one who made Evel Knievel ride those ramps toward some imagined payoff.

"I guess he calculated he would be a coward if he ever walked away," Ray Gunn said. "He never wanted to do that. Myself, I was from the country. Money and fame never mattered that much to me."

On the afternoon of October 13, 1968, still well removed from both money and fame, sometimes not making much more than a couple thousand bucks per show, the money tied to the gate receipts, Knievel dedicated a jump to his mother. He stopped at the Tahoe-Carson Speedway in Carson City, outside Reno, to jump ten cars. His mother was at the track along with his half-sisters Loretta and Kady. They had been in the crowd at Caesars Palace, so they knew that bad things could happen. The memory made everyone jumpy, especially his mother. She was so nervous at Caesars Palace that she couldn't even come out of the hotel to watch.

"It's okay," Loretta said to her mother. "He's done this a million times. He's dedicated the jump to you, made you stand up and wave to the crowd. It'll be fine."

Unknown to Loretta and Kady and their mother, there was one hitch in the approach that made this jump different. The dirt racetrack had a dip midway between Knievel's starting point and when he hit the ramp. He and Gunn had not been able to figure out the effects of the dip. Every time Knievel went into his approach, he lost speed on the downslope, then didn't have time to recapture what he had lost before he hit the ramp. They knew the problem, but had run out of time to work on it. Knievel said he still would be fine. He would make sure he did not lose speed going through the dip.

The afternoon was windy, but not windy enough to stop the show. Knievel went through his trial runs, came back to the appointed takeoff spot, this time for real, traveled halfway to the ramp, hit the dip, slowed down, tried to recover on the second half, and couldn't. The moment he left the ramp, the entire crowd knew that he would not make the jump successfully. The arc of his motorcycle indicated immediately that he would land very short of his target.

"He's dead," his mother screamed even before he hit the panel truck at the end of the line of cars and went flying.

The afternoon ended at the Washoe Medical Center, his mother holding his hand as he lay in yet another hospital bed. He underwent surgery for a broken left hip the next day, for a broken right collarbone later in the week. His discomfort was extended when he picked up a painful and life-threatening staph infection from a Foley catheter. His hospital stay was extended indefinitely.

"He was a sick guy," Ray Gunn said. "Just to visit him, I had to take off my clothes and wear one of those hospital uniforms."

No Jay Sarno appeared from Caesars Palace to provide financial assistance for the hospital bill this time. Any money from those Combined Insurance policies had been spent long ago. He was on his own. The racetrack promoter, in fact, declared in the newspaper that Knievel had signed a liability waiver as part of the contract. One day ran into another, as hospital time tends to do, and Knievel complained to everyone that he wanted to go back to Butte. When no plans were made for that to happen, he made his own plans.

Ray Gunn showed up at the hospital with a station wagon in the middle of the night. He collected Knievel in a wheelchair, padded quietly and deliberately through the hospital maze, careful to keep out of sight of nurses and doctors. Gunn almost lost his man when they reached the outside and the wheelchair stopped short and Knievel flew back through the air as if he had been shot off the motorcycle one more time, but eventually Gunn helped him back into the chair and they reached the station wagon. Knievel lay in the back, moaning. Gunn drove. They stopped in Twin Falls, Idaho, where Knievel knew a man who owned a mattress store. They picked up a mattress, put it in the back, much better, and completed the trip to Butte.

The Washoe Medical Center soon announced that it was seeking $1,808 for twenty-two days of care for the daredevil, but had slim hopes of success. Knievel claimed he was broke. The twenty-two days, added to the thirty-seven days at Southern Nevada Memorial in Las Vegas, meant that he had spent almost two months in Nevada hospitals in 1968.

He tried to perform one more jump before the end of the year. He set up a date in Portland at the Coliseum with Ted Pollock. A few days before the jump, no more than six weeks after two surgeries, he checked into a low-rent hotel in Portland. He looked terrible, looked like he couldn't walk, much less ride a motorcycle. He had a fever, pus was coming from open wounds. The staph infection would not leave.

"I'm fine," he assured Pollock, but as each day passed he looked less and less fine.

The promotion also was less than fine. Customers were not forming lines outside the box office. Pollock had paired him with a country music show that featured singer Molly Bee.

"How much have you brought in so far?" Knievel asked on the day of the show.

"Maybe $25,000," Pollock said. "No more than that."

"I'm not going to jump," Knievel decided. "It's not worth it."

Pollock had a partner in the promotion. Pollock saw Knievel's condition and felt sorry for the daredevil. Pollock's partner saw Knievel's condition and saw the promotion falling apart. He felt sorry for the promoters, not Knievel. He wanted to sue.

"Bill, just take a look at this guy, will you?" Pollock said. "If he goes out and kills himself, do you want that on your conscience? Look at him. He's in no shape to make this jump. Let it go, will you?"

The other promoter eventually agreed. He still was mad. He had one stipulation: he would not announce to the crowd that Knievel was sick, unable to perform. The people would get their money back, still get to see Molly Bee, not a bad deal, but he would not be the one to deliver all that news. Knievel's father, Bob Sr., had come up for the show. He did the job.

Knievel did not jump again until April 24, 1969. More than six months were swallowed up by the Bee Line Dragway crash and aftermath. How could his notoriety from Caesars Palace ever pay off if he couldn't work? He was broke again, slightly famous, but totally broke.

Then George Hamilton arrived.

Hamilton was thirty years old, the same age as Knievel, actually three months older. He was a bona fide movie star. Starting in 1952 when he was thirteen years old, cast as a servant to Lionel Barrymore in *Lone Star*, a western featuring Clark Gable and Ava Gardner, he already had appeared in eighteen movies. He was a leading man, handsome and certainly tanned, as most stories pointed out, urbane and charming, a bon vivant who had made gossip headlines when he dated Lynda Bird

Johnson while her father was in the White House. He probably was best known for his roles as an Ivy League smooth talker in *Where the Boys Are* in 1960 and as country music legend Hank Williams in *Your Cheatin' Heart* in 1964.

He was involved with assorted projects now, always looking for more. His immediate job was a role in *The Survivors*, with Lana Turner, the first miniseries that followed a story from beginning to end on network television. The producers wanted him to do some stunt that seemed a bit perilous to him. He asked for a stunt man to do the job. The producers suggested he hire that stunt man.

He tried to hire Evel Knievel.

"His name was bouncing around with some people I knew," Hamilton said. "They said there was this guy, Evel Knievel, wind him up and he crashes. How could you forget a name like that? He sounded perfect. I had my secretary track him down."

The phone dialogue went something like this:

QUESTION: Can you do this stunt? You'll have to do it in the next
 week or two.
ANSWER: I can do anything. I'm Evel Knievel.

Then he never showed up.

Knievel had returned to Los Angeles to appear at the ninth annual Custom Car, Motorcycle, and Dune Buggy Show at the Los Angeles Sports Arena, April 24–27, 1969. Actually, he appeared daily outside the west end of the Sports Arena and jumped eight cars at nine o'clock on Thursday and Friday nights, at three in the afternoon on the weekend.

This was his latest return to action. He still hadn't recovered fully from the staph infection. He was still on crutches from his broken hip. He had to be helped onto the motorcycle to ride. He was probably the unhealthiest daredevil in creation.

"In the past two years, I've had seven major injuries where I had to have major operations," he told the *Los Angeles Times*. "I've broken my left hip and pelvis twice each. I've also broken my left arm, my right ankle and foot and my right shoulder. And both wrists and knees. Besides that, I had one bad brain concussion. And I broke my back."

If there was some overstatement of his injuries, that was forgivable. He certainly was busted up. The *Times* noted that he might have more metal parts inside himself than inside his motorcycle.

"I have a problem with metal fatigue," he said. "The screws in my body keep busting, and they have to put in new ones."

Hamilton soon had forgotten about Knievel. Someone else did the stunt. A month passed. Maybe two. Maybe more. Hamilton received a phone call from Scotty, who guarded the front gate at Universal Studios. Scotty said, "A Mr. Knievel would like to see you."

"Send him up," Hamilton said.

"There's a problem," Scotty said.

The problem was that Knievel had arrived at the gate with two other guys in the big rig, his name and the world ramp-to-ramp record and the stated promise to do the canyon jump painted across the side. The big rig, Scotty said, would take up too much room inside the movie lot. No problem, Hamilton said, they could park outside and walk through the gate. Ah, another problem, Scotty said, Knievel couldn't walk.

The eventual outcome was that the two men in the truck parked the rig outside and carried Knievel to the office. That was how actor and daredevil met. The daredevil was delivered to his office like an animated side of beef.

The animated side of beef said his career was going great, that people wanted to see what he did. He had a number of jumps lined up.

"Looks like the last one didn't work out too well," the actor remarked.

From the beginning, Hamilton thought Knievel was fascinating. There was something very American about him, some chip-on-the-shoulder earnestness mixed with bullshit and adventure that always played well across the broad middle of the country. The more Hamilton heard him talk, the more he thought about tent evangelists and carnival barkers. Knievel said preposterous things, but he was dead serious when he said them. He wanted to jump the Grand Canyon on a motorcycle. He was serious.

"He was one of the slickest, maybe the slickest character I'd ever met," Hamilton said. "He was a con man, but it was all petty con. Do you know what I mean? He was one of those guys who would bet you in a bar that he had your name tattooed on his cock. Then he would whip it out, and he'd had the words 'Your' and 'Name' tattooed, just so he could win bets in bars. That kind of guy."

Hamilton signed him up to do some stunt in a week. Knievel said he was going in for surgery to remove "eleven and a half pounds of metal," but would be back and ready for the job. Hamilton was dubious. Eleven and a half pounds sounded like a lot of metal.

On the appointed day, the daredevil called from St. Joseph's Hospital in Burbank. Hamilton talked to him for a moment, but then heard a thud and the line went dead. When Hamilton finally got through to the room again, a nurse answered. She said Knievel had passed out, that was why the phone went dead.

This was another paragraph in an interesting story. Hamilton had been thinking about a movie that somehow involved this guy. The first thought was something about a whacked-out stunt man, but the more the actor saw Knievel in action—he passed out?—the more he became convinced that Knievel himself was the movie. Motorcycles. America. Insanity. Hamilton loved the package. After more than a little negotiation, he made a deal with Knievel, $25,000 for the rights to the daredevil's life story.

"I was happy when I got the rights," Hamilton said. "Then I said to myself, 'What the hell am I going to do with them?' "

The answer came from Joe Solomon, a grind-'em-out executive producer of B movies, many of them with motorcycle themes. Solomon saw the recent success of Peter Fonda's *Easy Rider*, which entranced critics and filled theaters in 1969, and lamented that he had featured Jack Nicholson in *Hells Angels on Wheels* only two years earlier. Now Nicholson was considered an easy winner of best supporting actor at the Oscars for *Easy Rider*. Joe Solomon wanted his own *Easy Rider*.

Hamilton said that was a large order. He couldn't promise another *Easy Rider*, but he thought *Evel Knievel* could be a very good movie.

"I want to make a movie about this guy that shows the insanity of America," Hamilton said. "Something about what our values are."

Solomon said that was fine as long as the picture came in on time, under budget, and had a bunch of motorcycles in it. The deal was made. The story of the daredevil from Butte—at least a version of it—was going to be on the big screen.

Putting together the varied pieces of the movie took over a year before filming began. Hamilton needed a script, a cast, a plan. He often needed to run ideas, situations, past Knievel, needed to get signatures on documents. The process invariably took longer than the actor thought it would. Knievel was back in action, jumping again, which meant that he often was back in inaction. He often was in the hospital.

"I'd have to get something done, and he'd be out of it," Hamilton said.

"He'd be in a hospital, and they'd have him on a morphine drip or something else to stop the pain. He was gone. You'd have to come back sometime later."

The deal with Triumph motorcycles had ended badly, and Knievel now rode a fat-assed American Eagle 750. The bike was the product of an old-line Italian manufacturer, Laverda, but had been imported recently to the United States under the American Eagle name. Knievel, by now the most recognizable motorcycle rider in the country, was a perfect choice as spokesman. The bike, alas, had been built for endurance racing. It dominated the European endurance circuit, but was not very good at jumping, flying.

Knievel couldn't handle the bike. Or maybe the bike simply couldn't handle the jumps. Take away the four days outside the L.A. Sports Arena, Knievel's understated debut with the American Eagle, and he crashed as often as he landed safely on the bike.

The first crash was back in Butte. On September 20, 1969, back in Naranche Stadium, the old football field for Butte High School, he attempted to clear sixteen Toyotas parked side by side in front of family and friends. He landed a little short, ran into a fence at the end of the field, and was thrown into it. He broke an ankle.

Dan Killoy, the longtime neighbor, visited him in the double-wide a few days later. Knievel was in a cast, but getting ready for a jump at Tri-Cities Speedway in West Richland, Washington, over the weekend. This would be seventeen Subarus.

"You're in a cast," Killoy said. "How can you do that?"

"I'll cut the cast off," Knievel said, "do the jump, then go to the hospital and get the cast put on again. No problem."

That was how he traveled for much of the next year. He never was healthy. For every jump that was a success—he made the trip over the seventeen Subarus in West Richland a week late after a cancellation due to high winds—he would add another broken bone to a crowded list. If he survived a jump of eighteen Mercury Cougars at Seattle International Raceway, despite a near wipeout in a thirteen-car practice run, he would break his collarbone when he came up short in Yakima trying to repeat his jump over thirteen Pepsi trucks. ("This time he wasn't drunk," promoter Ted Pollock said. "How do you figure it? When he was drunk, he made it. When he wasn't drunk, he got hurt.") If he survived in Vancouver, wearing a special brace as he cleared twelve cars, he crashed in a return to Seattle International, where he cleared nineteen Datsuns, but bounced off the safety van, wobbled and fell badly, got shipped off to the hospital with several broken ribs and compound fractures of the fourth and fifth vertebrae.

"I've had 12 major open reduction operations," Knievel reported to Charles Maher of the *Los Angeles Times* in a medical update from St. Elizabeth Hospital in Yakima. "That's when they cut you open and put a plate or a screw in. I've had about 35 or 40 screws put in me to hold the bones together."

Maher asked about the food at the many hospitals the daredevil had visited. The daredevil must be an expert on hospital food.

"I don't like any hospital food," he said. "If you're hungry enough, I guess you can eat it. But I'm a New York steak and lobster tails man myself. You don't see much of that in hospitals. They don't seem to go much for Oysters Rockefeller, either."

He gave a perfect description of his crashes to Jerry Uhrhammer, sports editor of the *Eugene* (Oregon) *Register-Guard*. He said if someone wanted to know what a single crash felt like, the someone should sit on the hood of his car, put a helmet on, and have his wife drive to a freeway. She should blow the horn when she got the speed up to ninety miles per hour.

"Then you hold your nose and fall off," Knievel said. "Then you'll know what it feels like."

That was exactly the feeling the daredevil had at his next jump, next crash, at Pocono International Raceway in Long Pond, Pennsylvania, on August 16, 1970. Doctors told him in Seattle in July that he would be out of action for six months with his injuries, basically a broken back. He distilled the six months into six weeks.

This was an important jump, first appearance on the eastern side of the Mississippi River. Thirteen cars. The result was not pretty.

"First the rear wheel . . . landed on the safety ramp and bucked the front wheel hard on the wooden slats," a report in *Saga* magazine said. "Knievel couldn't hold on to the handlebars after the terrific jolt and he went flying head first over the front wheel . . . he went bouncing down the ramp . . . tumbling like a rag doll."

The crash and description were similar to what happened at Caesars Palace. He finished with a broken right hand, broken sternum, three broken ribs, and a broken shoulder. He was, however, able to be lifted upright to walk to the start-finish line, climb a ladder, and address the crowd.

"This business is getting a little too rough for me," he said. "I don't know what happened. But a lot of times a guy runs short on nerve."

He would not jump again for four more months. The doctors in Seattle with their six-month estimate had not been wrong.

A story. One of the jumps he made successfully in the middle of this stretch of mishaps was an immediate and different addition to his public melodrama. Back on January 23, 1970, a Friday night, first jump of the year, Knievel tried to clear eleven cars (an indoor record) at the Cow Palace in San Francisco. He wound up slugging it out with a bunch of the Hells Angels, the nation's foremost motorcycle gang. It was another videotape moment.

"The announcer for the show had been drinking all night," Gene Sullivan said. "When Evel came on to do his jump, the announcer said something he shouldn't have said. He announced the canyon jump, and then said, 'If Evel Knievel makes this jump, he'll set back the Hells Angels one hundred years.' "

Sullivan was new to the Knievel operation. He was a big guy, fresh out of the Navy, where he had been the heavyweight boxing champion for the Seventh Fleet. His father was Prescott Sullivan, longtime sports columnist for the *San Francisco Examiner*. In the run-up to the jump, his father had gone to an interview session with Knievel. Son went along, just to listen.

When Knievel went into hyperbolic overdrive, the usual stuff, his code of honor, his aspirations, talk about Caesars Palace and the injuries, talk about the canyon, the words resonated with Sullivan. He told Knievel he liked the message and offered his services. Maybe this was the direction he was supposed to travel. Maybe Knievel needed a bodyguard, an inexpensive bodyguard at that, someone who wanted only a couple of hundred bucks a week to live. Maybe.

Knievel said he would think about it. Sullivan went to the Cow Palace. This was the first time he actually had seen Knievel jump.

"It was one of those providential things," Sullivan said.

Knievel and the Hells Angels had never had good thoughts about each other. Knievel always took great pains to say that he dressed in white leather, not black, because he did not want to be associated with the Angels and gangs and the dark side of motorcycling. The Angels always took great umbrage at those remarks. They also had been hounded, battered in the newspapers and on television for the past month in the Bay Area for their actions when they worked as security guards for $500 worth of beer at the now-infamous free concert at nearby Altamont Raceway in December. One of their members stabbed a spectator to death while the Rolling Stones sang, a violent and graphic incident captured on film for the documentary *Gimme Shelter.*

So when the half-buzzed announcer said what he said, there was a history. When Knievel came flying up the ramp for his jump, and when a Hells Angel came down from the stands and threw something at him—Gene Sullivan thought it was a wrench or maybe a pair of pliers—this was not exactly unexpected. The wrench, or maybe the pliers, missed Knievel. He hit the jump perfectly. He cleared the eleven cars and managed to stop himself in the dangerously short landing area. He then did a U-turn. He came back to the offending Hells Angel, whom he had spotted from the corner of his eye, jumped from his still-moving motorcycle, pushed the gang member against a concrete wall, and started to pummel him.

Four or five Hells Angels came to the defense of their man. Sullivan, who watched the whole mess develop in front of him, jumped to the defense of Knievel. He started whaling on a Hells Angel. Assorted spectators joined him. A donnybrook developed, something out of a Wild West saloon. The Angels eventually were routed, two hospitalized. Sullivan eventually shepherded Knievel back to the trailer and a few shots of Wild Turkey.

"You want a job?" Knievel asked.

"Sure," Sullivan said.

"You've got it."

The job started immediately. The worry was that the Angels would look for retribution. Knievel went to a friend's house in Sacramento, knocked on the door, and said he had to hide for a night because the Hells Angels were after him. Sullivan and Ray Gunn were left with the big trailer at the motel. The advertising message on the side did not seem like a good thing at the moment. The letters couldn't have been any larger. They were so bright they seemed like they were written in neon. The two men shared a room. They both were jumpy.

Unable to sleep, Sullivan went out to get something to eat. When he came back, Gunn was sleeping. Sullivan thought it would be fun to scare his new partner. He made a sharp noise. Gunn bolted upright, pulled a gun from under his pillow, and pointed it at the new bodyguard.

"Geez," Gunn said. "I almost shot you."

The Angels never did appear.

The screenplay for the movie was written two times during this period while Knievel alternately crashed and convalesced. The first attempt was by Alan Caillou, a writer whom executive producer Joe Solomon found. An Englishman with a broad mustache, a middle-aged guy who drove a period Bentley around Hollywood, a writer of men's adventure paperback novels under various nom de plumes, Caillou churned out an effort that George Hamilton couldn't stand. It was a straight-ahead portrayal of Knievel, sort of a World War II movie brought up to date, man in combat with death every day. Hamilton was distraught.

He petitioned Solomon to allow a rewrite. He promised that no characters would be changed, no expenses added. The rewrite would be painless to all finances. Solomon said that was fine, as long as the motorcycles remained.

Hamilton interviewed a bunch of the young emerging screenwriters, including George Lucas and Paul Schraeder and maybe even Spielberg. None of them seemed to get his idea. He then ran it past John Milius, laid out the plot and the peculiar American insanity to everything, the crazy man, the crazy country, a reflection of crazy national values.

"So tell it back to me," Hamilton said.

Milius described the story, the jumps, the injuries. He described the proposed canyon jump. He described the probable ending.

"The guy splatters on the other side," he said. "That's what America really wants to see. They want to see him splatter on the other side."

Perfect. Evel Knievel wasn't selling success! He was selling failure! Perfect. That was what America loved, the danger of it all. Hamilton set up the screenwriter in the house with the white walls and the Strauss waltzes, the Cuban cigars and the sunbathing women. The women were imported strictly for Milius.

"I knew a guy," Hamilton said. "I don't know where he got these women. I made one rule . . . Milius doesn't get to touch one of them until he's finished."

Hamilton was delighted with the product that quickly came from the arrangement. He read the screenplay and felt like "I had the jellyfish in my hand, but Milius gave it the sting." Proud of this coup, this script, Hamilton sent the pages to Knievel. He was shocked when Knievel called and started yelling. The script was terrible. The daredevil demanded that Hamilton come to the Hollywood Land Motel.

This was when Knievel pulled the gun on him and made him read.

"I don't think Knievel read very much, if at all," Hamilton said. "Someone had read the script for him and told him that it said bad things about his sister. I didn't know what the hell he was talking about. I think it might have been some of the stuff about kidnapping his wife.

"He pulled the gun, and I never read better, never talked faster. I explained the scenes to him. I finally convinced him that it was all right. He was making suggestions to me by the end."

The parts that Hamilton thought would bother Knievel most never were mentioned. Milius had drawn a self-absorbed, egotistical character, silly in a lot of ways. Crafty and crazy. Not a pleasant guy by any means. This was what should have set Knievel off, but Hamilton thought the subject of the movie never really understood what the movie was about. Knievel was worried about small deviances from facts.

"People are so close to something they sometimes can't see," Hamilton said. "The movie I did about Hank Williams was like that. Here was this tragic character, drank himself to death at the age of twenty-nine. He was pushed there first by his mother, who brought him into the bars to sing when he was thirteen years old, then kept there by his wife, who did the exact same thing. The women were the villains. His mother was dead when we did the movie, but his wife was alive and signed off on everything. She never saw what the story was.

"I don't think Knievel did either."

The two lines Hamilton liked best in the script were simple. They captured the wonder of Knievel's every performance to date, the surprise and relief at every finish. The movie would use Linda Evans's footage of the Caesars crash. After the crash, Knievel would lie on the pavement with his injuries. He would blink and smile.

"I'm alive," he would say.

"I'm alive," he would say again.

That was his triumph every time he performed. That was truth.

13 Action

The odd part of Knievel's red-white-and-blue motorcycle career, the words "America" and "American" mentioned virtually every time he spoke in public, was that he never had performed on an American motorcycle. From the first jump at Moses Lake on his Honda, through the jumps on Nortons and Triumphs and now the Italian Laverda 750s under the name "American Eagle," he had taken whatever small deal was available, always had gone for price over performance. He had risked his life on whatever discount equipment he could find.

The logical motorcycle for him always had been a Harley-Davidson, made in Milwaukee, Wisconsin. Harley-Davidson was the successful star-spangled American racing representative on the world stage. Knievel, alas, always made the company's executives nervous.

"Harley-Davidson was the most conservative company you could find," Duane Unkefer, advertising manager and promotions director in the seventies, said. "Extremely image-conscious. I said to my boss one day, 'I wouldn't mind buying one of those Datsun Z sports cars,' and he looked at me and said, 'Well, you'd have to pay for it in yen.'

"You couldn't wear a beard or long hair if you worked for Harley back then. You'd be fired in a moment. The word the company hated most was 'hog.' It hated that entire image of the motorcycle gangs. Fought against it."

Knievel was small and not very pleasant-looking potatoes to Harley in the past. He was too noisy, too wacky. Harley spent its promotional budget on the racing team. That was the image the company wanted.

The number-one Harley logo represented the success of the racing team. Knievel was a circus act.

Until now. The daredevil and the company had landed in a place where they suddenly could help each other.

Knievel had become the one motorcycle rider in America who couldn't be overlooked. With the movie on the way, with his appearance on all of the shows, he was more famous than all of the Harley racers put together. The company, at the same time, was struggling. The Honda campaign about meeting the nicest people on a Honda had been devastating. Attention had turned to those 150cc bikes, an entirely different look from Harley. Sales were down. Even the racing results were down. Harley was struggling on the track, which was why it had built the new XR750.

Enter Knievel. He sent word through racers he knew that he would love to ride the XR750. He was available now, his deal with American Eagle finished, as the importers of the Laverdas from Italy had gone broke. The business was being liquidated.

The Harley people were interested. Some of the Harley people were.

"I thought it was a great idea," Unkefer said. "Our dealers were screaming for help. They wanted us to do something to give the brand publicity. They were getting killed by Honda. They loved the idea of putting some Evel Knievel posters on their walls."

The person who had to be convinced was John Davidson, the Harley-Davidson president, a no-nonsense character who was the grand keeper of the company image. Unkefer and his boss, Charlie Thompson, and vice president Willy G. Davidson, John Davidson's brother, all argued hard for Knievel. Three against one, the president finally buckled. He did insist that one clause be added to the contract.

"There was a paragraph, a long paragraph, that detailed all the things Knievel couldn't do," Unkefer said. "If he went to jail, if there was a public scandal, an arrest for drunkenness, drugs, anything, the contract was finished. He couldn't spit on the street. There were a lot of ways out of the deal for the company."

Knievel received a chunk of money, but more importantly received the XR750 and whatever refinements to it that might follow. He was linked into the dealer network and would have local Harley mechanics at most of his events. He would have parts, service, backup motorcycles, at a moment's notice. He would have things he never had.

He also would have a version of safety. That was the most amazing result of the deal. The every-other-jump crashes would stop.

"I began work with him on his final jump of 1970, then worked with him for the next four years," Unkefer said. "I never really saw him crash. Some little things perhaps, but he never crashed."

The XR750 was a revelation. It was faster than any motorcycle Knievel had ridden. After some modifications in the first year, it was lighter than any motorcycle he had ridden. Factory riders on the bike dominated all levels of racing after 1972. Knievel found that he could gauge his speed better, was not surprised when he landed, could survive. This was the kind of bike he should have been riding all along.

"He carried a briefcase with him to all of his shows," Unkefer said. "One day he showed me what was inside. There were all these rods, all these screws and bolts. They were replacement parts for his body. If he crashed, he could tell the doctors which parts went where if the previous rods had been bent or screws had been lost. There must have been thirty-five, forty pieces in the briefcase. All of them sitting in red velvet."

His debut with the XR750 was in a show at the Lions Drag Strip outside Los Angeles. He jumped thirteen cars in front of 14,780 people on December 12, 1970. No problem. He had crashed in three of his previous four jumps, the final one in August when he cracked vertebrae, broke his shoulder and hand at Pocono. Nothing here. Nothing in his next two jumps of the new year at the Houston Astrodome. Nothing.

"I'm going to become the first motorcycle rider to make a million dollars a year," he proclaimed at the Astrodome to start 1971.

Who could argue? For once, his boast sounded reasonable. He was paid $25,000 for the two shows. ("Appearing both nights if he survives Friday's appearance," the advertisement read.) Maybe the ticket prices were $2, $3, and $4 to visit the self-proclaimed Eighth Wonder of the World, and maybe Jack Kochman's Hell Drivers also performed, and maybe there also was a demolition derby and a powder-puff derby, but an estimated 100,000 spectators appeared at the Astrodome over the two days. He had entered his first big-time stadium, and it was full. If he could stay healthy, yes, he could make a lot of money.

And now he could stay healthy.

The first important Knievel moment in the production of the movie with George Hamilton came on February 28, 1971. The script called for Hamilton/Knievel to reflect on his life while preparing for a world-record jump of nineteen cars, all American cars, not a Volkswagen or Datsun in the bunch, at the Ontario Motor Speedway outside Los Angeles. The story would jump back and forth from Ontario to the various bits of wackiness that had led to this moment. The finale would be the jump over the nineteen cars.

Filming already had begun at Ontario and on the MGM lot—Hamilton as Evel, twenty-four-year-old Sue Lyon, best known for her role as James Mason's shockingly underage lover in *Lolita*, cast as Linda Knievel—and this was the big-money camera shot. Knievel, the real Knievel, was supposed to jump over those real American cars before a sellout crowd of 78,810.

The people had been lured mostly by the first NASCAR Grand National race in track history, the Miller High Life 500, which would be won by A. J. Foyt with Buddy Baker second, Richard Petty third, but Knievel also was an attraction. His jump would take place before the stock car race, which had a $207,675 purse, richest in NASCAR history.

Hamilton spent the time before the jump with Knievel in the trailer/dressing room. The time did not go well. Wild Turkey was involved.

"Knievel was drinking and kept talking about the different things involved in the jump, aerodynamics, ballistics," Hamilton said. "He went on and on and on. I eventually decided he didn't give a shit about any of that. He was just getting drunk. That was why he was talking. He *was* drunk."

As the time approached to perform the jump, Knievel became skittish. He said that he might not be able to do it. The wind seemed excessive. Wind? Hamilton said there was no wind really. Knievel said the track conditions might not be right. What track conditions? Hamilton said the conditions were exactly what they were supposed to be. Everything was ready. Knievel finally said what he really meant.

He wanted more money to do the jump.

Hamilton was stunned. He pointed out that there was no more money. The budget under Joe Solomon had been stretched as far as it could go. Nothing else would arrive. The cast and crew still had to travel to Butte to film. There was no money. There also was no backup for this day, this crowd. Everything was in place. This was when the jump had to be done.

Knievel, dressed in his leathers already, said at last that maybe they would go outside and take a look at the setup. Then he would decide.

He did have one obvious problem. He had jumped nine cars a day earlier in a practice session at Ontario, and the handlebars had collapsed and he had broken his right hand. The hand was useless, but he did not give that as an excuse.

"How will you jump with a broken hand?" Hamilton asked.

"I'll tape it to the handlebars," Knievel said in a tone he would use with a schoolkid. "It's just logic, George. If your hand is broken, you tape it on."

When the actor and the daredevil stepped from the big rig, they were surrounded by photographers. The daredevil did not like being surrounded, didn't like people in his face. He told them to back off. They didn't back off fast enough. They were photographers. He swung his cane, hit one of them with force. The photographer went down. It was an ugly moment.

"Knievel had different canes," Hamilton said. "This one really was just a lead pipe. It could do some damage. There had been a thing, too, at the Astrodome where he had used that cane on somebody. It wasn't nice to see."

Knievel deemed the conditions right for the jump. Hamilton noticed that both the takeoff ramp and the landing ramp seemed off-center, not where they were supposed to be. Knievel said that was not a problem.

And so he jumped.

Drunk, with his right hand taped to the handlebars, he flawlessly cleared eighteen Dodge Colts and one Dodge van, not a Volkswagen or Datsun in the lot, to set another one of his world records. This one would remain for twenty-seven years until it was broken by daredevil Bubba Blackwell, who cleared twenty cars on a Harley XR750 on April 26, 1998, in Everett, Massachusetts. (Other riders jumped farther, jumped more cars, but on different, lighter equipment.)

Hamilton and the crew were relieved. They hadn't known what to expect. They had been ready for any result on the jump. They would have been able to adjust.

"I'd seen him get splattered once in Sacramento, so I knew what happened in that situation," the actor said. "It was a curious thing. He was hurt, and everyone was rushing around, and he looked up at me and winked. Like he was playing a game on everyone else. I couldn't figure that out."

The filming in Butte took place a month later, ten days of shots of Hamilton/Knievel kidnapping Sue Lyon/Linda, racing around the Richest Hill on Earth, police in pursuit, robbing stores, causing general mayhem. Locals were hired as extras, some with speaking parts. The director was Marvin Chomsky. He said Knievel made suggestions, but mostly quiet suggestions.

"The one thing he wanted to do was blow up city hall for a robbery scene," Chomsky said. "I told him we couldn't blow up the city hall. This was a movie. He said he could get some dynamite. He got some dynamite. I told him we couldn't blow up the city hall."

Local characters were hired to play local characters. The experience was pleasant for everybody. The city tried to help. Knievel showed actors the pleasures of the pork chop sandwich and the Montana Mary. Hamilton rode a motorcycle in a bunch of places where Knievel had ridden a motorcycle. He even picked up some Knievel-like injuries on the bike, separating a shoulder while he mastered the art.

"I never liked motorcycles," the actor said. "I did it, rode the thing at ninety miles per hour, but didn't like it. You're always an inch away from death on a motorcycle. Everyone I know who was involved with motorcycles wound up getting hurt. My son eventually lost his spleen on a motorcycle."

Hamilton rode the bike to the top of various ramps during the movie, part of the filming. He stopped before the takeoff point, looked at the distance to the other side. The thought of jumping on the bike was ridiculous.

" 'No way I'd do that,' " he told himself. "Say what you want about Knievel, you never could question his balls. You needed big balls to do what he did."

The movie opened on July 14, 1971, with a premiere at Grauman's Chinese Theater in Hollywood. Milius, the screenwriter, went in a limo that was behind George Hamilton's limo. Hamilton was dressed in character in the white leathers. A block from the theater, his limo stopped. Hamilton stepped out, put on his helmet, and jumped onto a waiting motorcycle. He rode the rest of the way on the bike, straight down the red carpet and onto a ramp. When he stopped, he was surrounded by people, mobbed by fans who wanted to shake his hand, touch him, simply be close.

This was different for him. The character trumped the actor.

"George wasn't George Hamilton anymore, he was Evel Knievel,"

Milius decided as he watched this unfold. "That was the reaction. You could see that he loved it. The attention. This was red meat for him. This was the red meat on his bones. It was the same for Evel.

"George and Evel, they were very well suited for each other. They were a couple of carny hustlers."

Knievel was in New York, in between his stops at Madison Square Garden and the Lancaster Speedway in Buffalo. He pumped the movie as he went from interview to interview.

"George Hamilton plays me in the movie, but all the jumping stunts I do," he said. "They've got no stunt men to double for me, and they never will get anyone to do so."

The reviews were not great. The *Chicago Tribune*, at the bottom of the pile, gave the offering one star, drivel, called it "the slow, dull treatment of one kook's life." The *Washington Post* said, "In order to get to the approximately four minutes (poorly photographed) of jump footage, consider what you have to sit through: 84 minutes of George Hamilton trying to change his image by riding a motorcycle—on top of acting out the neuroses and immature, self-centered activities of Knievel." The *Miami News* was kinder: "The film really is an attempt to characterize a real-life folk hero and the subject is fascinating enough to pull it off." A newspaper in Missouri called the story "a most amusing mixture of snippy arrogance and snappy humor."

The public seemed to like it okay. The film grossed $2,052,227 in the first twenty-one days of distribution, a solid figure since it was made for $750,000. It would wind up grossing somewhere around $15 million. The message Hamilton wanted to send about the American mind, the peculiar insanity of paying attention to something as peculiar and insane as motorcycle jumping, largely was missed. The way he had been typecast in the public mind was too much to overcome. People mostly focused on whether or not Hamilton should have played Knievel, and more often than not the verdict was that he was too good-looking, too refined, to be a motorcycle daredevil.

For everyone involved, except Knievel, this turned out to be another payday, another project, another number of days at the office. New projects awaited, turn the page. For Knievel, the effects of the movie were spectacular. He did not share in the profits, which bothered him, but the money arrived from other directions. This was the final big bounce off the publicity springboard he had discovered as he rolled across the parking lot at Caesars Palace. His name was wallpapered across America now, splashed on marquees, found in the movie listings in every small town, mentioned in coffee shops every morning.

He had moved into a different level of celebrity. He was no longer the scrappy second baseman, the local congressman, the bit player known only by theater aficionados. He walked with the home-run hitters now, with the Speaker of the House. He was the name on the front of the play-bill. Not only had he made the jump to the biggest arenas in the country, accompanied by the requisite boost in fees for his services (charging $15,000 and more for a jump now); he was able to live in an entirely different way.

True to form, he embraced his good fortune and doubled, tripled the bet. The clothes became flashier. The cars—and he always had been a sucker for the top-end cars, moving from Rolls to Rolls, Lincoln Mark III to Lincoln Mark III, making deals for cars even when he couldn't pay the rent—now became a never-ending string of impulse purchases, Ferraris and Maseratis, a good old Cadillac Eldorado every now and then, cars bought and discarded on a speculative whim. He always had liked golf, ever since his grandfather bought him a set of Wilson irons, but now he was able to attack the sport, bet on it, invent elaborate propositions. He always had liked women and a good night on the town. Well, the nights became longer and far more expensive.

The money that he never had now went through his hands as if it were on fire. He took the image that John Milius had typed for him, the out-of-control flamboyance, the eat-drink merriment, and not only lived up to it but expanded it. Life imitated art this time. Not the other way around. He was not the small-con character George Hamilton had met that first day at Universal Studios. Evel Knievel was on to the big con now.

"The movie definitely changed his life," Hamilton said. "He never would acknowledge that, but it did. It's one of those cases, I think, where if you give credit somewhere else, you feel it diminishes what you've done. Do you know what I mean? You like to think that you did everything yourself. He loved the idea of the movie in the beginning, then acted like it was signing an autograph or something. Just another thing. It wasn't just another thing. It changed his life."

The actor and the daredevil never had anything to do with each other once the movie ran its course. The daredevil grew to call the actor "kind of a pussy" in discussions. Indeed, he always downplayed the movie. He called the actor "my stand-in." The actor was not afraid to use the word "crazy" when he talked about the daredevil.

"I had a conversation with his grandmother when we were in Butte," Hamilton said. "She said that he had been a normal kid until he fell one day when he was ice skating, hit his head, was knocked out. He was always different after that. He didn't have the same equipment everybody else had. He saw life in an entirely different way."

If he could make the movie again, Hamilton said, he would make one change. He would play the character even further over the top. He would portray him as more arrogant, more demanding, more everything. Crazier.

A story. Nothing showed Knievel's rise to a new level of entertainment notoriety better than his trip to New York to play four nights at Madison Square Garden between July 8 and July 11, 1971. He was in the most famous arena in America in the biggest city in America, on display for the most jaded spectators in America. He was a long way from Butte and Moses Lake.

Maybe he shared the bill with Jack Kochman's Hell Drivers, and maybe they inherited the dirt on the Garden floor—and the flies in the Garden balcony—from the rodeo, which had just left town, but New York was New York. Knievel had brought Linda and the three kids with him. Ray Gunn had driven the big rig straight down Broadway. This was the big time.

"Evel Knievel is twice the man you or I am—he makes his living ripping off death while we're all trying to live without being ripped off," writer Philip Werber declared. "Evel is a man. He takes no shit from anyone, he fears nothing, for a dollar he'll jump over your hell while you cringe from your seat."

They didn't describe daredevils that way in the rest of the country. They did in the *Village Voice*. If Hollywood was where dreams were made, the movie and the invented story, this was where the nonfiction version was typed out. This was where the words were shipped to the provinces.

He was a gossip item . . .

"How does your wife feel about you risking your life?" syndicated columnist Earl Wilson asked, the question sent across the country.

"Who the hell cares," Knievel replied. "I wasn't put here to be the slave to any woman."

He was a self-contained business . . .

"I make half a million dollars a year," Knievel told Phil Thomas of the Associated Press, the answer sent across the country. "Except it depends on the year. Last year I didn't do too well because I broke my back twice and after that I got hit by a car while I was on my bike. That was a bad year."

He was a whole bunch of stuff that maybe even he hadn't considered. Or perhaps never phrased exactly the same way . . .

"Knievel is a lean, handsome man with curly hair, a hard-looking exterior, a quick temper, and a good deal of humor, perception and charm," writer James Stevenson decided.

> From the choppy years of his youth he has retained the wary eyes of a cardsharp, a thief's nerve, the combativeness of a brawler, the aplomb of a professional athlete, the flamboyant instincts of a promoter, and the glibness of a con man. There are trace elements of Robert Mitchum, Elvis Presley, Captain Ahab and an astronaut . . . His vanity and temperament are considered unusual even by show business standards, and he will give anybody bloody hell on a moment's notice. His courage speaks for itself.

This was part of a profile that ran in the July 24, 1971, *New Yorker*. Stevenson, on the way to a career as a prolific cartoonist, illustrator, and author of children's books, ate a couple of meals with Knievel, followed him around the Garden, watched the warm-up jump over ten cars (Knievel cleared the cars, but crashed into the far wall and collected a few more bruises because he couldn't stop) and the actual jump (a success, a strip of corrugated rubber put on the far side to help slow the bike).

Knievel went through his life story again, this time described how he gave up the life of crime while driving a Pontiac Bonneville across four states at 150 miles per hour as he was chased by police. He talked about starting both boys, Kelly and Robbie, on minibikes when they were five years old, putting them in a ditch and tying a rope to the minibikes so they wouldn't be able to go out of control. He talked about his grandparents, shooting ducks, working in the mines, jumping cars on a motorcycle, crashing nine times. He talked about the show he put on for the people at Madison Square Garden.

"They never saw anything like what I do," he told Stevenson. "And they'll never see it again."

The New Yorker. The most literary magazine in America. Address labels were put on the front covers, which featured a drawing of a leafy summer salad in a large bowl. The magazines were shipped across the country. The process of building a name in full public view continued. More words to more people.

Words were everywhere. Evel Knievel was everywhere.

14 Toys

In the fall of 1971, as the movie still played in drive-ins and theaters across the country, as *The New Yorker* with the salad on the cover still sat on tables in assorted dentists' waiting rooms, Knievel pulled up to a ninety-nine-year-old renovated carriage house in the Chicago suburb of Evanston, Illinois, for a business meeting. They were coming faster now, these business meetings, opportunities opening in a hurry, but none of them had brought the big financial payout that he hoped was out there.

The owner of the carriage house was a curious character named Marvin Glass. He, like any businessman, like Knievel, was exploring options, trying on another idea for proper size, wondering about the fit. Was there anything here? He was spinning the entreprenurial wheel one more time.

"Marvin didn't even know who Evel Knievel *was* at the beginning," Jeffery Breslow, one of Marvin's partners, present at the meeting, said. "A kid, I think it was the son of Marvin's accountant, got him interested, kept talking about the things Evel did. Marvin decided to bring Evel in for the meeting."

Glass was the president of Marvin Glass and Associates, the leading toy design business in the United States. He was a dynamic presence, regarded as a self-tortured genius in the field. He was a diagnosed paranoid schizophrenic, a tiny man, no more than five-foot-five, 130 pounds, an erratic buzz saw fueled on three packs of cigarettes and twelve cigars per day mixed with all the coffee a human being possibly could consume. At the age of fifty-eight, he was wrapping up his fourth marriage.

His fortunes had zigged and zagged through a career that started in 1948 when he had a couple of early hits with the Busy Biddee Chicken, a plastic hen that laid five marble eggs in succession, and the Yakity-Yak Talking Teeth, a windup set of chattering dentures that soon became a joke-store staple. The hits were followed by misses, which were followed by hits, then more misses, then hits again. A financial disaster like the production of a line of stained-glass, very Christian Christmas ornaments—Marvin learned, alas, as he sat in his stuffed warehouse, phone not ringing, that Christmas was not necessarily a religious holiday when people chose decorations for their trees—had to be offset by winners like Operation: A Skill Game Where You're the Doctor, or Rock'em, Sock'em Robots, or Super-Specs, an outrageous pair of joke sunglasses ten times the size of normal glasses.

His company headquarters at 815 North LaSalle Street, across from the Moody Bible Institute in downtown Chicago, was famous for its security. Approximately seventy-five people worked in various capacities trying to figure out what trick, what game, what toy, would capture the world's attention next. Everything was done in secrecy. Visitors were allowed to enter only after they stood in front of a television camera at the foot of a set of stairs, then were restricted to Marvin's office or conference rooms once they were buzzed inside. Designers in the brightly colored, seldom-seen work area were required to return their projects to one of two large bank safes at the end of the day. Marvin's office was in the center of the building, double-walled, no windows, a bunker inside a bunker.

If all of this mumbo-jumbo—partly Marvin's paranoia, partly show business, partly genuine concern about corporate espionage in a very competitive industry—added to his image as a toy genius, then so be it. The image was not bad for business. He sometimes sent his creations to the annual February toy fair in New York, the grand exposition where future products were unveiled, backed by armed guards. He sometimes sent voluptuous, top-heavy models instead of the guards. He himself showed up at least once with his latest creation inside a briefcase handcuffed to his wrist.

His home in Evanston, the ninety-nine-year-old renovated carriage house, was another part of the image. It was featured as the "Playboy Pad" of the May 1970 issue of *Playboy* magazine. The headline for the article was "Swinging in Suburbia," the reader's imagination left to supply the definition of the word "swing." The detailed description of the "emperor-sized ceramic Roman tub for eight" presumably was a clue.

"Distaff guests frolic in the huge ceramic-tile tub as the Jacuzzi whirlpool whips up bubbles," an unnamed correspondent reported.

> An elegant drink dispenser is close at hand. A complicated mechanism controls the colored-light system in the shower tub-room's ceiling; hues span the spectrum, gradually changing from warm red to deep violet and back again . . . Those more romantically inclined can relax just down the hall in the wood-paneled den where a blaze can be kindled in the fieldstone fireplace and libations can be mixed at the black leather–added bar that stands at the opposite end of the room.

One of the illustrations showed four smiling distaff guests enjoying the ceramic tub. Another showed a naked masseuse in the sauna. A third showed guests playing Funny Bones, a party game developed by Marvin for Parker Brothers.

The rest of the house was described with equal enthusiasm. The high-beamed ceilings in the living room. The two fireplaces capped by an enormous hood. The sculptures and paintings by Picasso, Dalí, Roualt, Frank Gallo. Wet bars everywhere. A grand piano. A high-fidelity system with controls built into the marble cocktail table. The magazine called the house "a live-in adult toy."

Marvin, it was obvious, liked women, liked a good cocktail, liked intrigue, romance, the battle, the chase. Marvin liked money. Not to save, but to spend, to indulge, to enjoy. Was it any surprise that Marvin was friends with his Chicago neighbor Hugh Hefner, the man who had typed this lifestyle into public acceptance? Marvin was a Playboy man.

"What is a Playboy?" the magazine asked in its "Playboy Philosophy" column as early as April 1956. "Is he simply a wastrel, a n'er-do-well, a fashionable bum? Far from it." The magazine explained:

> He can be a sharp-minded young business executive, a worker in the arts, a university professor, an architect or engineer. He can be many things, providing he possesses a certain point of view. He must see life not as a vale of tears, but as a happy time; he must take joy in his work, without regarding it as the end of all living;

he must be an alert man, an aware man, a man of taste, a man sensitive to pleasure, a man who—without acquiring the stigma of the voluptuary or dilettante—can live life to the hilt. This is the sort of man we mean when we use the word "playboy."

Marvin, of course, immediately liked Evel. Was there anyone else in creation who better "lived life to the hilt"? Evel, of course, liked Marvin. They were on the same glossy page.

"Evel impressed everyone in the room," Breslow said. "Everyone was charmed. There was an air of excitement about him. Articulate, very handsome. He'd done the Caesars Palace jump. He was interesting."

Marvin Glass had entered the meeting with a toy in mind, a toy that later would be called the Evel Knievel Stunt Cycle. The usual course for development of a product from the shop involved a bunch of designs, trial and error, finally resulting in the top-secret prototype that Marvin could sell to a big manufacturer after what he hoped would be a bidding war with other manufacturers. The manufacturer then would produce the toy and market it. Marvin's company by now was involved only in the research and design.

In this case, the research and design were minimal. The toy Marvin envisioned already existed in another form, a truck that he had sold to Ideal Toys. The key component was a gyroscope turned sideways, which acted as a powerful back wheel. The points at either end of the gyroscope were inserted into notches in a "power source," a plastic contraption that featured a crank. The gyroscope was slightly elevated. The child or adult in charge would crank as hard as he could, making the gyroscope spin faster and faster. When the cranking stopped, the rapidly spinning gyroscope would touch down and shoot the truck at great speed off the power source and across the floor.

The product had been a failure, lost in the ongoing traffic jam of toy trucks that flooded the market. Marvin still had hope for the concept. The speed should be attractive to kids. What if the gyroscope was the back wheel of a plastic motorcycle? What if the rider was a bendable rubber figure, dressed in red, white, and blue with a little plastic helmet, a little plastic cane, everything the same as worn by a caped hero who appeared on television? What if the bike could fly off ramps and over barriers and across Mom's freshly polished linoleum? What if the caped hero sometimes flipped and crashed, wow, and got back up and rode again? Marvin thought he could sell the same toy to Ideal all over again.

A deal was announced between Marvin and Knievel in the last week of November 1971. The two men posed for a publicity shot as Knievel signed the contract for personal promotion and licensing with Marvin Glass and Associates for "more than one million dollars." Marvin called Knievel "the last of the world's true gladiators," a line straight from the movie, and promised a future filled with Evel toys and other products.

"Few people have had as much impact on the American scene in the last decade as Knievel," Marvin said. "He is probably the first motorcyclist whose name has become a household word."

Ideal Toys, as Marvin suspected, quickly came aboard. Ideal's president, Lionel Weintraub, a few years earlier had rejected a proposal to produce GI Joe, the action figure, because he thought "boys won't play with a doll." GI Joe turned out to be a major hit, the equivalent to a boys' Barbie. Lionel wasn't going to make the same mistake twice. He too was educated in the popularity of Evel by the next generation, his son, Richie, a motorcycle-riding, guitar-playing teenager.

The deal, despite the exaggerated "million-dollar" figure, was modest. No one was making grand predictions. The teddy bear, produced in 1906, maybe America's favorite all-time toy, might have been a tribute to Teddy Roosevelt, but very few toys based on real-life people had been produced, and fewer had sold well. Ideal had to look back to its Shirley Temple doll in the thirties to see its last real-life success story. Take away some movie cowboys like Roy Rogers, Gene Autry, and Tom Mix from the fifties, who really were playing characters under their own names, and there were few modern precedents for the success of toys based on actual human beings. A comic-strip superhero or a cartoon character was a far better bet.

A March 5, 1960, article by Peter Wylie in the *Saturday Evening Post* on Marvin, entitled "Troubled King of Toys," spelled out the statistical realities for any toy in the marketplace. Over 200,000 toys were introduced at the New York toy fair in any year, but only 50,000 would be put into production. Only 200 of the 50,000 would make money. Only two or three would emerge at the front of the class, must-have selections on every Christmas list.

The first Ideal product, the Evel Knievel action figure, complete with white jumpsuit, white shoes, plastic helmet for vinyl head, and walking cane, whipped together in three months for the 1972 toy fair in February, turned out to be a solid item, but hardly a runaway hit. The Evel Knievel Stunt Cycle, which took a year to produce and get ready for the 1973 toy fair, was the big investment. It was anything but an assured commodity, another hopeful in a room full of hopefuls.

"I remember making my presentation to the buyer for Sears," Stewart Sims, Lionel Weintraub's son-in-law, said as he described the initial lack of interest. "He looked at me and said, 'Your toy might do all the things you say it will, but it will not be doing them in the Sears catalog.' "

No, but it surely would in the 1974 catalog. The Evel Knievel Stunt Cycle became the most popular toy in America for Christmas 1973, one of those damnable hot items that had to be tracked down, store after store, waiting list after waiting list. For girls, the most popular toy was Kenner's Baby Alive, the first doll to eat, chew, and fill up a diaper, but the Stunt Cycle captured the other side of the market.

The only reason Ideal didn't sell a million of the toys for Christmas 1973 was that Ideal couldn't make a million fast enough. The toy could have sold as much as twice that figure.

"I had to demonstrate the Stunt Cycle to the National Association of Broadcasters," Stewart Sims said. "You're in a room with all of these people. The rules were pretty strict. A toy had to do what it was advertised to do. You couldn't use fantasy to sell toys. You had to get down on your knees and show what the toy could do. If you can't get down on your knees, you probably shouldn't be in the toy business."

Sims demonstrated the many facts of the stunt cycle. (A few years later he would be back at the NAB, showing that Rubik's Cube actually could be solved.) Unlike GI Joe or other action figures, which required a lot of imagination, Evel Knievel could provide action himself. He could do something. Put him on the bike, crank up the gyro, the Energizer, as hard and fast as you could, stop cranking, let him go. He shot off the Energizer across linoleum floors, wood floors, driveways, stretches of concrete, any flat surface. The faster the Energizer had been cranked, the faster Evel Knievel traveled.

Adjust his position at the takeoff and he did a wheelie. Put up a ramp, he climbed the ramp and flew off into the unknown. Light something on fire, lay out a stretch of water in the middle of the track, shoot him out the window, shoot him off a roof, the evil possibilities for what could happen to Evel were endless. The crashes were wonderful. The motorcycle went flying. He went flying in a different direction. Maybe his helmet flew off in a third direction. He did the strangest things, landed in the strangest predicaments, and somehow always was able to get back on the bike. Exactly like the real-life character.

"Hold your breath, kids!" a full-page ad on the back cover of Marvel comic books proclaimed. "YOUR OWN EVEL KNIEVEL. MORE DARING THAN EVEL HIMSELF. Make him leap to fame on his stupendous STUNT CYCLE. He'll do wheelies! He'll do jumps! He powers away on his gyro-driven super bike. Stunts and tricks you wouldn't believe!"

"Jumps your set of encyclopedias volumes A through W," another ad said over a cartoon rendering of that very jump. "Sensational leaps over your neighborhood ditch."

The success of Christmas 1973 ("Everybody was clamoring for the toy," Stewart Sims said) opened up an endless string of possibilities for 1974, 1975, and beyond. Ideal would expand the line, expand again. The company would put out the Scramble Van, the Chopper Bike, the Gt Cycle, the Stunt and Crash Car playset, the Dragster, the Canyon Rig, the CB Van, the Sidewinder, the Stratocycle, the Trail Bike, the Funny Car, the Super Jet Cycle, the Skycycle, the Stunt Stadium, the Fast Tracker, the Road and Trail playset, the Stunt World playset, the Skull Canyon playset, and the Stunt Game, a board game. Evel Knievel would be at the center of each of these products, his name and picture across the top, the new signature "No. 1" associated with Harley-Davidson somewhere on the box.

He was a personal friend of the kids who owned the toy. They not only would put him into these perilous situations and he would survive, they would tuck him into bed at night. Man and plastic product were intertwined. Evel Knievel lived in Butte or Hollywood or wherever he lived. He also lived in the toy chest in the corner of the bedroom.

More than thirty years later, almost forty, the toy would still make these grown-up kids, now with their own families, smile. They would type out comments for Feeling Retro, a website for memories of the sixties and seventies.

"I used to race it from our living room to the kitchen," forty-one-year-old Lisa of North Carolina remembered. "Then I would yell, 'Hey, Mom, he broke every bone in his body.' To this day I tell everyone that this was one of my favorite toys."

"I remember back when I was five years old and living in Ft. Walton,

Florida," Tom, forty-two, said. "I was playing with my Evel Knievel and having him jump a ramp in the front hall way of our condo and having the front door as my stop. (Hay bales.) Well, after many successful jumps, I wound him up for one last jump. Off he goes and at that very moment my father came in and opened the front door and Evel flew right out the door and fell four stories to the parking lot below."

"I wound it up to full speed and then tapped the spinning back wheel on the back of my best mate's head (seemed like a great thing to do as a nine year old!)" said Mike, a forty-three-year-old from England. "The effect was immediate. My mate was almost scalped as reams of his 1970's style haircut were dragged into the mechanism. Not able to remove the bike from my bleeding and screaming mate, he ran home where his mother completed the job and gave him a bald spot 30 years too soon."

"I remember jumping Evel over 20 cases of beer at my friend's house, then flipping and smashing the bottom window of his mother's china cabinet," Dave, forty-three, said. "Toughest toy EVER!!"

"I actually prayed to Jesus for this toy," said forty-four-year-old Danny S. "Well, I am here to let you know that there is indeed a God because on Christmas morning, the 'Red Rider, Dual Action, Carbon-Firing BB Gun' of our generation, showed up, sure as thunder, under our tree upon my 5am wake-up . . . the memories of this greatest toy (my 'Rosebud') linger with me to this day."

The toy was the final piece of the perpetual dream for Knievel. This was the payoff. Fortune had joined fame. There never would be a public accounting of how much he would make—and he always would exaggerate numbers—but Ideal would say the toy made over $100 million, so if he made 10 percent of that he would have made $10 million. The success of the toy also brought other deals, negotiated by Marvin Glass and Associates, that would bring money from directions Knievel never had imagined. His name would be on bicycles, bedspreads, pinball machines, lunch boxes, candy bars, name a product, any product, an assortment of products. Some would sell, some would not. Money would be involved in all of them.

He was caught in a fat tornado of capitalism that visits very few people in their lives. He was in the highest demand.

"I was with him once, drinking," Skip Van Leeuwen said, describing how crazy the situation would become. "There were all these guys in another room. They'd paid $5,000 just to sit down with him, to make a presentation. That's $5,000 just to sit down. They were waiting, and we were drinking and he said, 'Fuck it, let's go play golf.' He told all those guys they would have to come back the next day. Just like that.

"He became so big. I worked with Mike Nesmith at one point. He was in the Monkees. I'd go out with him. I'd go out with Evel. There was no comparison in the attention they got. Evel was ten times as much. Crazy. Ten times as much as a Monkee."

The toy required very little change in Knievel's life. He was able to push ahead with whatever schedule he wanted. Just being himself, doing his shows, was the only public relations exposure the toy needed. Outside of a few business meetings, Knievel mostly had to cash the checks.

Stewart Sims was the first Ideal Toys executive to see Knievel jump, when he performed for two days at the Spectrum in Philadelphia, August 27–28, 1971. Sims came down from New York.

He found his man to be a bit standoffish, wary, an impression that people who went into business with him often described. Sims wound up spending the afternoon with Knievel as he visited half of the jewelry stores in Philadelphia. Karl Wallenda, the famous tightrope walker, also was in the show, and Knievel was determined to buy him a piece of jewelry as a gift. He was determined it would be the right piece of jewelry.

The spending already had begun.

"He always liked to let people know he was a big dick," Sims said. "He spent money. He liked to tell you he was a member of the Mile High Club [made love in an airplane], things like that. I never saw him dead drunk or anything, but he was hard to take. I always thought he was abusive. We were people who worked hard for him, and he never seemed to appreciate it."

One appearance Knievel would make for the toy was at the Macy's Thanksgiving Parade in New York in 1973. Sims arranged this, a coup of sorts, the first appearance by a toy in the parade. Knievel was supposed to appear in costume, do a few wheelies in front of the television cameras in front of the store in Herald Square, sell those toys. Martin Milner and Kent McCord, the two stars of *Adam 12*, would do the broadcast. Knievel would join the Rockettes, the Clydesdales, the Royal Lippizan Stallions, the Fifth Dimension, George Jones and Tammy Wynette, John Davidson as Prince Charming, and Tommy Tune and the Broadway cast of *See-Saw*, plus assorted balloons and marching bands.

The appearance became an adventure. Knievel drove cross-country from Butte, hauling the motorcycle. He was supposed to call Sims when he arrived. He never called. Sims phoned his hotel room again and again, received no answer. Wednesday night turned into the first hour of Thursday, Thanksgiving. Sims jumped into his car and drove into New York. He found Knievel in the hotel bar at 2:00 a.m., entertaining the crowd.

"I'm glad you're here, Stewart," Knievel said. "Because I don't think I'm going to be able to be in the parade tomorrow."

What?

"It's raining . . ."

Yes.

"I don't do wheelies in the rain. It's a safety thing."

What if . . . what if we got some pieces of plywood? Brought them out in front of the store?

"It's a safety thing. We should just cross our fingers, Stewart, and hope it stops raining."

The rain stopped. Knievel did the wheelies on national television. He came out to Sims's house on Long Island for Thanksgiving dinner. This was a big day. A month earlier, Sims's daughter had been born prematurely. She was ready to come home from the hospital. Sims waited for Knievel to arrive for dinner, while his wife picked up the baby. Sims and his wife waited for Knievel to arrive for dinner. The toy was that big.

Knievel carried the company for those first years. The ride always was shaky.

"One concern we always had was what we would do if he died," Sims said. "Part of his appeal was that he put himself in great danger and survived. What if he didn't survive? That was something we always took into account, that it was always possible that he could kill himself in what he was doing."

The people who died turned out to be the Marvin Glass and Associates people. Marvin himself died in January of 1974, age fifty-nine, a quick dance with cancer in the first flush of Knievel's success. He was replaced as president by Anson Isaacson, a man Knievel would call "my godfather" and his mentor in business dealings. Isaacson was shot to death in July of 1976 by one of the Marvin Glass toy designers, whose paranoia about all of the paranoia in the business had sent him into the office with a gun. He killed three people, wounded two more, then killed himself.

Knievel sold toys through everything that happened.

"Next year the Ideal Toy Company is going to make a lot of Evel

Knievel toys and I think they'll be something you'll be proud to have your children have," he said in a famous quote in a New York press conference. "One toy I'd like them to make is my own idea; I think it's the most super toy in the world. You wind it up, it goes like a little bugger, goes across the floor, and it grabs this little Barbie doll, throws her on the floor, gives her a little lovin', jumps back on the motorcycle and goes whizzing out the door screaming 'GI Joe is a faggot.' "

Toys. Who suspected that the pot at the end of the rainbow contained toys? Anson Isaacson once said that Knievel had "about twenty licensing arrangements now, which call for from 5 to 10 percent of the gross receipts." Who suspected that toys were so valuable?

A story. Knievel went for a business dinner one night in New York with the people from Ideal after the toy was established as a hit. The restaurant, Laurent, on East Fifty-sixth Street, was based on the dining rooms found in European grand hotels. It featured an adventurous menu, dark wood on the walls, ornately carved high ceilings, three climate-controlled cellars with over 45,000 bottles of wine. It was a place to see and be seen, a New York restaurant of the moment.

A dress code required all men to wear a jacket and tie. The toy executives wondered if this might force them to go somewhere else, with Knievel decked out in his usual high-collared Carnaby Street look, but he accepted a jacket and tie from the restaurant's collection.

He sat down at the head of a long table in the middle of the restaurant. The out-of-place jacket and the location of the table drew the attention of everyone in the room to him. He clearly was the guest of honor, a man who created a buzz of conversation wherever he went. He clearly was Evel Knievel. A number of diners came past and asked for his autograph. He signed, he talked. He was gracious and loud. Another famous man came to the table.

"Excuse me, Evel," he said. "I'm Richard Burton. I just saw you here and wanted to say hello. I'm a fan."

That was Richard Burton, the British actor. That was Richard Burton, sometimes the husband of Elizabeth Taylor, sometimes not. That was Richard Burton, probably as well known as anyone in the world at the moment.

"Well, Dick, nice to meet you," Knievel said. "Let me introduce you to the people in my toy company."

A few minutes later, a message came from another famous person. Salvador Dalí, the surrealist artist, known for his eccentric waxed mustache, for his paintings of limp wristwatches, for his flamboyance, was seated in a rear banquette. He was one of the three or four most successful living artists in the world. He would like to meet Evel Knievel.

"Sure," Knievel said. "Send him over."

The toy executives hurriedly told Knievel that Dalí was an older man. He was very well known, had created a style of art that was very popular. Perhaps it would be better if Knievel went over to Dalí's booth. Knievel agreed. He was gone for ten minutes, fifteen minutes, twenty. He returned.

"How'd it go?" Stewart Sims asked.

"Great," Knievel said. "I told him I had bought one of his paintings, had it back home in Butte. He liked that."

Pause.

Double pause.

"You know," the man who jumped across lines of parked cars on a motorcycle, who wanted to jump across a canyon, said, "those artists are some of the strangest people I've ever seen."

15 Famous

He stepped into his new situation as if it had been custom-made for him at some tailor's shop. Everything fit. This was the way he always had wanted to live, fast and rich and hedonistic. Borderline crazy. This was the traditional vision of good times that came out of long-ago Saturday nights in Butte when miners cashed their checks and blew the money as fast as they could on drink and women, gambling and nonsense, squeezed every bit of carnal pleasure possible out of a dollar, then returned to the dark hole when the dollars were gone. Fuck it. Have a good time. This was the life Knievel had tried to lead on credit and guile when he had little money. He could rip into it now.

"Do you fear anything?" writer Stephanie Fuller asked him as he prepared to jump ten cars twice daily at the Chicago Amphitheater as part of Cycle-Rama 71 at the start of his grand run. She meant crashing, dying, maybe hitting his head on the amphitheater roof because he had only twelve inches of clearance when he jumped.

"Yes," he said. "VD."

A television show, *The Beverly Hillbillies*, had appeared from 1962 to 1971 on CBS with great success. The plot revolved around the fact that redneck farmer Jed Clampett, played by Buddy Ebsen, struck oil in his backyard, became rich in an instant, and moved his family to Beverly Hills, California. The jokes came from how the family handled wealth in this sophisticated big-money setting. Knievel made the Clampetts look small-time and boring in his switch to wealth. He had practiced. He was living around Beverly Hills much of the time anyway before everything started.

His evolving dance with good fortune, starting in 1971, was nothing less than breathtaking (in either a good way or a bad way, depending on point of view) for anyone who followed it. As he grew bigger and bigger, richer and richer, he added and changed luxury cars in a hurry, bought mink and sable coats and designer clothes that startled the eye, bragged about his sexual conquests. He liked to show his $55,000 worth of diamond rings on his right hand alone, topped by a Baume & Mercier diamond watch. He had cheap replicas of the diamond rings made, then gave them away or hid them in bars and did magic tricks that made them appear.

He paid $100 to attendants when he pulled into parking lots, told them to keep the spaces open on all sides around his latest Maserati. He gave $100 tips to waiters and barmaids. He called the managers of restaurants to his table and said he wanted to buy a drink for everyone working in the kitchen. An hour later, he called the manager back and said he wanted to buy another drink for everyone in the kitchen.

He was always on the move, going, going, going. Since he wasn't in the hospital after every other jump anymore, he could work out a true schedule. He was in Agawam, Massachusetts, and Hutchinson, Kansas, out in Portland, Oregon, down in Tucson, back in Chicago, Oklahoma City, East St. Louis, Uniondale, New York, Cleveland, St. Paul, Cincinnati. He crisscrossed the United States, made money everywhere. He would jump in four different states within a single month. He would jump sometimes in the same city for three, four days in a row.

Every place he went, he blew through the premises like a force of nature. A force of nature with money to spend.

"He came to Seattle for us," Northwest promoter Ted Pollock said. "We were paying him $25,000. That was how far he had come. He eventually was too expensive for us after that. Anyway, he called and asked if I could pay him in cash. That was irregular, but I said it could be done. He jumped. I gave him the cash. I figured he needed it for something.

"He did. The next morning, he showed up to play golf at the Broadmoor in Colorado. He took the money out of his bag, the entire $25,000, and put it down on the first tee. He was ready to bet it all. And I think he did."

How had life changed? At two consecutive shows in the summer of

1972, planes that were leased to him, not motorcycles, were involved in crashes. He boasted that by the start of 1973 he "owned" eight planes, part of a project to start an air taxi service out of Butte that never really developed. He now flew to some appearances, leaving Ray Gunn or someone else to drive the big rig to the location.

The first crash happened on July 17 at Coon Rapids, Minnesota, at a drag strip where he was supposed to appear. A twin-engine Beechcraft owned by Knievel, piloted by a professional from Butte, tried to land on the strip and crashed into a trailer also owned by Knievel. The pilot was fine, but the daredevil said that the damage on the plane was $100,000, the damage on the trailer $1,000. At Knievel's next show, this time at Continental Divide Dragway in Castle Rock, Colorado, he himself crashed a 414 Cessna into a twenty-five-foot flagpole on the side of the drag strip. He complained that his "people" hadn't removed the pole.

The gathered crowd—the airplane that landed and crashed on the drag strip was a sudden, added part of the attraction—made the same startled noise it would make if he crashed on his jump. He was not injured, and the plane was only slightly injured, a broken wing light. He made the eleven-vehicle jump (four vans, four pickup trucks, three cars), waved to the crowd, got back into the Cessna, and flew out of the place. He boasted that he never had a Federal Aviation Administration license, but knew how to fly an airplane and did.

"I don't need a license to fly an airplane," he proclaimed to one interviewer. "I fly any damn place I want to. I fly from Seattle to Butte and Butte to Billings, Butte to Salt Lake City. What are they going to do? How can they stop me from flying around in the air up there? I mean, that's silly. I can fly a 747. There isn't anything I can't fly."

The rules that applied to everyone else did not apply to him. ("What I do, according to the laws of society, may not be exactly right," he told *Penthouse* magazine. "But the laws of society don't constitute my morals. I constitute 'em.") Celebrity was a golden pass to cut all lines. He used the pass.

He proclaimed that he had made love to over six hundred women, a figure that he was not afraid to say was growing rapidly. He proclaimed that he had made love to eight different women in one day. Was that a record? His modus operandi was basic. He set up shop in the noisiest, hottest bar in whatever city was his home for the night. He bought a round for the bar. He received an assortment of rounds in return. The people came to him. He was Evel Knievel, famous, straight from the television set, from the moving picture show, straight from the poster on your kid's bedroom wall. Adventure had begun.

"Men would offer him their wives," Jack Ferriter, a Butte guy who traveled with Knievel sometimes, said before he lapsed into a story that involved a woman in a red dress, her husband, Knievel, and an old-time hotel room with one of those transom windows over the door. "They thought it was an honor to give their wives to him. Women were all over him. They were attracted by the danger."

His major haunt in Los Angeles became Filthy McNasty's, a bar on Sunset Boulevard that in an earlier incarnation had been the Melody Lounge, inhabited by gangsters like Bugsy Siegel. In a later incarnation, it would be the Viper Room, owned by Johnny Depp. It was owned now by the McNasty brothers, Filthy and Wolfgang, Germans who had moved from Berlin as teenagers in 1956, found a foothold in the L.A. restaurant business, changed their names from Bartsch to McNasty, and lived their version of the American dream.

Phyllis Diller came to the bar sometimes, Little Richard, John Wayne even appeared. There was action every night of the week with loud bands, transvestite singers, mud wrestling, and a whole lot of Monte Rock III, who was a hairstylist, a singer, and mostly a flamboyant talk-show guest with Merv Griffin and Johnny Carson. Knievel fit into the picture nicely, as he left his latest extravagant automobile and a $100 bill with the valet parking attendant and signed on for the unfolding evening of high jinks.

The high jinks would go very late. The Sunset Boulevard location had to close at 2:00 a.m., but the brothers owned a second bar in North Hollywood, which was a private club. Filthy, who sometimes sang a tune of his own composition, "You're Breaking My Heart, You Tear It Apart, So Fuck You," during the proceedings, drove a black Cadillac hearse with a bright orange interior. He would fill the hearse with well-oiled women and drive them to the North Hollywood location. The men would follow, and the party would keep going until sunrise.

"Evel always would come," Wolfgang said. "He had the cane, filled with Wild Turkey. Always drank, but never was drunk. He mostly would come by himself to the bar. He would stay in a hotel on the strip. It was funny, if his wife was in town, she might come too. He would tell her what women he had seen, who he was with a night earlier. I never knew how he could do that."

Bob (left), brother Nic, and their mother, Ann, on a visit to Reno.

The young Bob in his grandmother's kitchen, next to the cabinet door he hit with his head.

Caesars Palace. Warming up.

High above the fountains . . . trouble ahead.

The trailer was his dressing room. His refuge
before and after he went to work.

Now, listen to me . . .

George Hamilton saw his movie as a commentary on American values. Critics mostly were not entertained.

He didn't want to go to the bottom of the canyon to pose, but the *Sports Illustrated* cover became the picture that was remembered from Snake River.

The long day at Snake River.

Five, four, three, two, one— Lift-off! Uh-oh . . .

The wrong side of the canyon.

Survives! Surrounded by mayhem upon his return.

He told Harry O he wouldn't pose with the gun and the bullets, but if Harry wanted to take a picture as he went to bed . . . well, that might be okay.

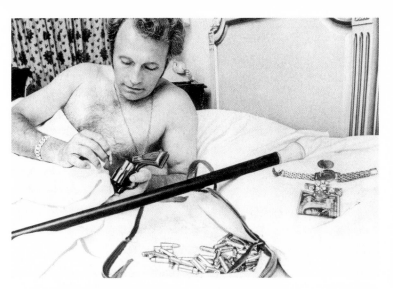

He played daredevil golf. Every shot was worth big money.

Selling, selling, selling. The talk shows seemed to have been invented just for him. Here he is on *The Tonight Show* with guest host Sammy Davis Jr.

Wembley

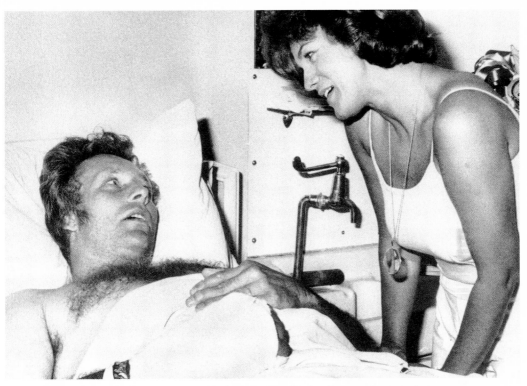

Actress Ann-Margret visits the famous daredevil in his London hospital room. The famous daredevil likes this.

Viva Knievel! The movie was supposed to start acting careers for both Knievel and model Lauren Hutton, but didn't do the job in either case.

The family gathers at Kings Island. Kelly, Linda, and Tracey visit the trailer before the show.

Robbie, ready to appear with
Dad at Kings Island.

Evel heads to jail. Inset: Shelly Saltman
after surgery, after the beating.

Linda would be there. Linda would be back in Butte with the kids. Knievel checked in and out of his different lives. Nobody said a word.

This was the seventies. He was a full-fledged man of his time. The time was out of control.

The plans for his oft-discussed, always-discussed canyon jump had continued through the bad times and into his new and ridiculously improved good times. He promised every year that the jump was imminent, scheduled for either the approaching Fourth of July or Labor Day, then adjusted when the actual date arrived. Every year he was like one of those end-of-the-world evangelists the day after Armageddon did not happen.

His first postponement, back in 1968, back while he was just returning to action from Caesars Palace and then the crash at Bee Line Dragway, back when he didn't have any real chance of clearing the distance, was the first of the disappointments. Not until three days prior to the proposed jump of the Grand Canyon near Page, Arizona, did local residents discover that the event was not going to happen.

Knievel said the villain was the Department of the Interior, notably Secretary Stewart Udall, which had rejected his request to jump from federal lands. The presence of a Navajo reservation, whose residents also wanted to be appeased, did not help. The jump could not take place.

"I guess they don't want him tearing across the canyon trailing a stream of flame and scaring the Indians," said Melvin Belli, noted defense attorney from San Francisco, hired to sue the Department of the Interior.

The choice of Belli was typical Knievel. The lawyer's most famous case, four years earlier, had been his pro bono defense of Jack Ruby, the accused assassin of accused assassin Lee Harvey Oswald. He always was in the news, with clients ranging from Lana Turner to Errol Flynn to Muhammad Ali. He brought Knievel into the news.

The suit never happened, though Knievel decried Udall's "decision" at all possible times. (Udall, contacted by writer Morris Alpern for *Argosy* magazine, said he never had met Knievel and always thought there was no real plan to jump the canyon, that Knievel simply used the department for publicity purposes.) Knievel wound up junking the idea of the Grand Canyon and in October of 1971 leased thirty-eight acres of pasture and brush, three years for $35,000, from farmer Tim Qualls on the edge of the Snake River Canyon, not too far from the town of Twin Falls, Idaho. Knievel had passed the canyon on motor trips with Ignatius and Emma as a boy, always remembered it. He soon told people that he had bought the land.

The crusade now became—because of Stewart Udall and that damned Department of Interior—a jump over the Snake River Canyon. Snake River was just as good, probably better. That was the new approach. The date of the proposed jump over this canyon was painted on the side of the Evel Knievel rig, then altered each time the event was postponed. This process brought great delight to Knievel's detractors at least once per year.

Progress, however, had been made. The handshake deal with Doug Malewicki, the builder of toy rockets in Phoenix, finally had produced a prototype vehicle designed to carry a grown man from Butte, Montana, across a canyon, any canyon, of his choosing. Four contentious years had passed, as Malewicki struggled to wring money out of Knievel. A sequence of bounced checks and broken promises stretched out the process, but the engineer had kept working in his spare time, followed his plan, and produced the seventeen-and-a-half-foot prototype rocket, called the X-1 Skycycle, and three much smaller test rockets.

On May 6, 1972, Knievel sponsored the Second Annual Snake River Motocross Championship races on his leased property and invited the press to the side of the canyon to see the prototype and witness the test firings of the smaller rockets. Malewicki estimated that $20,000 had been spent, none of the money on a salary for himself. He was hopeful about the test because he said Knievel had promised him a $5,000 bonus, plus expenses, if the rocket worked.

"The deal had changed over the years," Malewicki said. "It started out that I would get 30 percent of any profits, then 20, then 10, then 5. Now, I just wanted that bonus and expenses, go from there."

He felt that a major problem dealing with Knievel was being the same age. The daredevil never fully believed him, never gave him respect. Early in the development process, Malewicki had hired a scientist named Bob Truax to provide the engine that would propel the rocket. Shocked by estimates in the millions from aerospace companies to develop a jet propulsion system, he had been referred to Truax, a onetime colleague of rocket pioneer Robert Goddard. Truax was a Cold War expert who contributed to the development of the Polaris and Thor missiles, a man with a scientific imagination that had few boundaries. Truax had been fooling around with steam-power rocket engines for drag racer Walt Arfons. A Skycycle interested him.

"I didn't even know his background in the beginning," Malewicki said. "He had done all of these things with rockets. He was famous. I just knew that he'd been involved with the drag racer."

At fifty-five, Truax was twenty-one years older than Knievel and Malewicki. He was an average-sized man with a no-nonsense crew cut, a man of strong opinions. Knievel always was polite in dealing with him. Truax's words to Knievel seemed to matter. Malewicki's words to Knievel were the start of an argument much of the time.

The concept of the rocket had stayed the same: Malewicki had tried to build something that resembled a motorcycle. The prototype and the models each had two wheels, which kept the "cycle" in the name. They looked very much like rockets, however, with three fins on the back and a tapered nose in front. The X-1 was an impressive-looking machine.

The plan for the jump was that the rocket would be ignited, travel in increasing speeds up a ramp, shoot off the ramp and into the air above the canyon. Halfway across, two solid propellant rockets would be ignited, doubling the power, which would ensure that the rocket traveled into the airspace on the other side, where Knievel would eject from his cockpit and parachute to the ground. A drogue shoot would also be released from the rocket. Man and rocket would land somewhat simultaneously. Ta-da. Someone would play a John Philip Sousa patriotic march. Drinks would be served.

The test of the smaller rockets was a chance to see how well theory matched with reality. The X-1 was present only for show. Knievel posed inside. He would have to be on his knees in the cockpit, not sitting, to properly work the controls. The test rockets were all the same, affording a chance to test different trajectories. They were ignited one after another by Knievel, who pressed a button, surrounded by local kids holding their hands over their ears.

The first rocket, launched at a twenty-eight-degree angle, was almost across the canyon when the parachute was deployed, then it fell a few feet short and into the canyon. The angle was adjusted to forty-five degrees for the second launch. A camera also was added. This heavier rocket shot across the canyon and was traveling so fast that when the parachute came out, the chute was torn right off. The speeding rocket cleared the canyon edge easily, kept flying, and landed hard and out of eyesight. Not a great outcome if you were inside the cockpit.

The final rocket, minus the camera, also was ignited at a forty-five-degree angle. Everything seemed to work perfectly. The parachute deployed. The rocket slowly, safely, dropped to earth. A father and his son found it and returned it three hours later in fine shape.

"The rocket did what it was supposed to do," Malewicki said. "It was a success."

The success brought about a confrontation that had become inevitable. Malewicki wanted to be paid. Four years of increasing edginess had left the daredevil and the engineer in bad positions. The handshake in that hospital room in Phoenix was history from long ago. Malewicki wanted the $5,000 bonus, plus he wanted expenses.

Knievel balked. He came up with various reasons why the engineer should not receive either the bonus or expenses. Malewicki said he would not work on the project anymore unless he was paid. Knievel continued to balk, and a couple of weeks later Malewicki quit at the same time Knievel fired him. It was not a happy ending, no matter what version was told.

Knievel called Bob Truax the next day. He asked if the onetime NASA man would take over the project.

Truax said he would. He said he had some ideas.

Malewicki, mad, did what former employees do in most businesses: he took his talents across the street. He went to work for the competition. He went to work for "Super Joe" Einhorn.

One of the by-products of success, an annoying by-product to Knievel, was that other people had started to do what he did. New motorcycle jumpers seemed to appear on the scene every month, fearless characters fueled by the same economic desperation that Knievel had in the beginning, more than willing to risk their lives for the same tenuous benefits that he received. Cycle jumping was a growth industry.

There was no need to play in the minor leagues or sing in a string of roadhouses or sit in a classroom, bored, to perfect a talent in this business. Buy a motorcycle, buy a set of leathers, find some racetrack owner who needed one more attraction, line up the cars and ramp, take a deep breath (or a shot of Wild Turkey), and go. Become famous. Or not.

Bob Gill, a twenty-eight-year-old guy from St. Petersburg, Florida, already had jumped a canyon, Cajun Canyon outside New Orleans, 60 feet deep and 152 feet wide, on a Kawasaki 400 on April 16, 1972, three weeks before the Snake River test. He would jump a fleet of Ryder rental trucks for a television commercial the next year. Rex Blackwell and Gary Davis out of Phoenix performed in tandem as "the Flying Cycles." They roared at the same line of cars from different ends of the venue, hit the two ramps at the same time, and (hopefully) passed each other in mid-air and (hopefully) landed safely. A twenty-one-year-old named Bob Pleso from Ocala, Florida, promised to break all jumping records. A guy named Ted Keeper in Chicago drove around in a school bus that said "Ted Keeper Jumps Cheaper" on the side. He would put his life on the line for $50.

Jumpers were everywhere. A blond twenty-year-old from Phoenix, Debbie Lawler, had opened the business to women. A former model, she disclosed that she always wore her lucky orange brassiere when she jumped. Talk shows thought she was wonderful.

The best known of all the copycat jumpers was Super Joe Einhorn, a wild character from San Pedro, California. Divorced, broke, he truly had followed Knievel's route to fame, especially the part about stopping in assorted hospitals on the way. He had been in some spectacular crashes. At the Cow Palace, someone had spilled a soft drink in the lobby, and Einhorn's front wheel hit the spill in his approach and, whoa, that sent him out of control. His heart was pushed farther to the left side of his chest in the crash, and he said he now put his hand under his armpit when he recited the Pledge of Allegiance. In Sacramento he had landed short, and his Triumph 650 pretty much had disintegrated. In Charleston, South Carolina, he had jumped over a building, landed on his head, and broken his wrist, ankle, both shoulders, and a thumb. He had a lot of experience in the hospital.

"You come to and they're putting something in your eyes," Einhorn said, describing hospital time to reporter Dorothy Melland of the *Hutchinson* (Kansas) *News*. "They're always putting something in your eyes. Strange people are working over you. Then a doctor comes in and sits down and starts reading a list of injuries. He goes on and on. Broken back, dislocated shoulder, punctured lung. All that stuff. You lie there and think, 'Gee, that poor guy.' Then it dawns on you that the list is about your own injuries. And then you get scared."

The first rule for the new jumpers was to differentiate themselves from Knievel. Only Debbie Lawler stepped back, proclaimed that while she was the queen of cycle jumpers, Evel always would be the king. The rest of the jumpers routinely challenged Knievel. They boasted about how their jumps were different, more challenging. Both Gill and Pleso jumped with only a takeoff ramp, no landing ramp. More challenging. ("Ramp-to-ramp jumpers are a dime a dozen," Pleso said.) Blackwell and Davis flew past each other. Certainly different. Einhorn stretched paper across the top of the takeoff ramps between two poles, the way cheerleaders stretched paper in front of the entrance to the field before the big homecoming game, then he burst through on the way to his jump.

Knievel was painted as the old man at the age of thirty-five. His time was done. The new wave had arrived. This was a basic part of sales. Bigger. Faster. Better. New!

"Knievel is a fraud," Super Joe said in a prelude to a jump in Los Angeles. "He keeps talking about things, but he never does them. He's been talking about jumping a canyon for six years. The Grand Canyon, the Snake River, they're all the same, but Knievel hasn't jumped either yet.

"I honestly get mad when I read one claim after another that he's made. They're just not true. I challenged that big-mouth old-timer to a match jump-off. I suggested the pot we'd put up was $25,000 apiece, winner take all. He backed off, but there was good reason for him not to accept my challenge. The old man knew he couldn't make it."

Knievel was not happy with any of this. He grumbled, "I can spit further than that," on *Wide World of Sports* when Debbie Lawler broke his record at the Houston Astrodome. (He then realized his public relations mistake, invited her to a jump in Seattle, and presented her with a pink mink coat.) He appeared in Kansas City at a press conference to tell Gill to stop mentioning his name in all his promotions. He was not happy when Einhorn made the $25,000 challenge in a press conference in Sacramento, the money brought in from an armored car.

The competition promised other jumps. Gill said he had an offer to jump over the Rolling Stones while they played "Jumping Jack Flash." Einhorn looked into the possibility of jumping across Wall Street in New York from the roof of one building to the roof of another building. Or maybe he would jump across Niagara Falls, Canadian side to American side. Or maybe . . . he had interest in a canyon in Mexico.

The canyon in Mexico idea was where Doug Malewicki had become involved. He would help develop Einhorn's craft to clear that canyon. He was thinking about a kite attached to a motorcycle. He had thought about that when working out the rocket for Knievel. Investors had to be found. Knievel was not happy. He was not happy with any of this stuff.

In the final six months of 1972, his unhappiness allegedly was translated into grim action. The manager for Joe Einhorn was beaten and threatened in a San Francisco motel room. Bob Gill was beaten and threatened in a Kansas City hotel room. And Doug Malewicki, who had switched sides in the canyon-jumping business, was threatened near his own home. Knievel was not present at any of these events, but the men who were involved allegedly mentioned his name.

"The guy said, 'I'm supposed to kill you,'" Malewicki said. "'You should be dead right now. I felt sorry for you, though. You have a wife, children. I am going to do a favor for you. But you should do a favor for me too.'"

The speaker was a beefy man, middle-aged. He showed a gun for emphasis. His advice was that Malewicki should stop being involved with Einhorn in this project. The technology he used for Knievel should stay with Knievel. Was this too much to ask? Malewicki should consider himself warned. The beefy man left.

The engineer was not rattled. If the goal had been to scare him, it didn't work.

"I knew the guy wasn't going to kill me," he said. "If he was going to kill me, he never would have talked to me. It would have been over before I knew anything happened. He really didn't worry me for some reason."

The messages to both Einhorn's manager and Gill were allegedly the same message that Malewicki heard, but accompanied by punches or kicks. The FBI moved into the case under the Hobbs Act, which prohibits actual attempted robbery or extortion affecting interstate or foreign commerce. All parties were interviewed.

The redacted versions of the FBI reports would not surface publicly until 2008, almost forty years after the fact. One said that BLANK, presumably Einhorn's manager, said that he had discussed the $25,000 challenge with Knievel on the phone a number of times. On August 23, 1972, he received a severe beating from two men that required him to be hospitalized for two days. BLANK said that two weeks later he received a call from Knievel, who said he had no control over "the thing" that had happened, but that if BLANK told anyone, Knievel would fix it in twelve hours that BLANK would never walk again. A different BLANK in Kansas City, presumably Gill, said he was "scared to death" by his confrontation.

The FBI investigators wanted to find a connection between organized crime and Knievel. They thought that some of the venture capital for his jumps and other business deals was coming from mob characters in Chicago. They wanted to hang the beatings and threats on the mob characters.

"The FBI came to see me," Malewicki said. "I told them what happened. They showed me some pictures, but none of them was the guy who had approached me."

An agency review of Butte police files about Knievel was interesting. It found that he had indeed been a suspect in a string of robberies when he was a merchant policeman, and a large suspect in the robbery of the treasurer's office at the courthouse. He also had been flagged for a comment he made in 1962 to a bank official, wondering what the official would do if he, Knievel, wanted a large amount of money at that moment. The comment was thought threatening because he had no account at the bank, but no robbery followed.

Agents finally talked to Knievel on November 21, 1973, at O'Hare Airport in Chicago. He had called an FBI agent that morning and accused the agent, "in a very excited and occasionally vulgar manner," of trying to destroy his reputation by telling people that he was connected to organized crime. He said he was going to sue the agent and the FBI for $500,000.

By the afternoon meeting in the airport, he had calmed down. He retracted his threat to sue. He admitted making phone calls in the past to the different aggrieved parties, admitted that they were angry phone calls, but denied having anything to do with any of the physical confrontations. He said the confrontations probably came about because someone else also disliked the aggrieved parties.

The FBI tried to put together a case for a grand jury in San Francisco, but never nailed down enough facts. The attorney in charge of the San Francisco strike force was reassigned. The new attorney in charge looked at the files, decided there was not enough evidence to link any of the threats to organized crime. Knievel never was charged. None of this made the newspapers of the time. The public relations bullet was dodged.

"I later became great friends with Evel," Bob Gill said after the FBI report came out in 2008. He was unwilling to revisit any of the events. "He did that one bad thing with me, then did a thousand nice things after that. He apologized so many times I had to say, 'Stop it, will you, with the apologies?' "

A story. The job was not what Gene Sullivan thought it would be. The bodyguard who had joined the operation in San Francisco just in time to knock heads with those Hells Angels at the Cow Palace had expected that he would have to protect his client from bad people with foul intentions. He never thought that his client would be the bad person with foul intentions.

As weeks and months passed, as the money began to arrive, Sullivan found that he was on the wrong side of an assortment of late-night battles. Knievel would start the trouble, be in the wrong. Sullivan would have to stand beside him. He felt he was wearing a black hat instead of the white hat that had been promised. He didn't like it.

"I didn't feel like I was working for the same guy," Sullivan said. "I signed up to work for Bob Knievel from Butte, Montana. I liked that guy a lot. I worked now for Evel Knievel from Hollywood, California. I didn't like that guy as much. It was different."

Ray Gunn already had left. He quit one day in Phoenix when Knievel started complaining to a bunch of businessmen about something Gunn had done. Knievel said he was going to dock Gunn a week's pay. Gunn, who heard the comment, said that would not happen because he no longer worked for Evel Knievel. He quit right there, just like that, went home to Washington.

Virtually everyone who worked for Knievel was fired at one time or another or quit, that was part of working for him, but this was different. Gunn left and did not come back for a long time.

"Evel was great to be around most of the time," Sullivan said. "But he could be very demanding and had an extremely dark side too. Ray had been very close to him, but after Phoenix he never would have that same kind of devotion."

Sullivan was bothered by Ray's departure, bothered by the fights and arguments that Knievel started, bothered by the consistent immorality of the man. After a show in Sacramento, he handed in his notice. He came back a few weeks later, trucked a motorcycle out to Knievel in Detroit after an accident, but that was the end. Knievel wound up accusing him of trying to sabotage the jump in Phoenix after Gunn left. Sullivan told him that was ridiculous.

About a month later, living in Reno, wondering what to do next, Sullivan was invited to a breakfast sponsored by the Full Gospel Men's Fellowship. Entranced by the words of former California Angels outfielder Albie Pearson, he became a born-again Christian on the spot.

"You know, the Lord tells us in the Proverbs to depart from evil, so I did," Sullivan said. "I obeyed his word and departed from Evel."

After a few false starts, Sullivan settled on a career path. He became a cycle-jumper evangelist, touring the country, jumping cars, proselytizing, "Jumping for Jesus," as the advertisement still reads. He became part of the Knievel competition.

The new big-money life of Knievel was best exhibited in an event held at the Los Angeles Memorial Coliseum on February 18, 1973. He was a co-promoter, along with old friend J. C. Agajanian, of the world's richest demolition derby. Luxury cars like a new Rolls-Royce Silver Cloud, a Cadillac Eldorado, and a Lincoln Continental Mark IV would be placed in combat with twenty-seven other recent-model lesser sedans. After the destruction was complete, Knievel would jump over a pyramid of fifty junk cars.

There was a little something here for everyone. The day was called "Motorheroics.' "

"As soon as it was announced, we got such hate mail," J. C. Agajanian Jr. said. "A lot of it came from overseas. This was the decline of civilization. Americans were so . . . fill in the blanks. A guy wrote that anyone in Britain would give his eyeteeth just to sit in a car like the Rolls, not even drive it. And we were going to destroy it?"

ABC nevertheless bought the package for *Wide World of Sports*, Knievel's first appearance since his cameo debut five years earlier at Ascot. The Rolls was sent around the freeways of L.A., a sign on the side that said "This Car Will Be Destroyed on February 11, 1973," the date changed to a week later when rain postponed the first show. Knievel also took to the streets to promote the event. In the Maserati, he was clocked at 110 miles per hour on the Hollywood Freeway at one point.

His schedule was full. He paid a visit to Johnny Carson, where he told the host he was *not* suicidal. He put in some quality time with the McNasty brothers, who once had announced the news that "EVEL KNIEVEL IS DRUNK INSIDE" on their Sunset Boulevard sign. He dressed up in his mink coat with the sable collar and went to a sportscasters' luncheon at the Ram's Horn restaurant in Encino.

The luncheon did not turn out well. He shared the bill with UCLA basketball coach John Wooden, champion pole vaulter Steve Smith, and British heavyweight boxer Joe Bugner, among other people. As everybody else talked, Knievel formed the impression that he was viewed as a second-class citizen in this group, not as a true athlete. He addressed this impression when he finally went to the microphone. Some of the famous people already had departed.

"I heard some comments around here that what I do might be some kind of circus stunt," he said. "I'm sorry that John Wooden and Steve Smith already have left because I wanted them to hear this. First, I want to say that the least of my worries is what's going to happen next week. And the second-least of my worries is falling nineteen feet into a pile of sawdust.

"I want to talk to you about opponents. Now, there are a couple of you guys out there who wonder about that. And I would like you to tell me if you can find a tougher opponent than mine. Because my opponent is death."

The remarks, recorded by Charles T. Powers of the *Los Angeles Times*, left the room squirmy and silent. Knievel simply left the room. He had said what he wanted to say. The hell with those people. He didn't need any filter.

"My father sent me with him most of the week," Agajanian Jr. said. "I took him to a radio interview. I left while he was talking. He asked afterward where I was. I said I went to the bathroom. He said, 'Never get up and start walking around when I'm talking.'"

All the talk, all the publicity, did not bring out the crowd. Knievel and Agajanian said they had invested $200,000 in the show. They were hoping for 50,000 people, $8 per adult ticket. They got 23,764. The rainout hurt. Something hurt. Only the money from ABC saved them from taking a large financial hit.

The demolition derby had somewhat predictable results. Ken McCain of Fresno, who drove in derbies every week at Ascot and around the state, took the first prize of $7,000 in a 1973 Ford LTD. ("A lot of people are going to be surprised about those high-priced cars," Knievel had said. "It'll probably be some little Jap job that wins it.") In second place was a 1972 Mercury station wagon, also driven by a derby specialist. Knievel was right. The high-priced cars, driven by the high-priced racing talent, did not fare well.

The Rolls-Royce Silver Cloud fared worst of all. Bobby Unser, the Indy driver, was behind the wheel. The car quickly became hung up on a hay bale that was part of the out-of-bounds border. The motor died. The Rolls had an electric starter. The starter quit. The Rolls was done almost before the battle began. Assorted competitors crashed into the helpless luxury car, just for the hell of it, just for the show. Unser sat behind the wheel for the hits.

He had a short-fused personality that was a good match for Knievel. He was not happy. The cars, it should be mentioned, each ran on gas from a five-gallon can that had been secured in the backseat. This was a safety feature, the normal gas tanks left dry. Unser, as he left the Rolls, unhooked the gas line from the five-gallon can. When he was outside of the Rolls, he took out a cigarette lighter. He lit the lighter, threw it into the backseat. The Rolls went up in flames. It was a moment.

A delay developed between the derby and the jump. The last-minute subject again was money. Knievel had a disagreement with ABC. He said he had decided he wasn't going to perform. "I can't do this anymore," he said. The ABC people pleaded. The dispute eventually was ended.

Knievel came out of his trailer, jumped on the XR750, roared into the Coliseum, where he did some wheelies. He then went to the microphone. He now talked almost exactly like the character John Milius had created in the movie. He was a caricature of the caricature. He talked about the grand, oft-delayed jump at Snake River.

"You can say a lot of things about a man," he said. "You can say that he is a great race-car driver or a not-so-great race-car driver. You can say that he's been lucky, or else that he's broke or rich. You can say that he drives a big car or a little car. But you can say nothing better about a man than his word is 'as good as gold.' And I want to tell you something. If I jump that canyon and make it, when I land in that parachute I'll drop to both knees and I'll thank God Almighty that I'm alive. I'll grab a handful of Idaho dirt. If I miss and splatter myself against the canyon wall, I'll just get somewhere quicker where you're going someday and I'll wait for you.

"But remember something. Remember one thing. If you're ever at a party, or here in this great stadium at a ball game, or at home or in your office, and I happened to have missed on that jump and somebody says to you, 'That guy is a disgrace,' I'd like you to do me one favor. Say, 'Regardless of what Evel Knievel was, I saw him at the Los Angeles Coliseum. He said he was going to jump the canyon; he did; he kept his word.' And that's something you can say about very few men on the face of this earth.

"We've been here in Los Angeles for a while now, getting ready for this thing. It's been a good time. The women have come and gone. The parties have been great; the booze has flowed. But now it's time for me to do what I came here to do. Thank you."

A long, two-hundred-foot ski jump of sorts had been built to the top of the Coliseum at one end. He rode to the top, turned around, and came hurtling back down, trying to hit one hundred miles per hour before he reached the ramp at the twenty-yard line. The cars had been stacked three high in front of him, but had been compressed so they weren't much taller than a normal sedan. He cleared the pile easily, good landing. A parachute advertising Olympia beer popped out, and he kept moving, riding all the way up another ski jump at the other end of the stadium. The motorcycle slid at the top, but he gained control and came back.

"Another day, another dollar," he told ABC broadcaster Bill Fleming.

"You know, Evel, you're still shaking a little bit," Fleming, standing close to him, said.

"If you did what I did, Bill, you'd be shaking too," Knievel said.

16 Butte, MT (III)

A story. The sad thing happened on the Madison River in Ennis, Montana, on the morning of November 19, 1972. The irony was that after all of the danger, after all of the close calls, all the public conversation about the perils involved in his work, when death made an appearance in the midst of Knievel's ascendant rise, it came in a depressingly normal package. His father-in-law drowned in front of him, and there was nothing he could do to stop it.

The day started early, a duck-hunting trip with Kelly, now twelve, and Robbie, now ten, and Linda's father, sixty-three-year-old John Bork. Knievel and Bork now got along fine, thirteen years after one had married the other's daughter. The plan was for the men in the family to hunt, then meet up with Linda and daughter Tracey at Varney's Bridge in the afternoon. Ennis and the Madison River were perhaps seventy-five miles southwest of Butte.

Knievel and his father-in-law were lifelong hunters. They weren't doing anything unusual. This was a family outing, the type of event that the public forgot Knievel had, his life outside the leather jumpsuit and the fast lanes he found on the road after dark.

The accident happened in a moment. The thirteen-foot inflated boat the men were using hit a log and flipped. Everybody went flying. Knievel was able to grab Kelly. Bork was able to push Robbie to safety on top of the log, but was swept away by the current. He grabbed a branch for a half-second, then he was gone. Just like that.

"He had on heavy boots, and they filled up with water," Knievel told Pam Swiger of the *Montana Standard*. "I had on boots too, and I couldn't get to him. He never wore boots in a boat, but he just hadn't got around to taking them off."

Knievel and the two boys were able to find safety on a small island in the middle of the river. They proceeded to call out for help, but soon found they were very much alone. Knievel eventually left the boys on the island and found a spot to cross the river to find help. Horses were used to bring the boys to safety. Bork's body was found on a sandbar further down the river. The current had pulled him away, the boots had pulled him down.

"It was just a tragedy," Bob Pavlovich, Knievel's friend, a member of the state legislature, and the owner of the Met Tavern, said. "There wasn't any story. It just happened, awful."

No one ever had been killed in or at Knievel's many stunts, not even himself, no matter how he tried. Tragedy didn't need a challenge, an invitation. Sometimes it simply appeared.

"What kind of dreams do you have?" interviewer Joan Wixen would ask four years later.

"You know, there is one dream I keep having over and over," Knievel replied. "I relive the day my father-in-law drowned in a boat accident when he was with me and my two sons.

"I was torn between staying with the boys and trying to save him in the rushing water, and I stayed with my sons. Losing him in that river was probably the worst thing that ever happened to me. When I first married my wife, I wasn't at all close to him, but through the years we really formed a bond between us, and to this day I have never gotten over that accident and the feeling that maybe I could have done something to save him."

Butte was still a part of Knievel's life. This was his alternate universe, the place where he was husband and father, local boy who had made good despite a lot of grim predictions. This was still his home base, an increasingly silent partner in all that he did, but still a partner. He landed here when there was nowhere else on the schedule for him to land.

"You'd hear him come down the street with the Stutz Bearcat or whatever he was driving," Beverly Wulf, a neighbor on Parrot Street who babysat for the kids, said. "He was a show-off. Everything was for Bob. He'd hit the door, come from someplace, the first thing he'd say was, 'Kelly, get my suitcase, Robbie, get my golf clubs.'"

He was not a great husband, not a great father. Friends and enemies in Butte both would say, "He never should have gotten married." This opinion quickly would be followed by a nice word about his wife, something like, "Linda's the greatest, nicest girl in the world. She is going to go straight to heaven." The implication was that her perseverance, just living with this domineering man, would take care of any time she might be asked to serve in heaven's alternative.

Knievel insisted that Linda was off-limits for all interviews, off-limits even for pictures, so she was seen little, heard less. He would later explain that he didn't like the idea of divorce, someone else raising his kids. Indeed, the possibility of dying and being replaced was one of his oft-stated reasons for spending every dollar that came into his hands. He didn't like the idea of Linda being remarried to some banker, some businessman who would come onto the scene after Knievel perished in a stunt, some slob who would spend all the money, play with all the toys that Knievel had accumulated. Knievel dreamed about this foul event happening.

Linda, who admitted later that she should have gotten a divorce, had all the signs of an abused woman. She certainly was verbally abused. He barked, she jumped. He delivered his tortured explanations about why it was all right for him to sleep with other women, indeed, he glorified his relationships with them, boasted about them, while maintaining he could still love his wife, his "girl." Linda, at least in public, accepted it all, said nothing.

"I understand the romance, the balls-to-the-wall thing about him," one female neighbor said. "My father worked in the mines. I was, like, thirteen years old, and I said, 'Oh, boy, Evel's going to jump some more cars.' I was sort of sarcastic. My father was upset. He admired him. A lot of those guys in the mines did . . .

"But he beat his wife. That was not romance. Everyone in town knew it. What kind of a man does that? Linda is just the nicest person. Linda is class. Evel was not class."

His relationship with his kids also seemed to come out of a drill instructor's manual. He was autocratic, tough. The emerging defiant one was Robbie. Kelly and Tracey tended to follow his orders. Robbie would shake his head in agreement at whatever pronouncement his father made, then do exactly the opposite as soon as his father left. He was, more than one person said, exactly like his father, payback for a lifetime of bad behavior.

"That Robbie, he's driving me crazy," Knievel would say. He would mention that Robbie was bitten by a rottweiler as a young child. Maybe that was it. The rottweiler.

When he got around to putting some of his new money into a home for the family, Knievel mostly built a temple to himself. He picked the place, a nine-acre lot on the sixteenth fairway at the Butte Country Club, in April of 1972. He paid $100,000 for it in four installments to the Lakeshore Development Corporation over the next eight months. He then picked the style of the house, a ranch, and picked out the stone that should be used and picked out the curtains. If this was to be his dream house, then the features should come out of his own dream.

"I designed the whole thing," Knievel told Betty Sue Raymond, the women's editor of the *Montana Standard*, for a story on March 3, 1974.

Though finishing touches were still to be added when he showed Betty Sue the $200,000 house, most of the work already had been done. Knievel's sense of style—Linda told Betty Sue that he made great choices, even when he kept changing his mind—was obvious. The shag carpet that ran through the house was a burgundy wine color. The bathroom decor was a mixture of blacks and golds, right down to the black-and-gold fixtures. Heavy gold drapes were hung in the living room. A seven-foot circular bed dominated the bedroom, a mirrored headboard part of the picture. A giant cedar closet off the bedroom held Knievel's many fur coats.

"Grandma just loves to put on my mink coat and go in and lay on that king-sized bed," he said.

There was a room for Emma, for Grandma, when she wanted to stay. Ignatius had passed away in 1972. There were rooms for each of the kids, red fixtures in their bathroom. An artist was going to paint a picture of the sixteenth green at the Butte Country Club in the exercise room, a mural that would be in plain view while Knievel pounded golf balls off the Astroturf floor into a net. A stone wall surrounded the place, heavy wrought-iron gates in front, Knievel's signature "EK" prominent in the design. There would be stables, a putting green, a place to land a helicopter.

A second artist, not the one who painted the mural, worked with Montana travertine rock to create a picture of a man on a motorcycle behind the wet bar. The image of another man, no, probably the same man and same motorcycle, was created on the perimeter of the cathedral window in the living room. There was little doubt about who lived in this place and what he did for a living.

The house would become a stop for whatever tourists came through Butte, so Knievel added a guard shack in the front, staffed twenty-four hours per day. The locals mostly would drive past and wonder what was inside. The latest rumor was a heated horse arena. The house was a subject of conversation.

"I had a printing business," Mike Byrnes said. "Knievel called me up and asked if I could print some elaborate gold checks for him. He was smart. He knew that if he gave people a gold check with his signature on it, they might not cash it, save it for the autograph. I wasn't much interested in printing the checks, I wouldn't touch him with a ten-foot pole, but I wanted to see the place.

"I went in. He was sitting in the living room at a big glass table. There was a silver telephone. The phone rang. Evel listened. Then he said, 'I'm my own agent. I don't care if you worked with Sinatra and Dean Martin. Now get off my fucking phone.' "

The place where he could be found most often in Butte was outside his new living room window. The Butte Country Club was 6,343 yards of challenge, fun, aggravation, fast-talking, high-finance, white-knuckle excitement. The characters from the bars would gather when he was in town, and new characters would arrive, and golf would be played as if it were blood sport.

Knievel was on the course almost every day he was home. Noisy declarations would be made. Money in startling amounts would change hands. The daredevil would be the pacesetter, the trendsetter, the certified star of the show . . . which was exactly what he expected to be.

He played as low as a six or seven handicap at one time, fell all the way back to eighteen at another, but ability was almost a secondary asset in his version of the game. Composure was everything. How well could a man keep his hands steady when he played for money? How much money would make him shake? This was daredevil golf. Knievel claimed to reporters that he would play against Arnold Palmer, Jack Nicklaus, Lee Trevino, anyone, for $10,000 a hole. He said the famous golfers would shake like anyone else.

"They would find it different when they weren't playing for Bob

Hope's, Bing Crosby's, Glen Campbell's, Dean Martin's, or Andy Williams's money," he said. "It's different when it comes out of your own pocket when you lose.

"Everybody has his own choking price, but I play $2,000 a hole with two guys every day I play. And we pay $1,500 into the kitty for every sand trap you hit, every water hazard, and every out of bounds. I've lost $60,000 on a round of golf. When Nicklaus or Palmer says he 'lost' $10,000, he merely means he didn't win it. I lost it."

The side bets changed the way people played. That was the key to daredevil golf. The opponent, thinking about the money he could lose, would have to alter his game to stay away from the out of bounds, from the trap, from the water. The Knievel theory was that he, stout of heart, steady of hand, fat of wallet, would not be worried about these distractions.

The theory, alas, sometimes did not hold true.

"A guy once rode around in the cart with Knievel all day, didn't swing a club, and won $17,000 from him," Ed Zemljak said. "Knievel would keep making these bets . . . 'I'll get a par on this next hole' or 'I'll get out of this sand trap in one shot' . . . and kept losing them. The other guy never left the cart. He won $17,000 in eighteen holes."

Zemljak, who went to both grammar school and high school with Knievel in Butte, was a six-time state amateur champion in Montana. Knievel would sign him up to be his partner in assorted big-money matches. Zemljak wouldn't bet. Knievel would bet for both of them. Zemljak would find himself trying to make a putt for $5,000 of Knievel's money. It was a certain kind of pressure, putting for Knievel's money.

"I don't think I ever played a round of golf with him that he didn't break a club," Zemljak said. "You had to watch out. He'd throw the club at the golf cart. He threw a club at the cart once, a guy jumped out just in time. The club came right through the cart, in one side, out the other. Would have killed the guy.

"Knievel would break his putter mostly. But he'd also break the driver. He'd also break the irons. He broke just about all of them."

The daredevil would stop at one of the other houses along the course, run inside to call Linda in this pre-cell-phone age to have her bring another putter, driver, seven-iron, whatever he needed, from his own house. Sometimes he would tell her to bring another $2,000. She would find him on the course to replenish his supplies. He didn't drink much while he played, but when he hit the clubhouse, the Wild Turkey factor was added. Zemljak, who didn't drink, would hang around until the third or fourth shot of bourbon was served. Then he would make a fast exit.

"The fourth shot, that's when the fights would begin," Zemljak said. "He became a wild man. He was always fighting someone, arguing about something."

Knievel wanted the last word.

That fact was never in doubt.

"There was a Lebanese guy in town, did some work for me," Muzzy Faroni, owner of the Freeway Tavern, said. "I invited him out to play golf. He said he didn't play, but came out for the afternoon. We rode around in the cart. He handed me a club, and I said—Lebanese, he was dark— 'Hey, you're the first black caddie that ever has worked this country club.' We laughed. I told Evel on the phone that he didn't have everything in this town. I had the first black caddie at the Butte Country Club."

Two days later, Knievel returned the call. He said he had a surprise for Muzzy. Muzzy should be prepared.

Maybe a week later, two black men walked into the Freeway. If two Martians had done the same thing, it wouldn't have raised as many eyebrows in Butte. The two black men asked for Muzzy by name.

"This is Rabbit," one black man said. "I'm Killer. We're here to caddie for you and Mr. Knievel this weekend."

Rabbit was Gary Player's caddie on the PGA tour. Killer was Hale Irwin's caddie. The two men hung around for the week, carried bags at the country club, told a million stories. A fine time was had by all. Knievel had the last word.

He played in every celebrity pro-am across the country that would invite him. He would use old tricks if no invitation had been extended, call the organizers and use another voice to ask if Evel Knievel was going to be in the field. That would make your tournament worth attending! The organizers would call him and offer an invitation.

He would bring the boys from the Butte Country Club to the tournaments sometimes. He would have them caddie. Muzzy was his caddie for the pro-am in the Jackie Gleason Inverrary Classic in Florida. Knievel played in a foursome with Lee Trevino. Trying to sound important, Knievel ordered Muzzy to do some caddie-like duties and do them fast.

"Go fuck yourself," Muzzy said.

Trevino stared at the scene. He never had heard such a discourse between golfer and caddie.

Jack Ferriter found himself talking with Paul Hornung at some tournament. Bob Pavlovich, a longtime St. Louis Cardinals fan, found himself drinking with Stan Musial and Roger Maris. ("I thought I was in heaven.") Maybe a dozen of the boys, plus their wives, found themselves on a private plane to Fort Lauderdale.

"The plane was owned by Jerry Lee Lewis," Sandy Keith said. "Knievel told him he was interested in buying it and wanted to try it out. He took all of us to Florida, then he told Jerry Lee that he had decided against it."

The stories now involved all these famous names. The golf involved all these famous places. Arnold Palmer said . . . and then Doug Sanders had to write out a check . . . the golf outfits were elaborate. The golf clubs, the equipment, changed from week to week, new stuff replacing old stuff. The new life was a golf life. Evel Knievel played all of those places Bob Knievel only could dream about, the places in the magazines that you'd read in the pro shop. Better than that, sometimes he was in those magazines.

A bunch of guys dared him to jump his golf cart off a ledge on a steep par 3 at the Rivermont Country Club in Alpharetta, Georgia. The path between tee and green zigged and zagged down the hill. If he jumped from the middle of one zig over the ledge, he would pick up the path in the middle of the returning zag. The guys said this certainly would be an easy jump for a man of his talents.

"For days they dared me to make the jump, and when I came to the hole in a foul mood one afternoon—I wasn't playing well—I just went for it," Knievel told *Golf Digest* writer Guy Yocum. "Halfway down the hill I realized I'd made a mistake. You have no idea how unstable a three-wheel golf cart is when it becomes airborne. By the grace of God I made a perfect three-point landing, but the tires were like basketballs, and the cart jumped like an SOB. When I got the thing stopped, down by the green, I immediately got a royal chewing out from my wife. I couldn't blame her. She'd been in the passenger seat the whole time."

Maybe it happened. Maybe not.

Sounded great.

For the opening of the movie in Butte at the Fox Theater and the Motor-Vu Drive-In a couple of years earlier, where the lines of cars clogged up Harrison Avenue that night, bad as anyone could remember, mayor Mike Micone had proclaimed July 21, 1971, Evel Knievel Day. Part of the proclamation was that "Evel Knievel is requested to stay away from the city of Butte and to take his capricious and destructive acts elsewhere." That was a laugh, part hype for the movie, part look back at his larcenous past. The request, in truth, already had been granted. Knievel already had taken his capricious and destructive acts elsewhere.

He was gone far more than he was home.

The FBI, in one of its reports, would state that "REDACTED advised that while Knievel does maintain a residence in Butte, his family resides here permanently. Since he travels considerably, he is seldom seen in the area of Butte." REDACTED was right. Not only was Knievel on the road for his shows, he also spent those long stretches of Filthy McNasty time in Los Angeles, where he boasted about his ascent from the Hollywood Land Motel to the Saharan Motel to the Country Continental, and finally to a year-round bungalow at the Beverly Hills Hotel. He was no stranger to Las Vegas, where tales came back about his gambling moments, taking a hit on 20, spending the day betting thousand-dollar bills on the wheel of fortune, being outrageous. He was soon to learn the virtues of Florida in the winter.

Visits to Butte were noisy surprises now. He no longer was someone who other people expected to see on the street.

"I worked at the Montana Power Company," Tubie Johnson, teammate from the Butte Bombers days, said. "I went to the M&M for lunch. Bob came in, asked if it was all right to sit down with me. I said sure. I hadn't seen him for a while. He started talking about how he was going to jump over the Grand Canyon, and I said, 'Yeah, yeah,' and he said he was doing pretty good, and I said, 'Yeah, yeah,' and he said, did I see that colored guy at the end of the bar? That was his chauffeur. I said, 'No shit.' Then he asked me to come outside and see his purple Rolls-Royce and, sure enough, right around the corner at Park and Main there were three people just standing there, staring at it.

"He asked what time I got off work, and I said five, and he said he'd pick me up in the Rolls. Five o'clock, there he was. The colored guy was driving. I got in the back, and Bob gave me a cigar. We drove home in the purple Rolls-Royce, smoking cigars."

The locals would study the local boy when he came back for these short, electric bursts. They would remark on whether he had or hadn't changed. Most would argue that he had. Of course he had. He was goofy maybe in high school, but he had the chance to be elaborately goofy now. He certainly was taking advantage of it. He had no appreciation for other people's money when he was growing up. He had no appreciation for his own money now. He was out of control.

"He was like those kids from the ghetto who become rich and famous athletes," Dan Killoy, who had grown up in the same Parrot Street neighborhood, said. "He didn't know how to handle it too well. He had no common sense. One on one, he was a solid human being. Get him in a crowd, he spent his whole life trying to impress people."

The big emotion attached to Bob Knievel now in Butte mostly was curiosity. How the heck did all of this happen? The good citizens were alternately bemused and flabbergasted. They laughed at what they read and what they heard. The change in Bob Knievel's status was amazing. He was the one who made it big? Personal memories of that crazy son of a bitch Bob were attached to all of the things that that crazy son of a bitch Evel Knievel did now.

The private planes, the exotic cars, the jewelry, the sponsorships for everything he did . . .

"I was down at the Spot, a bar my friend owned," Clyde Kelley said. "Evel had come back from Caesars Palace, after being in the hospital for that long time. His trailers were parked outside the bar. I was outside looking at them. They looked good, painted a sort of purple color, but U-Haul at that time was using some kind of special paint that you couldn't paint over, no matter what you did. Sure enough, if you looked at Evel's trailers when the light hit a certain way, there was 'U-Haul.' He was driving around with those stolen trailers from U-Haul, all over the country."

The grand promotion for the death-defying moments, the money that was offered . . .

"Bob came into the Met Tavern one day," Dick Pickett said. "I had a motorcycle, one of those little rice burners. Not so little, really, but, you know, Japanese. Bob said, 'Give me the keys.' I said, 'Why?' He said, 'I have a bet going with those two guys over there from Helena that I won't drive at fifty miles per hour, doing a wheelie, standing on the seat with one leg. Give me the keys.' I gave him the keys.

"The entire bar went outside to watch this. He goes down Harrison Avenue, comes back once, turns around, comes back twice. This time he's really flying. Turned around the third time, and there he is. He pulls that sucker back into a wheelie. He's standing on the seat with one leg. Everybody from the bar claps. The guys from Helena didn't want to pay . . . but they paid. Oh, yeah, they paid."

Hometowns always have surrendered their local heroes to fame. That was always part of the deal. Politicians and athletes and singers and actors and corporate hotshots all had to move to a bigger place, a more celebrated stage to fulfill their dreams. This time, though, the local hero never really had been so heroic at home. The dream seemed kind of weird. The whole thing was weird.

A local Butte politician, Paul Hoelnstein, tried to start a tongue-in-cheek campaign to run Evel Knievel for president of the United States. Hoelnstein held a press conference at the old Metals Bank Building to start the process. The mayor also came to this event. Lapel buttons that read "Vote for Evel Knievel" were distributed. The potential candidate was called on the telephone in Atlanta and informed of the grassroots movement. Someone tried to get a few political facts straight.

"What's your party?" he was asked into the phone.

"Party?" Knievel replied through the speaker. "You bet! I'm ready. Where are you having it?"

A story. Somewhere during this time, Knievel met Elvis Presley. There was a pop culture inevitability to the moment. The daredevil from Butte, Montana, and the rock 'n' roll singer from Tupelo, Mississippi, wore the same showbiz clothes, worked the same fan base, even shared the same snarl when cornered. They were bound to bump into each other sometime, King Meets Last of the Gladiators, something like that. Flashbulbs would flash. Icons would smile under their piled-up hair.

The way it happened, though, was much quieter than that. Knievel's half-sister, Loretta Young, had begun to date Presley. She introduced her brother to her boyfriend. No cameras were present.

"Elvis was playing the Intercontinental Hotel in Las Vegas, which later became the Hilton," Loretta Young said. "My brother came to a show. We sat in one of those high booths up front. When Elvis went into his last song, his manager, Joe Esposito, got us, and we went back to the dressing room. Elvis changed clothes, and we all sat around and talked."

Loretta, tall, blond, very pretty, went out with Elvis for two and a half years. He picked her out of the Folies Bergere chorus line at the Desert Sands, asked her for a date between shows. She refused because she already had a date with Jerry van Dyke, Dick van Dyke's brother. Elvis persisted, came back the next night with yellow roses and a dinner invitation, and what was a girl to do? She was charmed.

He was funnier than the world knew. He was deeper than the world knew. He was, truth be told, a much sweeter spirit than her brother. Maybe the darkness would get him in the end, fame and drugs and deep-fried peanut butter and banana sandwiches, but not now. He still read the Bible every day.

"I found out what God's real name is," he declared one afternoon. "I read it in the Bible."

"What's His real name?" she asked.

"Hallowed."

"Hallowed? What kind of name is that?"

"I don't know, but it says it right here . . . 'Hallowed be Thy name.' "

The meeting with Loretta's brother went fine. Knievel always had been impressed by celebrity. Who was a bigger celebrity than Elvis? Knievel had a line about him that he repeated often—"I guess I thought I was Elvis Presley, but I'll tell you something. All Elvis did was stand on a stage and play a guitar. He never fell off on that pavement at no eighty miles per hour." All of which was true, especially the part about thinking he was Elvis.

"When he first got those white leathers, he said that he wanted to look like Elvis," Loretta Young said. "And he did. He even had a rabbit's foot for good luck. Elvis always had a rabbit's foot for good luck too, until one day he realized where the rabbit's feet came from. He said, 'Hey, wait a minute, this wasn't such good luck for the rabbit.' He stopped carrying them."

Elvis wanted to know what projects Evel had in the works. Evel told him about Snake River and the canyon. Elvis was impressed.

"How far is that?" he asked.

"It's over a mile."

"On a motorcycle?"

"No, I have this other thing. The Skycycle."

Knievel invited Presley to the jump, whenever it happened, at the close of the conversation. Presley said he'd be glad to go. The icons shook hands, went in different directions in the Las Vegas night.

Knievel called Loretta a while later, thanked her for the meeting. He was back in Butte and bragged about the round bed he had installed in the bedroom of his new house. Loretta told him that was very nice. She said Elvis had a round bed in his personal airplane.

"In his airplane?" Knievel said.

"And he has a chinchilla bedspread for it," his sister said.

"Chinchilla?"

Two weeks later, Knievel called again. He said, yes, he had had a chinchilla bedspread made for his round bed in Butte. He said that a chinchilla bedspread was toasty warm and comfortable on a cold winter's night.

"I know," Loretta said with a wicked laugh.

A story. Somewhere around this time, Jay Tamburina went to a dinner theater in Lincolnshire, Illinois, outside Chicago. He had been one of those salesmen with Knievel in the Combined Insurance days around Butte, one of the hard chargers who wanted to grow up to be district manager Alex Smith. Time had passed, and he was still with Combined and had reached his goal.

He went to the dinner theater with a couple of other district managers. A meeting was scheduled at the Combined home office the next day, so they took advantage of the opportunity for a night out. They had very good seats, close to the stage. The star of the show was George Hamilton. Three very pretty young women sat at the next table.

When the show was finished, Tamburina was moved to make a comment to the three women. He was not married at the time.

"It's funny," he said. "George Hamilton played Evel Knievel in that movie. I worked with Evel Knievel for a couple of years, selling insurance."

"Really," one of the women replied. "I'm George Hamilton's girlfriend. George loves talking about Evel Knievel."

She invited Tamburina to stick around, meet Hamilton, to talk about Evel. Tamburina accepted. The other two district managers peeled into the night.

The meeting with Hamilton went very well. There was a bunch of drinks, a bunch of conversation. One of the women peeled away. There was a band. Hamilton got up and danced with his girlfriend. When he came back, he suggested that Tamburina dance with the other woman, Mary.

Tamburina danced. He danced a few dances.

"Look, we're all going to the Playboy Club in Lake Geneva, Wisconsin. You should come with us," Hamilton then suggested. "Mary really likes you."

Temptation screamed through Tamburina's head, a freight train of pleasant thoughts that included sex, sex, maybe a little more sex, mixed with drinking and dancing. This was his Hollywood moment, George Hamilton and him, two beautiful women.

That other train chugged into the other side of his head, slow and steady, carrying a full load of Responsibility and Duty and all of that stuff. He couldn't stop its progress.

"I really can't go," he heard himself say to George Hamilton and the two beautiful women. "I have a meeting in the morning. I have to give a presentation."

He couldn't believe the words as he said them. He wouldn't believe them for the rest of his days. How stupid was he? This was the strangest decision he ever had made.

Bob Knievel never would have done that.

The best reports of the famous daredevil's popularity came from the emergency rooms. The children of America—mostly adolescents, but some younger, some much younger—would arrive with cuts and contusions, compound fractures and missing teeth, every now and then a badly injured internal organ. The dialogue between doctor and patient always would be the same.

"How'd you hurt yourself?"

"Well, I saw this guy on television . . ."

In Minneapolis, a nine-year-old cleared five garbage cans with his bicycle, but landed wrong and needed fifteen stitches and $400 worth of dental surgery. In Boise, Idaho, a sixteen-year-old cleared a ditch with his bike, but struck a house and suffered a severe concussion. In New York City, a nine-year-old drove his bike off a ramp and was impaled on his handlebars, suffering grave liver damage. In Salt Lake City, a seven-year-old girl, serious head trauma . . . in Brooklyn, a six-year-old, trying to clear three milk cases, critical condition . . . in Muncie, Indiana, a seven-year-old, impact so hard that his backbone "acted like a knife and cut his pancreas in half."

On and on it went. In Boston, three young doctors started writing down the case histories for the injuries they witnessed at Boston City Hospital. The reports were the same as everywhere else:

Case 1—MC, fourteen years old, had lacerations of the face and
   buckle fractures of the right digital radius and ulna. He had

accepted a dare to ride his bicycle over a plank pitched against sawhorses to land on a plank on the other side. He came up short.

Case 2—MB, fifteen, had fractures of both his right and left radius and a fracture of his mandibular symphasis. He pretty much had tried the same stunt as case 1, except he did it on a motorbike.

Case 3—JF, eleven, had numerous facial lacerations and two missing permanent front teeth. He and his friends had been riding their bikes down a wooden ski jump they built. He landed wrong, shot over the handlebars.

The three doctors, Joel Daven, J. F. O'Connor, and Roy Briggs, wrote a paper on the situation for *Pediatrics*, the official journal of the American Academy of Pediatrics. They pointed out the susceptibility of kids to what comes across the television screen, especially violent, risky acts performed by charismatic, heroic figures. The name of the paper was "The Consequences of Imitative Behavior in Children: The Evel Knievel Syndrome."

That was how famous Evel Knievel had become, how far away he was from home. He was from Butte, Montana, and he had his own syndrome.

17 Deals

The oft-promised canyon jump, no more than promotional whimsy for such a long time, a professionally painted line on the trailer, a subject for discussion on the talk shows, then not much more than a home workshop daydream for the rocket boys, Malewicki and Truax, finally became an actual possibility in the first months of 1974. That was when twenty-eight-year-old promoter Vince McMahon Jr. showed up in Butte.

Destined for substantial and curious levels of fame and fortune in future years as the head of World Wrestling Entertainment, where he would star as a villainous character in his own raucous productions, McMahon was at the beginning of his career in 1974. Fortune was the dimmest of lights in the distance. He lived with his wife and young kids in a trailer park in West Hartford, Connecticut, and ran wrestling shows on weekends in the state of Maine.

His father, Vince McMahon Sr., was a longtime promoter out of Washington, D.C. The wrestling map was sliced into a number of local fiefdoms, each part of the country run by a different operator, and Vince Sr. was responsible for all of the shows in the Northeast. Vince Jr. was a late addition to Vince Sr.'s life. He had lived with his divorced mother at first, never met his father until he was twelve, but now was determined to become an important part of the family business.

Enthusiasm was part of his nature. He bubbled with ideas for expansion on all levels, everything bigger, better, amped up, flamboyant. Vince Sr., a veteran of the wrestling wars (*his* father also had been a promoter) took a more cautious approach. Maine was a fine place for his son to get started. Maine. How much damage could he do in Maine?

For the younger McMahon, the trip to Butte was a way to break out of Maine. Knievel was his personal project. He had watched the *Wide World* jumps and was taken with Knievel's natural ease with the camera, with the life-or-death excitement that crackled off the television set as he shot off that ramp. Vince Jr. knew about the toys, the products, the George Hamilton movie. This was the stuff of the same youth market that he wanted not only to inhabit but to dominate with wrestling. The jump from one "sport" to the other did not seem like a big jump at all.

To him, Knievel very much resembled a wrestler with his over-the-top approach to life, with the clothes, the cars, the cocky pronouncements, the comic-strip exaggeration to everything he did. The daredevil had a substantial touch of Gorgeous George to him, worked with the same flair as the bleach-blond bad boy wrestler of the fifties who dispensed bobby pins, blew kisses to his fans, brought a revised importance to showmanship in the game. Knievel had some of the qualities of other wrestlers too.

"Argentine Rocca, one of our biggest stars, always had a saying about wrestlers," McMahon said. " 'Brains by the ounce, balls by the ton.' "

Potential promoter never had met potential client before the trip to Butte, had talked with him only once on the phone to set up the visit. Potential client was waiting at the airport. He was driving a customized white Cadillac that rode on oversized tires. The tires were so large that they couldn't complete certain turns.

"The tires would hit the wheel wells if you turned much at all," McMahon said. "So we drove some interesting routes through Butte that didn't need much turning. Everything had to be figured out. You knew he was a different kind of cat right there. A showman."

Knievel always had been wary of promoters, battled with all of them, broke with most of them at some point, even J. C. Agajanian. He prefered to run his own shows, but knew he needed outside help in a production as large as the canyon jump. He also needed outside financing. A lot of outside financing. The plan was to show the event on closed-circuit television in theaters and arenas across the country, something that had been done with varying rates of success for major boxing matches since the fifties. McMahon's father had been one of the distributors, one of the promoters for these broadcasts, so his company offered a history, a certain expertise.

The meeting went well. McMahon thought he saw the same charisma from Knievel in person that he had seen on television. Knievel thought he saw, at last, someone who might get this production rolling. McMahon went home to try to cajole his father into backing at least part of the show.

"The only thing that surprised me was the way Knievel treated his family," McMahon said. "I'd never seen anything like it. He was pretty dogmatic with his wife, ordering her around, and he wasn't all that kind to his kids. I kept wondering if this was a show he was putting on for the guy from New York or what it was. He was particularly rude to his wife."

McMahon wrote it off as cultural differences. Maybe this was the way marriages worked in Montana. Who could be sure? His unease surely wasn't enough to make him give up the idea of backing the show. The rest of Knievel was absolutely what he expected.

"He was a great self-promoter," McMahon said. "His instincts were great. He was one of those larger-than-life guys. He had courage and wasn't afraid to risk his life. Just the idea of getting into that thing, that rocket, and not knowing what would happen next . . . not many men would do that."

Vince McMahon Sr. did not share his son's enthusiasm. He didn't like the promotion, didn't like the unknown, untested, untried aspects of the show. A rocket, a canyon, and a goofball left a lot of possibilities for disaster. Who would pay good money to see this? Vince Sr. was fifty-nine years old, would be sixty by the time the rocket took off. He didn't need the bother.

In the end, though, to please his son, maybe to deliver a lesson, he agreed to bankroll 50 percent of the costs. This did not mean he was happy about doing it.

"He hated the canyon jump," Vince Jr. said. "I had a chance to sell our interest later on, and my father was yelling at me to make a deal. He said I should take any price, sell it all for a couple of dollars, give it away, just get out. I never did."

McMahon Sr. did try to give his son the best possible chance of success. In recruiting a 50 percent partner for the production, the father approached forty-three-year-old Bob Arum, the Harvard Law School graduate who had emerged as one of the leading boxing promoters in the world. The request was personal.

"I'd worked with Vince, the father," Arum said. "He was a good, good guy. He asked me to be part of the canyon jump to look out for his son.

He caught me at a good time. I didn't have anything going on. I was a little itchy for some action."

Arum had begun his career in the U.S. Attorney's Office in New York, where he was part of a task force investigation for the Internal Revenue Service into underworld influences in the boxing business, specifically the tax returns from the heavyweight title fight between Floyd Patterson and Sonny Liston. Studying the topic, he became fascinated with the mechanics of promoting big fights and the possibilities for financial success. He decided that he, a novice, could do a better job for everyone concerned than these old-line gangsters did. He quit the U.S. Attorney's Office, put together some ideas, and convinced pro football Hall of Fame running back Jim Brown, one of heavyweight champion Muhammad Ali's friends, to secure an audience with Ali's Muslim advisers. The interview led to Arum's role as promoter of the Ali–George Chuvalo fight in 1965, the first fight he ever had seen.

Nine years later, after a long and prosperous run with Ali, directly after Arum's company, Top Rank Inc., staged the second Ali-Frazier bout at Madison Square Garden on January 28, 1974, a twelve-round decision for Ali, the promoter suddenly found himself without his best client. Rival promoter Don King controlled present heavyweight champ George Foreman, and Ali had signed with King to fight Foreman in Kinshasa, Zaire, in "the Rumble in the Jungle" on October 30, 1974. Arum was on the sidelines.

Unless he went into the canyon jump business.

"Ali came to me, asking what to do," Arum said. "Don King and John Daly, the British promoter, had put together all of this money for Zaire. The fighters were guaranteed $5 million apiece. I told Ali, what the heck, take the money, and he did, but that still sort of stung. I was susceptible to doing something else. This was it."

He traveled to Cleveland with the younger McMahon and met with Knievel on the weekend of May 25–27, 1974. Knievel was appearing at Dragway 42 in nearby West Salem, Ohio, where he successfully jumped ten Mack trucks. Arum did not know much about Knievel, and Knievel did not know much about Arum. The meeting was not without its complications.

"There are three kinds of people I can't stand," Knievel said early in the conversation. "New Yorkers, lawyers, and Jews."

Arum was all three. Maybe the partnership would get no further than the introductions. He stuck around to find out. Was Knievel joking? Or was this how he really felt? This was interesting.

There was little doubt Arum came from an entirely different universe. His sensibilities, experiences, hell, his clothes, were entirely different. Arum was a city kid, born in Brooklyn, had lived in New York for most of his life. Yes, he was Jewish. Yes, he was a lawyer. He wore glasses, had gone to college, to law school. His mind ran in a certain direction. Yes, he worked for the negotiation, the adjustment, the business compromise. That was his training. He was as tough as Knievel. His toughness simply was seen in different arenas.

Don King, who soon became Arum's major competitor and sworn enemy, once described him to Vic Ziegel of *New York* magazine by telling a fable about an asp and an alligator. Arum was the asp in the story, a terrified creature who asks the alligator to give him a ride to the other side of the river because floodwaters are rising.

"I can't do that," the alligator says. "Because I know you'd bite me."

"I wouldn't do that," the asp replies. "If I bit you, we'd both drown. If you die, I die too."

The alligator appreciates the asp's logic. Gives him a ride. Halfway across the river, the asp bites the alligator on the back. The alligator screams.

"Why?" he says. "Now we're both going to die. Why would you do that?"

"I can't help it," the asp says. "I'm a snake."

"That's Arum," King told Ziegel, then shuffled metaphors thoroughly. "He sticks so many daggers in your back you look like a porcupine."

Knievel was a cowboy. That was Arum's opinion. The daredevil was bluster and force. Opinions flew off him in a constant storm. What was real? What wasn't? This moment's opinion could be replaced by the opinion of the next moment. The man was a whirlwind, a meteorological disturbance that moved through a perpetually hurried day. Nothing was subtle.

"He was with a whole coterie of people, ordering everybody around," Arum later said to a reporter in a description of that first meeting. "He never sat still for a minute. He kept giving speeches. At first, he never let me get a word in edgewise. I'm pretty forceful when I speak. I had come to Cleveland to put across my point, but Evel has a tendency to chop people up—not by doing a job on them, but by chopping them up and not letting them get in an idea or a thought of their own and just really using the person he is talking to as a platform to get his own ideas across."

The trick was to wait him out, not to argue. That was what Arum quickly decided. Argue and Knievel would balk, never budge. Much better to slip in a thought, let it percolate, let him find the logic for himself. A test, when Arum finally was able to speak a bit, was the proposed structure of the show that would surround the canyon jump.

The problem with the jump, with all of Knievel's jumps, was that they didn't take very long. They were finished in a matter of seconds. He could string out the process, ride back and forth on the motorcycle, do a few wheelies, warm up a few times before the actual attempt, but even that option would be missing from the canyon.

Knievel always had envisioned a short show that opened with a film about his life, maybe half an hour long, then the buildup to the jump, then the jump itself, then replays and interviews. Arum suggested—only suggested—that people would want more for their closed-circuit money. He suggested—that word again—that a number of daredevil acts perform before Evel closed the show. Like boxing, there would be an undercard. People would feel better about spending their money.

Knievel thought about it. Agreed.

"If you hit him too hard, he becomes so obstinate you can't do anything with him," Arum said. "But gradually, if he takes the time to sit by himself and think—he's an extremely intelligent guy—and when he eliminates his emotional initial reaction, the idea made a lot of sense and he went along with it."

By the end of the Cleveland visit, both men had thought about what the other one said and decided to do what made sense. Knievel felt confident that he wasn't going to be flimflammed by this fast talker from New York. The fast talker made business sense. Arum decided that he could live with the cowboy. He had lived with a variety of personalities in the boxing business, lived with Muhammad Ali. He could figure out how to live with this guy.

They shook hands on a deal.

The decision was made easy by the fact that ABC television also wanted to be part of the operation. The network had scored well in the ratings with the L.A. Coliseum jump on *Wide World of Sports* in November of 1973, then came back with a jump three months later on

February 17, 1974, from the Green Valley Raceway at North Richland Hills, Texas. Howard Cosell and Don Meredith were the announcers as Knievel tried to clear eleven Mack trucks. The presence of Cosell and Meredith, two of the three voices from *Monday Night Football*, still the hottest show on television after four seasons, showed the importance the network placed on the show.

> DANDY DON: This is really exciting to me. I've never really seen Evel jump. I've enjoyed talking to him. He's a very unusual fellow when you think about it. This is the guy who's going to jump over this canyon, the Devil Snake River, whatever the darn thing is . . . Snake Canyon River, that's it . . . but in any event, I don't really understand all this stuff. Why in the world does he do this, Howard?
>
> HOWARD: Well, he put it philosophically with the three basic questions of life, as he sees it. Where do you come from, what are you doing, and where do you go from here?
>
> DANDY DON: And here he comes right now.

The network was a natural partner for Snake River. Long seen as almost a comical third to NBC and CBS in the ratings competition that dominated all of television, ABC had found its place at last. Focusing on the baby boomer youth market, using game shows like *The Dating Game* and *The Newlywed Game*, comedies like *The Brady Bunch* and *Bewitched* (and *Happy Days*, scheduled to debut in the fall of 1974), and dramas like *The Mod Squad*, ABC was strong in sports, with *Monday Night Football* and *Wide World of Sports*, familiar with Evel, and full of big ideas for Snake River.

On April 6, 1974, the network recorded "California Jam," a West Coast answer to Woodstock at the Ontario Motor Speedway, and split it into four different shows. The festival—which featured Deep Purple; the Eagles; Black Sabbath; Earth, Wind, and Fire; and Emerson, Lake, and Palmer—drew over 250,000 people and, unlike Woodstock, ran without any major problems, even when Deep Purple guitarist Richie Blackmore blew up his gasoline-soaked amplifiers and caused a commotion.

The man who ran the show was Don E. Branker, a twenty-eight-year-old former musician and cowboy from California's San Joaquin Valley. He had the long blond hair and mustache of a musician, liked to dabble in the illegal substances he found around him, but had cowboy sensibilities when it came to hard work. ABC was impressed with the way he handled such a large event.

When California Jam ended, Branker found himself on a private jet with young network executives Dick Ebersol and Don Ohlmeyer, headed toward Twin Falls, Idaho, and Snake River. ABC gave him $10,000 to prepare a report on the feasibility of a rock festival on the far edge of the canyon. The network envisioned sort of a Woodstock-plus, great music added to the sight of America's daredevil shooting through the sky.

At Snake River, Branker combed the real estate that would be used on both sides of the canyon. The only discernible structure anywhere was a large dirt mound put together by Ray Gunn before he left, plus a steeply angled launch ramp on top of that. The far side of the canyon was desolate. It reminded Branker of what the surface of Mars must be like. He went home to California and typed out a ten-page report. His basic advice for the network was "no."

"Two things ruled it out in my mind," he said. "First was accessibility. The few roads were very small. There were no hotels to speak of. There was nowhere for people to stay, to eat, no ways to get around. Twin Falls was a town of maybe sixteen thousand. It could never handle the crowds they were talking about.

"The second thing was that the rocket had no guidance system. Nobody knew where it was going to land. How could you have all of those people over there, not knowing where the rocket would land? It was a disaster waiting to happen."

Branker sent the report to New York, cashed the check, thought he was done with the Snake River Canyon jump. A month later, he was its executive producer, headed back to Twin Falls to figure out how everything would work.

ABC had scrapped the rock concert, but was enthusiastic about the jump. It was now a partner with Arum and McMahon. The network would provide all of the production, plus concentrated pre-event publicity. The extent of ABC's involvement would be a secret. The promoters would have their own announcers for the closed-circuit shows in the theaters, but one week later ABC would put its version of the event on free television. The show had to be kept a secret—a situation that would become quite ungainly when trucks and cameras with ABC logos on the side appeared everywhere around the canyon—to protect the closed-circuit gate.

"We were pioneers in televising Evel's feats," ABC senior vice president

Jim Spence said, explaining the decision to join the promotion. "We had a good relationship with Arum because we'd worked with him in boxing. We were the only game in town—why CBS and NBC didn't want it, I don't know—so we were able to control the pricing. We got a fair rights fee. We thought it would do very well in the ratings."

"One of our producers, before the jump at the Coliseum, had said, 'You know who Knievel reminds me of? Conrad Birdie,' " Dennis Lewin, senior vice president for production at ABC, said. "So throughout the jump, we kept playing music from *Bye-Bye Birdie*, the musical. When he made the jump, we played 'We Love You, Birdie.' That's when we started dipping our toe into Evel Knievel."

Now the network was in much further.

Development of the Skycycle, an essential piece of the production, had gone slowly during the long wait for funding. Bob Truax instituted a no-money-no-work policy because he had such trouble getting promised checks from Knievel. Truax's curious scientific mind wouldn't let him stop altogether, so he still tinkered with the X-2, but he wouldn't add more helpers, buy more equipment, until he knew they would be covered financially.

Now, in May of 1974, the situation changed in an instant. The funds from ABC and Top Rank, etc., became capital to finish the X-2, then build a second, matching rocket. The production pace shifted from virtual standstill to everyday chaos. The September 8, 1974, launch date—no chance for postponement because of the closed-circuit production, tickets purchased, fans in their seats—meant that the project had to be completed in less than four frenzied months.

"We can hold the audience for about twenty minutes," Bob Arum told Truax, underlining the importance of staying on schedule. "After that, people start asking for their money back."

Truax's situation had changed since he started working on the rocket two years earlier. He had retired from the civil service in Potomac, Maryland, and recently relocated to Saratoga, California, with a plan to take a consulting job at a famous university like Stanford or with some high-tech company in "Silicon Valley," which was the new name for the area around San Jose. His first version of the X-2 pretty much had been completed in the backyard in Potomac, so he wound up transporting the rocket across the length of the United States.

This was done in a large trailer built to carry the steam-powered drag racer he had built for Walt Arfons. (The drag racer, certifiably fast, never had great success because of handling problems. It also left great puddles on the track, which forced postponement or cancellation of following races.) Truax hitched the trailer to his Ford Ranchero and clanged and banged across America, adventures and misadventures along the way, his cargo somehow intact and functional at the end.

The X-2 was a different rocket from the X-1 built by the departed Malewicki. Truax never liked the X-1, thought it didn't have enough power or safety considerations. Part of his new deal with Knievel was that he could start over again. He told Knievel that he would stay out of the public relations if Knievel would stay out of the engineering, pay in advance, and let him build a rocket that would get Knievel over the canyon safely. Knievel agreed to the terms.

Malewicki's X-1 had been stylish, sleek, had the two wheels that gave it at least some relationship to a motorcycle. The rocket had been destroyed by Truax in a test at Snake River on November 3, 1973, mostly done for promotional purposes in hopes of landing a sponsor. The tanks had been only half-filled, so the X-1 was doomed to fall into the canyon even before it took off. Truax worried for a minute that maybe the thing would get into the air, loop around, and come flying straight at the gathered group at the launch site, but the flight went fine. The rocket ran out of steam, flipped over, spun deep into the canyon, splashed into the river at the bottom.

Knievel, present for the launch, looked into the canyon. He cast out any grim thoughts when he spoke.

"This is a success," he said. "This was what we wanted to do."

The X-2 that Truax had built was not nearly as pretty, but more rugged. The body came from an old jet airplane wingtip that he had found at a salvage yard for $100. The fins were surplus helicopter fins that he had adapted. The autopilot came from an old Nike missile. The steam engine, more powerful than the one Truax had built for the X-1, was the same engine that he had used for the Arfons drag racer. The new rocket was a composite, put together from a lot of used parts. A bucket of bolts. That was what it was.

Now it sat in Truax's new backyard in Saratoga.

"Before long I was putting the finishing touches on the X-2," Truax wrote in an unpublished autobiography. "We had come this far on a very limited budget, but in May [1974], Knievel called me and told me to pull out all stops. He had found a sponsor with deep pockets . . . What followed were wondrous days. We never knew how long the project would take or what kind of difficulties we would encounter, so no effort less than the maximum would do. We worked until we were ready to drop."

The X-2 had to be finished, then test-fired, because Truax frankly wanted to see if his theories actually worked. A second X-2, what he called "the flight bird"—the rocket Knievel actually would ride—had to be built from scratch, adjustments made after the results of the test firing were known. Truax hired engineers, electricians, sheet-metal workers, a parachute expert, even his son and nephew, to get things done. He had as many as fifteen people on the job.

"We went from a lot of time, no money, to no time, a lot of money," engineer Facundo Campoy, who had worked with Truax from the beginning, said. "It was quite a change."

Innovation ruled. This was not NASA. To substitute for wind tunnel tests, the crew would tow the thirteen-foot rocket on a trailer up and down the freeways. ("Not ideal," Truax admitted.) To test the engine, the process was more complicated. Truax or someone would go to Pacific Rentals and rent a dump truck for the weekend, neglecting to mention the reason for the rental. A ramp then would be welded onto the truck, the rocket placed on the ramp. The crew would drive the dump truck and rocket to a drag strip, where the back of the truck would be raised to a fifty-seven-degree angle, the same angle as liftoff. The back axle would be locked, and the steam engine would be tested.

The water had to be heated to 600 degrees, which took a while, so the heating would begin before the crew and truck left from Truax's house. They stopped one day for gas, the attendant coming out of the station to service a dump truck with a rocket on the back. The rocket engine was bubbling and hissing.

"You guys steam-clean cars or something?" the attendant asked.

At the end of the weekend, the crew would remove the rocket, take off the ramp, paint over the spots where the welds had been, then try to dirty them up as if nothing happened. The owner of Pacific Rentals never said anything until he saw his truck—his truck?—and the rocket one night on the evening news.

"It's a complex vehicle, and all kinds of things could go wrong," Truax explained about his creation in an interview. "But if the engine valves work okay, if the vehicle doesn't roll over, if there's no major structural failure, if the parachutes deploy, if it comes down straight and hits level ground, if the damn thing doesn't fold up around Evel's neck, it's a success."

Work continued. That was the deal. The engineer engineered.

The star of the show went out to do the public relations.

18 America

The idea for the phony check came from the star of the show. The star of the show suggested that Bob Arum present him with a $6 million down payment on the certain Snake River Canyon fortune that would follow on September 8, 1974. The check would be the highlight of the press conference on June 24, 1974, to announce the event in New York City.

The promoter was not amused.

"Your guarantee is $225,000," he pointed out to the star of the show. "That's what we owe you. Not $6 million."

No, no, the check only would be for publicity purposes. This would be a flash of excitement, lending a touch of glamour to the proceedings. The assembled correspondents, sad sacks that they were in their gray and purposeless lives, would be thrilled to be in the room with just the idea of that much money. There already was one *Six Million Dollar Man*, the television show, with Lee Majors as Steve Austin, at the top of the ratings. Simply make another one.

"I wouldn't cash the check," Evel Knievel said. "You'd just present it to me. The way I figure it . . ."

And here Arum recounted the quote, years later, as he remembered it.

" 'If those two African Americans [George Foreman and Muhammad Ali, scheduled to fight on September 25] are going to be paid $5 million apiece to fight in Zaire, then I should be paid $6 million to jump a canyon in the United States,' " Arum said the star of the show said. "Except he used another word for 'African Americans.' "

Arum thought the check would be a good joke more than a promotional tool or headline on any stories. He went along with the idea, dragged public relations man Shelly Saltman with him to the Chase Manhattan Bank in the morning to see if they could rent or borrow a certified check for $6 million for an hour, maybe two, maybe with a couple of accompanying rented security guards for emphasis. When the bank turned down the proposal, Arum wrote the check himself from a Top Rank checkbook that never could cover that amount.

"It was a joke," Arum said. "A joke."

The press conference was held in the Belvedere Grill of the Rainbow Room on the sixty-fifth floor of Rockefeller Center. The turnout was terrific, another indication that all of those movies about New York sophistication weren't totally correct. Knievel, who only arrived in town at nine in the morning from Butte, then was forced to change in the car, entered the proceedings dressed in a white suit, red shoes, and a red shirt with an exaggerated collar. His cane and assorted jewelry completed the picture. Arum, introducing him in front of a large picture of Snake River Canyon, said, "On September 9 he will be the most famous person in the world." The crowd applauded the importance of the man, the projected moment, the jewelry, the cane, maybe the majesty of his red shoes.

"I don't know if I'm an athlete, a daredevil, a hoax, or just a nut," Knievel said. "But when I make that jump, I'll be competing against the toughest opponent of all—and that's death."

An intense promotional tour would start the next morning, an eye-popping, mind-numbing thirty-nine cities across the country in twelve days, so this was where he established the message he would hammer home to the American public. The major theme was not hard to discern.

"I'd say 5 percent of the people want to see me die," he said. "Forty-five percent don't want to see me die, but they want to be there if I do. And 50 percent are pulling for me."

"Whatever I get out of this thing, be it win, lose, no draw, because there can't be no draw, I deserve it because I've paid the price for success," he said. "If I miss it, I'll wait for you. Because dying is part of living. None of us are going to get out of here alive. If Mother Nature doesn't get you, Father Time will."

"Bob Truax says my chances are fifty-fifty . . . *if*," he said. "One, if the vehicle does not blow up on the launch ramp. Two, if it goes straight up in the air and does not flip over backwards and come back into the crowd. Three, if it goes 2,000 feet up at 350 miles per hour and goes across the canyon. Four, if the parachute systems open. Five, if, when they open, I come down on the other side and can stand the G forces. And six, if I can get out of the vehicle."

Death and disfigurement sat in the room as surely as they did when he was selling those Combined Insurance policies at the insane asylum in Warm Springs, Montana. Something bad could happen here. The good-looking man right in front of you, ladies and gentlemen, very well could be a walking, talking corpse. The name of the tour was "Evel Knievel Says Good-Bye," supposedly because he would retire after this jump, but if the paying customer wanted to infer another kind of good-bye, well, that was all right too.

Numbers associated with the production came out in a dizzying sequence that gave everything a certain authenticity. The Skycycle would be fired off a 108-foot ramp at a 56-degree angle . . . 15,000 pounds of jet horsepower . . . had to travel 1,400 feet . . . would be 500 feet down into the canyon . . . etc. Knievel had spent $500,000 for the development of the Skycycle . . . $300,000 for testing . . . $100,000 simply for concessions and latrines at the site! The numbers would change during the tour, some of them preposterous ($500,000 for the development of the Skycycle?), some of them rough estimates (500 feet down into the canyon), but they were rarely questioned. Delivery was everything. Any numbers sounded fine if they were delivered with style.

"Your own mental attitude is the one thing you possess over which you have complete control," Napoleon Hill and W. Clement Stone had advised. "Memorize: I feel healthy! I feel happy! I feel alive!"

The $6 million check was another number placed on top of the pile. Arum presented the check as if it were real. Knievel accepted it as if it were nothing more than justice for a man who was prepared to do the scary thing he was prepared to do. The check supposedly was a guarantee against 60 percent of the closed-circuit revenue. Top Rank and the promoters would receive the other 40 percent.

"Evel is being guaranteed the highest amount of money for any athlete or performer in the history of closed-circuit television or any other television," Arum said. "He is being guaranteed the sum of six million dollars, but believe me, we won't be happy until Evel's percentage goes to ten or eleven million dollars."

"I'll outdraw the Pro Bowl and the Super Bowl put together," Knievel said. "And I'll make more money than any heavyweight fighter in history."

Photographers took pictures of Knievel and Arum with the check. Photographers took pictures of Knievel alone, pointing at the picture of the canyon with his cane. Photographers took a lot of pictures. The dimensions for the possible live crowd were drawn in Woodstock numbers, 200,000 people or more. The record for a closed-circuit telecast was slightly over 1.5 million viewers for the first Ali-Frazier bout three years earlier, a record sure to be broken. Knievel promised a million-dollar party in Butte before he took off in the Skycycle, an armored truck following him everywhere, free drinks for the world. He invited the pope. He invited Elvis, Aristotle Onassis and Jackie, O. J. Simpson, Bart Starr, Mario Andretti, the queen of England. He invited the world. Life would be wonderful for the newest Six Million Dollar Man. If, of course, he survived.

"I'll be a winner," he promised. "I'll live like nobody else you've ever seen live. Lots of people who have a lot of dough like to put it in banks. I like to spend it. I figure if God wanted me to hang on to it, he'd have put handles on it."

Arum was amazed that no one questioned the check, no one questioned the numbers. The stories that ran the next day talked about the $6 million payment as if it were essential fact. The promotion was a staggering success already. The expenses for the show, the jump, the attraction, were being overestimated by as much as twenty-five times what they truly cost. No one was complaining. The show sounded like it was much bigger than it was.

"Dave Anderson put the $6 million figure in the *New York Times*," Arum said. "He would be mad at me forever for that. I told him it was a joke. He was not amused. He'd won the Pulitzer Prize, Dave Anderson. Everybody believed the check."

Not everybody. Not exactly.

After the press conference, Knievel and the promoters adjourned to the bar at the Regency Hotel, where he was staying. Somewhere in the proceedings, Knievel pulled the waiter close, told him he wanted to pay for the drinks, and asked if he could pay with a check. Knievel gave him the $6 million check. The waiter went all the way to the cashier before he noticed the number that was written on the check. He returned to Knievel and said he was sorry, but the hotel could not handle a check of this size.

"That's all right," Knievel said, taking another check out of his wallet.

This was the real Top Rank check for the real $225,000. The waiter came back again. The hotel couldn't handle this check either.

The tour began the next morning. First stop: Providence, Rhode Island. The mode of travel was a Lear jet, leased from a company in Dallas, repainted with Evel Knievel logos, renamed "the Montana State Rare Bird." (A lighthearted bill had been filed by Montana state senator Neil Lynch to give Knievel that designation.) The core group of travelers on the seven-seat plane, besides pilots Art Jones and Jerry Manthey, were Knievel; Arum; Shelly Saltman, the public relations man for Invest West Sports; an added financial backer, Zeke Rose, the public relations man for Ideal Toys; and Dick St. John, a lawyer for Knievel.

A crowd, estimated at two thousand people, was at La Guardia to see him leave. Another crowd, same size, was at T. F. Green Airport in Warwick, Rhode Island, to see him land. Both crowds were young, the types of crowds that would gather to spot music stars or Hollywood celebrities. A seventeen-year-old girl told the Associated Press in Warwick that she had told her boss that she needed the day off to attend a funeral. She did not feel she was lying.

"It will be the last chance we have to see him," she said, meaning Evel.

The jet hopped from Providence to Hartford, to Boston, to Albany, then Buffalo, before the day was done. Death came along for all of the rides, sat up front at Knievel's side at the press conferences, a half-beat away from dominating all conversations.

"Do you have a death wish?" was a question somewhere in the first wave of all questions.

"Yes, I do" always was the answer. "I want to die at 105 years old of natural causes in bed with two good-looking broads."

An extensive press kit—"It is not immodest to state that this kit represents the finest assembly of material ever prepared for the exhibitor's promotion of a closed-circuit television attraction," a press release for the press kit boasted—was given to each member of the media, a big pile left with each of the individual exhibitors.

The Knievel legend was replayed in the kit, easy alterations and all. He was in jail with Awful Knofel. He was in a coma after the failed jump at Caesars Palace. He was half-drunk in Moose's Place in Kalispell, Montana, when he saw that picture of the Grand Canyon. Facts didn't matter.

A series of press releases chronicled the exploits of various daredevils through history. Harry Houdini, the magician. Sir Edmund Hillary, the conqueror of Mount Everest. The Wallendas, the tightrope family dogged by tragedy. The idea was that newspapers could run a story a day about these people, to give the jump historical context. One of the stories was about Clem Sohn, a barnstorming air-show performer in the 1930s, a "kindred spirit" to Knievel.

"He [Sohn] perfected a set of homemade wings, lowered himself from an airplane, glided down from 20,000 feet to just 800 and then opened his parachute," the press release read. "But on April 25, 1937, Clem Sohn took one gamble too many. During an aerial show in Vincennes, France, his chute failed to open. At age 26, as 100,000 horrified spectators watched, Clem Sohn plunged to his death."

The operative word, again, was "death."

Pittsburgh, Cleveland, and Detroit were the major stops on the second day, Knievel's mortality put on display in each city. He sounded as if he knew Clem Sohn's story all too well.

"After all the backup systems I told you about, I have two more backup systems," Knievel said in Pittsburgh, or maybe it was Cleveland, or maybe it was Detroit. "I can say the Lord's Prayer in ten seconds, that's one. And if that doesn't work, I'm going to spit against the canyon wall just before I hit and turn around backwards, and they'll carve me into that baby like those presidents in South Dakota [at Mount Rushmore]."

These words were recorded by Shelly Saltman. One of the components of the tour, part of everyday life, quickly became Saltman's tape recorder. He recorded most of the question-and-answer stops, plus some casual conversation during the day. He was writing a book.

"I was part of the promotion for the Ali-Frazier fight in 1971 at Madison Square Garden," he said. "A couple of guys I worked with, Art Fisher and Neil Marshall, good guys, wrote a book about the promotion named *Garden of Innocence*. I read it, and it was fine, but I kept saying, 'I remember this,' or 'I was there for that,' and thinking I could have written that book. When this promotion came around, I decided to try it, to write a book just about the promotion. I cleared it with Evel, with his attorney, Fred Bezark. Evel was going to get some of the money if it ever was published."

Saltman, forty-three years old, was a California transplant, a chatterbox originally from Boston who thought he basically could sell anything to anybody. He had landed in Hollywood to work with Andy Williams, the singer, and had worked with clients from the Osmonds to Fabian to Muhammad Ali. He once had been part of a promotion to stage a boxing exhibition between Ali and Wilt Chamberlain, a fight that never happened.

Names of famous people were dropped into his typical conversation more often than pauses for punctuation. He was a nonstop optimist, a glad-hander of the first order, a promotional land mine, an explosion of good cheer put in places where he could do the most commercial good. His wife, Mollie, once had given him a set of California vanity license plates that read "CON MAN." He loved them.

Unlike Arum, he had run across Knievel years earlier. Back at the beginning, back when Knievel was going to do the shows at the Ascot Park racetrack for J. C. Agajanian, the daredevil appeared at a luncheon meeting of the Southern California Broadcasters Association. The site was Red Tracton's restaurant in Encino. Saltman was there.

He remembered that Knievel started doing wheelies in the parking lot, then on the street outside the restaurant, roaring up and down. He attracted a crowd that included the local police. They were going to give him a ticket, or maybe take him back to the station.

"A couple of broadcasters, Tom Kelly and Gil Stratton, talked to the police for him," Saltman said. "They were well-known guys. The police let him go."

Saltman remembered the afternoon as interesting, different. A book about promoting this guy did not seem like a bad idea. Things happened around him.

The size of the aircraft (everything so cramped that the pile of press releases had to be moved off the seat that converted to an emergency toilet when someone felt an emergency need) combined with the long sky-hop days to accelerate the socialization process for the group of travelers. Everyone came to know everyone else in a hurry.

Or at least everyone came to know the star of the show.

His whims, his moods, quickly dominated the small group. He was the cowboy, indeed, the one-man whirlwind that Arum first had described. Except he was whirling faster now. He delivered his pronouncements on all things. He did not ask for many questions from the floor. What he said—right down to his prediction for the weather—was the ultimate word. There was little doubt that he was in charge. This was the way he treated the boys from Butte. This apparently was the way he treated everyone.

The fact that he drank was not a surprise, since he readily had shown the features of his screw-top cane everywhere with great pride. The fact that he drank so much, starting with a double bourbon and soda for breakfast every day, was a great surprise. He charged the night hard, no matter where the plane landed, until three or four in the morning. He was back at seven or eight for takeoff, strapped into his seat with his breakfast double bourbon and soda. Cocktails pretty much were served on a twenty-four-hour basis.

His affection for pretty women also was not a mystery. He certainly had repeated it many times in public, the idea that he was married, loved his wife, but also kept an active and ever-growing list of conquests on the side. The sight of all this activity still could be unsettling. This was an intimate look at the sexual revolution.

"He tells me I should sit with this girl at the press conference," public relations man Joey Goldstein, hired to be part of the New York kick-off, said. "She's about nineteen years old, I figure, his girlfriend, and I'll say she might be the second-most-beautiful woman in the world only because there might be someone else in Tibet or somewhere who's just a little more beautiful. We sit at this table, and Evel is at the next table with his wife, and I guess everybody knows who everybody else is, and he gets up and talks about how he loves his family. It was all just strange."

Women treated him as if he were a rock star. He treated them as if they had damn good judgment. He was proud to be a sexist pig, a hedonist, a one-track mind. Women, despite whatever the two-year-old *Ms.* magazine and its editor, Gloria Steinem, said about liberation, were happy to know him.

By the end of the second day, Knievel had invited a female television reporter from Pittsburgh to join the group on the plane for a couple of days. Or maybe she invited herself. She was on the plane.

"She wanted the story," Saltman said. "And she got the story. Yes, she did."

When the television reporter left, she soon was replaced by the Avis attendant from Chicago, from Salt Lake, from wherever it was. Knievel invited her to come along, and she quit her job right there and was on the plane. When she left, it was time to fly to Butte and home and the family for a couple of days.

"Women just loved this guy," Bob Arum said. "They threw themselves at him. They loved the danger in him, I guess. I'd never seen anything like it."

"Women were crazy about him," Saltman agreed.

The biggest problem for the two promoters was to keep their man on schedule. He had a tendency to make changes in a moment, to order the hotel for the night to be switched from, say, Denver to Omaha to Kansas City because he knew some people in Kansas City. He ordered the pilots to detour at one point to Danville, Illinois, where he had them fly low over the headquarters of a friend, Watcha McCollum, a pilot, who wasn't even on the premises. He seemed to make changes sometimes simply to make changes, to prove that he was in charge. The pilots worried sometimes about what the Federal Aviation Administration might think about all this.

His phone calls could come at any time, deep into the night. The call could be about anything at all, large or small. He would say anything he wanted to anyone. In the middle of every press conference, he would stop to make a remark to Saltman—"Shelly, stop talking, will you?"—or to Zeke Rose, the man from Ideal Toys. He sometimes would call Saltman to his hotel room, then refuse to open the door, giving orders from the other side. He was equally hard on the pilots, hard on anyone who worked for him.

The rules did not go both ways. Saltman saved a note he and Zeke Rose received about that situation for the book.

> Don't ever insult or kidd [*sic*] me other than in private or we will have to part company.
>
> > Thank you,
> > Evel

At the end of the first week of the tour, the group made a side trip to Twin Falls. Part of the reason for the visit was for publicity, more pictures of Evel next to the canyon, an interview with AP writer Jurate Kazickas, but a larger part was to assure the sometimes jittery folk of Twin Falls that raping and pillaging would not take place on September 8. A public meeting was scheduled. Bob Arum had returned to the tour for the day simply for this stop. He wanted to make sure Knievel knew how important it was.

"Remember that anything you should say in criticism of Idaho or Twin Falls can hurt us," Arum said. "It can blow us out of the water."

Knievel, who in the past had called the people of the town "a bunch of cotton-spud farmers," was at his Sunday-school nicest when he talked with the mayor of Twin Falls, the county commissioner, and the assorted local makers and shakers. He not only volunteered to cap his on-site ticket sales at 50,000, after previously promising crowds from 100,000 to 200,000 people, but vowed that he would jump the canyon at midnight without any crowd at all if that was what it would take to make the Twin Falls people happy. He simply wanted to jump the canyon.

He said he would take out a county permit to stage a local gathering. He said he would donate $100,000 to the Idaho State Police and ask the troopers to "spend it all" to put away any motorcycle gang members who might make trouble. Anything else? He said he would do it.

"When I leave Twin Falls, I want to have the same smiles and friendly handshakes from the people as when I got there," he said.

This was the maddening magic he could perform in public. When he wanted to put on a suit of good nature and affability, he wore it better than just about anybody. He joked that if his safety systems didn't work, he would become a permanent member of the Blue Lakes Country Club, which was located on the canyon floor. The course would have a new sand trap the management "wouldn't believe."

The charm continued with the interview with the AP writer at the site. The key to all interviews with Knievel was talking to him when he was in a good mood. The trick was knowing when that might be.

"I'm so famous that if the youth of this country voted for President tomorrow, I'd probably win," he said to the reporter. "I have to have a 24-hour guard on my house in Butte, Montana, to protect my privacy. I make more money for a personal appearance than Elvis Presley and Liberace combined . . . I'm Evel Knievel."

"He's a supersensational showman," Saltman told the reporter. "He's outspoken, courageous, flamboyant. He has charisma, machismo, his own musk smell. He's articulate and handsome."

Saltman left out the part about being a big pain in the ass.

The visit to the Snake River site, despite Knievel's performance for the landed gentry of Twin Falls, was not a great moment for Arum. Clouds had been slipping into his mind all week about this promotion, about whether it was going to work, and now they would not leave. He was pretty much convinced that the enterprise was doomed.

The big talk about the $6 million check, about the billions of people who would watch this show from around the world, fell apart when you looked at the actual ramp and the facilities at the rim of the canyon. This was his first time at the site, the first time he saw exactly what he was selling. A county 4-H club fair looked more exciting. He was struck by the desolation. The ramp simply sat there, naked as a piece of construction equipment that had been abandoned in the desert.

"I'm fucked," he said to himself.

"It looked like the Toonerville Trolley," he later said. "There was nothing there. It was ludicrous. It was a big joke."

The press who came to Snake River would be skeptical and cynical, with good reason. Most reporters had the same well-worn eyes that Arum had. Slightly more than two months were left before the event. How could an attractive package of thrills, excitement, and derring-do be put together? How could this amateurish-looking rocket, straight from the pages of *Boys' Life* or *Popular Mechanics*, make anyone want to put up five or six bucks to stand around in some faraway arena? Selling this thing would defy the greatest salesmen in the world.

Another problem was Knievel. Arum's view of his star had worsened. This was more than any cultural differences. He now thought Knievel simply was crazy, out of his mind. The guy was a bully, a lout. His craftiness could be misjudged early in a relationship for intelligence and a certain wit, but that soon disappeared. The core person who remained was not a good person.

Arum kept comparing Knievel to Muhammad Ali. He had brought his two most famous clients together a week before the tour started at a party at Jimmy Weston's restaurant in New York. The purpose was to introduce Knievel and help promote a fight the next night between Joe Frazier and Jerry Quarry at Madison Square Garden. There was a pop-culture majesty to the moment, to be sure, the two great sports-page showmen of the time, maybe any time, thrown together, big mouth versus big mouth, just like that.

"You know what you are?" the boxer shouted. "You're the white Muhammad Ali."

"Then you're the black Evel Knievel," the daredevil shouted in return.

Everybody laughed in the restaurant, sounded great, certainly was the image most of America had of the two men, two peas from the same hyperbolic pod. But this was not true. That was what Arum decided. The two men were not even close.

He had been with Ali ten times as much as he had been with Knievel, twenty times as much, maybe a hundred times as much. Ali, for all of his noise, despite the nervous tremors he set off in certain sections of white America, always was a gentleman and a pussycat. Knievel had been more trouble in a week and a half than Ali had been in all the time Arum had known him.

"Ali was a kind, caring, warm person," Arum said. "This guy was the anti-Ali. He was a monster."

Funny, the solemn faces from the Nation of Islam, the so-called Black Muslims standing behind Ali with their suits and ties and sunglasses, were seen as a cause of concern in many parts of the country. Arum had worked with the Nation of Islam. Knievel was ten times, a hundred times the trouble.

Ali and the Muslims never drank, part of their religion. Knievel apparently drank all the time. Ali liked women, for sure, but worked with quiet discretion. "Give your number to Rahmann," he would say to an attractive woman, sending her to his brother. Knievel never was discreet.

"Ali and the Muslims were tame, tame, tame," the promoter said. "These were normal people, considerate people. They didn't hurt people's feelings just to hurt people's feelings. They weren't anything like this guy."

Two incidents quickly reinforced Arum's thoughts.

After the meeting in Twin Falls and the visit to the canyon site, Knievel and the tour group flew to Salt Lake City, where he was one of sixty recipients that night of the Golden Plate Award as a "Giant of Endeavor" by the American Academy of Achievement. It was a big-time award. Actor Jimmy Stewart, singer Paul Anka, Lorne Greene of *Bonanza*, rodeo star Larry Mahan, basketball player John Havlicek, actress Cloris Leachman, test pilot Chuck Yeager, and cartoonist Pat Oliphant were among the other recipients. The dinner drew over one thousand guests to the Salt Palace, where presenters included actress Helen Hayes and commentator Lowell Thomas. The guest speaker was special Watergate prosecutor Leon Jaworski, who told reporters he was "quite confident" that within two weeks the Supreme Court would force President Richard Nixon to turn over all secret recordings from the Oval Office.

Linda Knievel had joined the group in Butte a night earlier, made the trip to Twin Falls, then to Salt Lake City for the event. Her presence had brought a change to Knievel, quieted him down, but also had created the ominous quality that Vince McMahon had noticed. The air changed, not for the better, when he was around his wife. Linda, everyone thought, was quiet, lovely, very pretty, and overmatched. Everyone worried about her.

Getting on the plane the morning after the dinner, Knievel was cranky, upset that Linda wasn't moving fast enough. He gave her a spank on the bottom to make her move faster. Getting off the plane in Butte, he couldn't find his car keys and accused her of losing them. He dumped the contents of her pocketbook onto the tarmac in his search. He eventually found the keys in the pocket of a jacket that he had packed in his bag.

That night he invited Saltman and Zeke Rose and some other people to his house for dinner. He always had complained about Linda's cooking ("but I love her") as part of his discourses on marriage. Dinner wound up being served late, eleven o'clock, after Knievel spent a long day of golf and early night of drinking at the Butte Country Club. Linda served the meal, Knievel looked at one of the dishes—the peas?—and decided they weren't done enough or were done too much and threw them. Maybe he threw them at Linda. Maybe he threw them at the wall. He threw them. Linda locked herself in the bedroom. Dinner was a quiet affair.

"He's crazy," Bob Arum, who had left the tour again in Salt Lake, said when he heard this report. "Out of his mind."

The second incident came the following week in Austin, Texas. Knievel, for maybe the only time on the tour, went to bed early. The hotel where the group stayed featured a swimming pool. Some soldiers on leave from a nearby military base had met some girls and were in the pool at around eleven-thirty at night. They were having some fun, making some noise. Saltman and Zeke Rose and a couple of Knievel's friends from Butte also were in the pool. They were quieter, but also making noise.

A figure came out from one of the rooms in the hotel, yelling for everyone to keep it down. The figure then began shooting. The soldiers, the girls, Saltman and Rose and Knievel's friends all ran.

"It was crazy," Arum said. "People could have been killed. They were just kids having a good time."

The shooter was Knievel. He admitted that the next day. He said he also had called the police, telling them some people were making noise and an unidentified someone had shot at them to make them keep quiet. The shooting had worked, hadn't it? The pool was empty in a hurry. Quiet.

"A madman," Arum said when he heard this report.

His solace was that he "didn't have a lot of skin in the game," wasn't risking much of his own cash. Between Invest West and the sponsors like Mack Truck and Chuckles Candy and Ideal Toys, with ABC pretty much picking up the television costs, Arum would not be in much trouble no matter how much trouble developed with the promotion. The real risk belonged to the closed-circuit exhibitors across the country. If Arum supplied them with the event, Arum had done his job.

His one worry was whether or not Knievel went off into the sky. If the event didn't happen at all, that was when Arum would find financial disaster. The exhibitors would come after him. He had to get Knievel into the air. He had to hold his nose and keep going.

"We can do this," Shelly Saltman told him. "This is our job. We make bad people look good. And we're very good at our job."

The tour hopped one last time to an end in Seattle on July 12, 1974. There had been a break for the July Fourth weekend where Knievel was the grand marshal of the Butte parade. He did wheelies up and down the streets of his youth to standing ovations. Attendance jumped from 45,000 a year earlier to 70,000 this year, mostly because he was there. The only bump in the final week was when he blew off Portland, Oregon, as the plane was about to land because he didn't like the local closed-circuit promoter—"Fuck Portland," he said as the plane went back into the air—but that was minor.

Overall, by any public relations criteria, the tour was a great success. The total column inches in newspapers probably could stretch across the country. The star of the show was everywhere. The June issue of *Oui* magazine, for instance, had come out during the trip to match *Penthouse* with a long profile of him stuffed between a story on "Sex in the Soviet Union" and five pages of naked pictures of Sigmund Freud's niece. The big guns would unload during the coming seven and a half weeks. He would be on television more than the Marlboro Man.

The canyon jump at that moment was second only to Nixon's troubles with Watergate, the calls for resignation, as a subject for public discourse. Maybe it was first in a lot of homes. If there was anyone who hadn't heard about Snake River and what was going to happen on September 8, the person hadn't heard about anything, probably didn't know how to tie his shoes.

Not all memories of the tour were bad. Arum and Saltman were locked in for the rest of the promotional grind, working directly at the site, but Zeke Rose, the public relations man for Ideal Toys, pretty much was done. He had loved his time crisscrossing America with Knievel. He felt that Knievel had changed his life.

"I had been very businesslike, uptight," Rose said. "Watching Evel, I learned to relax, go with the flow. I learned to live on impulse a lot more. I'd never lived the way I did during those three weeks. It was very good for me."

Rose had brought his bag of toys off the plane at each stop, laying them out so the press could see what they looked like. He had answered questions. He had been associated with Knievel before the tour, so he was the only public relations representative who had a personal history with the guy. He had never minded the way Knievel operated in the past—the guy called him at four in the morning once to go shopping for an organ, still called him often in the middle of the night at home, which was okay except the phone was on his wife's side of the bed—and he liked this grand buildup to the grand moment. He had fallen into the frenzied rhythm of it all, the nonstop buzz. He had no doubt about what was going to happen next.

"I thought that after the jump Evel Knievel would have a ticker-tape parade through New York City," Zeke Rose said. "Just like Lindbergh. I really did."

19 Tests

On the morning of August 8, 1974, exactly one month before the launch of the Skycycle and its celebrated passenger across the Snake River Canyon—well, hopefully across the Snake River Canyon—Americans found a different daredevil on the front page of their newspapers. His name was Philippe Petit. He was a twenty-four-year-old Frenchman who was shown walking a tightrope strung between the twin towers of the World Trade Center 110 stories above Manhattan.

The picture did not tell the whole story. He not only walked on the wire while he held his long balancing pole, he danced on the wire, jumped on it, lay down on it. He laughed and smiled, did calisthenics, seemed to have a wonderful time. He began his journey at 7:00 a.m. and performed for an hour and fifteen minutes as traffic stopped below and commuters stopped and stared and marveled at what they saw while various law enforcement agencies tried to figure out a way to get him down.

"If I see three oranges, I have to juggle," he told reporters as he was dragged to Beekman Downtown Hospital for a mental evaluation after he finished. "If I see two towers I have to walk."

As the day progressed, more facts were discovered about Philippe Petit. He had come to the United States on a self-imposed mission to walk between the towers, but had been making a living as a street performer outside Lincoln Center and Madison Square Garden. He previously had walked on a tightrope between the two towers at the Cathedral of Notre Dame in Paris and between the two towers of the Sydney Harbor Bridge in Australia.

The latest walk was a group effort. Petit said he went to the World Trade Center at least two hundred times in three months to work out the logistics. As many as six friends posed as delivery men and hard-hat workers the previous day to enter the building with his equipment. They then hid themselves overnight on the two roofs. At sunrise, they fired an arrow from one roof to the other with a five-foot longbow. The arrow was attached to fishing line, which was attached to the cable. The cable then was strung between the two roofs . . . the show began.

"After the first crossing I look at the people, and that was fantastic," Petit said. "New York woke up and what did they discover? There was a high walker on the twin towers. I was not scared because it was a precise thing. I was dying of happiness."

Judged sane at the hospital, he was released from custody in the afternoon when Manhattan district attorney Richard H. Kuh declined to press charges. As part of the deal, Petit agreed to perform a free show at a lower altitude for children at Central Park at a later date.

The similarities in risk-taking to what the more prominent daredevil proposed to do in Idaho were obvious—"Combining the cunning of a second-story man with the nerve of an Evel Knievel, a French high-wire artist sneaked past guards at the World Trade Center, ran a cable between the top of its twin towers and tightrope-walked across it yesterday morning," Grace Lichtenstein wrote in the lead for the *New York Times*—but the dissimilarities in everything else were striking. Here was a man who took the risk simply for the excitement of it, who did it for free, climbed the mountain because it was in the vicinity. He was the counterculture daredevil, part of the peace and love generation that rejected materialism, part of the times that were a changin', uh-huh. He wore ballet slippers while he worked.

"I have no ambitions," he told the grand rush of reporters.

"What about dreams?" someone asked.

"I have a dream," he said. "Niagara Falls. I would like to cross the falls, but who knows? For that I need permission."

Knievel, despite his popularity with kids, was from a previous generation. The bottom line always counted. He reveled in materialism with his cars and airplanes, his extensive and expensive wardrobes. He was a red-white-and-blue American capitalist hero surrounded by noise and gasoline fumes, strength and power. He was not counter to the culture, he *was* the culture, front and center.

"This is a business, a big business, and a tough business," Knievel said in that *Penthouse* interview still on the stands. "I hope I make enough money in the next five years where I could shut [my boys] off maybe wanting to jump the motorcycle like I do because they're going to have to pay the price for success in this business and the price is getting half-killed. And I don't want my kids to do that. I'd rather have them go into some other business with the money that I make."

On the evening of August 8, 1974, the same people who read about Philippe Petit's walk on the tightrope in the morning sat in front of their television sets and watched their president resign. Ending a national melodrama that had lasted more than two years, his other options gone, one by one, Richard M. Nixon announced to the country that he would leave the White House the next day. He would be replaced by Vice President Gerald Ford.

Less than a week earlier, Nixon had insisted famously that "I am not a crook." He still defended his conduct during his 2,026 days in office and through the saga that began with a janitor discovering five burglars in the offices of the Democratic National Committee at the Watergate complex. He drew refuge in history:

"Sometimes I have succeeded and sometimes I have failed," the departing president said in his short television address, "but always I have taken heart from what Theodore Roosevelt said about the man in the arena: 'whose face is marred by dust and sweat and blood, who strives valiantly, who errs and comes short again and again because there is no effort without error and shortcoming, but who does actually strive to do the deeds, who knows the great enthusiasms, the great devotions, who spends himself in a worthy cause, who at the best knows in the end triumph of high achievements and who, at the worst, if he fails, at least fails while daring greatly.' "

If the words sounded familiar, there was a reason. This was a quote that Robert Craig Knievel also used often in press conferences to explain himself.

In the midst of the hoo-ha for the canyon jump, he had one last normal payday scheduled. He was supposed to jump thirteen Mack trucks on August 20, 1974, at the Canadian National Exposition in Toronto, sort of the state fair for all of Canada. Despite pleas from Arum to cancel the event, Knievel forged ahead. Part of the attraction was that both Kelly, now thirteen, and Robbie, eleven, would be allowed to perform with him, a first, everyone popping wheelies before Knievel did the big jump. Another part of the attraction was a $65,000 check.

"It's crazy," Arum said. "There's so much to lose if he gets hurt. This is not an easy jump."

Knievel turned the trip into a family outing. He left early with Linda and the kids, stopped for publicity interviews in Toronto, threw out the first pitch at a Cleveland Indians game, and was grand marshal for a parade in Akron before returning to Toronto for the jump. If Toronto went well, he was scheduled for a final pre-canyon press conference in New York the next day.

He was on his best insurance salesman behavior.

"If you put me in a rocket and send me at four hundred miles per hour and I have a chance to be killed . . . I'm interested," he told Toronto writers on his publicity stop when they asked if he had gone on any of the rides with his kids on the expo grounds. "But I don't want to go on the Wild Mouse."

He said that he never had jumped more than eleven Mack trucks, but what the heck, he might as well jump thirteen if he was going to do twelve. Thirteen was one of his lucky numbers. A few days earlier, August 13, he finally had received a permit to land on the far side of the canyon. The permit number was 1313. He would be fine with thirteen Mack trucks.

"I'll just come in here, get my leathers on, have a shot of Wild Turkey, and go out and do it," he said.

In Cleveland, he and the family were hustled from the airport to Municipal Stadium by helicopter, a grand entrance to throw out the first pitch before a crowd of 42,171 gathered for a "Rally Around Cleveland" promotion. Knievel said, "I've been all over the country, but it's the first time I've had a chance to see the great Cleveland Indians." The crowd roared. The great Cleveland Indians then proceeded to lose, 7–3, to the Texas Rangers.

The Toronto jump turned out fine. He took a rare practice run during the afternoon, nine trucks, then hit the marks perfectly that night before an estimated crowd of 21,000, which also had been drawn by an appearance of the Canadian rock group Lighthouse. (A night earlier the Lawrence Welk Orchestra, featuring Myron Floren, Joe Feeney, and the entire television cast, was the main Canadian National Exposition attraction.) Knievel seemed emotional and proud when he introduced his sons, then did wheelies with them. The action was filmed for *Wide World*, Keith Jackson at the microphone, and couldn't have looked better than it did.

"Knievel's 20-second sprint through the night air left him silhouetted against the blinking lights of the midway," reporter Stephen Handelman of the *Toronto Star* wrote. "A tiny, taut figure, he looked like one of the ride-and-motorcycle toys he sells across North America."

(One literal-minded reader objected to Handelman's sweet description. The reader did the math on the 112-foot leap and the 20-second flight. He might have found something. "Since this works out to a four miles per hour flight it appears that Knievel has achieved a startling break-through in motorcycle aerodynamics," assistant professor P. C. Stangeby of the Institute for Aerospace Studies at the University of Toronto wrote in a letter to the editor published a week later. "We look forward to further details.")

Knievel finished his night by pumping the canyon event. He continued to talk about the jump in ominous tones.

"You can say nothing better about a man than he kept his word, and regardless of my chances, I'll keep my word," Knievel said at the end. "It's all I have to look forward to now, that clear blue sky I'm going to be looking at from my Skycycle on September 8."

In the morning, as scheduled, he traveled to New York for the final big-city blitz. One of the interviews was with Milton Richman, sports columnist for United Press International. The interview took place in a helicopter as Knievel and family were taken from La Guardia Airport to midtown for a general press conference. The words were shouted because of the *wocka-wocka* sound of the helicopter rotors.

"How much do you think about whether you'll make it or not?" Richman asked, *wocka-wocka*, about the canyon jump.

"Enough," *wocka-wocka*, Knievel replied.

"Even when you lie in bed at night?"

"Sure," Knievel said. "It's all I can think about when I'm by myself like that. Whether everything is going to be okay or not. It gets worse as it gets closer."

Richman doggedly asked the tough question about Knievel's marriage, even with the family in the helicopter. How did he keep it together if he was seen in public with so many other women? Knievel thought about his answer.

"I've known women when I was younger, but my wife is my girl," he said, *wocka-wocka*. "We've been married for fifteen years now, and I've never had a better girl than the one I married."

At the press conference, he was asked about the well-publicized statements of Representative John Murphy (D-NY), who had promised to try to force the Federal Communications Commission to ban all coverage of the jump. Murphy called Knievel "a modern pied piper of suicidal mayhem." He said he had received "hundreds" of calls from concerned parents.

"One of the phone calls came from a parent who felt the promotion of this event was having a bad effect on young people and Mr. Knievel was a sick individual," Representative Murphy said. "The gentleman stated that he had asked his eight-year-old son when he was going back to school in September and the boy replied, 'The day after Evel gets killed.' "

Knievel was prepared for this question. He put on his angry face. He became Mr. Responsible, Mr. Control, the baseline product that he sold in the toy stores to the imaginations of America's children.

"I've traveled this country for eight years talking about automobile safety," he said. "I've also traveled this country eight years speaking to young people against narcotics. I wear a white suit when I ride my motorcycle, not a black one. Little kids don't run away from me, they identify with me."

He paused.

"You tell that congressman to go straight to hell," Knievel said.

Sixteen days were left before the canyon extravaganza.

Work on the Skycycle, the rocket, had hit a snag. Truax and his helpers transported the test version of the X-2 from Saratoga, California, to the canyon in the first week of August, where they hoped to fire the thing into the air, accumulate the data from either a success or a failure, bring that data back to California, and complete the final version of the second X-2 rocket, the one Knievel would ride. This did not happen on schedule.

One problem was that the promoters and Knievel didn't want a test shot fired. They were terrified that some news organization, any news organization, might take a picture of a rocket blithely flying over the canyon. That, Bob Arum said, would kill the event. The attraction was whether or not the famous daredevil was going to be splattered on the canyon wall. If a rocket was shown on the nightly news zipping over the thing like the 8:50 commuter train arriving from Scarsdale, well, the attraction was gone. Nobody would buy a ticket.

The second problem, which developed as Truax argued that a test flight was absolutely necessary for Knievel's safety, was that static test firings of the rocket did not go well at the launch site. An autopilot had been installed so Knievel didn't have to do anything, simply take the ride as if he were sitting on top of a fat Roman candle, but the autopilot was balky. The electrical system worked erratically.

Truax and company had to sort through a solution because the autopilot expert in California had gone on vacation. All of this took time. Another problem was discovered with the shear diaphragm that blocked the nozzle where the steam was released to shoot the rocket into the air. A second diaphragm had to be made—difficult because there were no machine shop facilities in Twin Falls—and added. More time. Then there were problems in the electrical connections with the parachute system, even though the parachute hadn't been installed. Again, more time.

"What if we don't make it?" Truax would ask himself when he woke up in the middle of the night and thought about his tight schedule.

Knievel came down from Butte to sit in the rocket on the launch pad, try the fit, which turned out to be snug. He had trouble getting in and getting out, but didn't seem worried. He wasn't big on practice.

The original rocket plan, the safest plan, would have put him in a closed cockpit that he could eject from the rocket in one piece, same as jet pilots did, separate parachute from the rocket, separate landing, but cost considerations had canceled out that possibility from the beginning. Now that cost considerations had been eliminated, it was too late to go back to the better plan. An order for a cockpit that could be ejected had to be placed with the manufacturer two years before delivery.

The result was the open cockpit design. Knievel sat on a seat that had been taken from a go-kart. The parachute contraption, built by Ron Chase and a separate company from El Monte, California, would work with the entire rocket, not just the cockpit. Knievel would have to ride his craft wherever or however it went. The parachute system, though, was all theory.

"We never practiced with the parachute attached," Bill Sprow, one of the engineers with Truax, said. "The rocket would blow a lot of dust and debris around when we'd test. We didn't want the parachute system, which had a lot of smaller parts, to be affected by that."

Early on the morning of August 25, 1974, not long after sunrise, at least three weeks later than they planned, Truax and his team finally fired off the test rocket, the first model of the X-2. Arum and Knievel finally had been convinced that the test was a necessity, that Knievel's life would be in jeopardy without it. Everything was done in secret. Not only was the press not allowed, no one in the press even was told that this test might happen. If the flight was successful, the plan was to deny that it ever took place.

The plan did not have to be put into action. The test was a failure.

The parachute system, attached for the flight, malfunctioned. Almost as soon as the rocket left the launch pad, the parachute deployed. The trip was doomed ten yards into the flight. The rocket went straight until the chute was fully open, then it shifted from horizontal to vertical and made a long, slow trip to the bottom and a final splash. This time, unlike the X-1 when it crashed, the fins were visible, sticking up from the water, so the rocket could be recovered and brought back by helicopter.

A medical dummy, the same height and weight as Knievel, nicknamed "Good Galahad" by Truax, had been the passenger. The medical dummy was also recovered, intact.

"The combined cost of both vehicles which have gone into the Snake River is almost $500,000," Knievel, now the next passenger on the next trip, told the Associated Press. "This makes the Snake River the richest river in the state of Idaho. In fact, there is a rumor that all the trout are turning to gold."

The figure was an exaggeration by five—the rocket that went into the river and the rocket that he would ride cost no more than $100,000 together to build—but the picture of the two rockets ending in the river had to be disconcerting. Knievel said, "The third time's a charm," but there clearly were issues to resolve and not a lot of time to resolve them.

Truax asked for a postponement of a week or two, but Knievel told him that wasn't an option. ("Do the best you can," he said. "I would have survived that last test.") The flight had to go on September 8. Truax and his crew returned to California and went into round-the-clock over-drive. He decided to junk the autopilot, which meant he ripped out all of the electrical instrumentation. Knievel now would operate the parachute manually with a spring-loaded deadman control. He would hold on to a lever, and if he should black out from the G forces involved at liftoff, his hand would go limp and the lever would open the chute.

A bunch of other changes also were made as the engineers worked and worked. Truax and Sprow haunted the military salvage yards of the West Coast, looking for parts they needed. Knievel called and wanted a 35mm Nikon camera installed, part of a deal he had made. The camera was installed. The entire experience was like pulling an all-night study session on the eve of the big test. The participants knew they could do better if they had more time, but there was no time. They had to do the best they could.

"I'm not sure how Knievel felt about any of this," Bill Sprow said. "He was a promoter, and you never knew what to believe from him, but I'm sure that test didn't do anything for his confidence in us. We were trying to put that rocket on the other side. And we didn't."

On the afternoon of the test, August 25, 1974, another event happened in Bruceton Mills, West Virginia, that didn't help Knievel's confidence. Bob Gill, part of the competition, one of the cycle jumpers the FBI thought had been muscled by Knievel's associates, failed in an attempt to jump from one side of Appalachia Lake to the other side. He landed short, hit the wall of the riverbank head-on. He was thrown onto the land. His back was broken. He was paralyzed below the waist.

Three weeks earlier, on August 4, another member of the competition, Bob Pleso, had crashed at a drag strip in Phoenix City, Alabama. Outspoken, Pleso had derided Knievel's efforts at Snake River before his own jump. He said, "For $6 million all he's doing is rocketing off a ramp . . . pulling a rip cord, and then he and his Skycycle will float like a feather to the ground." Pleso then stepped onto his motorcycle, tried to clear a record thirty cars, landed on the twenty-ninth, was thrown forty feet in the air, landed on his neck, and skidded for twenty feet. He died in surgery two hours later.

The daredevil business was in a bad stretch everywhere a man looked.

A story. Before he went back to Butte, Knievel was scheduled to pose for the cover of *Sports Illustrated* for the September 2 issue, part of the last burst of pre-jump publicity. Heinz Kleutmeier, the *SI* photographer, convinced him that the best shot would be on the floor of the canyon, the long walls splashed with sunshine, the white knight in front of the natural wonder that was his opponent. Knievel agreed, but kept canceling the slotted times for the shoot.

Kleutmeier made one more appointment, rented a helicopter and pilot to take them down to the floor. Knievel still stalled, dawdled over breakfast. They were in the middle of a restaurant not far from the rim of the canyon. The clock already was running on the helicopter rental. Kleutmeier went to his last psychological ploy.

"You're scared, aren't you?" the photographer said.

"I'm not scared," Knievel said.

"Sure you are," Kleutmeier said. "You're scared to go down into that canyon in a helicopter. I can see it in you."

"Fuck you," the daredevil said. "I'm not scared. We can go down right now."

And they did. And the picture became the most famous shot of the entire production, a portrait, Evel in his leathers, a man and his canyon.

A story. Bob Wussler, head of CBS Sports, always had wanted a piece of the Evel Knievel franchise. *The CBS Sports Spectacular*, the network's sports anthology show, was a pallid and irregular competitor to *Wide World*, often dumped off the seasonal schedule for football or basketball, never able to grab the same identity as the weekly "thrill of victory, agony of defeat." *Wide World* invariably tapped into the more popular events—Knievel's jumps, replays of Ali fights, international track competitions—leaving CBS a step behind.

With ABC locked in for the Snake River jump, CBS again was consigned to the sidelines of a major event. Then an opening suddenly appeared.

"I went to lunch at a watering hole named Mercurio's, across the street from CBS headquarters," Kevin O'Malley, then a young producer at the network, said later. "I ran into Jack Price, who handled a lot of the closed-circuit business for Bob Arum and Top Rank. We got talking about Snake River, which he was working on."

Price mentioned "that kooky thing that the attorney general of Idaho was trying to do." O'Malley innocently asked, "What kooky thing would that be?" A couple of hours later, he was on an airplane. By nine-thirty that night he was in Boise, ready to write a check for $50,000 to ensure that CBS would be able to cover the canyon jump as it happened.

The story was that the land on the far side of the canyon, the proposed landing area for the Skycycle, belonged to the state of Idaho. The Idaho attorney general, always looking for revenue, announced that he would grant access to the land to news agencies for a fee. The plan was to auction off the rights to take pictures. The attorney general was not thinking about live television at the time, more about local stations and still-cameramen, but CBS now asked, "What about a television network?" Wasn't CBS a news agency?

The network's idea was to cover the canyon jump as a news event. The $50,000 was their auction offer. There would, of course, be grand repercussions. Top Rank's closed-circuit audience probably would disappear, as would the ABC audience for the replay a week later, but CBS would be a hero to the public, providing a live home telecast for free. The state of Idaho would be $50,000 richer.

"There was a precedent," O'Malley said. "The Rose Bowl Parade, for instance, was covered on different channels. The Macy's Thanksgiving Parade was covered on different channels. These were public events on city streets. If you could make a deal with the city to set up your cameras, you had a right to show what went past."

O'Malley laid out the idea for his boss. Wussler loved it. That was why everything happened so fast. O'Malley was spinning from the speed.

"I get into Boise that night," he said. "I'd had to pack in a hurry, had to borrow $500 from a CBS lawyer because this was way before ATM machines arrived and there wasn't time to go to a bank. You know those displays at the airport, where you push a button to get a reservation at a hotel? Those had been invented. There were two options in Boise. I think I pushed the button that was lit. The woman comes on the phone and asks whether I want the deluxe room for $35 or the executive for $43. I ask, 'What's the difference?' She says the executive has a Jacuzzi. I figure, eight dollars, what the heck. I check in, get to my room, can't find the lights. It's dark. I fall into the Jacuzzi and almost kill myself."

A hearing already was scheduled for the next day, August 28, 1974, in Boise, the state capital. Bids would be accepted the day after that. The process was taking place eleven days before the jump. Somewhere during the night, Knievel's Twin Falls attorney, Jim May, was called by a friend who had information that O'Malley was in town and CBS was trying to execute this flanking maneuver to televise the jump.

May and Don Branker, the twenty-eight-year-old long-haired producer from California, were on a private plane at sunrise, heading to Boise. Branker even wore a sports coat for the occasion. The hearing was held in the capitol building, chaired by Lieutenant Governor Jack Murphy. The feeling from the beginning was that this was a pro-forma affair, that the deal with CBS pretty much was done.

When Murphy finally asked if anyone was in the room representing Knievel, it was a surprise when Branker stepped away from a back wall and walked to the front. He told the state officials that Top Rank owned the exclusive television rights to the event and if they were not honored, lawsuits would be filed everywhere. He then asked for a lunchtime recess to be able to call Top Rank president Bob Arum in New York. The request was granted.

"I want your permission to cancel the jump," Branker told Arum after outlining the problem. "I want full authority to say we're going to cancel the jump."

"Cancel the jump?" Arum said. "We can't do that. We've got too much invested."

"I know that," Branker said. "But do they know it?"

"You're talking about a million-dollar gamble here. Let me try to call Wussler."

Arum called. He argued. Wussler wouldn't budge. Arum called Branker. "Do what you have to do," he said.

Back at the hearing, Branker argued that Evel Knievel was a performer, no different from a singer, and the canyon jump was a performance, and Top Rank owned the rights to that performance, no different from a concert. O'Malley argued that the Snake River Canyon jump was a news event and CBS was in the business of bringing news to its viewers. Branker asked what O'Malley would think if an ABC crew showed up and started to broadcast the U.S. Open golf tournament, which CBS owned. O'Malley said that was different, that CBS had bought rights to all of the camera positions on the golf course. Branker asked, "What if we filmed from a blimp? From a helicopter?"

Branker's final argument centered on a prize bull that got loose from a pasture. If someone came upon that bull, could that someone take it and sell it? No, of course not. The someone didn't own the bull. The television rights for the canyon jump were the same as the bull. Top Rank owned them, and if anyone else, i.e., the state of Idaho, sold them, lawsuits would come down like rain.

Branker returned to the back of the room, where attorney May heartily shook his hand. The rock promoter felt like an exhausted Clarence Darrow.

The hearing was finished, the auction still scheduled for the next day, but something had changed. Branker overheard O'Malley talking on a pay phone about "some hippie talking about prize bulls . . ." The next day CBS withdrew from the scene. There were no bids to televise from the far side of the canyon.

The show was a show, not news. ABC and Top Rank owned the show.

"We were really getting a lot of heat from theater owners across the country [who had committed to show the jump], and we had a very tender situation on our hands," Wussler said in New York. "It got to be a larger issue than it ever should have become. But we've had a very interesting time for the past forty-eight hours."

A final bit of business, maybe monkey business, had to be cleared up in Butte before attention could shift to Twin Falls and Snake River: Knievel had to stage his million-dollar party. The promise of a gala blowout had been a constant on the Evel Knievel Says Good-Bye Tour. Invitations had been extended to gossip-column celebrities who ranged from Elvis to the pope to Jackie Onassis, a party like no one ever had seen, a ramble through the assorted nightspots of Knievel's youth trailed by that Brinks truck and a quickly shrinking pile of money. A million bucks. What kind of good times could a million bucks buy in Butte? A beer cost less than a buck.

Bars like the Freeway Tavern, owned by Muzzy Faroni and Judo Stanisich, had been getting calls for weeks, locals wondering when they should appear. Muzzy and Judo, whoever answered the phone, said to hang loose and pay attention. There was no set date. There really was no plan. Bob would have the party when he felt like having the party.

Uh-oh.

He decided sometime during the day of September 2, 1974, that he felt like having the party on the night of September 2, 1974, six days before the rocket launch. This was Labor Day. He also apparently decided that the million-dollar price figure might have been a bit of an exaggeration. The party didn't begin until after eleven o'clock that night.

"We got a call," Muzzy Faroni said, "that he was coming."

The day had been spent at the Butte Country Club, where the Evel Knievel Classic Golf Tournament took place. Elvis, despite a special printed invitation to the tournament and the jump, just for him, had declined the offer to visit the festivities, and Jackie O and the pope and Sinatra and Muhammad Ali and Elizabeth Taylor also, alas, had other important engagements, so the two celebrities in town were heavyweight boxing legend Joe Louis and aging tennis notable Bobby Riggs. The sixty-year-old Louis, beset with Internal Revenue Service problems, still worked as a greeter at Caesars Palace and no doubt was paid to take a quick hop from Vegas on a Lear jet for the event. Riggs, fifty-six, still was in the news from his losing match a year earlier in the Astrodome against

Billie Jean King, 6–4, 6–3, 6–3, in the celebrated "Battle of the Sexes." He also still was on the payroll for the Welch Candy Company, advertising Sugar Daddy, a caramel lollipop. Riggs wore a yellow-and-red Sugar Daddy track suit every day to promote the product. The Welch Candy Company also was a sponsor of the canyon jump, a logo for Chuckles on every piece of Knievel's equipment to promote that product, so a certain synergy existed here. So, yes, Riggs also was being paid.

The celebrity golf tournament featured two paid celebrities. Plus Knievel.

"Before the tournament began, Evel came up to Joe Louis and said, 'Joe, I need a little help,' " Bob Arum said later. " 'These are my people in Butte. Could you do me a favor, just knock a few out of bounds here and there? To make me look good.' I heard him say this. Joe didn't know what to say. The idea was so foreign to him. He stuttered, Joe did, so he said, 'I-I-I coul-coul-couldn't do that.' I'll always remember that."

Knievel played in a foursome with Louis, Riggs, and Ed Zemljak. It was daredevil golf all the way, bets everywhere. Knievel soon discovered that Louis was not so good that he purposely had to hit bad shots. He hit more than enough on his own.

"I'll bet you $50 you can't put the ball on the green," Knievel said at the two-hundred-yard, par 3 sixth hole. "I'll pay you on September ninth [the day after the canyon jump]."

"If I knock this on the green, I'll ride with you on the eighth," Louis said before his shot landed just short.

Riggs, a golf hustler, a tennis hustler, a hustler's hustler, set up a bet with Knievel that if either of them shot 37 on the par 35 back nine, the other one would pay $5,000 for the pleasure of seeing the feat happen. Knievel went over. Riggs chipped in from the fringe on the eighteenth hole to shoot 37. Ed Zemljak saw Knievel write another check to another opponent after another round.

The golf tournament dissolved into the always-raucous golf tournament banquet, which dissolved into the million-dollar party, which was no longer a million-dollar party. Knievel and Riggs and Arum arrived together in a jeep at the Freeway a few minutes before midnight. The place was packed, word out, maybe three hundred people, maybe more, elbow to elbow, filling every inch of the small bar room, but they were not people Knievel knew. The people Knievel knew mostly were home in bed. These were kids, most of them underage.

"Drinks for everybody," Knievel shouted.

The pandemonium that followed was what would be expected from the combination of free beer and young drinkers. The Freeway was over-whelmed as the young drinkers took as many beers as they could as fast as they could. On a normal night the bar was known for its pork chop sandwich, a Butte staple invented by the proprietors of a restaurant called Pork Chop John's, but perfected here when Muzzy hired John's chef for $5,000 just to bring the recipe. There were no pork chop sandwiches now. There was only beer.

The kids whooped and laughed and pissed in the parking lot. They took every beer the Freeway had and then followed their pied pipers, Evel and the guy in the Sugar Daddy warm-up suit, who now were in a police cruiser headed to the Acoma Lounge and Supper Club in the middle of town. The police cruiser was flashing the lights and using the siren and headed the wrong way up Montana Street.

"There was nobody in the bar, a Monday night after midnight, and then the party arrived," Jimmy Sheehan, one of two bartenders at the Acoma, said. "It was the craziest thing ever. By the time Evel got there, he had to fight his way in. Bobby Riggs, they just passed him through the crowd and over the bar. Then he goes to stand, and he stands on a box that collapses, and he falls right down."

The scene at the Freeway was repeated at the Acoma with mixed drinks added here. Owner Sandy Keith, Knievel's onetime commanding officer in the National Guard, said, "Give 'em anything they want." A polka band played "The Caissons Go Rolling Along" as the crowd cleared out every bottle in the place. Kids stood on top of the piano bar. Kids stood on top of the banquettes. Kids stood everywhere. They chugged drinks from the two tall Galliano bottles that had been in the bar forever.

One of Knievel's better Butte escapades had started in the Acoma. Drinking in the bar one day, he looked across Wyoming Street at the nine-story Finlen Hotel, the tallest building in town, maybe all of Montana, and made a bet that he could drive his motorcycle through the lobby, onto the elevator, up nine floors, onto the roof, do a lap, then be back on the elevator, down nine floors, back in the lobby, back out the door, and free by the time the police arrived. The key to the bet was that the police station was located within a block of the hotel.

"And he did it," Jimmy Sheehan said. "By the time the police arrived, he was gone."

Now he was with the police. The next stop was Bob Pavlovich's bar, the Met Tavern. More of the same. Then to the El Mar Lounge, a country-and-western bar for a final stop. One reporter, Joe Eszterhas of *Rolling Stone* magazine, chronicled the entire party parade. He noted that the herd of youthful drinkers became more and more sparse at the last two stops, more beer thrown at each other than drunk at the Met, an older crowd at the El Mar already, the kids not really welcome at two or three in the morning.

"Evel Knievel is a motherfucker," one kid shouted in a party-ending stretch of dialogue from the El Mar reported by Eszterhas.

"He'd be the best fuck your mother ever had," one of the resident old-timers replied.

That seemed to be a fine and appropriate good-night.

The million-dollar good time was a bust. Sandy Keith at the Acoma said that Knievel had "rung up a $4,000 bill in an hour." He said this with a certain admiration, but if the bill was the same at the other three bars, and it probably was less because the Acoma was the site of the mixed-drink open bar, the total for the night was $16,000. The million-dollar party came up $986,000 short. There was no Brinks truck. Take away Bobby Riggs and his Sugar Daddy outfit and there were no celebrities. (Joe Louis went to bed.) There weren't even friends and associates of Knievel. There were just the underage kids and the daredevil.

The pope and Elvis and Liz Taylor and John Wayne and the rest of the invitees apparently knew what they were doing.

20 Twin Falls, ID (I)

An eclectic cross-section of American journalism formed one of the first waves of outsiders to hit Twin Falls and Snake River as the event grew closer and closer. The publicists for Top Rank said with breathless importance that they had issued over 130 press credentials to publications ranging from the *New York Times* and *Washington Post* to *Time* magazine and *Mother Jones* and the *Wall Street Journal*. Adding photographers, radio personnel, and technicians, the credentials figure went past 300.

"I just okayed a guy from Kokomo, Indiana," veteran fight publicist Harold Conrad, a confidant of Ernest Hemingway in the old days, brought on as part of the promotion, said. "The guy does a talk show. Last night every call was on Knievel. His boss said, 'Get out there and cover this thing.' "

Unsure how to treat the man and the event, different editors had made different personnel choices for the assignment. Sportswriters were sent to cover "Man vs. Canyon" as if it were the Super Bowl, the World Series, another Ohio State–Michigan battle for Big Ten football supremacy. Science reporters, the same people who had covered rocket launches from Cape Canaveral and the landing on the moon, were sent to cover the technical aspects. ABC prominently added Dr. Jules Bergman, its voice-of-authority science expert, to the broadcast crew. A final group of writers included sob sisters, metropolitan columnists, entertainment reporters, and television writers. These people primarily were interested in celebrity and/or death.

The canyon jump was a convention of journalistic cynics.

"Do you know how they write 'motherfucker' now in my paper?" *New York Daily News* sob sister Theo Wilson asked a disparate group within this disparate group.

She had covered the arrival of the Beatles in the United States, the Charles Manson trial, the Sam Sheppard trial, the trials of Sirhan Sirhan and Angela Davis. She recently had been covering the news generated by the Pentagon Papers. No one answered her motherfucker question.

"They write it 'blank-blank-blank-blank-blank-blank fucker,' " Wilson said with a pleasant smile.

The logistics for covering the present blank-blank-blank-blank-blank-blank fucker and his attempt to jump this large hole in the ground were not great. There were so few motel rooms in the area that some reporters stayed in Burley, forty miles away from the canyon. The promoters, through Bob Arum and Shelly Saltman, exaggerated all aspects of the production. Money figures were exaggerated. Early ticket sales were exaggerated. Exaggerations were exaggerated. Burt Reynolds was coming! Maybe John Wayne! Truth was hard to find.

Knievel was unpredictable. He split his time between Butte and the Blue Lakes Inn in Twin Falls, flown back and forth in a leased Lear jet piloted by his friend, now air transport chauffeur, Watcha McCollum. Sometimes Watcha wore a red velvet dinner jacket while he worked. Sometimes Watcha and Evel, as they arrived from Butte or departed to Butte in the Lear, buzzed the large tent where the reporters worked. The promoters promised press conferences with Knievel most days, but most days the conferences never happened. When they did happen, they never happened at the prescribed time.

The man of the moment was seen mostly in flashes. He carried his magic cane and seemed to be in an angry hurry, barking at the people who worked for him. He was not afraid of using the magic cane to open a path. He also was seen late at night, ordering another round of drinks for the bar at the Blue Lakes Inn, making pronouncements, giving more commands, nuzzling with assorted women who were not his wife, sometimes when his wife was in a room down the hall.

The journalistic cynics were not impressed.

"Bobby Knievel might have been the worst creep I ever met . . . ," freelance writer Bill Cardoso, formerly of the *Boston Globe*, later wrote. "A philanderer and a bully. None of which, of course, should be held against a man. But he blew my vote of confidence because in public life he was a hungry spokesman against these evils. Whenever and wherever he could find an audience. Mr. Red-White-and-Blue. What an asshole."

"The contest is Evel Knievel versus the canyon," Wells Twombley, sports columnist for the *San Francisco Examiner*, said in words that were soon copied into a bunch of newspapers across the country. "The canyon is the sentimental favorite."

"I thought Knievel was a bully, abusive in his tone," Joe Eszterhas of *Rolling Stone* said. "He was one of those guys who acted like he was the star and everyone else didn't matter. I thought he was a bully and a prick."

Eszterhas had started to form his opinion on the party crawl in Butte and reaffirmed it daily at the canyon. Twenty-nine years old, the future Hollywood screenwriter already had written a critically acclaimed non-fiction book about murder and the conflict between youth and authority in a small town in Missouri, *Charlie Simpson's Apocalypse*. When he approached *Rolling Stone* editor Jann Wenner with the idea of covering Knievel and the canyon, Wenner said, "Great, go do it." He could write as much as he wanted.

"I thought the story was larger than Knievel by himself," Eszterhas said. "I wanted to do this gigantic picture of Americana. The whole panorama of Idaho and farms and motorcycles and kids, this event with Knievel at the center of it."

Not all of the press for Knievel was bad. There were a few writers who painted the man of the moment as the next Lindbergh, or at least a sports-page, wacky reincarnation of him. (Lindbergh had died in Hawaii a week earlier at the age of seventy-two, putting him in people's minds.) There were a number of writers, a majority, who started out intrigued by Knievel and the production, but who grew more and more disillusioned as the big day approached. (Why are all of those trucks with ABC logos here when Top Rank says the event never will be on free TV? Hmmmm.) There were writers who had disliked Knievel's act before they even arrived. (Death for sale. Gross.)

"I hope he doesn't die," one of this group said. "Because then he'll be seen as a martyr."

The big journalistic wonder was whether this was a fraud, a fix. Was Knievel going to be shot into the air, land on the other side, free and easy, and chuckle as he walked to the bank? The worry was that everyone—writers and the general public included—was being hood-winked.

The promoters' and Knievel's constant overstatements of the money involved were a negative here. If all this money had been spent, wouldn't the danger have been engineered out of the equation? The sentence that was heard most often was that if NASA could put a man on the moon, surely these guys could get Knievel across the canyon.

The promoters tried to strike down this kind of talk since it was a brushfire that could burn down the entire production. Bob Arum was moved to put on a show-and-tell demonstration after using up all his words.

"Look at that," the promoter said, pointing at the 13-foot rocket and the 108-foot launch rail and the wide and deep expanse of the canyon. "If it's a fraud, it's a fraud. Let it speak for itself."

The rocket looked very small.

The citizens of Twin Falls never really had wanted the event to come to their town. They accepted it as if it were a large tablespoonful of castor oil, somehow good for them, but never liked the thought of what was to come. Now, as the date approached in a time-warp hurry and as hairy strangers appeared on fat-boy motorcycles that fumed and belched, well, worry and fear took charge again.

The citizens of Twin Falls might not have spent a lot of time in the outside world, but they had seen movies. Bad things could come from this invasion.

"I don't like it," Mrs. John Blasius, longtime resident, told the *Twin Falls Times-Herald*. "I'm afraid someone's going to get hurt. It could be on the canyon. It could be riots in town. We have the word that they're going to barricade the liquor store and all the sporting goods stores. I just think it's foolish. A lot could happen to the town. They're going to have all these hippie motorcyclists in here for this."

"They should control the drinking," her husband added. "If they've been drinking, they can't handle them all. It may help the town, yet it could be overdone, too."

The town was small, maybe 21,000 people in a county that contained only 44,000 people. The *Los Angeles Times* pointed out that there were 46 churches, 15 parks, and 14 Negroes in Twin Falls. The idea that as many as 50,000 people might arrive was scary enough, but the kind of people who might arrive was even scarier. This was seen as an invasion of Visigoths, or maybe a spaceship settling down at Shoshone Falls, a

212-foot drop, bigger than Niagara Falls, don't you know, and dispensing platoons of alien beings.

Rumors began as soon as the visitors arrived and set up camp by the falls. Housewives were supposedly raped. Property supposedly was destroyed. The sheriff's department investigated, said the rumors were groundless—skinny dipping perhaps, but no rapes reported anywhere. People still worried. The population was filled with hunters, gun owners, and the rumor here was that local sales were brisk in both guns and ammo. The possibility of shoot-outs between cowboy hunters and big-city motorcycle gang members was mentioned.

"Any time a town doubles, triples or quadruples its population, there are going to be problems with security, traffic flow, shortages . . . ," businessman Jerry McBratney, one of the cooler voices, said. "Whether we like it or not, the jump is scheduled. I have mixed emotions about the thing, but there are problems with any big crowd."

Twin Falls County sheriff Paul Corder deputized forty citizens as special officers for the weekend to augment his normal roster of sixteen. Thirty-four state police would arrive to direct traffic on the crowded roads. The National Guard would set up a command center next to the sheriff's office, and units were asked to hold drills on the weekend of the jump, alerted that they might be called.

The Magic Valley Hospital in Twin Falls made disaster plans. The hospital had 120 beds but could handle only a maximum of ten people at a time in its emergency room. The emergency room staff was doubled, from one doctor to two. Five hospitals were put on alert for overflow. A big worry was that people would fall into the canyon.

"Our local people, who know the canyon, sometimes fall over, so what are you going to do with strangers?" Sheriff Corder said. "That canyon could be a problem. There will be people all along the canyon with no respect for it."

A temporary air traffic control tower was brought in for the Twin Falls City-County Airport, which normally had no need for a tower. The Federal Aviation Administration, which would man the temporary structure, announced that air travel on Sunday would be restricted to 8,000 feet above sea level, 3,900 feet above the jump. The X-2 Skycycle, classified as an aircraft by the FAA, was exempt from this ruling.

Security for the site was left to the promoters, who were supposed to hire their own guards. This included the 38 acres around the rocket that were leased to Knievel and the adjoining 216 acres retained by farmer

Tim Qualls. These latter acres were available to campers, $40 for the weekend, a stiff price. Qualls told reporters that no comparisons should be drawn between himself and Max Yasgur, who leased his dairy farm in upstate Bethel, New York, for Woodstock. Yasgur became so supportive of his hippie visitors, providing them with free food, water, and dairy milk, that *Rolling Stone* had published a full-page obituary when he died in 1973. Qualls said he was not Max Yasgur.

"I've got a reputation for being mean and ornery, and I aim to keep it," Tim Qualls said.

The Twin Falls County Fair, normally the biggest event in the area, also was scheduled for September 4–7. With an annual four-day attendance between 70,000 and 100,000 joined by Knievel's projected 50,000 gathering at the canyon jump, this would be an unprecedented influx of people. Sheriff Corder reported that his extra men would patrol not only the fair but rural areas to make sure people could attend the fair without worry of being robbed. This did not stop some 4-H livestock exhibitors from threatening to pull out of competition. They were worried about the safety of their animals.

Sheriff Corder said that the fair never had brought many problems, that it was local people, like a big family get-together. He wasn't sure what problems the motorcycle people would bring.

"There's no telling what kind of people we'll have to look out for," he said. "We'll have to rely on the state cops to help out."

A separate universe was created at the edge of that canyon. That was the situation. The concession stands already had been set up. (Hamburgers were a dollar, hot dogs 50 cents, beer at 40 and 50 cents per can, $2.50 for a six-pack, $9 for a case. Commemorative statues in gold, silver, or bronze were $150,000, $22,500, or $5,000. An Evel Knievel belt buckle was $40, a commemorative coin $3.) Drinking fountains had been brought to the site. Two hundred portable toilets had been brought to the site.

What next? The people of Twin Falls could only wonder.

Jerry Swensen, owner of a local meat market, had a history of making a comment about life and times in his weekly advertisements in the *Times-Herald*. He made one about all of this, said in his ad that the promotion was "all a put-on" and that Evel Knievel was "full of baloney." He nevertheless promised to present Knievel with a twenty-pound baloney if the jump was successful.

A few days before the jump, who came into the store? Swensen was in

Salt Lake City, where his wife was in a hospital recovering from a brain tumor. His father, Sherman, was behind the counter. The man of the moment, the famous daredevil, the public figure who television commentator Geraldo Rivera said just the other day was more popular than Ted Kennedy, John Lennon, or David Cassidy of the Partridge Family, went to the case, picked up a twenty-pound baloney, and slammed it down in front of Sherman Swensen.

"You know what you can do with your baloney, don't you?" he said.

He walked out the door.

Sherman put the baloney back in the case.

The man of the moment was becoming unhinged by what he faced. That was the feeling of the promoters as they worked through the final days. The man of the moment was scared out of his mind. He was zipping back and forth to Butte on the Lear jet. He was drinking a lot. He was spending a lot of time with a good-looking young woman who said she once was Miss Beauty Queen or maybe Miss Junior Miss Beauty Queen, something like that. Other women from his past also had arrived and shared his attention. The TV reporter from the airplane. She was around.

He was frenetic, worse with each day, hour, minute. He would talk about his family and how much he wanted to be with them, how worried Linda and the kids were. He would order another round, kiss another woman. He would talk about his friends, the people from Butte, how much they always meant to him. He would explode at some small thing they did.

"All the people he was with, the hangers-on," Bob Arum said, "he abused them terribly."

Filthy McNasty and his brother, Wolfgang, arrived from Los Angeles. They had made their reservations long in advance at the Blue Lakes Inn. Knievel came to them and said they couldn't stay at the inn. He said he needed their rooms.

"Go fuck yourself," Wolfgang said.

They stayed in their rooms.

There was a dinner for the promotion staff at the Blue Lakes Inn. Facundo Campoy, one of the engineers who had worked with Bob Truax from the beginning, brought along two young guys who had helped at the site. Knievel yelled at him from the head table.

"Who are these guys?" he asked. "They weren't invited."

"They've worked every day since we got here."

"Not invited. Get 'em out of here."

Campoy and the two young guys left. Knievel sort of apologized the next day. Campoy said that it was fine. He was a professional. He did not have to get along with the person in charge to do a good job.

A general end-of-the-world feel had come over the entire operation. Nerves were stretched. People acted in ways they never had acted. Maybe it was the isolation, everyone gathered in the middle of this rural nowhere. Maybe it was the realization that this weird promotion actually was going to take place, that a human being actually was going to risk his life for entertainment, yucks, jollies. Maybe it was the realization that the weird promotion, whether the star lived or died, probably was going to finish as a large financial egg.

First reports of ticket sales around the country were not good. Boxing telecasts in theaters had a history of being a last-minute purchase, an impulse buy, but that was boxing. This was a different sort of cat. Not good. The tickets for the site, the live attraction, also had not sold. Knievel's big show for the Twin Falls citizens of cutting off ticket sales at 50,000, even though he could sell 200,000, seemed ludicrous. If 15,000 people appeared, it would be a miracle. The timing pretty much was that if people weren't here by now, they probably weren't coming.

"Knievel played it all wrong," Bob Arum said. "He didn't think about kids when he did his promotion. His appeal mainly was to kids with the toys, television. Despite ABC and *Sports Illustrated* making this some kind of sports event, this was a kid event.

"Knievel wouldn't shut up about how he was going to die. The more he talked about dying, the worse it was. What parent was going to let his kid go somewhere to watch someone die? This wasn't a kid-friendly event."

There were no kids at the site. If there were, Mom and Dad grabbed them by the hand and turned around in a hurry. The people who bought tickets were predominantly bikers. The event looked more like the annual motorcycle rally in Sturgis, South Dakota, than a family picnic. These were hard-core party people. This was a full-blown party atmosphere. The end-of-the-world atmosphere extended everywhere in the vicinity.

"Forget Knievel, forget making money," Arum said. "The one perk was that the sex was unbelievable. I had been separated from my wife, and Twin Falls, Idaho, was like a Mormon place or something, and all of these women were so caught up in the jump, everybody—I mean everybody—was pushing women away. Great-looking women. And when the jump actually took place, the place was overrun with all of these women, and all these nerdy writers suddenly were the attraction, covering the event. It was one orgy, that's what it was. It wasn't even an orgy, it was 'Hey, you want to get laid?' No problem, right.

"We had the U.S. women's ski team acting as our official hostesses. Suzy Chafee, Suzy Chapstick in the commercials. Anyone wanted a massage, they gave 'em a massage. It was wild."

One question Arum was asked often was about whether he was promoting a suicide. (See? Not kid-friendly.) He said he wasn't. He said there was no blood on his hands, no matter what happened.

"If there's a fatality Sunday, I don't think we've promoted a suicide," the promoter said. "Knievel was determined to do this crazy stunt."

Could he have done it without you?

"Sure. He couldn't have done the same promotion. He couldn't have made as much money, but he could have done it. He *would* have done it. He had been talking about it for six years. He was determined to go through with it. He made the decision. All we did was give him a good promotion."

Arum said the rocket would lift off on time, no matter what the wind speed was, no matter what the weather was. Rocket designer Bob Truax said a twenty-mile-per-hour wind was a maximum. Anything higher would force a postponement. Arum said that Knievel would be in charge of that and that only a hurricane would bring a postponement. Twin Falls did not have a lot of hurricanes. He also said television coverage would stay with the event no matter what happened.

The rocket people did busy work around the X-2. They had finished all changes despite the tight schedule. They fretted now about whether everything worked, but they felt reasonably secure with what they had done. Former astronaut Jim Lovell, commander of the first spacecraft to orbit the moon, was part of the closed-circuit broadcast team. He took a look at the X-2 and said that he would travel in it if Knievel had second thoughts. Facundo Campoy and Bill Sprow also said they would fly in the X-2.

"I'd been a drag racer in speedboats until my wife made me give it up," Campoy said. "In one season in my division, nine of the twelve racers were killed. So maybe I had a different perspective."

Truax was one dissenter. He said he built rockets, didn't fly in them. His estimates on Knievel's chances had varied during the rounds of interviews, but he had settled on sixty-forty odds that Knievel survived. He said that Knievel had the same chances as a good test pilot in a new, untried plane.

"If you were going to give me $6 million for doing it, I'd say, 'Nothing doing,' " Truax said. "It's a dangerous thing."

Knievel heard all of this talk, the pros and cons of whether he would survive. Jimmy the Greek had arrived at the site, unbidden, simply to fuel his own publicity machine, and while he wouldn't predict a life-or-death outcome, he did say that "the odds are three-to-one Knievel is crazy." There probably would be more speculation about the man of the moment's fate in the next forty-eight hours than there ever had been about any man of any moment.

One of the more bizarre additions to the conversation was a six-foot-tall, one-ton tombstone delivered from the Rock of Ages Corporation in Barre, Vermont. The company said it was a commemorative stone for the jump, but not a lot of imagination was needed to envision another use.

Knievel had the required imagination. He silenced a dinner table conversation at the Blue Lakes Inn when he read a quote from Jack London that he wanted inscribed on the side of the stone. Jim May, the Twin Falls lawyer, had found the quote.

"I would rather be ashes than dust," Knievel read. "I would rather that my spark burn out in a brilliant blaze, than be stilled by dry rot. I would rather be a superb meteor than a sleepy and permanent planet. The proper function is to live, not to exist."

Pause.

"That's it," Knievel said. "That's me."

The man of the moment's edginess became public on Friday afternoon. This was the dress rehearsal for Sunday's launch. He was lifted to the X-2 early by a giant crane, swung through the air in a bosun's chair, then caught and helped into the cramped cockpit, where he sat for forty-five minutes in the sunshine at the fifty-six-degree launch angle. That meant he was almost flipped upside down. An ignition test was run on the steam engine and failed—five-four-three-two-one-*clink*—then worked on a second try. Knievel was left to fidget and sweat while other people hurried around him.

He was in his full all-American flight uniform, modeled on his racing leathers. He wore the flight helmet. Blood flowed to his upside-down head. More blood flowed. While his eyes stared straight at the blue Idaho sky, he obviously thought about the possibilities after the rocket was launched for real in two days. The possibilities did not seem great.

"I've created a monster," he said later, "and I don't know how to handle it."

At ground level, as Evel sat upside down, the first battalions of true Evel believers had arrived. They were not a pretty sight, these believers, dirty and self-medicated, pushing against the cyclone fence erected to keep them away from the rocket, biker guys and biker chicks, pleading and snarling. One woman, spaced out and topless, a crucifix bouncing between her breasts as she rode atop her boyfriend's shoulders, was called "the Hollow Lady" by Eszterhas and "the Quaalude Queen" by Cardoso. She fit either description. A young guy, also on top of someone's shoulders, named himself "the State Pig of Montana." "I'm the State Pig of Montana," he said, again and again. He was covered in dirt, presumably as filthy as any state pig of Montana should be.

The Quaalude Queen and the State Pig kept up a constant clatter of "Evel, Evel, the tribes have assembled," calling to the man of the moment, who probably couldn't hear them, hung up in the sky. The Queen added the fact that she loved him and would be proud to share her love with him. The State Pig continued to state that he was the state pig. The man of the moment finally saw and heard all this when he came down from the rocket with his blood still filling his cranky head. He told one of the guards that if any of the screamers made a move to climb to the rocket to "blow their goddamned heads off."

And then he made a strange remark.

"Look at this," he said, loud enough for promoter Arum and anyone else to hear. "Sunday is the greatest day of my life, and it's run by a bunch of goddamned New York Jews."

Arum tried to shuffle the words off ("My values are different from his—he's a cowboy"), but they hung around like an unpleasant odor. What was that? "Bunch of goddamned New York Jews"? Things did not improve when Knievel returned to his trailer.

This was supposed to be the time, finally, when he sat for an interview. He went into the trailer. The ragged clot of press people closed around the door, a crowd, cameras and microphones sticking out from all sides. The plan was for Knievel to sit down on the steps on a red-white-and-blue throw rug hastily supplied by Shelly Saltman. The plan, alas, would put him out of sight from reporters and, more importantly, cameramen in the back rows.

"Have him stand," Jim Watt, an NBC cameraman out of Los Angeles, suggested to Saltman.

Before Saltman could reply, Knievel popped out of the door. He had heard the request and did not like it.

"If I want to sit down, I'm going to sit down," he said.

"Out," he then said to Watt. "Out."

Out? A strange dance began as Knievel turned and went back inside the door, then burst out again and said to Saltman, "Tell him the next time he looks at me to have a smile on his face," and then to Watt, "I'm not an actor, Mr. Cameraman, do you understand that?" and then Watt replied, "That's right." And then it seemed finished, and then Knievel pushed it one more step. He said, directly to Watt again, "I said, 'Have a smile on your face.' " Watt said years later, "I had just come back from working in Vietnam. I probably told him to go fuck himself," but what he really said was, "I don't smile for anybody." It meant the same thing.

Watt was a smaller man. He was hamstrung by his equipment. Knievel bounced off the steps of the trailer, swinging the cane. He had a good angle. He hit Watt's camera. He hit Watt's shoulders. He knocked Watt to the ground. He stood over the cameraman.

"Get him out," Knievel said. "Out! I don't need any crap from a cameraman like you."

"I can't go without my camera," Watt said.

"I'll stick it in your ear if you're not careful," Knievel said as other parties finally moved between the two men.

Not only was this ugliness, it was ugliness witnessed by the people who were sending all of those words across the country. Knievel clomped back into his trailer. Watt picked himself up and walked away with his broken camera. There were assorted guesses that this was part of the hype, a first cousin to those fights at the weigh-in between two boxers—They Really Don't Like Each Other!—to promote the big heavyweight fight. Watt, though, made it seem real. He was a real cameraman, whacked for trying to do his job, nothing else. Knievel also made it seem real. He was out of control.

After a while, he came back and *sat down* on the stairs and tried to explain himself. He was more restrained than he had been all day. Almost calm.

"I think all of you here now know, regardless of what two or three jackasses might say or have said, out of the millions of legitimate press people in the world, what this thing is," he said. "It's a monster. I think you all know now by looking at me that I wish I didn't have to do this and wish I wasn't here. But I'm going to, and I'm trying to keep my wits about me . . . and you're all welcome to film whatever you want as long as you're here to help me. If anybody doesn't want to help me, I'll go after them and throw them out, just like I did the last guy."

He went over to the fence and talked with his constituents at the end of the interview. The State Pig of Montana was happy. The Quaalude Queen was happy. The man of the moment stepped onto the waiting helicopter, Watcha McCollum at the controls, and away they went.

A story. The person who hated Knievel most was Don Branker. Arum privately had decided that "I never would root for someone to die, couldn't do that, but I wouldn't mind seeing this guy bounced around a little bit in that rocket," but mostly kept his opinions to himself. He still had to sell tickets. Branker did not have that problem. The twenty-eight-year-old rock 'n' roll site manager, running on overdrive every day, worried not only about whether or not Knievel would get inside the rocket, but also about details like providing one portable toilet for every five women in the crowd, one more for every ten men. The theatrics had worn him down. He'd had enough.

His relationship with Knievel was terrible. Knievel wrote him off from the beginning as a long-haired hippie asshole, a characterization that put him near the bottom of all shit lists. Every suggestion Branker made wound up in a battle. One fight led into another. Knievel thought Branker didn't know anything. Branker thought Knievel was an idiot.

When he was approached by Eszterhas for an interview in *Rolling Stone*, the rock 'n' roll guy let his opinions roll. He sat next to the rocket and talked into a tape recorder and vented:

> I got into this thing because I wanted to get away from Watergate and everything it was doing to my head. I'd promoted over 400 rock and roll concerts and I was the producer for California Jam in Ontario and I'd promoted the Stones, the Dead and Alice Cooper. I got involved in this too, I suppose, because I wanted to do an event that had nothing to do with rock and roll.
>
> I hadn't met Knievel, but I knew that he is as important to little

kids today as Ted Williams and Mickey Mantle were in my child-hood. He interested me sociologically that way. I also realized that you can walk into just about any house in America today and sooner or later hear the name Evel Knievel. It's crazy, but it's America. Maybe it's part of an escape syndrome. Maybe America just badly needs a hero.

So I came out here months ago and started setting things up here as a producer for Top Rank. I'm not going to kid anyone, Top Rank gave me a contract for a lot of money, but also I felt what I was doing was important. I was working with a community and putting it through tremendous changes very fast. And I realized that after the jump is over, I'll go back to L.A., but the people in this community will still have to live here. I tried my best to keep that in mind as I worked with them.

Finally I met the star. I watched Knievel and for a while I thought him the most charismatic man I ever met and that includes both Jagger and Dylan. I'd watch him go into a room and his presence would fill it up. He'd become everything going on in that room.

After I worked with him a while, though, I started noticing certain things. He has a real tendency to exaggerate, more than any person I've ever met. In addition to that, he himself believes everything he says. Where I come from, that's a pathological liar. He would say these things that were lies so emphatically that he just about made you believe them—even though you knew they were lies. And in this respect his power of the press blew me out. It seems to me he scares the press and they end up eating out of his hand because he strikes some bully chord in them. Since most newspeople I've met aren't exactly heroic, they just let themselves be run over.

I noticed all the hypocrisies too. He flaunts other chicks more than any other performer I've met. Yet he stands for a conservative Americanism. Like I've seen him go into a crowd where he hears somebody yell "Fuck!" and he'll say: "You shouldn't cuss around women and children." Then an hour later I'll see him tongue-lash some guy and call him every kind of asshole with the guy's girl right next to him.

I noticed other things too. Like the fact the guy has a tendency not to pay his bills. Guys come in here saying—I still haven't got that check he said he'd send me. Little guys who don't make a lot of money. Yet he'll flaunt his diamond rings at them. And stupid, needless lies. Like he went around the country saying for a while that all the tickets to the site had been sold so nobody else can get in. I think he's still lying about that. He says now that 50,000 people will come here. I'm guessing 10,000.

He's also full of prejudices. I'm a freak and I get the feeling he doesn't quite trust me because my hair is long. A couple of weeks ago I hosted a network thing on TV, *In Concert,* and I had the O'Jays and Flash Cadillac on, and Evel heard I'd be on TV and he said he'd watch me. He did too. He called me and said—"I like what you do, but get rid of all that music. The hell with that rock and roll. I hate that rock and roll. I'll make a Skycycle believer out of you yet."

His emotions are erratic. He'll call people twenty-four hours a day, for example, any time of the night, and start yelling about some little thing that hasn't been done. He can be sitting at a table, and he'll be complimenting the guy sitting at his left and smiling, and suddenly he'll turn to the guy on his right without breaking stride and say something like—"You damn no good son of a bitch, you didn't do this or that. I'm gonna kick your ass!"

One of the things I discovered after working here a couple of months is that the promoters and Top Rank aren't exactly running the show. Evel is. All of it. Every single detail. He doesn't trust anybody about anything. He wants to do everything himself, and his response to everything is money. That's his only concern—money. How many dollars will it cost? And how many dollars will it bring in?

Take this whole security issue. I stay awake nights worrying about people going over the rim Sunday because the security is woefully bad. Irresponsibly bad. And it's directly Evel's fault. I had to fight him to get a public-address system for Sunday. I want a guy to get on the PA every few minutes and tell the people to stay the hell back from the rim. It will be a kind of psychological conditioning. So I went to Evil and hassled, and he said—"How much is it going to cost?" And I told him $18,000, and he said—"Hell no, to hell with it, that's too much money."

I finally talked him into it. "How's it going to look if people get killed Sunday?" I asked him. I said—"If just one person dies out here, the whole thing won't be worth it." That line didn't seem to cut much ice with him.

I tried to talk him into putting another fence along the rim for Sunday, but he won't go for that. One fence is enough, he says, and he keeps talking about the security men who'll be up here. "The fence costs too much," he says. I tried to argue with him, but he just said—"It's my show, not yours!"

I wish this thing was over with. To tell you the truth, he scares me now. What's even scarier, I think, is that he really believes he's going to be the president of the United States someday. I'm not kidding. I've heard him talk about it. The Knievel toys are the biggest-selling toys since the Barbie doll, and the way he figures it, ten, fifteen years from now those kids are your voting majority. He'll become a crusader like Oral Roberts in politics and talk about decency for America. If that ever happens, I'm going to tell a lot of people about how, back in Idaho, when he wasn't a candidate for president, he was more worried about his damn money than about people's lives.

The scene with the cameraman, Jim Watt, was a final disturbing bit of evidence for Branker. Knievel was the ultimate bad guy. That was Branker's opinion. That was why he did what he did that night.

One of the loose ends of the promotion that had to be tied in a hurry involved Miss Beauty Queen, Miss Junior Miss Beauty Queen, whatever she was. The young woman, the girl, starry-eyed and excited by all that was happening, apparently wrote a love note to the man of the moment. The man of the moment's wife discovered the note and was offended. The man of the moment instructed Bob Arum to slip Miss Beauty Queen $200 and send her back to wherever she was from. Miss Beauty Queen found another place to go.

"I took her back to my room at the Blue Lakes Inn," Don Branker said, "and I fucked her. Out of spite I fucked her. I fucked Evel Knievel's girlfriend for spite."

Branker's parents had come into town. They spotted him with Miss Beauty Queen the next morning and knew that he stayed with her all night in his room. He was married at the time, a wife back in California.

"What are you doing?" his mother asked.

Her son really couldn't explain.

The next night, the night before the jump, there was no time for sex or spite. Branker was called to the launch site from an organizational meeting at the Blue Lakes Inn. He had hired a local Indian called Chief Red Cloud to help with the many problems that might develop in Twin Falls. The Chief had done good work, especially calming the local population, but this was a different problem than had been anticipated.

"You better get out here," Chief Red Cloud said. "There's a riot going on."

Branker drove his rental car over the bouncy, bumpy dirt road to the site. There were no lights at the site except in the trailers the promoters used as offices and the spotlights on the ABC trucks and the rocket. Everything else was wilderness dark, darker than dark. Branker's headlights, when he pulled in, gave him flashes of what was taking place. People were moving. Noises of destruction were coming from assorted locations. Anarchy.

He drove fast, fast as he could, to the trailer. Tommy Frazier, brother of former heavyweight champion Joe Frazier, was there. He had been hired by Top Rank as security. Chief Red Cloud was there. Filthy McNasty, for some reason, was there. He had showed up, driving the Cadillac hearse with the name of his bar on the side. A few other people were there. Bob Arum and Shelly Saltman were on their way.

This was a definite crisis situation.

"It was right out of a movie," Branker said. "If you told people, they wouldn't believe it. The first thing I saw . . . they'd literally torn the top off a beer truck. They were throwing cases of beer out of the truck. People were running everywhere with cases of beer. It was 'Mad Max Meets Evel Knievel.' "

Second sight was worse than first sight. Screams came from the darkness, female screams. Cheers. More screams. More destruction. Fires were started. Portable toilets on fire. Concession stands on fire. The people in the Qualls family's fields—how many people? a lot—were drunk and high and doing whatever they wanted to do, and there was no one to stop them. The people apparently had been upset by the $40 fee to park, about the prices for the beer, thought they were being gouged. They gouged back. Or maybe they simply wanted a party. Beer was now free.

Branker had hired some shotgun-carrying guards for the day, but they were gone. Who knew where they went, intimidated by the crowd. There were no guards. The one weapon available was a pistol that one of them had left in the trailer. Branker took charge of the gun.

He had supervised the installation of fences at the site. Most of them were along the edge of the canyon, the two-fence system that hopefully would stop people from falling over the edge if they surged forward when the rocket took off. He'd had another fence constructed around the rocket, the television equipment, and the trailers. This had created a compound.

The rioters had control of the rest of the site, the dark part. They would make a move sometime toward the compound, the lit-up part, for total control. That was to be expected.

Arum called the governor of Idaho, asked about the possibility of the National Guard coming onto the scene. The governor said that could happen, but if it did, the rocket launch certainly would not take place. Branker called the adjutant general of the National Guard. The adjutant general said the Guard had to protect the town in case there was a riot, not the promotion. There would, in short, be no help from the National Guard.

"So it was us," Branker said.

When the rioters came, he and Chief Red Cloud went outside to the fence for the confrontation. Branker carried the gun. He has been asked through the years how many rioters were involved. His answer has been, "Maybe five thousand," but he never has been sure. Did Custer count the Indians? The one thing he knew at the time was that there were a lot more enemies than there were bullets in his gun.

A leader seemed to step forward from the crowd. Again, like a movie. A couple of lieutenants seemed to be behind him. They said they were going to tear down the fence and come into the compound. Branker stepped closer with the gun by his side and said they were not.

"You've got a gun," the leader said, a slurred mouth at work underneath bloodshot eyeballs. "There's a lot of us out here, and you can't get us all. We're going to throw you into the canyon."

Is this really happening? Branker wondered. If it was a movie, then he should answer with the appropriate lines of dialogue.

"You know what, somebody might throw me into the canyon, but it won't be you," he said. "You and your two buddies behind you, I'm going to put two bullets each in your heads. I want to make sure you're dead. You will be dead."

The dramatic pause followed.

Yes?

"We'll be back as soon as the sun comes up," the leader said. "Real soon. We'll be back."

The rioters went in other riot directions that involved more beer. The trouble was averted for the moment. The future? Branker and now Arum and the Top Rank people worried. Even if the rioters didn't return, more security somehow was needed. The National Guard was out. What would happen in the morning at the jump? Even if the 50,000 proposed attendance figure was now preposterous, 15,000 people, 10,000 people would be a challenge. Certainly 5,000 people had been.

Branker had been in a couple of verbal confrontations during the preceding days with some huge biker. The guy seemed to be a Hells Angel. Branker thought about him now. He told himself the guy would be laughing at him if he could see the situation he was in.

Branker said that out loud.

"Too bad the big Hells Angel guy wasn't here," he said. "He would have had a laugh."

Chief Red Cloud said he had seen the Hells Angel and his friends set up a camp at Shoshone Falls. Really? An idea clicked inside Branker's head. He grabbed the Indian, jumped into the rental car, spotted a man in his headlights carrying six cases of beer, three under each arm, very hard to do, blew past, and headed to Shoshone Falls.

The negotiations did not last long. Branker offered $1,000 of free beer, plus free food, if the Hells Angel guy would collect his Hells Angels friends in the morning and have them work as guards for the canyon jump. They also would be stationed along the fences, best seats in the canyon. The Hells Angel guy agreed. He and the other bikers weren't really Hells Angels—most of them were from Denver and groups like the Chosen Ones, the Brothers Fast, the Terranauts, the Captain Americas—but "Hells Angels" seemed to be a fine, all-encompassing term.

"Where do you want us, boss man?" he said.

At sunrise, the Angels or whatever they were arrived at the site, a line of large men on motorcycles, normally a small town's worst nightmare. They were hungry.

"Give 'em what they want," Bob Arum said in the small kitchen in the compound.

"We're not serving breakfast yet," the cook said.

"Motherfucker," Arum said in a loud voice, "serve 'em breakfast."

And so it began. The Hells Angels or whatever they were ate breakfast. They were given pieces of red cloth to tie around some part of their bodies to show that they were official guards. The day of the great canyon jump had arrived.

21 Whoosh

The man of the moment made the moment a family affair. If this was going to be his last day on earth, then he would go out looking like a church deacon. Linda and the three kids would be there. His mother would be there from Reno. His father had been there all week. ("Bob always had to have a challenge," his dad said at a press conference, sounding a bit like Ward Cleaver. "I tried to discourage him for years for fear of injury.") His eighty-one-year-old grandmother, Emma, would be there. His half-sisters would be there from both sides of the family tree. His cousin, Father Jerry Sullivan, a Catholic priest from Carroll College in Helena, Montana, would give the benediction before liftoff.

His lawyers, accountants, bartenders, friends, and fellow reprobates from long ago had appeared already at the site. Bus trips had gone down from Butte. There had been a mass migration from the city, people driving the 364 miles in five, six, seven hours, depending on speed. The Butte High band had gone down to play the National Anthem. Everyone had assembled, former promoters, fans, everyone . . . Ray Gunn, his first assistant from Moses Lake in the early days, had returned for the show, friends again, signed up now to watch the jump from a helicopter and carry a bottle of Wild Turkey to the other side for an instant celebration.

The day would be part wake, part wedding reception, an all-time Humpty Dumpty experience. The broken pieces of Robert Craig Knievel's life would be put together for this one time as they never had been put together, not once, in all of his years.

He would fly from Butte in the Lear in the morning with his family. Watcha would be at the controls and would buzz the crowd at the canyon, a dramatic touch. Watcha and everybody else would switch to a helicopter at the Twin Falls City-County Airport, arrive at the site to great applause, and the man of the moment would put on the flight suit in his trailer, and the show would begin.

Unless, of course, he canceled the show.

"I have two demands that if you don't meet I'll cancel the show," Knievel said in an early morning phone call to Bob Arum from Butte.

Arum prepared for the worst.

"First," Knievel said, "I want to have all the press meet my helicopter when it lands. I want to make a statement."

Arum said that would be impossible. Moving the entire press corps through the crowd could start a riot. (Another riot.) What he could do was bring Knievel to the press tent. That was possible. Knievel could make his statement that way. Same result.

Knievel agreed.

"Second," he said. "I want you to bring your two sons to my trailer before the jump. I want to say some words to them before the jump because people are going to blame you for my death and I want them to know it was my idea. And I want them to sit with my family at the jump."

"Done," Arum said, figuring that the two boys, ages eleven and nine, would do what he told them. "I'll get them there."

Knievel seemed sentimental in everything he did that morning. He seemed to be turning off the lights, locking all the doors. Just in case. He had a picture of the canyon, just the canyon, no Skycycle or ramp, that he secretly signed, "Linda, I love you," across the blue sky. He told Kelly, his oldest son, last thing before everybody left Butte for the jump, to pretend to go back into the house for his shaving kit and hang the picture on the bedroom wall. He wanted that waiting for his wife if somehow the results turned out badly.

Even when he arrived at the site—plane flight, helicopter, there—he was sentimental. Even when he talked to the press.

"When I weighed last night all the good things and the bad things that were said, it came out a million to three for the good," he told the press after he landed in Watcha's helicopter. "So I hope all your landings in life are happy ones—and I thank you from the bottom of my heart."

Could this be the same man who had been such a terror for the previous week?

"He apparently has not read all of the papers," one of the cynics suggested within the hearing of Charles Maher of the *L.A. Times*.

"I think he's making his peace," another cynic said.

This was his good-bye to his adversaries. He went inside his trailer to get dressed and say good-bye to his family. And to Bob Arum's sons.

The crowd was somewhere between 10,000 and 15,000 people, far fewer than Knievel or the promoters had expected, but still a nightmare. These were the same hard-living characters who had run wild a night earlier, now joined by reinforcements who doubled or tripled their number. The burnt-out chemical toilets and the knocked-down concession stands were a testament to the work these people could do. The toilets that weren't burnt out and the concessions that weren't knocked down were incredibly busy.

The temperature hung around 90 degrees, all sunshine. A strong wind, as much as twenty miles per hour, whipped clouds of dust everywhere. The heat and the dust made a man want another beer. Or convinced a woman to take her shirt off. Both acts happened quite often. The women were encouraged by more than one sign that read "Show Us Your Tits."

The crowd was forced to provide much of its own entertainment. The preliminary acts—Karl Wallenda walked on the high wire, Gil Eagles rode a motorcycle blindfolded along the rim of the canyon, a man named Sensational Parker swung over the edge on an eighty-foot pole, and the Great Manzini escaped from a straitjacket while he was hung upside down over the canyon from a burning rope—were performed out of sight from the live crowd, staged only for the closed-circuit viewers across the country. Fenced off from the compound and the rocket and any activity around it, with only the few remaining concession stands to visit, with no security except at the fences, the crowd improvised. Freely.

"These young girls . . . these beautiful young girls . . . were saying that they wanted to give blow jobs for Evel," Bob Arum said. "And they did. Right there. Blow jobs for Evel. It was an amazing thing to see."

One of the few live attractions was the Butte High School marching band and the accompanying Purple B's Drill Team. Knievel had requested the presence of the band, even requested that certain songs be played, and had put up $2,200 to make the trip happen. Ken Berg, the twenty-six-year-old band director in his first year at the school, had pulled all the pieces together. It was quite a task. He was in charge now of over one hundred kids dressed in heavy purple-and-silver uniforms topped by heavy fur hats that were over a foot and a half tall. The band had left Butte at midnight in buses, ridden for seven hours, and appeared at the site at sunrise. The return trip would start immediately after the liftoff. The buses were expected back in Butte around 2:00 a.m.

"It was a lot of work," Berg said, an understatement. "I probably saw less of what happened that day than anyone. I was worried the whole time about those kids."

The crowd, well, members of the crowd made comments about the Butte High School band. The comments were not nice. The Purple B's Drill Team, girls, had their butts pinched. Lewd suggestions were made to all females in uniform. Director Berg had to keep photographers away from the drill team because the photographers were trying to take shots from ground level, up the high school girls' legs. The band already had planned to take part in the Rose Bowl parade in Pasadena on January 1, 1975, appropriate monies having been raised. This was not the Rose Bowl parade.

"We were a bunch of naive band students," flute player Judy Staudinger, whose brother played the drums, said. "This was not a very naive crowd."

The kids were mostly terrified. They had never seen anything like what they saw now. Kim Ungerman, a photographer for the *Montana Standard*, stood on the announcer's platform to take a group picture of the band in formation. He said he could see four fights taking place in the crowd at one time, one that involved eleven of the motorcycle gang security officers. There was little water on the site, less food. The purple suits weighed a thousand pounds apiece. No one had slept. The ticket-holders were upset because the band was on the far side of the first fence, a prime location. The ticket-holders said more nasty things.

At one point a riot seemed to be developing, an assault on the fence. Someone from the promotion quickly asked the Butte band to play a song, any song. Berg whipped the troops together. They played a special Evel Knievel song they had learned for the trip. The music, curiously, seemed to quiet the crowd. The promoter asked the band to keep playing.

"We played 'Come On, Baby, Light My Fire,' " Judy Staudinger said. "I remember that. It seemed to fit."

The only celebrities who had appeared were President Gerald Ford's two sons and singer Claudine Longet and her boyfriend, skier Spider Sabich. (The couple would be in the news a year and a half later when Longet shot and killed Sabich in their Aspen, Colorado, home. After a front-page trial, she was convicted of negligent homicide.) The location was too remote to attract most celebrities. Then again, the location was too remote to attract most people. There were few places to stay, few big-city resources for travelers.

Duane Unkefer, who handled Knievel's dealings with Harley-Davidson, described the problems as well as anyone. He was in charge of a group of Harley executives and their wives who had flown in for the event. Harley had removed itself from the production—the rocket was not a motorcycle, not even close—but the company logo had been slapped on the side of the thing and Evel was their man, so the executives followed.

The accommodations, alas, were terrible, a roadside motel that was miles from the jump site, then a yellow school bus early in the morning for a ride to the launch. This was the only transportation Unkefer could find for his bosses and their wives. After an interminable ride in two-lane traffic, the bus bounced over the dirt road to the jump site, then pulled up maybe twenty feet from the canyon, which was as close as the bus could go. There were no such things as reserved seats or luxury boxes for canyon jumps.

The executives were parked here in the middle of the masses. The masses pounded on the side of the school bus, drank, cussed, stirred up a bunch of dust. Unkefer stepped out of the bus to see what he could see.

"They mostly were all males, but there were a couple of women too," he reported. "Right near me, three or four guys, big guys, grabbed one of the women and ripped all of her clothes off. Just like that. Then they held her in the air. Horizontal."

And then a succession of other males proceeded to have oral sex with the woman, who did not seem to mind. Unkefer looked back into the bus. All of the executives and all of their wives had witnessed this display.

"I wondered," he said, "what my future with the company might be."

A picture of that horizontal naked woman, or perhaps another horizontal naked woman, would appear in an article about the jump a week later in *Sports Illustrated*. The caption would read: "The biker crowd does its own launching." High school boys would study this picture endlessly in school libraries in coming weeks.

Heinz Kleutmeier, the *SI* photographer for the Evel Knievel cover, had come back to Snake River for the jump. He had flown in from Madison, Wisconsin, where he had been part of a project for *Life* magazine called "One Day in the Life of America." Over one hundred photographers had been sent across the country to take pictures of various people and events on September 5, 1974, a random date chosen to represent the everyday hum of the country at work.

Kleutmeier's assignment was at a high school in Madison, then at a college bar at the University of Wisconsin. The magazine would choose 208 shots from over 1.5 million photographs taken across the nation. The format would be so successful that it would be expanded in future years to fill best-selling coffee-table books.

The magazine noted that on September 5, 1974, no different from any other day in America, about 8,600 babies would be born, 5,400 people would die, 2,500 would get divorced, and 6,300 would get married. There was no real news. The date was selected because, "in the period after Labor Day each year, summer is put away, school begins, the tempo is up. In many ways it is the year's real beginning."

Three days later at Snake River there was this different dynamic at work. Kleutmeier was stunned by the difference. The universal was replaced by the bizarre. "One canyon jump" was added to the list of births, deaths, marriages, and divorces. One guy would be shot into the unknown. Chaos seemed to be everywhere.

Kleutmeier tried to inject a small bit of common sense into the proceedings.

"You're going back to the bottom of the canyon," the photographer told his assistant when they arrived at the site. "That's where I want you for the jump."

The assistant objected. The sun was brutal. The bottom of the canyon would be hot, dirty, and totally without merit. Nothing would happen there.

"No, that's where the story is going to be," Kleutmeier said, thinking about the test shot he had witnessed. "I saw the test. That's where this guy is going to land."

This was a different One Day in the Life of America. Yes, it was.

The ceremonies before the launch were part halftime at the Super Bowl, part High Mass in the Roman Catholic Church. The broadcaster for the closed-circuit show was David Frost, the thirty-five-year-old British talk show host, noted as an interviewer of political figures and fiancé of actress Diahann Carroll. Three years in the future he would do interviews with Richard Nixon that would help explain what had happened in the past couple of years. His color man now was Jim Lovell, the decorated American astronaut.

"This is reminiscent of the early *Mercury* days," Lovell said, presumably talking about rockets, overlooking what was happening with the crowd around the launch site.

Knievel came out of his trailer and bounded up the dirt hill that was the base for the launch ramp. He looked clean and perfect in his red-white-and-blue flight suit, the copy of his motorcycle leathers. He was a Saturday morning cartoon brought to life. A well-dressed, but worried Saturday morning cartoon. He shook a few hands on the way to meet Frost on a platform at the top of the hill overlooking the canyon.

Frost seemed nonplussed to be asking questions of a man who might be dead within the next five or ten minutes. Knievel talked in solemn tones, which befit a man who might be dead in the next five or ten minutes. It was not the greatest interview in interview history.

"How have you prepared yourself physically and mentally for this?" Frost asked in the midst of his questions.

"David, I don't drink very much," Knievel said. "And I *never* have taken a narcotic."

"Do you have any advice for people out there?"

"Live like you were made to live. Don't take a narcotic."

Frost's final question was whether or not Knievel was afraid at this moment. Knievel gave a lengthy answer that mentioned God and Old Glory, Jesus and living "in a country like this."

"I think that a man was put here to live, not just exist, and today is the proudest day of my life," he said in conclusion. "I'm living a dream that they thought never could be done, but it'll be done."

He stood with Frost on the platform for the benediction, delivered by his cousin ("Guide him to a successful landing, Lord, whether it be on earth or in Heaven" Father Sullivan said), shook hands with Bob Truax ("Don't pull that chute until the right time" Truax said), then was carried through the air slowly in the bosun's chair hung from the crane. He could have climbed the stairs to the rocket, no problem, but a sponsor had supplied the crane, plus money, so he rode the crane. An Evel Knievel song, John Culliton Mahoney's "Ballad of Evel Knievel," was played over the loudspeaker during the trip ("A strong yet simple man, riding on the edge of danger"). The poem "Why," which Knievel read often before his jumps and claimed he had written, was read while he was helped into the Skycycle ("To be a man and do my best is my only quest").

There would be debate later about his condition when he went into the cockpit. There would be people who claimed he was drunk, blitzed on shots of Wild Turkey when he went in. There would be other people who declared he was perfectly fine. There would not be a consensus. He definitely was scared, nervous.

"He's sitting in the thing, and he's out of it," Arum said. "He didn't even recognize me. He was scared shit out of his mind. I wished him good luck."

"He was okay," Facundo Campoy, who wiped his face and then helped him put on the flight helmet, said. "He was alert. He heard me. He wasn't drunk. No. He was okay."

The most important fact for everyone involved in the promotion was that he was inside the cockpit. The show would happen. More than one of the promoters during the closing weeks had doubted that this moment ever would take place.

"There was a big guard with a cowboy hat and a shotgun right next to the rocket," Don Branker said. "Everyone thought he was there to protect Knievel. I told him he was there to threaten to shoot Knievel if Knievel tried to climb out of that thing."

David Frost said the announcers would be silent for the countdown.

"Happy landings, Evel," he said.

Ten . . .

The time was 3:36 in the afternoon of September 8, 1974. The numbers came through the radio in the pilot helmet clamped tight over the man of the moment's troubled head. No stopping now. He was going to travel over Snake River Canyon in this bucket of previously used bolts. Or not.

There was no turning back now. He was strapped into this compartment in the front end of this retread airplane fuel tank that had been salvaged from a government junkyard, one of those fuel tanks you see on the wingtips of fighter planes or private jets, a fuel tank that cost no more than $100 as scrap metal. He waited to be blasted into the sky. Maybe blasted to smithereens. Blasted in some manner or shape or form. That was for sure.

The fuel tank, which was supposed to be a rocket of course, had been altered, painted, given some kind of "jet propulsion" system, a set of surplus helicopter fins had been stuck on the side, and some corporate logos had been added to complete the red-white-and-blue American commercial package, but truth was truth: he was riding a homemade piece of shit. Three smart kids with an *Encyclopedia Brittanica* and a whole lot of spare time could have made this thing. Shot it off from their backyard.

Nine . . .

The sense of doom that had been an undigested worry in his stomach for the longest time had grown and grown in the past months, days, hours, and now, in the final minutes and seconds, it filled his entire body, gushed out, covered his every word and action. He was a dead man.

He had talked so much about the risk, the peril involved, while selling this event, this stunt, this whatever it was across the country, that he had convinced himself. He was a goner. He had created his own demise, built it from scratch, from an idea in his head to a public extravaganza televised around the world. "Man Kills Himself." Come on, folks. Get your money up. Bring the wife and kids.

"Right now I don't think I've got better than a fifty-fifty chance of making it," he had told Robert Boyle of *Sports Illustrated*. "It's an awful feeling. I can't sleep nights. I toss and turn, and all I can see is that big ugly hole in the ground grinning up at me like a death's head. You know, I've always been concerned about kids—not just my own three, but all kids—what kind of an image I'm providing for them, what kind of an inspiration. I don't know now. Maybe I'm leading them down a path to self-destruction. Our house in Butte is surrounded night and day by people wanting to take a look at me, to take something as a souvenir. And that damn little Robbie of mine, the 11-year-old, you know what he's gone and done, He has got a big old sign out in front that says 'SEE EVEL JR JUMP—25 CENTS.' It's not a good thing."

Eight . . .

Push the button. That was all he had to do. Push the button and away he went. He had little control over what happened next. He had no steering wheel. He had no gears to shift. Nothing. He was so cramped he couldn't put his arms out and attempt to fly as a last gasp if trouble arose. The last-resort personal parachute hanging from his chest was nuisance rather than comfort. He had his hand on the lever for the drogue shoot, that was it. Wait ten seconds after liftoff and let it go. It would work without him if he passed out. He really was a passenger, not a driver.

When he pushed that one button in front of him, the plug would be pulled on the seventy-seven-gallon boiler underneath, the water inside superheated in the past fourteen hours to 475 degrees, and 5,000 pounds of steam pressure would be released. The old airplane fuel tank . . . okay, the rocket . . . the rocket would be traveling at 200 miles per hour by the time it reached the end of the 108-foot ramp into the sky, traveling as fast as 400 miles per hour when it hit the height of its arc, 2,000 feet in the air. (Plus the 540-foot drop into the canyon. That meant he would be almost half a mile off the ground.) If all went well, the drogue parachute and then the big parachute would deploy from the back of the rocket, and he would slow down as he reached the other side. He would be traveling no more than fifteen miles per hour when a pointed shock absorber, sort of a pogo stick on the front of the rocket, would cushion the landing on the moonscape on the other side.

This, of course, was all hypothesis. No one ever had done this.

Seven . . .

Maybe the rocket would blow up when he pushed the button. That was a possibility. Maybe the rocket would flip in midair, go out of control, plunge straight down. Maybe there wouldn't be enough power, the rocket limping over the edge of the canyon, *bang* and *crash* and *bang* and *crash* all the way to the bottom. Maybe the parachute wouldn't open and there would be too much power, the rocket shooting off to God knows where and landing God knows where. Maybe. Maybe. Maybe. Maybe the pressure from the liftoff, the G forces, would cause a heart attack. Simple as that.

He could die by fire. He could drown in the Snake River. He could die from internal or external injuries. The permutations of death seemed endless. He could break his neck. Some jagged piece of something could cut him in two. He could be paralyzed for life. Anything. He was a crash-test fucking dummy, a passenger, along for the ride. He could be scared to death right now, before anything happened. Is anyone literally scared to death?

Someone had written that he would be like a guy with a firecracker stuck up his butt. That was a good description. Now the firecracker was going to be lit.

Six . . .

He had left a letter for the citizens of Butte on the front page of the *Montana Standard* two days before the jump.

Citizens of Butte

After being close to home for the past days, hearing and seeing much evident thoughts of all of you, I have wondered, especially these last few days as the jump time grows closer, how to let you know my feelings.

Today under my name on the Skycycle X2, there is a sign that says "City of Butte, Mont., Richest Hill on Earth." For me, it not only means richest for ore deposits, it also means richest for the friends and loved ones that I have.

On Sunday, about 3:20 p.m., Butte time, the countdown will start for a Skycycle shot the world thought could not be done.

I know that there are many of you in this little City that I call home who always knew that some how I'd get a chance to realize my Impossible Dream.

When the launch control center gives me in my helmet-radio earphones "T minus 10 seconds to blastoff," I'll give you the "thumbs up" sign. That will be my way of saying Thanks!

Evel

Five . . .

He had carried this thing to the limit. No doubt about that. Straight from Good Time Charlie Shelton's couch in Kalispell all the way to this phantasmagorical sideshow that had stopped the world in its tracks. Pretty good. Pretty damn good. Talk about a good sales pitch.

The canyon was part of the basic package from that Kalispell night forward. Never let it go. He talked coast to coast about jumping the canyon. He talked about it when he was poor, everybody living in the trailer, Linda and the kids picking oranges from some guy's grove, just to have something to eat. He talked about it when he was famous, filling the Astrodome, filling Madison Square Garden, his name on the marquee, dinner delivered now by room service. He talked about it before the shows and after the shows, talked about it in press conferences and at testimonial dinners, talked about it on *Wide World of Sports*. Talked about it on *American Bandstand*.

Maybe the name of the canyon changed during those eight years from the Grand Canyon to Snake River because of circumstances. Maybe the motorcycle jump became a rocket jump because of simple physics. The double-dare never changed: he would jump a canyon. He jumped cars and trucks and buses in a line, jumped the fountains at Caesars Palace. No matter what he jumped and no matter how he landed—and he'd landed badly, broken most of the big bones in his body, spent maybe three of the past eight years in hospitals—the canyon was the ultimate challenge. He talked about it in the hospitals as soon as he could talk.

And here he was.

Four . . .

The money wasn't nearly as much as he'd thought it would be. The crowd wasn't nearly as large as he'd thought it would be. The pope hadn't appeared. Nor had President Gerald Ford. Nor had Elvis or John Wayne or Muhammad Ali or most of the people on the invited list. That was okay. The hell with it. The television cameras were here and 260 sites around the country would show this thing live on pay-per-view, and ABC would show it on film next week on *Wide World.* David Frost and Jules Bergman and Jim Lovell, who went to the moon, were here to do the play-by-play, and for this moment on this one afternoon all of America would wonder what was happening out here in the middle of nowhere. Would he win or lose, live or die? All of America would wonder. Want to know.

The press, okay, hadn't been good. Someone had written, and everyone else had copied, that line that said, "The canyon was the sentimental favorite." The guy from the *Washington Post* lamented that "brutality is big business and suicide attempts can be marketed in a big way in America." Jimmy the Greek, the oddsmaker, had said that thing about "three-to-one this guy is crazy." Bob Truax, he said he wouldn't ride in what he had built.

Voices of negativity came from everywhere.

Three . . .

You know what? Fuck all of those people. Fuck Jimmy the Greek. Fuck Truax. Fuck the bastards with their typewriters, clickety-clacking away, making fun of him with their big words, throwing up their hands in horror about what might happen, screaming about the money he was going to make, acting like he was stealing from cookie jars and piggy banks that belonged to old widows. Fuck the promoters, all taking their bites, not worrying a bit about whether he lived or died. Fuck the hippies and the draft dodgers, who couldn't care less about him. Fuck the fatsos in their living rooms, staring at the blue light every night, grazing, feeding their faces, and never taking a chance. Fuck anyone who thought he was going to die. Fuck anyone who wanted to tell him how to live.

He was Evel Knievel. He was "the Last of the Gladiators." He was "the King of the Stunt Men." If life could be measured by wealth and possessions, he had a hell of a life. He had a good-looking wife and three healthy kids. He had all the pussy on the side a man ever could imagine. He had a Cadillac, a Lincoln, two Ferraris, a $400,000 house on a golf course. He had jewelry. A movie had been made about his life. He knew famous people, and they knew him. Name a restaurant, a bar, a gas station, or a city hall in the United States of America, and he could walk in tomorrow and everything would stop and everybody would know his name and everybody would smile. He was Evel Knievel. Kids loved him. They followed him wherever he went, did what he did, wanted to grow up to be just like him. Businessmen stood in line, paid money simply to talk to him for fifteen minutes. If he put his name on their product, it flew off the shelves. He went to bed as late as he wanted, played golf when he wanted, ate what he wanted, drank Wild Turkey or Jack Daniel's just about every day of his life, starting before noon. He had it running through his body right now, mixing with the adrenaline and the fear. He was Evel Knievel, and he didn't have to take shit from anyone. Did he mention the pussy on the side?

Fuck 'em all.

Two . . .

He never had been a religious man, he was more of a fatalist in everything he did. Whatever happened was what was bound to happen. He did talk to God for a second now. He said, "God, take care of me." He definitely wanted to live. Take care of me. Take care of me. Take care.

The rocket was set at that 56-degree angle at the bottom of that 108-foot ramp. The sky was all he could see in front of him, blue sky with a few faraway clouds, the sky a kid would draw in third grade, fat yellow sun with rays coming out from the side, a picture that maybe would be hung on the wall in the classroom on the night that parents would visit the teachers. Nice picture, kid.

One . . .

He pushed the button.

22 Twin Falls, ID (II)

The naked eye saw that something was not right almost from the beginning. The fabric, the white blur . . . what was that? . . . began to unfurl from the back of the rocket. The parachute. That was what it was. The drogue parachute began to unfurl. The liftoff looked fine, the rocket going off in an impressive *whoosh*, shot out of a steam cloud. There was enough power, hell, that rocket could have made that flight easily, but when the fabric, the parachute, the drogue parachute, the little parachute, started coming out even before the rocket left the 108-foot track, that was that. The flight was doomed. Over before it started.

On a windless day, or with a wind at his back, Knievel maybe could have completed the trip anyway, chute or no chute. The liftoff was that powerful. On this day, the eighteen- to twenty-mile-per-hour wind came straight at him, a second element to slow his progress. By the time the rocket cleared the other side—and it did clear the other side, high in the air, "sort of like a Harmon Killebrew pop fly" someone wrote—the drogue chute, the little chute, had pulled out the main parachute, and together, along with the wind, they won the arm-wrestling match with the steam power that had started the flight. The rocket rolled, virtually stopped, then flipped downward. The parachute, carried by the wind, pulled the X-2 backward, over the canyon again. The rocket also slowly started to head downward, head first, as if it had jumped off a diving board in slow motion. Jesus Christ, the man of the moment was going to land in the river.

He's dead.

That was the thought in the Knievel family group as everyone strained forward to see what would happen next.

He's dead.

That was the thought in the press tent. Maybe the thing was for real, after all. The cynics wondered if they had been too hard, too flippant in their writings. The laughs had disappeared.

He's dead.

That was what the crowd thought as people started to move forward for a better look. For $25, shit, you ought to be able to see if the guy was dead.

In the simulation on Friday, Knievel had been slow getting out of the harness in the open cockpit. The problem was that the clips between the harness and his flight suit were in the wrong place. Someone who could sew had been called to adjust the clips on the flight suit. The someone had done this on Saturday, but hadn't realized that Knievel had two suits. Only one suit was altered. Today, early, Knievel had spilled something or simply found a smudge of dirt on the first flight suit. He switched to the second suit, the one where the clips had not been adjusted. The problem was discovered when he was snapped into place in the rocket, too late to fix. His vanity, changing suits, might now cost him his life. As the rocket was about to slide past the rim of the canyon, disappear from view, the last picture showed him struggling furiously to get free. If he was going to land in the water, he had to be able to get out of the cockpit.

Now, nothing could be seen.

Nothing.

"His engine's out," Lovell, the astronaut, said on closed-circuit. "He's dropping at seventeen feet per second. But from this angle, we can't see."

Nothing.

None of the many cameras could be trained on what was happening. One camera showed a helicopter hovering near the bank of the near side of the canyon. Two men were rowing a boat furiously in that direction. The river was fifteen to eighteen feet deep, certainly deep enough for a man to drown. Where were the powerboats? The angle showed only rocks on the near side of the canyon. The camera was unable to pick up the near part of the river and the near shore.

One of the broadcasters—Arum never had said which one—had declared that he would stop talking if Knievel died. He would not do play-by-play of a man dying. David Frost was silent.

"David, I'm very scared," Lovell, the astronaut, said.

Nothing.

"Why is it taking so long?" Linda Knievel asked as she took her kids, all crying, from the family area to be closer to the press tent, hoping to see a televised picture. "Get your butts in gear."

"What happened?" she asked someone else. "Did he open the parachutes by mistake?"

"Stop your crying," Shelly Saltman said to the three kids. "Your dad's going to be all right. He's fine."

Saltman admitted later he lied.

Nothing.

Nothing. Nothing. Nothing.

The Butte High School band had a good view of the liftoff, the opening of the parachute, the turn downward, and then the disappearance beyond the canyon rim. Kids began to cry, especially girls. Evel Knievel was dead. Director Berg now had this problem to handle. He would have to talk with the band members about mortality and risks and . . . he suddenly had a more immediate problem.

The band was situated between the fence and the canyon. That had been a worry all day. He had spent the last eight hours watching the kids, making sure that none of them went too close to the edge. Now he looked back toward the crowd and saw an unsettling sight. The gathering of louts, emboldened by the disappearance of the rocket, or maybe simply wanting to get a closer look, had torn down the fences and was headed this way toward the edge of the canyon. The Butte High School band was in the way.

Berg furiously ordered the band into a closed formation like a wedge. He tried to make sure everyone was accounted for, near as he could tell, and ordered the band to march forward toward the buses in the parking lot. The wedge went against the unruly Visigoths heading for the canyon. The two sides crashed into each other, headed in their different directions. The Visigoths, unorganized, gave way.

"When we got through the crowd," Ken Berg said, "I just kept the kids marching right to the buses. I just wanted to get everybody out of there."

Don Branker had hurried from the family viewing area, where he watched the liftoff next to Linda and the kids, to get to the ABC control truck. He wanted to see different pictures. Maybe fifteen monitors showed shots around the site. While other eyes scanned for the shot that none of the monitors had, the X-2 Skycycle and Knievel, Branker was more interested in the action around the edge of the canyon. Yes, the fans had broken through one fence, two fences, and were headed to the edge. This was the worst possible situation, one of those tragedies you always read about at religious celebrations in India or somewhere, hundreds of people killed in a crowd panic. He envisioned a great loss of life. Right here.

Then an amazing thing happened.

Branker saw it again and again. The Hells Angels, the motorcycle guys, whoever they were, held their ground. The last-ditch security guards, themselves the people the promoters had feared the most in their planning, stood on the far side of the broken fences and through menace or charm or force, whatever was needed, calmed whoever came at them. These beefy, bearded outlaws with their tattoos and ponytails, their leather and denim, were the quiet heroes of the entire production. There and there and there, Branker saw them stop the charge or catch some people at the end of the charge and throw them back into the crowd, safe from being pushed over the side.

"They were terrific, these guys," he said. "No $1,000 for beer plus free food ever had been spent better."

Bob Arum looked down at the crowd from the control tower, where he had watched the liftoff, saw the chaos, and suddenly was forced to smile. Here came his two sons. They had been sketchy about the idea of going to Knievel's trailer, listening to his absolution for their father—"A lot of people are going to hate your father, but it's not his fault"—and they definitely didn't want to watch the jump with his family. That was the last place they wanted to be if he died.

Arum had forced them to go, simply to ease Knievel's scattered disposition. Now, when it appeared the worst might have happened, his sons were making their escape back to the TV tower. Good for them.

The lack of information was a strange addition to the event. With cameras everywhere, all of them focused on this one man in a small area, how could he go missing? Yet he did. Like a quarter that had rolled under the couch, had to be there, he somehow couldn't be seen, couldn't be found.

And then he was.

"I think Evel's getting into the helicopter!" Lovell, the astronaut, shouted on the broadcast.

Sure enough. There he was.

He was alive.

The camera angle never did allow a picture of the rocket, which had bounced off an outcropping on the near side of the canyon, ricocheted, fallen fifty feet more, finally come to rest in some brush a few feet from the Snake River. The rescue happened out of sight. Knievel continued in his attempt to unlatch the damn harness after the crash. He was in a panic. He had cut his nose trying to pull off the visor on his flight helmet without unlocking it. His legs ached from a first jolt at liftoff when they were slammed into the hatch. His body ached from the landing. Another jolt.

The first people to reach him were Bob Garrison, a seven-foot-tall skin diver, and John Hood, a forty-eight-year-old guy from Trenton, New Jersey, who worked for Knievel. Hood had been lowered from the rescue helicopter on a rope.

"Are you hurt?" Garrison asked.

"No," Knievel said.

"Can you move your arms?"

He moved his arms.

"How about your back?"

He tested his back.

"I'm ready," Knievel said.

Garrison and Hood cut the daredevil from his harness. Yes, he might have died if he'd landed in the water, unable to unbuckle the harness, but the buckled harness probably had saved his life in this situation. If he had been able to free himself, he might have been thrown out of the cockpit when the rocket hit the first rock or when it landed. Even if he hadn't been thrown out of the cockpit, if he hadn't been locked in, secure, he would have slid forward on impact and been mangled with the front of the rocket. Either way would have brought serious injury. The mistake with the suit actually saved him. He stayed in place.

Hood pulled him from the rocket, placed him in a boat, then they transferred him to the rescue helicopter. Knievel waved to the closed-circuit camera from the boat to show he was all right. He took Hood's place in the helicopter. The pilot said he would come back for Hood. He then took Knievel to the launch site.

The amount of time involved, all of this happening, was startling. Sixteen minutes after the man of the moment had blasted off in the rocket, scared to his core, then possibly dead, he now was back. He jumped off the chopper and into the chaos at the site. From a distance, yes, he almost looked like Lindbergh at Le Bourget Airfield in Paris. A sixteen-minute Charles Lindbergh perhaps. The fences were down, and as the helicopter immediately went back into the air, the crowd came around him in drunken congratulations. He was surrounded, a white dot in a small sea of ants.

Sixteen minutes.

No time had passed. A lifetime had passed.

Sixteen minutes.

David Frost greeted him, and Jules Bergman of ABC was right there too, and they asked questions as he moved back up the hill toward the same spot up where he had left Frost. People jostled and bounced all around them, but a couple of the shotgun-carrying guards cleared a path.

Knievel seemed more than a little disoriented, and very tired. He basically had no idea what had happened with the rocket. He hadn't even realized that the parachute released early. Did he release the chute himself? He did not know. When his view from the cockpit had become a view of the canyon and not the blue sky, that was when he had worried. He had thought he was going to die in the water, yes. He was very lucky, yes.

"Both Ron Chase [who designed the parachute system] and Bob Truax told me that if I saw the canyon wall to get the hell out," he said. "That's what I was trying to do."

After the quick interviews, he went through the crowd to his reunion with Linda and the kids in the trailer. After the trailer, he came out, threw a cane to the crowd, not the real one, a fake, which started yet another fight among the rabble. The cane was eventually broken into smaller pieces for the many members of the congregation, somewhat like relics of the true cross. He moved onto the helicopter with Linda and the three kids, off with Watcha again to the Blue Lakes Inn.

Done.

"I'm so glad it's over," eighty-one-year-old Emma Knievel told the Associated Press. "And if there's a party tonight, I'll be there with bells on."

The outcome was deemed very strange. If the battle had been between life and death, success and failure, this somehow felt like a tie. Maybe even worse. He hadn't killed himself, which was a good thing of course, but he also hadn't done what he'd set out to do, which was clear the canyon. There was no resolution.

"When you stop to think about it, this was the best thing that could have happened," Jimmy the Greek said. "It shows he could have gotten killed. It wasn't a rip-off."

Maybe. Something still felt fishy, even if nothing was. America does not react well to failure in any form. The same press tent cynics who sucked in their breaths when the rocket went down now exhaled doubts. Could it all have been a plot, a scam? Did Knievel release that lever for the drogue chute just to save his ass? Could this have been scripted, all the way to the rescue? Was he ever in any real danger? The veterans of closed-circuit boxing shows remembered that championship fights usually ended with an intriguing story line to promote the next closed-circuit fight. An odor often accompanied the finish to championship fights. Was that the case here? A rematch? Smelled like it.

Clouding the situation were immediate quotes from both rocket engineer Truax and operations director Branker that they thought Knievel had released the lever by mistake (Truax) or on purpose (Branker). Both men retracted their observations, but the words added to the general feeling of dissatisfaction.

The truth, soon discovered by Truax when he looked at video replays, was that the top of the canister containing the drogue chute had been blown off by the force of the liftoff. The problem was as simple as that. The engineers never had run a single test, not even a static test, with the canister and chute attached. It was a curious decision, since parachute problems had plagued both of the test launches, but the madcap rush to the finish was blamed. Nobody had checked out the parachute arrangement. A blunder.

"It was our fault" was Truax's assessment. "He did everything he was supposed to do. He showed courage and performed like a good test pilot. I'm sure he did not release the chute prematurely. But he thought he did at first. He came in and said, 'What did I do wrong?' It was a mechanical failure."

At dinner at the Blue Lakes Inn a few days earlier, Knievel had presented a $100,000 check to Truax that he vowed to sign if the jump went successfully and he was alive. In a quieter moment after the jump, Truax ripped up the check in Knievel's presence, said he wouldn't take it. This was much to the consternation of assistants Facundo Campoy and Bill Sprow, who had been scheduled to receive substantial parts of that payment. They thought Truax was trying to ingratiate himself to pursue some further project. They wanted their money.

Nobody was really happy anywhere about the result. Nobody except Knievel.

"People were praying, and God made the wind blow, and I landed on the bank," he said. "I would have been dead if I landed in the water."

A story. John Hood was still on the bottom of the canyon next to the Skycycle. After he had helped pull Knievel from the cockpit, he had surrendered his seat in the rescue helicopter. The pilot said he would return. He did not mention when that would happen. Hood waited and waited, and the helicopter did not come back. He waited some more, and the helicopter still did not come back. Darkness arrived. This brought the realization that the helicopter was not going to come back.

He was on the bottom of the canyon for the night.

Strangely, he was not alone. There was a guy from Connecticut and a couple of other guys in the area who did not introduce themselves. They had climbed down to avoid the $25 ticket price, yet see the rocket take off. The show had come to them, better seats than they ever imagined. Everybody seemed to have been drinking.

Hood moved off to the side, made a fire. He took the parachute from the rocket, the parachute that in the end had doomed the flight, and made a bed and blanket out of it. He thought mostly about what he would say to the pilot, the son of a bitch who had left him there, but he also thought about his time with Knievel.

Funny how things worked out. He lived in Trenton, New Jersey, was a motorcycle racer for Harley when he was younger, steady appearances at Langhorne Speedway, Harrisburg, Williamsburg, plus two times down at Daytona, good stuff, then he ran the service department in a Honda dealership. He was intrigued with the events that took place at Caesars Palace back in '67 and '68. He liked the idea of the canyon jump. After Knievel was mangled when he jumped the fountains, Hood sent him a letter volunteering to replace him on the Skycycle, whatever that was, and jump the canyon. Knievel sent a letter back, thanked him for his interest, but said the canyon jump was his own challenge and he was going to do it himself.

Four years later, at a small track in West Windsor, New Jersey, Hood met Knievel. The daredevil had switched to the newer version of the Harley XR750 and was doing some practice jumps at the track with the new motorcycle. The two men talked, and Knievel said he needed someone to drive his big rig, with its thirty-two-foot chassis and thirty-foot coach, so long it was illegal in most states, up to Buffalo for a show. This was July of 1971. Hood did the job, and then Knievel said he needed someone to drive the rig to Wilkes-Barre, and Hood, who was divorced, back living with his mother, did that job too. He had been with Knievel ever since.

It was a business arrangement, no doubt about that. He already had quit twice, been convinced to come back. He was like Ray Gunn, who had the job before him. He knew there would be some blowup moment that would end it all.

"Knievel's just an unreasonable character," he decided. "That's the way it is."

When dawn came, Hood decided to get the hell out of the canyon. He had brought his climbing rope and belt with him on the rescue, not knowing what kinds of trouble he would find with Knievel. This was the trouble. He left the other souls at the bottom of the canyon and worked his way, careful step by careful step, up the 540-foot climb to the top. He tried not to look back.

When he hit the top, made it, he beheld an amazing sight. The chemical toilets all had been burned. The concession stands all had been burned. A 1974 Cadillac Eldorado, the odometer stopped forever at 1,037 miles, had been burned, torched. Fires still smoldered. Litter was everywhere. The scene was a vision of the end of the world.

"It was like there'd been a great battle in a great war," John Hood said.

He started looking for that pilot who had forgotten him. He was thinking about punching the guy in the nose.

The aftermath of the jump was the final nightmare. One more night of anarchy. The fever that broke out in the crowd when Knievel went into the canyon, then grew when the fences went down and everyone rushed to the rim to get a better view, continued to roar until it simply roared itself out.

The bizarre result, mixed with an anger about the ticket prices, mixed with the day or days of drink and drugs and unchecked abandon, left various spectators in various states. Some trudged home. Some waited for the crowd to disperse. Some continued to go wild.

"I'll always remember that a lot of the people, when it was announced that Evel was safe, were not happy," Judy Staudinger from the Butte High School band said. "We couldn't believe that. They wanted him to die. They were shouting that the whole thing was a rip-off, a fraud. How could you have been rooting for someone to die?"

Everything that could be burned was burned. Everything that could be trashed was trashed. Broken pipes from the water fountains sent water everywhere. The chemical toilets burned in a row.

The ABC production crew was not saved from trouble. When Knievel went into the canyon, people broke through the fence and tried to climb the staging that was used as the control tower. The climbing soon switched to violence, destruction. The people took over the tower after the show was done.

"There were a lot of spaced-out idiots with knives," ABC unit manager Bill Farrell told the *New York Times*. "They cut wires, smashed equipment, ripped off headsets. Our guys had to abandon the site."

"They took out everything that would burn," one concessionaire said. He estimated he had lost $10,000 in equipment.

The only security, once again, was provided by the few paid guards the promoters had hired. The Hells Angels guards departed once Knievel was back from the canyon, job done. No reinforcements arrived. The paid security guards were no match for the remaining "spaced-out idiots."

"We could have held them off if we had any help from downtown," security guard Courtney Krest said. "We thought we had enough help on hand, but all we could do was pull back and guard the launch area."

A man named Don Hanley wound up as the last employee on the promotion's payroll at the site. A Butte guy, a builder of race cars, he once had built some cars for Knievel's father. When the canyon jump preparations moved into the building stage, he had come to Twin Falls to construct the 108-foot track and the wooden tower around it. He had put in the fences and the water fountains, done a bunch of things around the site.

He watched the jump from the other side of the canyon with Knievel's father. They had a good view of the entire descent. ("I never thought he was going to die," Knievel's father told reporters. "I did think he was going into the water.") When they saw that Knievel was all right, Hanley looked back up at the rim of the canyon. All he saw was people.

"Where the hell did they come from?" he said.

Back at the site, his job was to take as much of the equipment as he could salvage back to Twin Falls to a warehouse. He made one trip, when there still were a lot of people at the site. He made a second trip when there were not many people. He came back, maybe three in the morning, for a third load and was stopped at the entrance to the site by a sheriff's deputy.

"You can't go in there," the deputy said.

"I have to go in there," Hanley said. "I have to bring out some more stuff."

"They're burning everything in there. There's a riot."

"Why don't you guys go in and stop it?"

"We can't. We have reports that the Hells Angels are going to burn down Twin Falls."

"What about the people in there?"

"We're going to capture them on their way out."

The conversation was heading nowhere. Hanley repeated that he had to go back inside, riot or no riot. The deputy told him he was putting himself in peril because there would be no help.

"Don't you dare call us," the deputy said. "Because we won't go in there."

Hanley drove the bumpy road to the site. He counted fourteen separate fires, but didn't see any people. The people all had gone. No, that was not right. When he reached the compound, or what was left of the compound, he found one last Visigoth, shirt off, climbing up and down the 108-foot track. He was carrying a flare, putting the fire to the ramp, which wouldn't burn because it was metal.

Hanley called to the man, told him to come back down. The man obeyed. He stood in front of Hanley, swaying, a long day of substance abuse behind him. Hanley took the flare from the man's hand, told him to go home. The man started walking.

One guy with a flare. That was the deputy sheriff's riot. The Hells Angels did not burn down Twin Falls. Hanley took his third load, some balled-up fencing that had been ripped from the poles, some of the telephones that had been scattered everywhere. He came back to the site again at sunrise for more. He was there when John Hood arrived from the rim of the canyon.

"What are you doing here?" Hanley said, surprised.

"I'm looking for that chopper pilot," John Hood said.

The big news in the newspapers the next morning was not the canyon jump. That was a final indignity. In an attempt to lessen the amount of criticism he might receive, President Gerald Ford chose Sunday morning to announce that he had pardoned Richard Nixon "for all offenses which he may have committed or taken part in from a period from January 20, 1969, through August 9, 1974." The attempt did not work. The move drew a storm of criticism across the country, headlines and commentary everywhere.

The photographs and stories from the canyon jump, which sometimes had been called "the Event of the Century" by the promoters, were forced lower or even off the front page. A bigger event had happened on the same day as the event of the century.

The man of the moment commented on none of this. He flew back to Butte with Linda and the kids in the Lear jet on Monday morning. A crowd that the *Montana Standard* estimated at one thousand people greeted him at Bert Mooney Airport. He walked off the runway, picked up a handful of gravel, Butte gravel, damn it, kissed it, and threw the stones high in the air. He shook hands with everyone in sight as if he were a politician returning from an important trip, a serviceman back from a foreign war, a daredevil back from a canyon jump.

"I'm tired, but I'll be all right in a couple of days," he told the crowd. "That's a very minor injury. I've been hurt worse in other jumps. I'm happy to be alive.

"I'm back home for the fall, the hunting season, Christmas and so on. But I feel I don't want to try the canyon again.

"Thank you all."

His voice cracked at the end. That was what the *Montana Standard* said.

23 Rebound

A column entitled "Sports Line" was a nationally syndicated feature that appeared in many sports pages in midsize and smaller newspapers across the country in the seventies. Readers submitted questions by phone or through the mail to their local daily, and some smart-ass somewhere delivered a smart-ass answer in the column. The format was a printed precursor to sports talk radio.

On February 6, 1975, the following exchange took place in "Sports Line" in the *Charleston* (West Virginia) *Daily Mail*, among other papers:

Q. Can you please tell me what the great "King of the Stuntmen," Evel Knievel, has been doing since the Snake River jump? Also, does Evel plan to jump his motorcycles over any cars or trucks in the future?

> L.T.
> Tarrytown, N.Y.

A. His highness has been counting his money since Snake River. There was a lot less to count, incidentally, than announced. Evel's cut finally came to around $600,000. Our source says the misfire, which resulted in his parachuting dizzily down the canyon, left him badly shaken for the first time. No more cars or trucks for a while. When his nerves are steady again, Evel says he will ride his skycycle over Mount Fujiyama, near Tokyo.

Four months had passed since the bizarre Sunday afternoon at the canyon, and this was the first official "Where Are They Now?" or "Whatever Became Of?" entry in the Knievel saga. The unbylined smart-ass from Smart-Ass Central (in answer to the next question, "Does anybody really know what Portland Trail Blazer basketball star Bill Walton's trouble is?" the SA's answer was: "Walton's great contribution to sport so far has been to dispel the idea that your typical problem athlete is that way because he's black") had some of his facts right, some wrong, most a half-turn from the truth.

His highness was not sitting at home, counting his dollars and licking any and all wounds. Yes, he might have been bruised in the wallet, more than disappointed about the financial outcome, and his reputation might have taken a coast-to-coast pummeling for his cantankerous, snarling approach at Snake River, followed by the odd finish, but his ego had emerged untouched, unscathed, ultimately undaunted. He was not hard to find.

He was everywhere.

He was playing tennis in Dayton, Ohio, paired with professional Jack Kramer against Bobby Riggs and television talk show host Phil Donahue. ("I haven't played tennis very much," Knievel admitted.) He was traveling with college senior football players from the East-West Game to visit kids in Shriners Hospital in San Francisco. In Seattle he was presenting the *Seattle Post-Intelligencer*'s award for athlete of the year from the state of Washington to bowler Earl Anthony at a banquet. Shyness, never a problem, had not intruded now. Everywhere Knievel went he gave speeches, signed autographs, shook hands. He also played golf. He definitely played golf.

In a three-week stretch in January, he probably played more golf than Jack Nicklaus. He probably played against Jack Nicklaus. He played in the pro-am at the Phoenix Open. He played in the pro-am at the Dean Martin Tucson Open. He played in the Joe Louis Open in San Dimas, California. He played in celebrity fields that included Bob Hope, Glen Campbell, McLean Stevenson, Maury Wills, Forrest Tucker, Dean Martin, Joe Namath, Hank Aaron, Jack Lemmon, and Lawrence Welk.

The Modern Great American Fame Machine, powered by the instant recognition of television, did not stop for one bad review, or one dropped pass, or even apparently one bad Skycycle trip. A familiar face was a familiar face, no matter what happened. The salesman in Knievel recognized this fact, and he returned to pre-canyon form to sell his basic product, himself. He cavorted. He charmed. He brought out the old W. Clement Stone, Combined Insurance Positive Mental Attitude (PMA). On the eve of the Tucson Open, he dropped one aphorism after another from the podium before a crowd of 1,200 at the Tucson Conquistadores Annual Sports Banquet.

"The price you pay for success in this country is too great."

(Applause.)

"No one is ever really sincere. The farmers are praying for rain, and on the same day the golfers are praying for sunshine."

(Applause.)

"Success is when you wake up in the morning and are happy with what you see in the mirror."

(Standing ovation at end.)

He acted in public as if the events at the canyon never had happened. Okay, maybe they had happened, but they hadn't happened the way everyone else described them. Knievel left the bad parts out of his personal narrative. The canyon was still a snarling behemoth, unconquered by mere men. He had tried, damn it, valiant and bold, and if he hadn't succeeded, so be it. He was the Red Sox, losing to the rich and all-powerful Yankees in the bottom of the ninth, not some flimflam man leaving town in a hurry. He not only still was alive, but still had his dignity.

If there had been any thoughts that he would move into a prolonged period of hibernation, they had disappeared by Christmas. An eighteen-foot-tall Santa, giving a peace sign, rode a twenty-foot-long motorcycle on the lawn in Butte, surrounded by thirty-five thousand lights strung on thirteen trees. This was not the house of a man trying to hide from people.

Two days after Christmas, before the decorations even came down, he was on the road, acting as if nothing bad ever had happened. The Butte Junior Chamber of Commerce had nominated him in November as a candidate for the United States Jaycees Ten Outstanding Young Men of the Year. (He didn't make the final cut.) He was loved somewhere.

That other public figure who had been in the news on Labor Day, the pardoned Mr. Nixon, had declared in 1968 that he was "tanned, ready, and rested" when he came back from political oblivion to win the White House. This public figure was ready and rested, now working on that tan.

"Now the question arises: how do you identify the stars?" sportswriter John Lankford asked in the *Tucson Daily Citizen* on January 16, 1975, after he followed a fivesome that included Knievel, singer Glen Campbell, actor Greg Morris of *Mission Impossible*, golfer Bobby Nichols, and a local businessman around the golf course at the Dean Martin Tucson Open.

Knievel and Campbell are the stars of this group. On every hole, young and old clamored for their autographs, stopped them in their tracks, the wife or girlfriend posing with an arm around the waist while the husband or boyfriend snapped color Polaroids or Instamatics for posterity. The heavies of the entertainment world (Knievel is a strange mixture, really, of entertainment and sport) take the celebrity thing in stride. They have a way of signing autographs and being friendly in the face of exploding cameras without missing a step between tee and green.

The Negative Mental Attitude of the canyon jump was gone. The Positive Mental Attitude was back.

Lankford reported that on the sixth tee Knievel offered to bet Greg Morris $100 on who would hit the longer drive. Morris declined. Knievel then topped his shot, hit a ground ball. On the next hole, he wanted to bet Glen Campbell $1,000 that he could get down in two shots from 130 yards away from the green. Campbell also declined. Knievel got down in three.

The PMA not only was back, it was in familiar overdrive.

This did not mean that nothing had changed. Despite his selective memory of what happened, the dark moments from Snake River still hung around his name. The story quickly had emerged after the rocket failure that the $6 million check was promotional nonsense, that the actual takeout for Knievel was around $600,000, and that even that figure probably was inflated. Bob Arum said his company, Top Rank, cleared about $150,000. Promoters and speculators on all levels of involvement had taken a communal bath.

The canyon jump was a failure on all levels.

"Never in our wildest dreams did we think so few people would watch the event," Arum said. "We were very, very disappointed by ticket sales."

The goal had been to attract 1.8 million people to 350 theaters across North America at an average ticket price of $10. The final number of theaters shrunk before the event even occurred to 260. The number of people shrunk to less than 500,000 on the day it occurred. The hope for big profits, the big kill, enough money to last a lifetime, disappeared.

The results on the artistic side were as bad as the results on the financial side. Maybe worse. While publications like *Time* magazine and *Sports Illustrated*, perhaps sheepish about the attention they had paid to the event prior to liftoff, pulled their punches with phrases like "a nifty failure" (*SI*) and "a bizarre spectacle garnished with machismo and the threat of death" (*Time*), there were writers, like Dan Sellard of the *Eugene* (Oregon) *Register-Guard*, who called Knievel "a star-spangled slob."

"I'm hoping you do retire," Sellard advised. "Take your $6 million check and disappear. We need somebody better for a hero."

Bernie Milligan, sports columnist of the *Van Nuys News*, said, "Knievel's pre-thing remarks, threats, promises, predictions and brags, when analyzed in retrospect, show that the entire performance above and into the Snake River near Twin Falls, Idaho, was Much Ado About Nothing." Milligan called the show "a dud, about as thrill-defying as it was death-defying."

"The hustle won't work twice," the *Idaho State Journal* proclaimed from its editorial page.

> The magic in the idea has fled. Knievel might try it all again and draw only yawns. Who cares? Even before the abortive rocket shot, the tawdry trappings and the cheap carnival air surrounding the production had begun to wear . . . If Knievel does defy reason and try another canyon jump, we hope he will choose another site far away from Idaho. We shouldn't have to put up with it more than once in any man's lifetime.

The pile of bad reviews was capped off by Joe Eszterhas's unfettered dissection of Snake River in the November 7, 1974, issue of *Rolling Stone* magazine. Titled "King of the Goons," the story ran for 35,000 words, the size of half a novel, covered 22 pages, and simply killed all aspects of the production. Without the pressure of a daily deadline, and working with an open-ended expense account, Eszterhas had been able to observe and record the excesses, the weirdness, the mud and nonsense attached to the scene, not to mention the ongoing hubris of the leading man.

"After a few minutes, with two or three thousand people still there, Evel Knievel climbs into his helicopter and Whatchamacallit takes him back to the Blue Lakes Inn," Eszterhas wrote in his closing section.

As I watch the helicopter take off and the dust swirl and listen to those unending "Eeeeeeeeeeeeevel! Knieeeeeeeeeeevel!" screams, I realize it is time for a final tally. So I check my list.

The million dollar party wasn't a million dollar party.

The test failures weren't test failures.

The Skycycle wasn't a cycle.

The $6 million check turned into rubber.

The 200,000 people turned into 50,000 people.

The 50,000 people turned into 15,000 people.

Elvis Presley turned into an invisible being. So did John Wayne. So did Steve McQueen. So did Dustin Hoffman . . .

The public-relations men turned into misinformation men.

The reporters turned into public-relations men.

The jump turned into a nosedive.

The abyss turned out to be harmless.

The Event of the Century turned out to be a farce.

I turned into a social leper.

The star turned into a palooka . . .

In the pop-culture pages of the newspaper/magazine where new music had been found and legitimized biweekly since 1967, where Dr. Hunter S. Thompson dueled with Richard Nixon, where rolling papers and hemp products were advertised, where trends and fashion were established for the sixties and seventies youth market, Knievel ultimately was painted as not only a fraud but a low-life boor. Dr. Hook and the Medicine Show had sung the Shel Silverstein lyrics "And we keep getting' richer, but we can't get our picture/On the cover of *Rolling Stone*," a top-forty salute to the magazine's power. The cover illustration by artist Ray Domingo on this issue showed a cartoon cowboy Knievel, King of the Goons, riding a cartoon rocket the magazine noted "may look like a bomb . . . in fact, may look suspiciously like Slim Pickens riding an A-bomb to his and the world's doom in the last scene of *Dr. Strangelove*." This was not the kind of exposure Dr. Hook was singing about.

Eszterhas, years later, remembered that "an Evel Knievel Alert" was posted in the magazine's offices in San Francisco. Some phone calls had been made, allegedly from Knievel. Some threats had been made about physical revenge. Staffers were told to alert authorities if Knievel was spotted on the premises.

Nothing happened, but the depth of Knievel's anger would be shown thirty-three years later. In 2007, writer Peter Relic would ask to interview him for *Rolling Stone*. Knievel would decline because the magazine "in 1974 sent 'a shit named Joe Eszterhas' to write about Snake River, 'The King of the Goons,' a story that 'hurt very, very much and I know a thing or two about pain.' "

In public, though, after the jump, he stayed away from the fight. He said nothing. Even the greatly reduced paycheck didn't seem to bother him. He had survived Snake River in a lot of ways.

"What the hell," he told Jurate Kazickas of the Associated Press in Butte two weeks after the event. "I'm still alive, I have the blue Montana sky. What do I need all that money for?"

The challenge was how to reconstruct his career, how to attract a paying crowd to watch him perform again. No matter how much attention he received at a golf tournament, he definitely was overcooked and damaged goods for the American public. Asking for an autograph was one piece of business. Forking over more money to keep the King of the Daredevils' opulent kingdom solvent was quite another.

"When you charge a guy $25 for a ticket, you've got to give more than five seconds of action," twenty-one-year-old Bruce Cougan of Seattle had explained to the AP at Snake River. "I know lots of people who wouldn't pay to see him jump over a garbage can after this."

No matter what death-defying stunt Knievel proposed, no matter how kooky, crazy, intrinsically challenging it might be, the public presumably would not bite. Throughout his travels, the canyon had been promoted as his ultimate test. If the ultimate test had been such a bomb, how could a new ultimate test be sold? Then again, how could anything less than the canyon, say, another night jumping over used cars at some dragway, be sold? America presumably would scratch, yawn, reach for the *TV Guide* to find other alternatives.

This was a real problem. The answer was simple and brilliant: forget the old public, the World's Greatest Daredevil would work an entirely new public. He would appear in another country.

Assorted deals had been proposed during the buildup to Snake River, and while many of them had been pulled back a few seconds after the rocket's inglorious landing, more than a few were still available. The thought of re-creating the Knievel commercial demand from the beginning in a new country, new market, was intoxicating. Even with the travails at the canyon, the Ideal Toys collection of motorcycle and jump toys had been the favorite Christmas choice of American boys for 1974 and had "outsold Barbie four to one," Knievel boasted.

At the end of October, the first foreign possibility was slipped into the newspapers. The destination would be Japan. Another daredevil, the thirty-year-old son of a World War II kamikaze pilot, would try to rocket over Mount Fujiyama, a 12,388-foot-tall volcanic mountain sixty miles southwest of Tokyo. Bob Truax would build a new Skycycle. Knievel would publicize the event by appearing in a minimum of five, maximum of ten motorcycle jumps around the country. The jumps would be over no more than thirteen vehicles.

"I don't give a damn what kind or what size vehicles they are," Knievel said. "I'll get $45,000 per jump against 50 percent of the gross gate receipts."

Though he claimed to have sold one of the battered test Skycycles to Japanese interests for $265,000, plans for the production never proceeded much further. The appropriate financial backing never arrived. The name of the daredevil son of the kamikaze pilot was never announced. By January 1975, Japan was forgotten and Knievel had a new and better destination in mind. He was going to London. He was going to jump over the River Thames.

The proposal was put forward by British promoter John Daly. Knievel would be back in the Skycycle. He would take off from Battersea Park, travel somewhere between 250 and 500 yards across the famous river, then land on the grounds of the Royal Hospital in Chelsea. The *New York Times* on January 8, 1975, quoted a British government official who was skeptical about the attempt, noting the various permits required, plus, "if he [Knievel] falls into the river, the permission of the Water Authority and the Pollution Authority also would be required," but the presence of Daly in the operation gave it some substance.

Thirty-seven years old, the son of a dockworker, Daly was another former insurance salesman who had found success in the entertainment world. During his two-year stint with Canada Life, he had befriended actor David Hemmings, then became his manager. When Hemmings reached the big time in Michelangelo Antonioni's 1966 hit *Blow-Up*, he and Daly used the financial capital to form a talent agency called Hemdale, which soon managed rock acts like Yes and Black Sabbath, owned the worldwide rights to the musical *Oliver!*, and moved into movie production.

Daly bought out Hemmings in 1971 and in the last two years had backed the London stage production of the musical *Grease* (starring the understudy to Barry Bostwick on Broadway, newcomer Richard Gere) and had just completed production on Ken Russell's movie version of *Tommy*, the rock opera by the Who. Despite a major fire on the set, which was a pier in Hampshire, and despite the presence of Ann-Margret, Oliver Reed, Roger Daltry, Keith Moon, Pete Townshend, Tina Turner, Elton John, and Jack Nicholson in the cast, the film was only Daly's second-most-exciting business enterprise in 1974. He was also, you might remember, Don King's partner in "the Rumble in the Jungle," Muhammad Ali's eight-round knockout upset of George Foreman ("If Evel Knievel can make that jump, I can whip George Foreman's rump," Ali had predicted) on October 30, 1974, in Kinshasa, Zaire.

That event, which featured the birth of the rope-a-dope, the machinations of Zaire's dictator, Mobutu Sese Seko, and countless plot lines, not only had been a boxing version of Snake River Canyon but also impacted Snake River Canyon. Bob Arum, remember, had been free and inclined to work with Knievel because Muhammad Ali had followed the money—mostly money raised by John Daly—to Don King. Knievel, remember, had been moved to invent the phony $6 million paycheck for Snake River because Ali and Foreman both were promised $5 million, again, money mostly raised by John Daly.

Now Daly, with his ability to raise money for curious events, was drawn to Evel Knievel for his next promotion, and Knievel was drawn to Daly. On February 14, 1975, the two men met at the Regency Hotel at 560 Park Avenue in New York City to iron out details. Included in the meeting was Bob Arum.

The promotional world was small and incestuous. The people involved in it were, if nothing else, resilient.

"Now listen, here's the way the tour's going to be," Knievel said the next day in his suite at the Regency. "I have a few ideas that are going to be great for publicity. First, we'll get a girl to go to the highest building in London. You get all the press and television cameras there, and we'll get the girl to slowly take all her clothes off and throw them onto the sidewalk off the top of the building. When she's finally naked, she throws her arms in the air and shouts, 'Don't miss Evel Knievel at Wembley Stadium . . .'"

And so it began again.

"The other thing I need are six Rolls-Royces," Knievel continued. "What I'll do is this. Each week I wreck one. Some I'll drive into a wall at sixty, seventy miles per hour—not dangerous, really—and some I'll drive into the Thames. We'll get a headline every week, 'Evel Knievel Wrecks Another Rolls,' and each time we'll have a picture . . ."

The deal had been made, indeed, with Daly. His management team of George Miller, American representative Fred Schier, and advertising director Howard Gottlieb mingled in the suite with Arum, with Zeke Rose, with Jonathan Martin of ABC, with Fred Bezark, with John Hood and assorted other characters.

Though the press still was fed the story of the great blast-off over the Thames—"I know I can make it across," Knievel told the *Washington Post*, adding, "This time I'll see that they fix the damned parachute"—the venue and the challenge quickly were changed. Wembley Stadium (capacity: 82,000), England's national athletic home field, site of the track and field competition for the 1948 Olympics, called by soccer superstar Pelé "the cathedral of football, the capitol of football, the heart of football," became the place. Thirteen red British buses, single-deckers, not the double-deckers of London postcards, became the opponent. The daredevil half-astronaut became a motorcycle rider again.

He would take a familiar route to international fame. This would be Caesars Palace with a British accent.

"The European people are very stuffy and very dry," Knievel explained in the suite, half of the people there from Europe, virtually all of them with a greater knowledge of the continent than he had. "They are serious people, don't look for a free laugh. They have seen guys strapped into cars jump off a ramp over two or three cars, land on another ramp, and they say, 'Wasn't that great?' but they've never seen a guy hang on to the handlebars of a motorcycle and go over thirteen buses. They know there's no bullshit involved, and if you have any apprehension about what European people will think, you can forget them. I'm the greatest stuntman and daredevil in the world."

Among the group who knew better but nevertheless nodded in unison at this European appraisal by the boss were Brian Cartmell and Harry Ormesher. Cartmell had been hired by John Daly to run the publicity for the event. Cartmell then had hired Ormesher, a London sports photographer known as Harry O, later to become a famous fashion photographer, to take pictures. The two were destined to become Knievel's tour guides to London, a somewhat smaller version of the Lear jet tour of the United States before Snake River.

This was their first view of their man. He seemed a bit excitable. Was this the way he always acted? They didn't have to wait long to see what kind of high maintenance would be involved.

"Look, you guys, I'll tell you who I'm bringing with me to England," Knievel said. "It's going to be a helluva show. There's this guy called . . ."

The phone rang. Knievel paused.

"Somebody stop that fucking phone . . ."

He began talking again.

"Yeah, there's this guy called . . ."

The phone rang again.

"I told you to stop that fucking phone . . ."

He moved in a flash, grabbed the phone with both hands. He looked as if he were going to throw it, kick it, strangle it into submission. This was the intermittent rage that was familiar to anyone who had worked at Snake River. Anything was possible.

"I don't like to be interrupted when I'm speaking!"

John Hood took the phone from him, took the receiver off the hook. The room had grown very quiet. Would he strangle Hood and the phone at the same time? Everybody waited.

"Don't let the fucking thing ring again."

And then it was done.

"Now, I was telling you about a guy named Orval Kisselburg," Knievel continued. "You have to see what he does. He shoves a stick of dynamite up his ass and blows himself forty feet into the air!"

Done.

Cartmell and Ormesher looked at each other. They had the same thought.

"The guy was out of his mind," Ormesher said. "We were dealing with some American madman."

Knievel laid out the plan. He would bring Kisselburg to Wembley. He would recruit Butch Wilhelm, the midget, again. He would put on a show these Brits never had thought about, much less seen. The big trucks would be shipped by boat, his customized Cadillac pickup added to the lot. He would fly down another godforsaken ramp, gun that Harley, sail it across however many buses were set in front of him, land on the other side. He could do that.

The date for Wembley would be May 26 at 2:30 p.m., a Monday, the spring bank holiday, also celebrated as Whitsun Monday in Great Britain, the first Monday after Pentecost. Knievel would bring his caravan of thrills to ten other sites around the British Isles, smaller jumps in succeeding weeks in places like Bristol and Birmingham, Glasgow and Manchester, Blackpool and Nottingham, usually two shows a day, afternoon and evening.

It was his most ambitious schedule in years. He would be paid $450,000 for the tour. If all went as well as everyone predicted, he would continue across the English Channel and through the rest of Europe, play a string of dates on the continent before a triumphant return to the United States.

"Are the women in England as beautiful as they say?" he asked Cartmell.

"Yes," the publicity man replied. "They are called English roses."

"Good," Knievel said. "I'll water a few of them."

Cartmell, who looked a bit like John Cleese, top banana of the *Monty Python Flying Circus*, the BBC hit comedy show, was a former Fleet Street reporter who knew what sold and what didn't sell in Great Britain. He had worked with assorted celebrities and politicians, dusting off their résumés. He once brought the last living relative of Napoleon Bonaparte and the last living relative of Admiral Horatio Nelson together to play the new board game, Trafalgar, near the site of the famous sea battle off the coast of Spain. The publicity picture, taken by Harry O, ran in every paper in England and France.

Knievel presented some obvious public relations challenges. Though he thought every Englishman and certainly every English rose knew all about him, he was mistaken. The average London resident had no idea who or what Evel Knievel might be. The canyon jump had stirred little interest. The presence of English commentator David Frost at Snake River was seen as more interesting than anything Knievel did.

Cartmell would have to blitz the British press to draw any kind of a crowd to Wembley's vast spectator terraces. He would have to work around Knievel instead of with Knievel if the naked woman on the building, something out of the 1930s, was supposed to be a grand promotional idea. He would have to make his own ideas appear to be Knievel's ideas. Suggestion was needed much more than argument with this character.

An example, a test case, soon arrived. The conversation in the crowded penthouse had taken an inevitable turn toward the thousands of dollars in diamonds that the daredevil was wearing. He freely explained the logic behind them yet again, a man buying diamonds when he can't get insurance. He told his little stories about each piece of jewelry. He said a woman a few nights earlier said the diamond on his left hand was so large that she thought it was a portable television set. He estimated the value of the diamonds at $600,000.

"What happens if you get mugged?" Harry O asked with great logic. "Where's your insurance then?"

"Then this is my insurance," Knievel said.

He pulled a snub-nosed .38 Smith and Wesson revolver from his jacket. He pointed it straight at Harry O. He said the gun was loaded.

"I sleep with this baby under my pillow every night in case some dumb jerk gets the idea of robbing me," he said.

Harry O, once his nerves settled, suggested that a picture of Knievel loading the .38 Smith and Wesson at night, maybe with some money and jewels sprinkled around the bed, would be a great publicity shot. Papers everywhere in England would use it. Knievel immediately said the picture was impossible. He didn't pose for pictures. Didn't do it. Wouldn't do it. Not for anyone.

"I don't pose for pictures," Knievel said. End of story.

Harry O thought about that. Cartmell thought.

"Evel," the photographer said after a while, "what if I showed up just as you were going to bed? Took a picture of what you were doing before you went to bed? Maybe caught you when you were loading the gun? That wouldn't be posing."

Knievel considered the request.

"I'll be taking a nap tomorrow afternoon," he said. "If you were around, I suppose you could take the picture."

Sure enough, the jewels were spread out on the bed the next afternoon. The money, augmented by a couple of thousand-dollar bills, brought by Arum from the bank just for the picture, were spread on the bed. Sure enough, Knievel loaded the gun. He was shirtless and serious. Bullets were spread out on the bed. He looked like Clyde Barrow getting ready for work. The picture eventually would be seen everywhere.

"That's the way you had to work with him," Harry O said years later. "Make him think everything was his idea."

Another example: Ormesher also had asked Knievel if he did physical workouts to stay in shape. Knievel said that of course he did. Ormesher asked when Knievel might be working out. Knievel said, oddly enough, that he might be working out just prior to loading his gun. Ormesher said that would be another great candid shot. Knievel agreed.

"Freddie," he then said, turning to Fred Bezark, the lawyer. "Buy me a gym suit and some sneakers. I need 'em by noon tomorrow."

The two Brits also accompanied their man on his business travels. He was in New York for the annual toy fair at the mammoth International Toy Center at 200 Fifth Avenue. Ormesher added some shots on the street when Knievel took over a pneumatic drill and a hard hat from a construction crew and started drilling. (No one mentioned that he started drilling at a spot that already had been patched with new tar.) Cartmell added some stories when Knievel went into Tiffany's on Fifth Avenue and tried to buy the Tiffany Diamond for a million dollars. ("It's not for sale, sir," the clerk said. "Let's get the fuck out of here," Knievel said.) There was also a chance to look at the client onstage as he charmed two thousand toy wholesalers, telling them about the tour of Great Britain and defending the perils of Snake River.

"If I had made it," he said, "everyone would have said it was easy."

The European tour would be a chance to create new fans and possibly bring back the disenchanted. The challenge was familiar. The format was familiar. No button to push here. No bucket of bolts. He could do what he always had done to make himself famous, get on that bike and fly. The people of the British Isles would be certifiably amazed. Amazed and grateful.

"If it wasn't for America," Knievel informed Cartmell and Harry O, "you two would be Krauts."

"How'd you work that out?" one of them said.

"Because, you stupid son of a bitch, we won the fucking war for you," Knievel said. "It was our bombers that flattened the Kraut cities, and it was our destroyers that sank all of those submarines. If it was up to me, I'd have let you all rot . . . what do you think of that?"

Would he say stuff like this in England? Cartmell wondered.

"Here's what I think," the publicity man replied, maybe out loud, but also maybe only in his mind. "You don't know your history from your arse."

The fun had begun.

24 Wembley

He arrived in London on May 6, 1975, which gave him almost three weeks to promote the May 26 jump at Wembley. The tour would continue from there for the next two months, finishing with a week in Blackpool at the end of July. There was no need to hold back.

"I hope to make a sincere effort to become the world's first private astronaut," he announced at a first press conference the next day at the Inn on the Park across from Kensington Gardens.

The selling went from there. Knievel might have been unknown in Great Britain, but he was made for the British tabloid press. He spoke only in headlines, dressed only in his flamboyant outfits, carried the cane, drove around in the candy apple red customized Cadillac pickup truck. Cartmell pounded out press releases, one after another, took his one New York interview with the daredevil and cut it into individual pieces for the many London newspapers to digest and distribute. Cartmell was not afraid to use the magic promotional word.

"I suppose you might even say that his closest friend is Death, because Death has been a regular companion of Evel for quite some years now and Evel expects one day to get more than just a handshake from Death, a permanent hug," the PR man typed. "He has maintained many times that his idea of heaven is to arrive there in the prime of life, with plenty of vehicles to jump, where there are great golf courses, some good-looking girls and where there is plenty of sunshine. He has never visited Britain, but he is hoping to meet our Queen, the Duke of Edinburgh and other members of the Royal Family."

Knievel met Harry O at Wembley one morning and told him to take only one picture. That was a shot, the thirteen buses in a line, Knievel standing at the far end of that line. He was a speck, dwarfed by the obstacle that confronted him. Got that? It was a heck of a shot. He had never jumped thirteen buses. Nobody had. Knievel said he was done posing.

"It would be great if you did a wheelie tomorrow morning in front of Buckingham Palace," Harry O said. "Sort of 'This is the first thing the Queen saw when she started her day.' "

Knievel refused.

"Elvis Presley never did a wheelie in front of Buckingham Palace when he came to London," he said. "I'm not going to do one either."

He did take a walk around the Tower of London and assorted spots for *Wide World of Sports*, which would broadcast the jump on a delayed telecast the following Saturday. He also did a press conference and jumping exhibition in the parking lot, the car park, outside Wembley.

The jump was minor, a ramp on one side, room for a van or two in the middle, a ramp on the other side. Pictures were taken, polite applause given. Knievel went back to talking in tabloid headlines.

Harry O, left with nothing to do for the moment while Knievel entertained the reporters, looked at the ramps and the distance in between, looked again, and asked another photographer if he could borrow his motorcycle. Harry O knew how to ride a motorcycle a little bit, and of course he tested the ramp, made the same little jump that Knievel had made, then returned the bike to its owner. Knievel was not happy.

"You're showing me up," he said when he found Harry O alone.

"I just did a jump," Harry O said.

"Well, don't ever do it again."

Knievel was a single man for the trip; Linda and the kids were expected to join him later in the tour. He lived like a single man in a suite at the Tower Hotel overlooking the Thames. There was golf. There were women, drinks, howling at the same moon in a different country.

John Hood had shipped the equipment by boat out of New York, a three-week trip, everything packed into the sixty-three feet of Mack Truck. Knievel told him to get arrested when he drove the rig into London.

"Go down some side street where you get stuck," Knievel said. "Back up traffic everywhere. Let the cops come and impound the equipment. Let them drive it away. Make sure the press is there to get pictures of everything. It'll be great publicity."

Hood decided not to do this.

"I talked to some people at the docks," he said. "They told me that if the trucks were impounded, we wouldn't see them for a long, long time. I drove through Trafalgar Square, had a couple of pictures taken, but that was it."

The extravagant publicity plot—Hood remembered Knievel once proposed a fake car crash with George Hamilton in L.A., a fake kidnapping of some star in Las Vegas to get extra press—wasn't needed in this case. The press releases and the pictures did the job. Nothing more than Knievel being himself was enough to make the British take notice.

"He is one of the few old fashioned showmen around today, an heir to a great circus tradition, the dare-devil prepared to disregard his own safety to reassure thousands that man can still achieve success against his environment," Geoffery Wansell wrote in the staid *Guardian*. "It is the same calculated risk that has captured the imagination and drawn gasps from millions since Leotard the acrobat invented the flying trapeze in 1859, and Charles Blondin walked across the Niagara Falls on a high wire that same year."

"He carefully unscrews the gold, diamond-encrusted clasp of his cane," Michael O'Flaherty of the not-so-staid *Daily Express* wrote. "Pours himself a measure of Montana Mary—a potentially explosive mixture of Wild Turkey bourbon, vodka, tomato juice and beer. Checks that the .38 Smith and Wesson is loaded. And puts his life savings—or some of them—under the pillow.

"It is bedtime for Evel Knievel, stuntman extraordinaire, who makes a living courting death."

Who could resist that? Harry O's "unposed" picture of Knievel as he loaded the gun ran next to the text.

Over 70,000 people would show up at Wembley on the given day. This was for an event that measured zero interest at the start. None. Knievel sometimes claimed later that the crowd was 102,000 people, an inflated figure, but there definitely were a lot of people in the stadium. Over 70,000.

A story. Knievel played golf virtually every day. Harry O, the photographer, and Cartmell, the publicity man, played with him at the Wentworth Club with its three courses stuffed into the Surrey heathland outside London. John Hood came along, his job now to carry a

King Edward VII cigar box that was used to hold money for all the bets. Knievel instigated bets for everything, bets for each hole, bets for most shots, bets and more bets. The usual daredevil golf.

He talked early in the match with Charlie, his venerable and toothless English caddie. Charlie had seen the group arrive in the dressed-up, customized, oversized Cadillac truck, a vehicle seen as often in England as a spaceship from the left side of Mars. Charlie was impressed.

"What other cars do you own?" he asked.

Knievel went through a list of the rolling stock at the moment back in Butte. He mentioned the two Ferraris and the two Cadillacs and the Porsche. Along with eleven horses and nine dogs.

"The car you should have is a Lamborghini Espada," Charlie said.

"Why is that?" Knievel asked.

"Because it's the best car in the world," Charlie said. "A man of your stature should own the best car in the world."

Evel considered this information for a moment. He decided that Charlie was right in both statements. The Lamborghini was the best car in the world, and, yes, a man of his stature should own one.

"John," he said to John Hood, "go buy me a Lamborghini."

Hood left with the King Edward VII cigar box. The foursome continued its round. Everyone had to keep track of his own bets. At the eighteenth hole, John Hood waited at the green. He told his boss that there were no Lamborghinis for sale in London, but he had found one in Brighton. The color was red. The price was 15,000 pounds. The exchange rate was 2.37 U.S. dollars to one pound.

"Let's get it," Knievel said.

And he did.

Frank Gifford, the former football player for the New York Giants, famous now as the Monday night play-by-play man with Cosell and Meredith, was the *Wide World of Sports* broadcaster for the jump. He had become friends with Knievel, spent regular time with him beyond the normal ABC meetings. He liked Knievel, liked his style.

"He was a little wacko," Gifford said. "Drinking Wild Turkey out of his cane. I kind of admired him."

The night before the jump, Knievel asked the forty-four-year-old Gifford to have dinner with him. They went to a restaurant where Knievel soon was surrounded by Brits. He told his stories, drank Wild Turkey straight from the cane, drank an assortment of other drinks that arrived at the table. Dinner was followed by visits to a string of pubs, more drinks, which were followed by some driving range moments on the banks of the Thames. Knievel had been looking at the river for three weeks and had a bag of balls and a five-iron with him. He was going to hit golf balls across the Thames.

(This wasn't the first time he had hit golf balls across the Thames. Sitting in his suite at the hotel, he had convinced Harry O to go with him a few days earlier. Harry O agreed. Knievel brought his clubs and some balls, and they went to the elevator. He pushed the button that would take them up. *Up?* Knievel said they would be hitting the balls from the roof. And they did.)

"This is crazy," Gifford decided after watching a number of balls disappear into the dark, presumably landing on the other side of the river (not a particularly hard shot).

He hailed a cab and went home. Knievel kept hitting balls. No camera was kept on whatever he did next. No clock was kept on when he returned to his suite. The only record of the rest of the evening was kept in his eyeballs. They looked like maps of downtown London the next morning, crisscrossed with many red, bloodshot lines. He was a mess.

Gifford was with him when he took his first look at the buses and the ramp. The setup. Knievel had a familiar prediction.

"I can't do this," he told Gifford.

Gifford had the same reaction John Derek had had when Knievel made a similar statement the night before the jump at Caesars Palace over seven years earlier. What do you mean you can't do this? If you can't do it, then don't even try. Pull the plug right now.

"I can't do that," Knievel said.

Take a couple of buses out of the line. Easy.

"I can't do that," Knievel said.

He said that there was not enough room on the takeoff ramp to get up to speed. The ramp was one of those ski slope deals, starting at the top of the stands, the same kind of steep ramp he had driven into the L.A. Coliseum to jump over the fifty crushed cars in a pile. That was a smaller jump. There wasn't room here to get enough speed to clear the buses.

He said that was too bad, but he still would do the jump.

Gifford, like John Derek, wanted nothing to do with a stunt that was this risky. Are we encouraging this? Are we exploiting this? He didn't want to be part of a televised death. Panicked, he searched for Doug Wilson, the producer. He explained his worries. Doug Wilson became worried. They went back to see Knievel at his trailer.

They knocked on the door. No answer. Knocked on the door again. No answer. Opened the door. Knievel was asleep.

Gifford woke him up. Asked how he felt now.

Knievel said he was fine. He would find the speed somewhere.

The show would take place.

Gifford still wasn't sure about any of this, still was nervous, but at the appointed time, twenty minutes after four on a Monday afternoon in London, he was in his yellow ABC blazer. Knievel was in a new set of leathers, blue, just for Wembley, with enormous white French cuffs. He was doing some wheelies, then his two-warm-up trips down the ski slope, stop, down the ski slope, stop.

"I was talking with him today, and he looked out at the seventy thousand people here and said, 'What does a man have to do to get this many people together?' " Gifford said on television. "I said, 'Evel, you're doing it.' "

This was the largest live crowd that ever had seen him perform, the largest by far. This was the crowd that should have been at Snake River, kids and families. The prices ran from three to eight U.S. dollars for the show. Affordable. This was his public relations masterpiece. Right here.

He came down the ramp on that third trip, after he gave a thumbs-up to television to let the producers know this was for real, tried to get the speed up to somewhere between 93 and 95 miles per hour, the number he felt would give him a distance of 130 feet, enough to clear the buses. Failed.

The parabola was all wrong from the beginning. Too flat. Too flat. Too short. He came down hard on the front wheel on the plywood safety extension that covered the top of the last two buses. Same as Caesars Palace. Blam. The thirteenth bus. The motorcycle bounced high in the air. He was thrown forward.

There was a moment, perhaps, when he could have saved himself . . . he tried to hang on, tried to hang on, tried . . . but then he was gone. Over the handlebars, flipped, flying, gone. He landed and rolled over and rolled again, and the motorcycle followed him, stalked him, seemed to know what it was doing. Mad. Same as Caesars Palace.

When he stopped rolling, the motorcycle rolled on top of him.

"He's down and he is hurt," Gifford said on the telecast. "Oh my God."

John Hood was the first one to Knievel. He pulled the motorcycle off Knievel's legs. Frank Gifford was close behind.

Gifford was terrified. He saw a bone sticking out of Knievel's hand. He saw blood coming from Knievel's mouth. Gifford thought he not only had been part of a televised death, he was part of a televised death of a friend. The crash was violent and stunning. How could anyone survive? Knievel had almost landed at Gifford's feet when he finally stopped.

The announcer dropped his microphone and bent down and was only slightly heartened by the fact that Knievel was trying to speak. This would be the daredevil's dying declaration, possibly his last words. Gifford listened very hard because he wanted to make sure he heard exactly what Knievel said.

"Frank . . . ," Knievel said.

"Yes, Evel," Gifford said.

"Get that broad out of my room," Knievel said.

The scene that followed was dramatic, melodramatic, serious, yet strange, part B movie, part Oberammergau Passion Play, part Road Runner cartoon, the part when the dazed coyote, *boinnnnnnnng*, tries to recover from his latest colossal mishap. Hood removed Knievel's helmet. Knievel was shifted carefully to a stretcher, carried toward an ambulance. The crowd was beginning to cheer. He was alive.

He didn't want to go to the ambulance. He wanted to go to the ramp, wanted to talk to the people. He wanted a microphone. Forget the blood, the bone in his hand. The route was turned toward the ramp. Room was cleared with each step. The microphone was brought close. Knievel asked to be helped up. The process was very slow.

When he finally stood, one arm over the shoulder of promoter John Daly for balance and strength, he made his announcement.

"Ladies and gentlemen of this wonderful country," he said into the microphone, "I have to tell you that you are the last people in the world who will see me jump. Because I will never, ever, ever jump again. I'm through."

The reaction from the English crowd was mixed. There were as many boos as there were cheers, a lot of people who thought this was an act. He really wasn't hurt, couldn't be hurt. He was up there talking. This was bad theater. That was what it was.

The people around him knew differently.

He clearly was injured. He was in a lot of pain, winced every time he moved. His hair was everywhere, his face as dirty as if he had come from eight hours in those Butte mines. He should have been somewhere in the middle of the city now, siren blaring, headed toward an emergency room. He was here. He wanted to walk off the ramp.

Walk off the ramp? Gifford suggested that he had done enough. He should get on the stretcher.

"Help me walk off the ramp," Knievel said.

"I got you, buddy," Gifford said.

He walked off the ramp. Progress was very slow, Gifford at one side, John Hood at the other side, but he walked. Every time he paused, someone would suggest the stretcher. Every time someone suggested the stretcher, Knievel would plead his case.

"I want to walk out . . .

"Please help me out . . .

"I want to walk out . . .

"Please.

"I want to tell you something, Frank. I don't know how I got here. I'm hurt awful bad.

"I walked in, I want to walk out."

He eventually was put on the stretcher, lifted into the ambulance, taken to the Royal London Hospital in Whitechapel, a two-hour trip through traffic. He was diagnosed with a broken right hand, a compressed fracture of the fourth and fifth vertebrae in the lower part of his spine, a fractured left pelvis, and a 7¾-inch split in his right pelvis.

Once again, his injuries, as serious as they were, did not match the impact of the pictures of the crash that gave him the injuries. The entire stretch of film—the crash, the dialogue, the words to the crowd, the way he looked—this again was stuff that never had been seen on television. This was more than reality. This was hyper-reality. He looked as if he were dead.

"He's lying there, broken this, broken that, instinctively he says, 'I gotta talk to the crowd,' " producer Doug Wilson said. "It was part showmanship, I guess, but part knowing who he was."

In the hospital in succeeding days, Knievel blamed the "idiot mechanic," who would have been Hood. He said the gears in the bike had been set up wrong for the jump, that a counter shift should have been added. He said that a different gearbox had been ordered from New Jersey too late, never reached London in time.

He also said that the size of the London buses was a problem. The American bus was eight feet wide. The London bus was eight and a half feet wide. Six inches per bus, thirteen buses. That came out to a six-and-a-half-foot difference. Give him the extra six and a half feet and he would have made the jump perfectly. Give him different gears, based on the knowledge that the buses were wider, and he would have made the jump perfectly.

The idiot mechanic kept quiet at the time because he was in need of a job, but pointed out a couple of things years later. The first was that Knievel had practiced only once, and that was that time for the press in the parking lot. He jumped the couple of vans, that was it, and even then was more interested in "a couple of girls that were around" than what he was doing in practice. The second thing was that this was the first time in his life that Knievel ever talked about technical things.

He was not a technical man. He basically used two Harley XR750 bikes for his shows, one bike for wheelies, the other for jumps. The wheelie bike was geared lower so it was easier for him to flip the front end upward and ride that way. The jumping bike was set up with higher gears for the speed necessary to make the jump. No specifics for each jump ever were determined for the jumping bike. The jumping bike was the jumping bike. No gearboxes were ordered from New Jersey.

The miss was no different from any of Knievel's misses—it was a miscalculation by Knievel. He still had no speedometer on the bike, no tachometer, no research, nothing, he jumped totally on instinct and feel. His feeling was wrong here. The buses were higher than American buses, as well as wider. That was his problem this time. He didn't go high enough, didn't go far enough. He was bounced in the air and didn't, couldn't, hang on. This crash was no different from the many crashes in the old days. He didn't have enough information.

"You look at those jumpers who came after him," John Hood said. "They had everything figured out. He just didn't want to know."

The retirement lasted three days. The *Wide World* show wouldn't be seen until Saturday, and on Thursday, at five-thirty in the morning, Doug Wilson's phone rang in New York. Wilson had returned home to edit. Knievel told him to make a big edit. Wilson should cut out that whole speech to the crowd. Turned out Knievel didn't mean it. He wasn't going to retire. The speech would look stupid.

"No, it won't," Wilson said. "We'll say something. People will understand."

"You can't run it," Knievel said.

"We're going to run it," Wilson said.

Knievel became angry. He threatened to sue Wilson, to sue ABC, to
sue everybody concerned if the speech ran. Wilson told him that the
speech would be fine. Go ahead and sue.

On Saturday the show ran, the retirement speech ran. The tape was
spellbinding. Again, like Caesars Palace, this was something that people
did not see in the technology of 1975. This was different. This was exciting. Argue the morality of what this guy did for a living, fine, but admit
that this was some kind of show. He walked in, and he was going to walk
out. After the flop at the canyon, this was the rebound of Evel Knievel.
This was his best moment.

"He never apologized for yelling at me, threatening to sue," Wilson
said. "But when he came back from England, Jim McKay met him at the
airport to do an interview for us. Evel was on a gurney, but he had his
helmet with him from the jump. He said, 'Give this to Doug.' That was
the closest he could come to an apology."

He had been in the hospital for eleven days, then back at the Tower
Hotel for five more before coming back home on June 10, 1975. Linda
had hurried to London along with Kelly and Robbie. They accompanied
him back to New York and then to Butte, where he was scheduled for
three more weeks of bed rest. He said he would return to London in the
fall to tackle those buses again.

"You told seventy thousand people you were going to retire," a reporter
said at John F. Kennedy Airport. "How can you say now that you're
going back?"

"I don't care what I say," Knievel said from the gurney. "The schedule
calls for me to jump again in September."

A story. The Lamborghini was parked in front of the Tower Hotel
the entire time he was in the hospital. Management liked the idea of a
famous, expensive car in the front driveway, so it never was moved during Knievel's recuperation. When he came back, he and any visitors to
his suite could look down at the car. It was easy to spot. The color, yes,
was a bright red.

"Come on, we're going for a ride," Knievel said one day during his recuperation to Harry O. "We're going for a drive."

"You can't drive," Harry O said. "You have that broken back. Or whatever it is."

"No, you're going to drive. I'm going for the ride."

Knievel needed help to get dressed, help to get out of the room in a wheelchair. He needed help, from the two men who carried him, to get into the car. Harry got into the driver's seat, which was on the right side like the rest of the cars in England.

As they drove along, Harry feeling out the temperament of this cheetah of an automobile, Knievel became impatient. The speed limit on the highway was, say, seventy miles per hour. Harry would not go over the speed limit. English laws were tough.

"Come on," Knievel said.

No.

"Come on."

No.

Knievel somehow worked his right leg over to Harry's side, worked his right foot over to Harry's foot on the gas pedal. Knievel's foot stepped hard on Harry's foot. The speed shot up to 100, 110, 120 miles per hour. Harry screamed.

He was convinced (again) that Knievel was out of his mind.

The site of the rematch turned out to be Cincinnati, not London. The buses turned out to be Greyhounds, not the red buses shown in travelogues for the British Isles. The month turned out to be October, not September. The jump turned out to be Evel Knievel's final probe of the far limits of his chosen profession.

He was back at an amusement park, back in the carnival smells of corn dogs and onion rings, back in the shadow of giant roller coasters, back in the weird reflections of fun-house mirrors. The European excursion lasted exactly one afternoon. He was home. The old market, Middle America, was opened again.

"I'd been looking for some big production," Jim Gruber, a former minor league ballplayer, now the manager of promotions and special events for Kings Island, said. "Somehow Evel Knievel got in my mind. I thought that we could do that."

Knievel had appeared at the Soap Box Derby in August in Akron,

Ohio, and Gruber had gone to check him out. Gruber's big worry was that the daredevil was some kind of wildman, someone who could turn into a public relations nightmare. He was surprised at how personable Knievel was, at his message of safety to kids. This was exactly what he wanted for the amusement park.

Kings Island had been open for only three years. Located twenty-six miles northeast of Cincinnati in Mason, Ohio, the park featured a one-third-size replica of the Eiffel Tower and a set of fountains that matched the fountains at Caesars Palace. Fountains-Caesars-Knievel, it all made sense.

After the requisite trip to Butte and the requisite unorthodox negotiations (Knievel handed $100 to the waitress in the cocktail lounge at the War Bonnet Hotel in Butte and told her to give it to a noisy man at a nearby table if he promised to just shut up for the next hour), the deal was done. The announcement of the jump was made in the closing minutes of an ABC special, *Portrait of a Daredevil*.

"We got our man," Jim Gruber said.

Knievel came into town two weeks before the jump. His approach here was entirely different from his approach in London. Or at Snake River. Or, for that matter, anyplace else. He was all business. For the first time in his career, possibly the first time in his life, he brought caution into his operation. The jump over fourteen Greyhounds scared him. He resembled a normal, everyday human being considering this jump. Holy shit, this was a long way.

There was a reason for this caution. He had decided that this would be the final long jump of his career, the final attempt for any kind of record. The possible consequences, this one last time, suddenly were frightening. He didn't want Fate to nab him on the way out the door.

"I'm convinced that he was serious about this being his last jump," Gruber later told *Cincinnati* magazine. "He was just too cautious, too nervous. About half the time in his practice jumps he was coming down on his front wheel instead of the back."

Practice jumps. That was how serious this was.

Kings Island management provided him with a helicopter for his time around Cincinnati. He flew over the site of the jump every day and made changes in the way the ramps were being set up. He asked for the ramps to be elevated. He then asked for the ramps to be lowered. Up, down, halfway. Yes. He then asked for the ramps to be widened. He asked for a bridge to be built over a culvert. He asked for a guard rail to be removed so he would have a longer landing area, straight into a street. He asked for guards to block off the street when he jumped. Just in case.

His mind seemed to hop from worry to worry. He asked for the ramps to be painted. He asked for the helicopter to hover over the ramps to dry the paint so he could practice. Nothing was right. He jumped over five, six, seven buses in a practice. He asked that the buses be parked so close together that they would scrape the paint off each other. He never had done stuff like this.

"He didn't like being banged up anymore," a friend said. "He really loved golf more than anything. It killed him when he was banged up and couldn't play."

He had turned thirty-seven years old eight days before the October 25, 1975, date of the jump. Ten years had passed since that first shaky leap in Moses Lake across the bag of rattlesnakes and the sleepy mountain lions. The words he blurted in London about retiring had left a residue. London had felt different. Every other time he had crashed through the years, he had been on a path, building toward the canyon jump that was going to be the ultimate challenge. Crazy as it sounded, crazy as it played out, he'd had the canyon as a goal. There was no ultimate challenge anymore. There was no goal.

Retirement wasn't such a bad idea.

"It hasn't come easy," he told reporters during the week, summing up his career. "Look at these scars."

He pulled off the top of his jumpsuit, showed all the zigs and zags from his many operations. The question always was about how many bones he had broken. The answers varied—at the end of his career, he would settle on thirty-seven major bones, fourteen operations—but the scars alone were warning enough to keep most sensible people out of the daredevil business.

For the first time, he seemed to be thinking right along with the sensible people. His body was still banged up from Wembley. He would have to give himself a shot of Xylocaine to numb the pain just to get through the jump. The dotted lines were leading to an ending he did not want to see. That was the only ending possible if he kept pushing his limits.

"To pay the price would be just too great," he said. "Never again am I going to jump this far. I like it here. I like to be among you humans."

The crowd was a disappointment. Attendance for this final record jump was 25,000, a number that was diminished by the fact that 20,000 of the people had simply paid four bucks more than the basic $8 fee to enter the park and ride the rides. Management had hoped for a much larger turnout—the area was set up to hold 70,000 people—but the day was lousy, dark and cold, intermittent rain, and the jump was shown live on *Wide World of Sports*.

John Hood had quit after the London crash, but Knievel had asked him to come back. ("I had to come back," Hood said. "I was the only one who knew where the trucks were in London. The only thing I'd sent back right after the show was the Lamborghini.") Roger Reiman, the Daytona champion, also had returned as another mechanic to adjust the gears. The gears were now important. Everything was important.

On the morning of the actual jump, Knievel had practiced again, something he never did. He cleared ten buses this time, fine-tuning. Even as he took the microphone to talk to the crowd, moments before the actual jump, he still was tuning. He asked the Kings Island crew to remove the extra length of plywood ramp they had installed going out onto the street through the hole where the guard rail was removed.

"With the threat of rain gone," he said, "I think it would be safer without the plywood."

He promised to make "the best jump and the safest jump of my life," and away he went. One pass, two passes, three passes, thumbs-up, he came down the adjusted ramp, over the elevated ramp (this part adjusted to half the height of the buses because it sat on flatbed trailers), then up the final ramp and into the sky.

For a half-second, a second, it looked as if he might flip backward. The front end this time was high, too high, an obvious overcompensation for the crash in London when the front wheel landed first. The balance of the motorcycle was out of whack. Backward seemed to be the easier direction to travel, ass over nearest teakettle.

Then he brought the front end down.

But not too much.

The motorcycle landed on the back wheel in the middle of the safety plywood that had been extended onto the roof of the fourteenth bus.

The front wheel landed.

Perfect.

He shot off the end of the ramp and through the hole in the guard rail. Turned around in the street.

Done.

"If a man is a real professional, he has to realize he cannot go beyond a point of no return and a motorcycle doesn't have wings on it," he told the crowd. "I am going to continue to perform around the world with my two sons, but I have jumped far enough. I am going to walk away from here along with you, and I hope to come back and walk away year after year. That's a professional."

Done.

Or so he said.

Fifty-two percent of all televisions in America were tuned to *Wide World of Sports* when Knievel jumped at Kings Island. An estimated 55 million people watched in the middle of a Saturday afternoon. This ultimately would be the highest-rated show (22.3) in *Wide World*'s forty-five-year history from 1961 to 2006.

25 Fort Lauderdale, FL

The night was still alive, even if the bars in Fort Lauderdale were not. The famous daredevil and a longtime friend from Butte, Ron Phillips, had met two women, and the famous daredevil said they should move the party to his lavish hotel lodgings at the Bahia Mar Beach Resort. This was a fine idea, except the hotel thought the daredevil had checked out. Some other well-heeled visitor now occupied the lavish lodgings. No rooms were available. Not even for the famous daredevil.

His reaction to this news was a surprise. There was no reaction. He didn't get angry at all. The famous daredevil, Mr. Evel Knievel, simply suggested everyone follow him. There was a backup plan.

He had been thinking he might buy a boat, you see, and the Bahia Mar Beach Resort was planted next to the Intracoastal Waterway, and boats were docked along the marina, big boats, yachts, and one of them surely would be for sale because boats always were for sale. Sure enough, the search party of two men and two women found a boat, a yacht, that had a "For Sale" sign on the side.

Knievel knocked on the door, the hatch, whatever it was called. The time roughly was three o'clock in the morning. The owner of the yacht appeared after a long stretch of knocks. He was not happy when he appeared.

"I want to buy your boat," the daredevil said. "How much do you want for it?"

The sleepy-eyed owner named a figure.

"I'll buy it," the daredevil said. "I won't argue about price. I'll pay just what you want . . . with one condition. I'll give you a check . . . and you get off the boat. Right now."

The deal was done. Just like that. The owner took the check, woke up his family, and they gathered up their belongings and left, as if they were refugees fleeing an impending invasion. The daredevil and Ron Phillips and the two women settled in for the night.

"The next morning," Phillips said, "Bob decided we should take our first boat ride."

This was complicated by the fact that the boat the daredevil had purchased was an eighty-seven-foot Broward yacht, which was a large boat. Only a licensed captain could operate a yacht this size. The daredevil found a captain at the marina, and the party went out for a pleasant day on the high seas. On the way back, a problem developed. The captain steered the boat to one side in the waterway and stopped to make room for another boat coming in the opposite direction. The daredevil was not pleased.

"Just keep going," he said. "The hell with them."

The captain politely explained a few nautical rules. One was that a smaller boat always had to make way for a larger boat. This had not been an issue all day, owing to the size of the daredevil's new boat, but the boat that now was passing was larger. The eighty-seven-foot boat had to surrender the right of way.

The next move was inevitable. The daredevil went onto the boat market in the succeeding days. He discovered the availability of a Feadship, which was 116 feet long. Feadships (built by First Export Association of Dutch Shipbuilders) had been sold over the years to people like Henry Ford, Malcolm Forbes, and Arthur Godfrey. This was one of the biggest yachts in the world at the time.

The daredevil, of course, wanted the Feadship. On the day the deal was supposed to be completed, papers signed, cash exchanged, Skip Van Leeuwen, one of the long-ago motorcycle racers at Ascot, a short-term member of the Hollywood Motorcycle Daredevils, was Knievel's guest in Fort Lauderdale. The daredevil had given him a stateroom on the eighty-seven-foot boat, the Broward. A painted wooden sign with Van Leeuwen's name was even hung on the stateroom door, a sure sign of nautical stature.

The two men now went together to pick up the new boat, the truly big boat. Van Leeuwen's head was spinning.

"Some papers have to be signed, and Bob has to give this salesman a

$635,000 check," Van Leeuwen said. "Bob writes the check. This was a Saturday. The salesman said the bank wasn't open, so he couldn't take the check. The deal would have to be put off until Monday."

The daredevil did not like this. He steamed and stewed and took out his car keys. He hung them in front of the boat salesman's face.

"These are the keys to my Bentley, which is worth $165,000," the daredevil said. "You hold on to the keys until Monday. If the check doesn't go through, you keep the car. All right?"

The boat salesman agreed. He took the keys.

"Now get the fuck off my boat," the daredevil said.

He would call the Feadship the *Evel Eye 1* and the eighty-seven-foot Broward also would become the *Evel Eye 1*, and in rapid order an array of service boats would be added, an eventual Evel Knievel armada of thirteen *Evel Eye 1*s. Finding a place to put this many boats became a problem, so he bought a house at 2824 N.E. Twenty-eighth Street in Fort Lauderdale on the Intracoastal Waterway with three hundred feet of docking space. He not only was a boat owner, he was one of the biggest boat owners in the United States.

The new passion for boats fit in with his assembled other passions for planes, cars, jewelry, flashy clothes, large tips ("Here's $100, watch my car"), golf, large gambling bets, diamond-studded canes, Wild Turkey, well-endowed women, and any other loud and ostentatious gewgaws that might come into his line of vision. These might have been frivolous attachments for another man, but for him they were business expenses.

He was Evel Knievel. This was the way he was supposed to live.

"I'm a retired millionaire," he replied when one reporter asked what to call him if he wasn't going to jump anymore.

The idea was that he would stay in the news. Maybe he no longer would place his testicles directly on the line, attempt those life-or-death jumps that would scare away eight out of any average cat's nine lives, just the idea of them, but he would not leave the public sight. He would jump a little, put on some different kinds of shows every now and then, but the important thing was that he would still be Evel Knievel, larger than life. People would want to be him because he would live out their dreams for them.

He was a public personality. That was how it worked. He was a character in everybody's living room. Example A of this life came on November 9, 1975, two weeks after the successful Kings Island jump. He was the subject of a *Dean Martin Celebrity Roast*.

This one-hour show on NBC was a staple of the network's lineup. The format was familiar. Dean drank a bit, smoked a bit, and laughed real hard. Knievel, the roastee, the man of the hour, sat next to the podium at a long table on the stage at the ballroom at the MGM Grand in Las Vegas. Assorted other public personalities at the table came to the podium to make gentle fun of him. These people ran from Milton Berle to Glen Campbell to Dr. Joyce Brothers, from Nipsey Russell to Ernest Borgnine to Don Rickles to Senator Barry Goldwater, from McLean Stevenson to William Conrad to Foster Brooks and Ruth Buzzi.

"Evel, a lot of people will be forever grateful to you for everything you've done for them," Ernest Borgnine said. "Especially the thirty-three doctors' children you personally put through college."

"This man has so much metal in his body, they just came up with a new disease for him," Milton Berle said. "Terminal Rust."

"How do you like the outfit he's wearing?" Georgia Engle of *The Mary Tyler Moore Show* asked. "It looks like Liberace's underwear."

This was what you did as a personality. You got together with the other personalities, and America watched and envied, and the money kept rolling into your many accounts. You were a product. People bought you after a while. You were a brand name. There was no better quality than consumer loyalty. Knievel understood this.

"Kids look up to me more than anyone in the world," he told show business interviewer Bob Thomas of the Associated Press. "Sure, they respect Muhammad Ali, but not every kid wants to be a fighter. They all want to jump motorcycles and cars.

"I tell people I'm Evel Knievel, but I'm not necessarily evil. I want to do good with my life. Mostly I want to reach kids and tell them the dangers of narcotics. That's the biggest crusade of my life."

The money and the business offers still came from all directions. Checks—substantial checks—would arrive from anywhere. From Europe. From the Middle East. From the Far East. These would be fat sums of money attached to some product attached to one famous man in America. Surprises. Thank you very much.

Knievel brought his old friend from Butte, Louie Markovich, George Markovich's brother, down to Florida simply to pre-interview people who wanted to do business. Was there any merit to the deal? Louie would decide if Evel should decide. That was how many offers there were.

"A lot of them sounded good," Markovich said. "All kinds of things. I remember something from Aruba. They wanted Evel to come down, sign some autographs, appear in the casinos. See how it went. That sounded really good, but I don't know what happened. I don't think anything ever came of it."

The leased Lear jet was ready to go at any hour, day or night, to any place in the country. A call from Knievel to the hangar was all it took and everyone was in New York. There he was, riding a bicycle through Central Park to promote bicycle safety. Oops, there he was in Las Vegas for some other damn thing. For relaxation, he was standing behind three different blackjack tables at once, making thousand-dollar side bets on two-dollar hands played by senior citizens. Lost $15,000 in five minutes. Who cares? He was off tomorrow for another celebrity golf tournament in Palm Springs, for a talk show in L.A., for something.

Linda would come down to Florida for a week, two weeks, mostly without the kids. She and her husband would go down the Intrascoastal in the Feadship, dock for a week in Miami. Then she would go back to Butte. He never went to Butte much these days, but when he did he went to his personal bank vault.

The vault was inside the office building he had commissioned next to the Met Tavern, across Harrison Avenue from the Civic Center. The building was substantial, a real office building with a real office where his secretary, Meg Meagher, handled real business. The vault was also substantial, looked very much like one of those places Knievel would have robbed in the old days. The door to the vault had gold lettering that read "Evel Knievel National Bank. Savings. Absolutely No Loans." Money was piled randomly on the floor. He would tell visitors that they were looking at over a million dollars. He sometimes would bring people into the vault so everybody could throw the money into the air and sit underneath the shower of cold, hard cash. There were a lot of one-dollar bills in the vault.

"I tell people there are no withdrawals, no interest," he said. "All they get is a wish of good luck from me."

This personality business was a full-time job. Only once was there talk about actual investments. Even that did not last long.

"We went to New Orleans," Markovich said. "There was a guy who owned thirty-three racetracks. He wanted Evel to be involved in some housing complex with him. Evel brought in Leslie Nielsen, the actor. We played golf every day for a week. Leslie Nielsen was my partner. Evel played with the guy who owned thirty-three racetracks. I don't know how it all came out. I think maybe the guy had something to do with the mob."

In New Orleans, golf with Leslie Nielsen. In Florida, golf with Jackie Gleason, a neighbor. In Los Angeles, golf with Flip Wilson. Hell, golf with all kinds of people. Knievel joined the Lakeside Golf Club right at the edge of Hollywood, the celebrated club where Bing Crosby and W. C. Fields and Johnny Weismuller and all kinds of people once belonged. Personalities.

He was one of them.

"So he's driving one of the boats," a Fort Lauderdale friend said. "There's a restaurant on the Intracoastal where the owner had pissed him off for some reason. There are all these signs near the restaurant that this is a 'No Wake' zone. There are tables and chairs, people eating, right on the dock. This is lunchtime. Evel guns it! The water comes up like a tsunami. Knocks over tables and chairs. Dinners go flying. Gets everyone wet. He just keeps on going."

Wasn't that what personalities did? That was what this one did. Spending money and leaving a big wake were part of his job.

A story. Dee Robinson was a thirty-year-old college senior at the University of Maryland. For her final year, she had taken advantage of a partnership program with the Art Institute in Fort Lauderdale to study interior design in Florida. She read a story in the local newspaper about an upcoming roast of Knievel at a celebrated Fort Lauderdale disco. He always had intrigued her. She had ridden Harleys with her dad when she was young, knew a bit about motorcycles, still rode one.

Even though she was supposed to study for a test the next day, she went to the disco on the appointed night. Evel Knievel. What the heck. The place was filled, packed, and she was lost in the back, couldn't see, but then a good-natured bartender asked if she wanted to stand on the bar. She stood on the bar. She could see and, yes, be seen. She was a pretty woman.

Midway through the proceedings—she thought the guest of honor looked uncomfortable up there at the head table, pinned down for a bunch of speeches—a man came up to her, said he was Mr. Knievel's bodyguard, and that Mr. Knievel had spotted her and would like to invite her to a party back at his yacht after the roast. If she accepted, the bodyguard said he would drive her to the yacht.

"I have a test in the morning," Dee Robinson said first to herself.

"But it's Evel Knievel," she said second to herself. "It's a chance to meet Evel Knievel and see his yacht."

"Sure," she said to the bodyguard.

The 116-foot yacht, the Feadship, *Evel Eye 1*, was appropriately amazing. The night was amazing. Maybe twelve people had come from the roast, and Knievel gave them a tour, and then everybody hung around the deck and had drinks and hors d'oeuvres. Robinson, single, by herself, stayed in the background until the bodyguard came to her again and said Mr. Knievel would like to talk to her in the pilothouse.

The meeting went fine, better than fine. Knievel was locked into his charming gear, personality turned to glib and sociable. Robinson slipped into the same gear. Somewhere in the conversation Knievel asked her what she did for a living.

Not wanting to admit that she was still a college student, her education delayed by time in the military, she skipped a step and said she was an interior designer. Knievel was delighted. He asked her questions about design, about her career path. She made up answers. Knievel stayed delighted.

"Here," he finally said as he went to his special Evel Knievel checkbook, filled out one of his special Evel Knievel gold checks. "I want to hire you as a designer. I want you to start working on my yacht."

He handed her the check. She stared at the amount, the $10,000 down payment. Amazing. Knievel had only two demands for the renovation. Both involved the sleeping quarters. The first was that the bed had to be at least seven feet wide, large enough that he could fit comfortably between three women on each side. The second was that a secret compartment had to be built somewhere close to the bed.

"What will you put in the secret compartment?" Robinson asked, thinking about size.

"I'll need room for a half-gallon of Wild Turkey," Knievel said. "And for Bruno."

"Who's Bruno?"

"My .357 Magnum."

Oh.

She went back to the Art Institute the next day, didn't do well on the test, then told her teachers she needed some time off because she had a job redecorating Evel Knievel's yacht, the *Evel Eye 1*, the Feadship. She also said, since most of the teachers worked on the side, that she probably could hire some of them along the way. Which she did.

The job became her senior project. She arrived at the house on N.E. Twenty-eighth Street every day on her motorcycle, supervised the renovations. Knievel introduced her to people as "my interior designer." She somehow fit two queen mattresses into the sleeping quarters for Knievel's proposed ménage à sept gatherings. She created the secret place for the Wild Turkey and Bruno. She had all of the carpets ripped out, replaced with patterns that included the initials "EK." She added a life-sized steel statue of Knievel on a motorcycle. She added a helicopter landing pad for special occasions, because you never know. She did whatever the boss wanted, spent a lot of money.

"He was like the dog from Aesop's Fables, the one who sees his reflection in the water while he's crossing the bridge," she said. "The dog is carrying a bone in his mouth. When he sees the reflection, what he thinks is another dog with another bone, a bigger bone, he becomes jealous and begins to bark. His bone slips out of his mouth and goes into the water. Instead of two bones, he has no bone at all. That was Evel and his boats. He was always chasing the next thing that looked even bigger and better. Chasing the illusion. Just because he could."

One day he came aboard the yacht with a cypress clock he'd been given at some dinner. He liked the clock, wanted to hang it in the new interior.

"Where do you think it should go?" he asked.

"I don't know," she said.

Every place seemed taken. The clock didn't fit. Knievel said he'd make it fit. He got a hammer and some nails. He nailed the clock into the ceiling of the sleeping quarters.

"There," he said. "People will see it."

"Yes, they will," Robinson agreed.

"I never told him that I was still in school or that this was my first job," she said. "By the time I was finished, I had graduated from college and was in business for myself. I was an interior decorator for yachts. I'd gotten other jobs from my first one."

Knievel had other plans too. He talked about building a new house in Fort Lauderdale. He wanted Robinson to do the special design work. First order of business would be ordering fourteen stained-glass windows to depict some of his jumps. Was this okay? She said stained glass would be fine. Would the windows depict only the successful jumps or the unsuccessful ones too? He told her not to be fresh.

He finally jumped again in Worcester, Massachusetts, of all places, on October 11, 1976. This was almost a year after the jump at Kings Island and was only his third jump in the two years since Snake River. He also signed for two jumps at the end of the month at the Kingdome in Seattle. All of these events fit inside his new pulled-back, cautious schedule. He was scheduled to jump thirteen U-Haul trucks in Worcester, ten Greyhound buses per night in Seattle.

His younger son, Robbie, now fourteen years old, would make his jumping debut in Worcester. From the beginning, Robbie was the one who had wanted the daredevil life, the one who had the gene that made him challenge anything or anyone in his path, the gene that his father had. They had rubbed against each other from the start, father and son, collided, essentially because they were the same headstrong, obstinate character. The people in Butte who saw it mostly said about the father, "Uh-huh, that's just what he deserves."

Robbie had been onstage before, at both Toronto and Kings Island, doing wheelies, but this would be his first jump over anything. The hurdle of choice was four of those U-Haul trucks. His father had talked for years about how he didn't want his sons to follow his career path, but now he didn't seem to mind. He saw the possibility that Robbie could replace him as the star in the business and he, the semi-retired star, could manage that business and maybe perform a little. Robbie would be the daredevil. He would be the personality.

Kelly, the older son, now sixteen, already had decided to retire from the act. He was more interested in the business side of the operation. His father could help there too.

"Here was Evel's basic negotiation," a friend said. "The promoters would come in with their contracts, drawn up by lawyers. Evel would let them talk, explain everything, then he would turn his copy of the contract over. He would list '1-2-3,' and he would write, 'Up-Front, Percentage, Guarantee.' 'That's my contract,' he would say. 'Let's start with number one. That would be in cash. Right now.'

"He once had me make a copy of the promoters' proposed contract. Then, when everybody was sitting around the table, he took the original copy and ripped it up. The promoters were shocked. He went into 1-2-3. Finally he brought out the copy of the original contract."

The Worcester contract and the Worcester show were weird from the beginning. The promoter, Abe Ford, was an old-time wrestling guy from Boston. He originally had talked about putting the show in Foxboro at Schaefer Stadium, where the New England Patriots played. That was a stadium that seated sixty thousand people, a big-time event, but then the deal fell apart. Abe Ford convinced Knievel to go to Fitton Field, where Holy Cross played college football, a field with an old-time wooden grandstand that seated twenty thousand people. This became a not-so-big-time event. Ford said he had to stage some kind of show somewhere to recoup the money that he had put into the potential Foxboro show. Knievel agreed to the new deal.

He was supposed to jump the thirteen U-Haul trucks on Saturday, but the show was rained out, postponed to Monday afternoon, Columbus Day. The weather was fine on Monday, but the new Knievel brought out his new worries. The invincibility definitely was gone. He looked at the football field, a diagonal path set up to give him the most speed going into the jump, and he looked at the thirteen U-Haul trucks, and he pulled three of them out of the line. The ninety-five-foot jump became seventy-five feet. He mentioned the rainy weather and not enough room to get up to speed, even with the diagonal, as his reasons.

Even then he did a series of practice jumps, two jumps over four trucks, three more over seven trucks, before he successfully jumped the ten trucks. (Robbie successfully jumped the four trucks.) The crowd was only nine thousand people, and the receipts, at the end, had disappeared. Abe Ford and the other promoters also had disappeared. Knievel claimed he had lost between $20,000 and $30,000.

Since the show was in the afternoon, he had time to go to Boston and search for Abe Ford. Luckily for Ford, and probably for Knievel, the search was fruitless.

"He had that second cane, you know," John Hood said. "The one that was really a lead pipe, disguised as a cane. He was not afraid to use it. He'd broken some promoter's leg with it."

In Seattle on September 29 and 30, 1976, the careful Knievel also appeared. He looked at the ten buses in the Kingdome, looked at the ramp, and pulled three of the buses out of the line. He jumped seven both days, the second day live on *Wide World of Sports*. His shoulder hurt after the second jump, and he went straight to the hospital, where he was released with no more than a shoulder strain.

This performance turned out to be his final jump on *Wide World*. He had been part of seventeen of the show's telecasts in ten years. He was seen as an ABC attraction as much as Fonzie or Barney Miller or Robert Blake as Baretta. He had helped bring the network back to life. The network had given him life. It had been a great arrangement. He had ABC president Roone Arledge's private phone number and was not afraid to use it.

"We'd have some argument about sports," Louie Markovich said. "Who played center field for the Yankees, quarterback for the Packers in 1935. Something like that. Evel would say, 'I'll call Roone. He'll know.' "

The network still considered him a personality, still bounced ideas around, had plans to use him in various situations, would use him at the Kentucky Derby in the next year, but the jumps were finished. ABC executives pretty much agreed that part of his career was finished.

"I think there was an overall feeling that it was done," Jim Spence said. "What else was there to do?"

Ta-da.

Enter CBS.

The network that had lusted after Knievel for its *CBS Sports Spectacular*, that had tried to broadcast the canyon jump as news, now picked him up as entertainment. The sports department had no say, yes or no, in the matter. The network bought a privately produced special, a Hollywood sort of extravaganza, that featured the famous daredevil and assorted other daredevils. The network bought trouble that it never had imagined.

Yes, it did.

The famous daredevil bought it too.

26 Chicago, IL

The show was called "Evel Knievel's Death Defiers." The date of the broadcast was set for January 31, 1977, a Monday night, 8:30 to 10:00 p.m. on the East Coast, Knievel's first jump on prime-time television. A number of daredevils were scheduled to perform their sundry death-defying feats. Knievel would finish the night "by attempting to jump over the world's largest indoor saltwater pool, which will be filled with man-eating killer sharks," according to a press release.

Man-eating killer sharks had been the American demon of choice for the past three years since the publication of Peter Benchley's surprise best-seller, *Jaws*, in February of 1974. The book went to the top of the *New York Times* fiction list for forty-four straight weeks, eventually selling over 20 million copies. This led to the Steven Spielberg movie, starring Roy Scheider, Robert Shaw, and Richard Dreyfuss, which was the box-office hit of the summer of 1975 and earned over $470 million worldwide. The ominous theme from the movie had become part of an ongoing sketch starring Chevy Chase as "the Land Shark" on the hit television show *Saturday Night Live*, now in its second season, and a *Jaws* 2 sequel soon would begin filming, and on and on it went. Shark chic was everywhere.

The Knievel jump was a heavy-handed attempt to carve out a slice of this public fascination. A commercial scheduled to run in the days preceding the telecast would paint a picture of the battle between the fearsome sharks and the familiar daredevil in his white leathers. The announcer would describe Knievel's leap and the trouble that lurked below and warn that, "if he doesn't make it, water wings won't work."

The attempt would take place at the old Chicago Amphitheater, a place where he jumped before, famous as the site of the protest-filled, riot-filled 1968 Democratic Party Convention, a hulk of a building located on the edge of the now-closed stockyards on the South Side. The independent producer would be Marty Pasetta Productions, credited with six Oscar awards telecasts, seven Grammy telecasts, plus the Elvis Presley comeback special, *Aloha from Hawaii*, that was bounced off the satellite on January 14, 1973, to the largest worldwide television audience in history. The hosts would be Telly Savalas, the actor who played the top-rated private detective Kojak on television, and actress Jill St. John, famous as a James Bond girlfriend in the movie *Diamonds Are Forever*.

Marty Pasetta himself would be the executive producer. Michael Seligman, a rising star in the specials business, would be the producer. The show would have that mashed-together television buzz of an awards show, a halftime at the Rose Bowl, a true made-for-the-medium event. The ratings would be unbelievable. Sequels would follow. Everyone would have fun, make money.

Or maybe not. Seligman was the first to realize that a potential disaster lay ahead. He went to visit Knievel a few weeks before the jump in Fort Lauderdale.

The two men had met once before in Los Angeles at Dino's Lodge, the bar owned by singer Dean Martin at 8524 Sunset Boulevard. Still a stop on any Hollywood tour because it had been the site of the opening credits for the hit television series, *77 Sunset Strip* (1958 to 1964), the bar was built on the side of a hill. While the famous entrance was at street level, the back of the building dropped two flights lower.

That was why Knievel dared Seligman to jump out the back window. First night they met, just talking, drinking cocktails, that was the challenge: jump, do it now, go ahead. There was no predicting how far a man might travel before he landed in the dark, not to mention what the conditions might be for that landing.

"You should do it," Knievel said. "If you're going to work with daredevils, you should be a daredevil yourself."

"I'm a Jew," Seligman said. "Jews don't jump out of windows. We hire people to jump out of windows. We hire our daredevils."

Knievel laughed. Seligman laughed. They seemed to get along. Seligman's wife was pregnant with his daughter-to-be. Knievel suggested the daughter-to-be should be named Evelette. Everyone laughed again.

Now that the producer had to visit the daredevil in Florida to work out details of the telecast, it seemed natural to accept an invitation to stay for the night aboard the *Evel Eye 1*, even though he also could stay with his parents, who lived in Fort Lauderdale. The night sounded pleasant. He and his parents could go to a large dinner with Knievel and his family; then he could go back to the yacht with Evel.

"The dinner was fine," Seligman said years later. "Nothing was out of the ordinary. Then we got back to the boat. He'd been drinking. I went to bed, and he started beating up his wife and his children. It was terrible. I didn't see it firsthand, no, but I heard all of it. I heard the yelling, and I heard the slaps, and then I heard the crying. I heard his wife, Linda, crying. I heard the kids crying."

In the middle of the night Seligman quietly gathered his things and left the boat. He went to stay with his parents.

Nothing was funny now. From the moment the show was conceived, it had contained an inherent possibility for trouble, the chance that any of the live acts could draw an instant cloud over the proceedings with a bad result. Scenarios had been created for what to do in each case, how to handle hospital situations, how even to handle death. (The first move in all fatalities would be to switch to a commercial or a string of commercials.) Now there was the additional worry that the star of the show, the guy whose name was in the title, was a time bomb. Evel Knievel was seen again as a jerk. The shark tank people had come to the same conclusion as the Snake River rocket launch people.

"He was just an awful guy," Michael Seligman said.

A press conference was held on January 25, 1977, six days before the event, in the Beverly Room of the Conrad-Hilton Hotel in Chicago to start the publicity buildup. A miniature tank that contained thirteen plastic man-eating miniature sharks had been installed in the room. A miniature Knievel, the Ideal Toys version, built to scale, sat on a miniature motorcycle on a miniature plastic ramp next to the tank. This way the real Knievel could explain the jump to the reporters in the packed room, move the model of himself and the motorcycle over the models of the fearsome sharks with his hand, land safe on the miniature other side, and . . . never mind.

The real Knievel did not appear for the press conference at the scheduled start time. No one knew where he was. The guess was that he was somewhere between Fort Lauderdale and the Conrad-Hilton. The guess covered a lot of the United States.

Everybody waited. Time passed.

"We were in contact with him all day yesterday," Joey Goldstein, brought in from New York to handle the public relations, said. "We lost contact with him last night."

Everybody waited. Time passed.

"He is what he is," Marty Pasetta, executive producer, said, taking the podium, trying to make unpredictability a virtue. "Knowing Evel, he could very well come walking into this press conference or he could very well not come walking into this room."

Time passed . . .

Pasetta tried to press ahead, detailing the other acts that would appear on the show. Karl Wallenda, the most familiar name on the list, would appear from Miami, where he would walk a wire stretched between hotels, from the Eden Roc to the Fontainebleau. Dave Merrifield, also in Miami, would perform on a trapeze that hung from a helicopter, his act providing incredible background shots of the city. Ron Phillips, Knievel's buddy from Butte, would drive a skimobile off a ski jump in Lincolnshire, Illinois, watch out below. Orval Kisselburg, a daredevil who had known Knievel almost since the beginning, would blow himself up with an act called "the Russian Death Chair" at the same location. Finally, "Jumping Joe" Gerlach would jump off the roof of the Chicago Amphitheater itself, an eighty-four-foot drop, to a three-foot sponge on the street.

The media crowd, grumpy now, began laughing. Each act seemed more bizarre than the previous one. The possibility of Jumping Joe Gerlach jumping off the roof of the Amphitheater into a three-foot sponge on the street sounded more silly than terrifying. The entire show sounded silly. Dark humor.

Time passed . . .

Pasetta, at the end of his presentation, was handed a note from a messenger. The note, read aloud by the producer, said, "This is a more dangerous jump than Snake River Canyon or any of my other jumps. Signed, Evel Knievel." No one believed it was real.

Knievel never appeared.

The grumpy people went home.

A reporter called Joey Goldstein the next day to see if the press agent ever did contact his client. Goldstein said he had. Knievel was still in Fort

Lauderdale. The reporter asked what the daredevil's excuse was for missing the press conference. Goldstein, fed up with Knievel for the second time in his life after his experiences with the Snake River tour, went contrary to normal press agent procedure: he told the truth. He said Knievel told him, among other things, "I'm sick and tired of dealing with Jews."

Maybe Knievel had said it only for Goldstein's benefit, a personal ethnic dig. Maybe it was no more than an insensitive joke. Maybe, too, he meant it. Whichever the case, printed in a Chicago newspaper the next day, along with the previous Snake River quote about the three things in life he hated most—"lawyers, New Yorkers, and Jews"—it read like he meant every word of it.

The star of "Evel Knievel's Death Defiers" was left to scramble long-distance in denial. He said he had received ninety-one phone calls from people who were upset with him. He said he never said the words. Never would. He had a wisdom tooth that was giving him hell. That was why he didn't go to the press conference. He had a lot of friends who were Jews. He made a list, including Howard Cosell, and said he owed all his success to these people. He said he himself was probably a Jew because he "believed in life."

"If any son of a bitch in Chicago says I'm anti-Semitic," he said, "I'm going to beat the shit out of him."

He said he was on his way to Chicago.

A couple of problems also had developed with Knievel's opponents in this venture. That would be the sharks.

The first problem was that local animal rights people were worried about possible injuries to the animals. The city's Commission on Animal Care and Control said it might have to stop the show. ("What do we do if he falls into the tank and the sharks attack?" David R. Lee, executive director of the commission, asked. "To save his life we may have to destroy all these creatures.") The animal rights people were waiting for any legal missteps, ready to call a halt to the proceedings in a moment.

The second problem was whether there were going to be any proceedings. The people in charge of catching the sharks in the Florida Keys were worried about whether or not they could find enough sharks, and then if the sharks would look fierce enough. The press releases promised thirteen man-eaters in the tank.

"We've got four acceptable animals, maybe five," shark expert Gerrit Klay reported to Red Smith, columnist at the *New York Times*, from the Shark Quarium in Marathon, Florida, a week before the event. "The weather's been terrible."

The sharks were going to be far from man-eaters. The biggest boxes Klay had for shipping the animals to Chicago were eight feet long. He was hoping to catch lemon sharks or blue sharks, but pretty much was looking for anything with a dorsal fin. There would be no white sharks, like the killer in the movie *Jaws*. White sharks can be as large as thirty-six feet long. There also would be no danger.

"If Evel Knievel should fall in," shark expert Klay said, "he'd spook these animals right out of the pool."

The Smith article was syndicated across the country. Marty Pasetta was forced to scramble again. He described to reporters the size of the saltwater pool that was being built, ninety feet by fifty feet, four feet deep. For the animal rights people, he described the care that would be taken with the sharks, the twenty-five thousand pounds of salt and the varieties of chemicals that would be put into the water to create a familiar environment. For the potentially bloodthirsty viewers, he described the dangers involved. The sharks definitely would be lemon sharks. They all would be at least ten feet long. They wouldn't have been fed for three days before the jump. They would be "mean."

"Jacques Cousteau," Marty Pasetta said, "assured us that lemons are mean."

Knievel finally appeared in Chicago on Friday, did the local *Phil Donahue Show*, did *AM Chicago* and other television. He said again that he was not anti-Semitic. He promoted the jump, did his job. The sharks finally appeared on Saturday and were released into "the world's largest indoor saltwater pool." They definitely were a long way from home. Chicago was in the midst of a record forty-five-day stretch when the temperature would not move above 32 degrees. The temperature outside two days earlier was a record –13 degrees, the coldest day in the coldest month in Chicago weather history. The wind chill was –60 degrees.

The chill now extended to the show itself. Who wanted to come out of the house? Pasetta's staff was distributing free tickets to Chicago high schools in an attempt to draw any kind of a crowd. Ticket sales were almost nonexistent.

"This time the sharks are going to be the good guys," sports columnist Robert Markus wrote in the *Chicago Tribune*.

> Ever since Peter Benchley wrote "Jaws," sharks have been painted as the heavies, certainly an unfair picture.
> Sharks are like everyone else. There's good and bad in all of them, Personally, I never met a shark I didn't like. But I've met some people I didn't like.
> One of them is going to jump a motorcycle over a tankful of teeth in the Amphitheatre on Monday night. His name is Evel Knievel and everyone I know is rooting for the sharks.

The play-by-play announcer assigned to the jump was thirty-eight-year-old Brent Musburger. He had become CBS's prominent sports voice, front and center for the past two years as the anchor of *NFL Today*, the pro football show that dominated the Sunday ratings with a cast that also featured former Miss America Phyllis George, former Philadelphia Eagle Irv Cross, and Jimmy the Greek. Musburger was a Montana native, grew up in Big Timber, which was located between Bozeman and Billings, so he found a measure of acceptance from Knievel.

"We always could talk about Montana, it was an easy entrée," Musburger said. "I'd met him at some kind of event a few years earlier in New York. Maybe when he announced that he was going to jump the canyon. I didn't know him well, but I had memories of Butte from when I was a kid. We could talk about Butte. There were some good restaurants in Butte. I'd go there with my parents."

Gary Deeb, the television critic for the *Tribune*, wrote a column that killed the idea of the Death Defiers ("So now it's CBS succumbing to the sleazy lure of Knievel in a mad effort to boost prime-time numbers") and lamented the presence of Musburger, a serious voice in this unserious project. Musburger was not chagrined. He had appeared in a number of unserious projects.

"It was the era of trash sports, baby," he said. "It was like the Wild West. I'd been to Rio de Janeiro to broadcast Steve McPeak's walk on a tightrope over a canyon. I'd been to the Mojave Desert to see this guy, 'the Human Fly,' walk on the wings of a jet . . .

"The Human Fly. They put me up in a cherry-picker for that one. I'm up there, trying to see what he's doing as the plane comes closer to the abandoned airport where we were. I can't see anything. I'm just making shit up. The UCLA band was down on the ground. They'd been brought out just for this. They were in a formation that said, 'GO FLY.' He comes by, does what he was supposed to do. I shout, 'Nice run, Fly.' I have no idea what I'm talking about. I read later that the UCLA band sued because it hadn't been paid."

To Musburger, this event promised to fit into the same book of off-the-wall trash memories. How do you broadcast this thing? "Heeeerrre he comes . . . the sharks look hungry!" Marty Pasetta promised that paramedics and scuba divers would be on hand in case they were needed. An ambulance would be on the premises. If, perchance, Knievel did land in the tank and the sharks began to tear him to pieces, a special camera had been located underwater to record the action.

Musburger, the day before the show, looked down into the tank. He was surprised. He thought the sharks looked like minnows. He did not feel afraid. This was the challenge? Maybe, with the right camera angle, it would look better. He hoped so. He went back to his hotel to get ready for the big night ahead.

This was a mistake. He missed the action. Evel Knievel crashed and landed in the hospital before the event even began. Even the Human Fly hadn't done that.

"I wasn't there in the afternoon," Musburger said, "but I guess the director wanted Evel to do a practice run. He went to the trailer, where Evel was drinking Jack Daniel's with another guy. They'd been drinking for a while. The director said he wanted Evel to do the practice run. Evel told the guy to go to hell. The director said if Evel didn't do the practice run, there would be no show. So Evel punched the director, just whacked him, sent the guy spinning out the door of the trailer, right down the stairs.

"Then he put on his helmet, said something like, 'You want a practice run? I'll give you a practice run.' He went over to the bike, kicked the starter, jumped into the saddle. Cameramen scrambled to get to their equipment. And he just took off. And he crashed. Went over the side. He was drunk, and he crashed the motorcycle. It was something straight out of Hollywood. They carried him off to the hospital."

Musburger's account of the events was backward. Other accounts flipped the scene 180 degrees: Knievel wanted to do a practice run, the producers didn't. He was drinking, drunk. There was an argument. According to Michael Seligman, Knievel pushed Marty Pasetta against the wall of the trailer, said something like, "I don't care what you want, I'm doing a practice run." Pasetta was left in pain in the trailer. Knievel stormed off, jumped on the bike, crashed, landed in even more pain than Marty Pasetta.

"Thank goodness we were ready for anything," Seligman said. "We had all the cameras in position. We were rolling. We had all the angles covered except from the cameraman Knievel crashed into."

A third version of the argument inserted Sandy Wernick, part of the production staff, into the role of the pushee in the trailer. Wernick, according to this story, tried to convince Knievel not to take a practice jump because it would jeopardize the prime-time show. The two men argued. Knievel finally asked Wernick if he was a Jew. Wernick said he was. Knievel pushed him, went out, and crashed.

Wernick, over thirty years later, now the manager of comedian Adam Sandler, refused to talk about the moment. Pasetta, retired, also refused.

"He has never talked about the Death Defiers show," his spokesperson said. "And he never will."

The result of the incident—and everyone agreed there was an incident that involved a push, anger, then the crash—was the same in all of the stories: Knievel was in the hospital. This was different from any of the crashes he had suffered in the past. The easy jump, no more than ninety feet in the original plan, the distance in baseball from home plate to first base, had been made easier when he pulled a safety deck into place that shortened the distance to sixty-four feet, roughly the distance from home plate to the pitcher's mound. The idea that he could not make that jump was almost inconceivable.

Yet he crashed.

He easily cleared the pool of sleeping, docile sharks, but seemed to turn the handlebars in midflight. He hit the landing hard, tried to correct his path, and overcorrected. He took a hard right off the elevated ramp, went through a barrier, clipped a twenty-nine-year-old cameraman from Arlington Heights named Thomas Geren, who was filming the jump and had no idea what was coming. The motorcycle flipped, and Knievel went flying as it went upside down, everything out of control, and landed on concrete.

He was taken to the Michael Reese Medical Center on the South Side, where he was diagnosed with a broken clavicle, broken right forearm, wrist and leg contusions, and bruises. (Geren also was taken to the hospital, but released with minor injuries.) Somewhere on the ambulance ride, or perhaps in the emergency room while he was having his injuries treated, Knievel figured out an explanation for what had just happened. He figured out a doozy.

He wasn't drunk. He was a hero! He had crashed in the afternoon to save innocent people, paying customers, who would be in the crowd at night. He had decided a day earlier that a crash was inevitable because the setup in the Amphitheater was too confined, too cramped, not right. Simply to get enough room to gather enough speed, a hole had been made in the Amphitheater wall. He would have to fly through the hole, onto the ramp, over the sharks, and then land on a ramp that went upward again, over some seats. It all was crazy. Rather than force the promoters to make the jump safe or for him to decide not to jump at all, back out of his contract, he took things into his own hands.

"I knew there was going to be an accident, and the show couldn't be canceled," he said from his hospital bed. "So I decided to take what was coming to me, and I didn't want to see anyone else hurt. I made the practice run before an empty house so no parents or children would be hurt."

He not only removed all blame from himself, but turned himself into Audie Murphy, Congressional Medal of Honor winner, jumping on a ticking hand grenade to save the rest of the platoon. This was grand, audacious stuff.

"I knew when I saw it all squeezed together yesterday that it wasn't going to work," he continued. "When we put it all together, the tank, the ramp, and the ski slope, it was too cramped. I fell Sunday when I took a practice run up the ski slope. I knew as soon as I saw it that it was too steep to climb.

"I'm not placing the blame on anybody or anything. It was a combination of pressure and faulty, hasty preparation. Because of the ski jump construction, I felt someone would have been killed. It was my obligation to make it safe, and there was a misunderstanding between the production company and myself. ·

"The show had to come off, but I couldn't take a chance with people's lives. So I told the cameras to roll and took the run."

He was treated at the Michael Reese Center by Carlton West, a thirty-three-year-old black orthopedic physician. West had been put on alert, told that business might be arriving from that Death Defier show at the Amphitheater. He still was surprised when the emergency room began to fill with hubbub.

"I didn't have time to think about Evel Knievel as a celebrity," he told

Jet magazine. "I guess I started to think about it after all the reporters and the cameras came."

The angle for the *Jet* story, the magazine part of John H. Johnson's African American publishing empire based in Chicago, basically was Black Doctor Treats Famous White Man, still seen as news in 1977. The reporter wanted to know if Knievel had mentioned Dr. West's race. Dr. West said he certainly had.

"His comments regarding that were actually complimentary," Dr. West said. "But I think my youthful appearance was more striking than my color."

"I've been accused of being an anti-Semite by some newspapers, but that's not true," Knievel told the magazine. "When I was a little boy, the only man I wanted to be like was Joe Louis. I think he's done more for race relations in this country than anybody."

So there.

Left without the main attraction for "Evel Knievel's Death Defiers," Evel Knievel, Marty Pasetta Productions, and CBS were forced to improvise. There were no thoughts of cancellation, but adjustments certainly had to be made. The film from the different camera locations was edited in a hurry, a package prepared for the show. A camera crew was sent to the Michael Reese Center to be ready for live updates and an interview with the injured star from his hospital bed. Telly Savalas and Jill St. John were briefed, told they had to ad-lib a lot.

Pasetta, who hoped that news of Knievel's premature crash would not be known until showtime, ordered that the press be kept from the Amphitheater until the last minute. Since the general public and the press could be confused for each other, the general public also was kept from the Amphitheater until the last minute. Since the general public in this case mostly consisted of high school kids with free tickets, and since the temperature outside was well below freezing, an unruly situation quickly developed. The first riot outside the Amphitheater since the 1968 convention became a possibility.

"Let 'em in," management decided after some angry moments.

The show that followed was a mishmash of mistakes, an artistic disaster. Savalas and St. John struggled. They looked like they were a weekend replacement anchor team at a small station in the Midwest, unprepared, off stride from the beginning. All dialogue was stiff. The film of Knievel's crash was shown. The daredevil was interviewed a number of times from the hospital. Savalas kept saying, "It's only orthopedic," about Knievel's injuries. Whatever that meant.

With Knievel out of action, the Death Defiers took on added importance. They were the live action. This became another mess. The first Death Defier scheduled to perform live was Wallenda, walking the tightrope between the two hotels in Miami. The problem was that he hadn't even arrived at the hotels on time. He was caught somewhere on the streets of Miami in a traffic jam. He would perform later in the show, but the schedule had to be ripped up again. Savalas and St. John kept ad-libbing. Commercials came at strange times. Everything was strange.

"I was at the top of the ski jump, waiting with my snowmobile," Ron Phillips said later. "It was so cold up there, waiting and waiting. All the snow around the base of the snowmobile had turned to ice. I didn't know that."

Wired for sound, able to hear the broadcast through a plug in his ear, able to talk into a little microphone, Phillips received word that he should go. He had made a few practice runs earlier, no problem, but now when he started moving and stepped onto the footpegs to lift himself, one leg slipped on the ice that had formed on the footpeg. That caused him to let off the throttle, and by the time he was able to give the machine more gas, he knew that he would not be traveling fast enough, which was fifty miles per hour, when he hit the edge of the ski jump. He knew he would crash.

He went off the edge of the jump. He bailed. He went one way, the machine luckily went another. He landed lucky, on his back. Sort of lucky. Nothing had been broken, but the air in his body had been expelled by the force of his landing. He couldn't talk.

"Are you all right, Ron?" Jill St. John asked in his ear from Chicago.

No answer.

"Was that the practice jump we just saw, Ron? . . . Ron? . . . Was that the practice jump?"

The air came back into Phillips's body.

"You gotta be shitting me," he said from the ice and snow.

The Russian Death Chair was another problem. Kisselburg was receiving only $5,000 from Knievel for his act, but now he was the star of the show, the grand finale. He was very nervous. After all of his time on tour, all of the stunts, this was his first time on national television. This was also his first time in a tuxedo.

"Orval always dressed as a clown when he performed," Ron Phillips said, "but Evel told him this was national television and he couldn't dress 'like a fucking clown' and had to wear a tuxedo. I don't think he knew what a tuxedo was when Evel said it."

Phillips took Kisselburg to a tuxedo rental establishment, told him to say if anyone asked that he was going to a wedding. Fitted, dressed for the big night, he added another extra for his performance. In his normal act, he blew himself into the air with three sticks of dynamite. For national television, he decided to add a fourth stick for a bigger blast, a record.

The trick was to place a fifty-pound bag of cement over the dynamite. As part of the finer print in the laws of physics, a cone of silence, maybe two feet by two feet, exists over the exploding dynamite. Stay inside the cone, put something in your ears to absorb the noise, fly into the air, and be all right.

Kisselburg always put cotton in his ears. He had been told that ear plugs could be blown straight into your brain by impact, so cotton seemed to be a better choice. As everybody hurried on this night, though, schedules out of whack, he had forgotten to put the cotton in his ears. He realized this . . . five, four, three . . . as the countdown came and he girded himself for the blast.

"Here was this guy, in the middle of a field in Skokie, Illinois, or wherever, strapped to a chair with three or four sticks of dynamite strapped to the seat," Musburger, who now had to broadcast this part of the show, said. "He was going to blow himself up. It was a challenge to broadcast. How do you do play-by-play of something like that? 'There he is, ladies and gentlemen, his finger is moving closer to the button . . . ' What if it all goes wrong?"

The four-sticks-of-dynamite explosion was bigger than the three-sticks-of-dynamite explosion, bigger than Kisselburg had imagined it would be. He went flying, ten feet, fifteen feet, twenty feet into the air. The fifty pounds of cement, in addition to absorbing a bunch of the concussion, split open to cover the scene with a gray dust that covered everything. Including Orval Kisselburg.

He was knocked silly, stretched out on the cold ground, and his hearing was gone. Phillips and the EMTs on duty ran to him and finally got him to his feet . . . "He's alive!" Brent Musburger exulted on the broadcast from the Amphitheater . . . and tried to get him to get inside an ambulance. Kisselburg, uninsured in the daredevil business, refused. He figured his hearing would return as soon as the ringing stopped.

The only other problem was that rented tuxedo.

"It looked like shredded wheat," Phillips said.

He and Kisselburg zipped the suit into the handy carrying case, took the carrying case back to the rental place, and left in a hurry. Never heard from the people again.

The reviews of the show were terrible. Joan Ryan of the *Washington Post* said, "Evel Knievel's Death Defiers now must be considered the worst TV program ever" (against a lot of stiff competition). The worries of the animal rights people were justified as half of the sharks died. Only twelve sharks, in the end, had arrived for the show, not the unlucky thirteen that were advertised. One died before the show, so that left eleven in the tank when Knievel shot off the ramp and crashed. One died when the pool was being drained, another died from bites it had received in the tank from another shark, and three died in transit to their future home in Boston at the New England Aquarium.

"I'll tell you, I'll never work with TV people again," shark expert Klay said, angry that he'd had only three days to prepare the water for his clients instead of the promised ten to fourteen days. "They went back on their word."

The final verdict on the show came, however, in the weekly Tuesday meeting at CBS headquarters in New York that autocratic network chief William S. Paley held with his department heads. Careers, lives, were known to change in an instant in these meetings. Bob Wussler and his people at CBS Sports were terrified. They suspected they could be fired.

Paley, according to one account, went through some other business until he reached the Death Defiers. He looked at the Nielsen ratings numbers and said something like, "Pretty good. If we can improve our production qualities the next time, perhaps Death Defiers II can be even better."

The numbers were everything.

"That's television," Michael Seligman, who has produced the Oscar awards show since 1979, the Emmys since 1996, said. "It's all about the numbers."

"Your act was sensational!" Seligman and Pasetta wrote in a co-signed letter to Orval Kisselburg a month later. "As you know, the show had the highest ratings on CBS this year, a 50 share."

27 Hollywood, CA

His residence when he was in Los Angeles, okay, in Hollywood, now was the Sheraton Universal Hotel. He could sit in his suite in the twenty-story hotel, located on a hill overlooking Universal City, and almost be able to see the old Hollywoodland Motel on Ventura Boulevard where he had spent his early days in the city. He could think about how far the trip had been from one stop to the other.

His neighbor was Telly Savalas, the host of the ill-fated sharks spectacular, a perpetual resident of the Sheraton because it was close to the Universal lot where he filmed *Kojak*. The hotel also was convenient for Knievel when he filmed an episode of *The Bionic Woman* with Lindsay Wagner at the beginning of the month, September of 1977, at Universal. He liked the hotel. He sometimes stayed for weeks in a row.

A funny thing had happened during that *Bionic Woman* show. He was on the set, and some guy came to him and asked for his car keys. The guy said the Stutz d'Italia roadster, the Stutz valued at $129,500, was blocking traffic. Knievel flipped the keys to him, and the guy tried to steal the car, just drive it away. A security guard tried to stop him, and the guy panicked. He crashed the Stutz, the $129,500 Stutz, into the front gate.

Just today the studio had settled on a figure of $9,588 to pay for the damages. Very good. Maybe it was an omen.

There had been a run of not-so-good in the past year. Start with the shark fiasco. Continue with the movie, *Viva Knievel!*, with Lauren Hutton and Gene Kelly and Red Buttons and all those people. It opened in the beginning of June and pretty much was a bomb. The critics hated it, hated him. The public never showed up. The toys . . . the toys looked like they needed a boost too. Lee Majors, the Six Million Dollar Man, had taken control in the sales figures for two Christmases now. What did Lee Majors ever do?

Then there was the Internal Revenue Service, always on his back. And some guy in Twin Falls said he hadn't been paid for the chemical toilets. And even old Watcha McCollum, the pilot from Snake River, was looking for money, said, "Knievel not only doesn't know the meaning of the word 'fear,' he also doesn't know the meaning of 'accounts payable.' " Very funny.

Maybe this payoff for the Stutz was a start. Maybe the critics would love the *Bionic Woman* episode when it played in a couple of weeks. Maybe the deal he had signed with Ralph Andrews Productions right here in L.A. would develop some great television ideas. Maybe there would be another movie, though probably not right away. Maybe the revenue stream would get back to its normal flow. Maybe.

He was here anyway. Hollywood. This was where deals happened.

He had lived long enough and tipped heavily enough at the Sheraton Universal that he knew the different people who worked the different jobs in the hotel. That was why he nodded hello to the cashier in the gift shop, looked toward the rack of paperback books, and said on this fine day, "Do you have something new I'm going to like?" That was why the cashier said, "No, but I have something new you're *not* going to like."

The book was *Evel Knievel on Tour*, which promised on its front paperback cover that it would tell "the Inside Stuff on the High-Flying Daredevil No PG-Rated Movie Could Ever Show." The cashier said the book was trash. The High-Flying Daredevil put down the buck-and-a-half price, plus state and local tax, and took the trash to his suite.

Nothing ever would be the same again.

The author was Shelly Saltman, the chatterbox publicity man from the Snake River tour, then at the canyon. He shared the credit with someone named Maury Green. Saltman had mentioned more than once to Knievel on the private jet during the tour that he was going to write a book, but three years had passed. The timing seemed strange.

Why did he wait so long?

"I had the tapes and was going to do the book, but then I was involved in other things," Saltman said years later. "I sort of forgot about it. Then

I was talking with some people one night, talking the way I normally do, and Maury Green, a writer, was there, and he asked, with all my stories about famous people, if I ever had thought about doing a book. I said, 'It's funny that you ask that.' We eventually put together the book."

The tale basically was a chronicle of the tour, the book the publicist had said he wanted to do. Knievel's words, Knievel's deeds and misdeeds. Saltman's observations were woven together, stop by stop, for 205 pages. As often happens with books, especially mass-market paperbacks, the most provocative writing was on the covers. The back cover promised even more than the front cover did.

"They say that it takes a hustler to know one, and Saltman got to know Evel Knievel very well," the text read. "On a breakneck nationwide tour to promote the Snake River Canyon jump, Shelly got a good, honest look at the man behind the myth. Here's everything that goes on behind the scenes—big money, big wheeling and dealing, big hoaxes, parties, booze and broads—AS AMERICA'S SUPER-STUNTMAN WAGS HIS TONGUE AND SHAKES HIS FIST AT DEATH FOR THE SHEER, CRAZY, MONEY-MAKING HELL OF IT!"

Though Saltman certainly did not draw a flattering portrait of Knievel—various episodes on the tour were recounted, from the pistol shots into the hotel pool in Austin to the various incivilities toward Linda in Butte—friends of Knievel who later read the book found nothing wrong. The character painted in the pages was the character they knew. Maybe Saltman could have been nicer in some descriptions, but this was Knievel. Things that the daredevil said in the book were things his friends had heard him say for years. This was him.

Knievel did not agree.

He would later say the book was "a filthy lie" and "pornography." He would claim the book insulted his mother, wife, and children and portrayed him as "an alcoholic, a pill addict, and an anti-Semite and an immoral person." He would make the book sound as if it was the worst thing ever written about anyone in the history of the written word.

There was no record of how long it took him to reach this conclusion, how long it took to read the book. There was a chance that he did not even read it, relying on other people to tell him how terrible it was, though he did give a copy of *Evel Knievel on Tour* a few years later to a friend in Butte and the friend found a number of underlines and notes in the margins that indicated Knievel had read the book with great interest. Or at least parts of it.

"Some pages were ripped out too," the friend, Joe Little, said. "I have to think those were the ones that really got him mad."

On the very first page of the book, in the very first paragraph, Knievel found exception. This was a page that was an extension, really, of the front cover, a browser's inducement to buy the product in his hands. Under the headline "X-Rated Evel," Saltman offered three paragraphs of quotes from the subject.

"I've made love to more beautiful women than all you guys put together even know," the first paragraph read. "Hell, I never knew a broad who wasn't a pushover . . . I've got more broads than you ever saw . . . *Penthouse* knows it, *Playboy* knows it, and now you know it . . . even my wife knows it and my grandmother knows it. I don't bullshit anyone."

The headline was underlined. Assorted words in the paragraph were underlined. The words "Constitutes Adultery" were printed in ballpoint pen at the top of the page. Underlines and comments continued throughout the book. "This Is A Lie And Not Accurate" was followed by "Lies, Lies," which was followed by "Lies, Lies, Lies." A quote on page 169, where Knievel complained to producers about appearing after Burt Reynolds on *The Tonight Show* ("That fucking Burt Reynolds, why the hell should he go first?"), was underlined with the comment, "Never Said It To Anyone."

Even Saltman's final sentence in the book, which expressed joy at Knievel's survival at Snake River ("I fell into the arms of Evel Knievel's father and cried my eyes out, I was so glad to see that god-damned, cantankerous son of a bitch alive and well"), was found offensive. The phrase "son of a bitch" was underlined, the word "Insult" printed underneath.

Again, there was no record of how long these feelings were allowed to marinate after reading. There was no record of how much drinking took place, how much Wild Turkey was consumed during the marinating process. There was, however, a record of Knievel's feelings at times in his life about the First Amendment: he was not a big fan.

George Hamilton had seen that when he first brought the movie script for *Evel Knievel* to Knievel's low-rent motel room and was forced to read at gunpoint. Joe Eszterhas had a glimpse when his unflattering *Rolling Stone* article was published and he received phone calls that put the magazine's offices on "Evel Knievel Alert." Automotive writer Joe Scalzo also had felt the heat.

Scalzo, who wrote for assorted publications and had written a number of auto sports books, wrote a couple of paperbacks, *Evel Knievel* and

Evel Knievel and Other Daredevils in the run-up to the canyon jump. These were the first books written about Knievel, pretty much the only books before Saltman's effort. They did not make Knievel happy.

He called Scalzo to make his displeasure known.

"You're a rip-off prick," he said to begin the conversation.

The words came out in an angry hurry. Knievel said he would sue for all royalties from the books, plus damages for using his name without permission. The bluster continued for an appropriate length of time, Scalzo unable to get in much of a rebuttal, or even to mention that First Amendment thing, before Knievel abruptly hung up. Scalzo never heard from him again.

The legal threats did not bother the writer much because he knew the books were not defamatory in any way. No court would rule against him. The belligerence did not bother the writer either, because he was in California and Knievel was calling from Butte, Montana. A punch in the nose could not travel from Butte, Montana, to California.

That was not the case, alas, with Shelly Saltman. He worked about fifteen miles from the Sheraton Universal. Not a bad drive at all if you caught the L.A. traffic just right.

Saltman now was at 20th Century Fox, where he was a vice president in the telecommunications department. He had taken the job because he was tired of the travel involved with sports promotions and ready for a different, corporate kind of challenge. His department worked with the new concept of made-for-TV movies for HBO and other cable channels and with another new concept, the sale of existing movies to companies that would put them on VHS and Betamax tapes to sell (or rent) for home viewing.

The offices were on the 20th Century lot, famous for all the movies that had been filmed there, a touch of glamour, and Saltman was on his way to the famous studio commissary shortly after noon on September 21, 1977. He was his enthusiastic self, tracking down a rumor that the commissary now had a frozen yogurt machine. He would see if that was true. Now, though, he spotted Evel Knievel coming toward him. He was not surprised. All kinds of famous people came to the 20th Century lot. He smiled.

"Hey, Evel," he said.

This was when someone grabbed him from behind, threw him to the ground, and held him there. What the hell? Saltman looked up and saw Knievel swinging a metal baseball bat at his head. What the hell?

"I'm going to kill you, you son of a bitch," Knievel said. "For what you wrote about my mother."

That was what Saltman heard. Just in time, the blow coming toward his head, he was able to free his arms and hold them in front of his face. The blow shattered his left arm and his right wrist. Or if it didn't, the subsequent blows did.

"I'm going to kill you," Saltman heard.

Whack.

"I'm going to kill you."

Whack.

Somewhere in the beating, Saltman passed out. What happened after that, he didn't know. Knievel obviously stopped swinging after a while. He and his accomplice walked away, off the 20th Century lot. No one stopped them.

"There were a number of witnesses, but nobody stepped in," Saltman later said. "This was a movie lot. People were used to seeing all kinds of things happening around them. None of them thought this was real. They thought it was another scene from another movie."

When the executive on the ground in the pool of blood didn't get off the ground and head for a sandwich, people grew suspicious. What the hell? When he continued to lie there, his friend Alan Rice decided this was for real. He lifted Saltman into a golf cart and took him to the medical office on the lot, where an ambulance was called. The police also were called and told that Evel Knievel had beaten the bejeezus out of a man right here at 20th Century Fox.

Saltman was taken to Los Angeles New Hospital. A warrant was put out for Knievel's arrest. Saltman didn't awaken until after surgery had been done on his left arm. The arm was in a large cast.

"I don't know the provocation," Saltman told reporters. "But I assume it had something to do with the book."

Alan Rice had called Saltman's wife, Mollie, with the news. She thought the two men were playing a joke. Tell the truth, Shelly was going to be late for dinner? At sundown, Yom Kippur would begin. He was supposed to be home for dinner with her entire family. Now he was going to be late?

In Las Vegas, Bob Arum already was at services at his synagogue. He was called to the rabbi's office for an important phone call. The phone call was from Shelly.

"Shelly says, 'Watch yourself,' " Arum said. " 'Evel attacked me with a baseball bat, and now he may be coming after you.' I wasn't too worried. Evel didn't know what synagogue I went to."

Knievel was stopped by police that night at the Lankershim Boulevard on-ramp to the Hollywood Freeway. He wasn't exactly trying to hide, riding in the refurbished $129,500 Stutz with a bodyguard. He was tailed by a car that contained his lawyer. He explained that he was on his way to the West Los Angeles police station to surrender. The police redirected him to the North Hollywood station, then to West Los Angeles, where he was booked.

Stan Rosenfeld, a young publicist in Hollywood, had been hired recently to work with Knievel in various movie projects. The work really hadn't begun, so he didn't know much about Knievel. The start of his education was a phone call during the afternoon from Rona Barrett, the print and television gossip queen.

"Do you have a statement about Evel Knievel?" she asked.

"A statement of what about Evel Knievel?" Rosenfeld answered.

"He just took a baseball bat to Shelly Saltman's arm."

"And then, as they say, hilarity ensued," Rosenfeld said years later, describing the situation.

He and Knievel prepared a statement for reporters at the station. Rosenfeld read Knievel's words, "I stand by what I did," and Knievel's appraisal of the book as "a filthy lie" that called him "an alcoholic, a pill addict, an anti-Semite and immoral person."

The daredevil was booked on suspicion of assault with a deadly weapon. He was released on $1,000 bail, told to appear next Wednesday for arraignment in West Los Angeles Municipal Court. The booking process did not take long. Knievel answered one question on the way out the door, wearing sunglasses, looking harried.

"What are you going to do tonight?" a reporter asked.

"I'm going to have me a good time tonight," he said. "Like I do every night . . ."

A story. An item had appeared in newspapers across Montana on the morning of September 21, 1977, the same day he attacked Saltman and was arrested. The Montana chapter of the national Multiple Sclerosis

Society announced that Evel Knievel had agreed once again to be honorary chairman of the state's annual MS READ-a-thon.

The READ-a-thon was a reading competition. For thirty days, students would read as many books, magazines, and newspaper articles as possible. Parents and sponsors would contribute a certain amount of money to the MS Society for each book a child read. Prizes would be awarded to the biggest readers.

"READ-a-thon is a great incentive to encourage children to read and that's important in a time when TV and many, many other conflicts seem to draw them away from good reading habits," Knievel said in the press release. "We feel that if a child can read for 30 days, that child will always be a good reader."

A story. After the attack and before he surrendered, Knievel made a call to Dee Robinson, his "decorator" back in Fort Lauderdale. He told her that some problems had arisen, so plans for the new house with the fourteen stained-glass windows were going to have to be shut down for a few weeks. Nothing major was happening, understand, just a few problems that he would work out.

"What kind of problems?" she asked.

"Oh, you'll find out," he said. "Soon enough."

She found out the next morning. She was in a convenience store and noticed the front page of a newspaper. She couldn't believe the story. A baseball bat? An attack? A few days later another unbelievable story emerged.

Mike Anderson, the captain of the *Evel Eye 1*, told her that the owner of the boat wanted to meet her. She said she knew the owner, Evel. No, Anderson said, Evel only leased the boat. The real owner had stepped forward and was taking back control. Payments had been missed. Evel never had been the owner, no matter what he said.

Robinson met with the real owner, who was not a happy man. He said she had "ruined" his boat. She apologized. She said that she had thought Evel was the owner. She followed his orders. The real owner said he now had a set of different orders. He would hire her to make the boat look "exactly" the way it looked before the sleeps-seven bed and the helicopter landing pad and the sculpture and all the rest had been added. Could she do that? She could.

The first job of her career was redecorating Evel Knievel's yacht. The second job was removing all of the decorations she had done in her first job. She never worked for Evel Knievel again, didn't see him for more than a decade.

The famous daredevil hired Paul Caruso, a big-time Hollywood attorney, to represent him. Caruso had worked with a number of celebrity clients, including James Mason, Zsa Zsa Gabor, Jane Russell, Brenda Vaccaro, Kirk Douglas, and Elroy "Crazy Legs" Hirsch. He successfully had defended actor and war hero Audie Murphy on a charge of attempted murder against a dog trainer who allegedly brutalized Murphy's dog and romanced his girlfriend. The key to the defense was Caruso's contention that Murphy, credited with killing 282 German soldiers in a day to win the Congressional Medal of Honor, couldn't have fired four times at the dog trainer and missed. Not guilty.

Knievel's defense for beating Saltman came straight out of Butte, Montana: I kicked his ass because he deserved it. There was no debate about whether the daredevil had done the deed. Too many people had seen him do it for that. The explanation he offered was that he was justified in doing what he did. Anyone in Butte would see that.

"It was the way we grew up," Louie Markovich, the longtime friend, said. "You could get away with a lot of things in Butte, but one thing you never could do was bring family into something. As soon as you brought family in, it was a whole different story. I think that was because so many kids came from such bad family situations. They didn't have a father, didn't have a mother. Bob didn't have either growing up, but he never talked about it. Never talked about his mother. Never once. Nobody ever asked him about her. Because they knew . . .

"He wasn't educated, Bob. He dropped out of school. When the guy talked about his mother, I think that put him over the top. You didn't talk about family like that."

"I think he thought he was going to be seen as a hero," Jim Blankenship, another old friend from Butte, said. "A bunch of books had been written about celebrities. Tough things. He was going to show that one celebrity wasn't going to take this. He would take matters into his own hands."

The victim became the villain when Knievel took the case to the public. Whose side are you on, the famous daredevil or the creep writer? Knievel was Buford Pusser, walking tall. He was Gary Cooper at high noon, Dirty Harry, Gene Hackman in *The French Connection*. He was on the side of good, of justice.

"Because of what I did in this matter, I will never lose the love and respect of my family and friends," he said. "I have personal convictions that must not be violated by anyone."

He brought this defiant attitude with him to the courtroom when he was arraigned on October 12, 1977. (A two-week delay had been granted to allow attorney Caruso to familiarize himself with the case.) Knievel said he wanted to plead guilty. He did what the policemen said he did. Saltman deserved it. End of case. Defendant would take his punishment.

Caruso acted stunned at this development. He said that he had advised Knievel to plead not guilty because there were ramifications to any civil trial that might follow. He asked for a day to consult with his client. Judge Frances Rothschild granted the delay. She said that she had never come across such a situation in her West Los Angeles court.

The next day Caruso announced to the court that he was resigning as Knievel's attorney. Knievel announced to the court that he pleaded guilty, but acted because Sheldon Saltman had written "a vicious book of pornography" about him. He said that he had broken Saltman's arms "because you write with your hands." Judge Rothschild scheduled the sentencing for a month later in Superior Court.

Saltman, still in the hospital, was amazed at all of this. Knievel's strategy seemed to work. That's the way it seemed, reading the newspapers. His side of the story was everywhere. Saltman's was nowhere. There were things he would like to point out, but no one seemed to ask.

Like, first of all, the slander about Knievel's mother. The only mention of Knievel's mother in the entire book was "Evel wouldn't stay in Denver, because his real mother lived there and he didn't want to see her. 'My mother's never taken care of me,' he said. 'I'm taking care of the woman that raised me, my grandmother, and that's all there is to it, you dig?' " That was the righteous cause for a beating? That?

A second thing: Knievel didn't attack Saltman's arms. He, the victim, put his arms up in self-defense. If Knievel's planned path with the baseball bat had been unimpeded, the bat would have landed directly on Saltman's head. This was attempted murder. Nothing less. Why wasn't it being prosecuted as attempted murder?

A third thing: the accomplice. Why was nobody trying to find the accomplice? Knievel mumbled something about not knowing the guy and something else about never ever saying the guy's name. Nobody seemed to care about the accomplice. Nobody seemed to care about the seriousness of the crime.

Saltman was confused about the entire business. He couldn't believe any of it had happened.

"I went through stages," he said. "Like you read about with rape victims. First, I felt sorry for myself. Why did this happen to me? Then fear. Is this guy going to come back and finish the job? Then anger. My son was a water polo player at Arizona State, a big kid, and I guess his teammates had to stop him from getting on a plane with a baseball bat and come looking for Knievel. I was glad that didn't happen, but for the first time in my life there was someone I could have killed. I had never felt that.

"The final stage, and this took a while, was pity. This guy just blew up a good life."

The sentencing took place on November 14, 1977. Knievel was handed 180 days in Los Angeles County Jail, plus three years' probation. He could have been sentenced to a maximum of four years in state prison or to the one year recommended by the district attorney and deputy probation officer Ann Burnett for "a cowardly act. This was not even a one-on-one confrontation." The sentence was seen as lenient.

Judge Edward Rafeedie, while he said that "long ago we abandoned the concept of frontier justice here in California and in the civilized world," also praised Knievel's guilty plea. He said, "It is very refreshing for the court to have a defendant charged with a serious crime walk in and openly admit his guilt." Knievel said he thought the judge was "fair" on the way out of court.

The idea of six months in jail did not seem to bother him. He would set off on a trip through the California penal system that was alternately comic, embarrassing, and flat-out sad. It was a *Hogan's Heroes, McHale's Navy* sort of sitcom wackiness that grabbed headlines and attention on the surface, that crazy old Evel Knievel, but a tale of further self-destruction underneath. What he didn't realize was that the train of slowly accumulated gravy was leaving the station, taking away the pieces of the extravagant life he had built, and try as he might, he would not know how to stop it. The old tricks didn't work anymore.

Public perception had changed. He convinced no one with his boasts of frontier justice. He tried to say that he needed assistance because his hands were still broken from the shark tank crash, but no one believed him. Two-on-one was two-on-one. America didn't like that.

The swings with that baseball bat had put him on the other side of an invisible fence. He simply didn't count the way he once counted. He had been heading toward the back edge of celebrity anyway, his age against him, his act suddenly shopworn, especially with the shark fiasco in Chicago, but now he officially was damaged goods, yesterday's news, a treacherously loose cannon, and ultimately a bad guy. The votes were in.

"The biggest problem with fame is people begin to think everything is forever," Stan Rosenfeld said years later, after representing actors George Clooney, Charlie Sheen, and an A-list group of Hollywood stars. "Fame and all the things that come with it are lent to you. You don't own them. You have to pay rent. And when you don't pay the rent—and people know when you don't—everything can disappear. You kill your franchise."

A story in the *National Enquirer* that appeared in his last days of freedom, "Evel Knievel's Lavish Lifestyle," proved to be a final celebration of his affluence. Harry O's shot of Evel loading the .38 Smith and Wesson ("I don't pose for anyone!") sat nicely under the headline. A picture of the recently departed *Evel Eye 1* Feadship was included, along with a picture of Evel leaning against the front fender of one of his Ferraris. Though the story mentioned the subject's upcoming incarceration, the tone was curious, as if nothing had happened, a celebration of his good fortune and fiscal folly.

"I met the shah the other day, and he said, 'You bought more planes in one day than I've bought!' " the prisoner-to-be said, meaning the Shah of Iran, the richest man in the world.

Knievel listed, one more time, the spoils of his profession. He claimed, yes, he once bought seven airplanes from Beech Aircraft at one time, once owned a total of eleven airplanes, two of them Lear jets. He once, of course, also owned thirteen boats, headed by the Feadship, which he admitted had been leased and now had been returned. ("I gave it back to the guy I leased it from because I felt sorry for him—he's going through a divorce.") He rounded off the estimates for the jewelry and the cars, but did say he had a late addition to his garage, the $129,500 white-and-gold Stutz convertible, the only convertible Stutz ever made. He claimed he had paid $675,000 in taxes the previous year.

The story read like a trip through life's checkout lane. This was the pile of high-calorie stuff that had been amassed. A careful reader noted that there wasn't a fruit or vegetable involved.

"If I lost it all tomorrow, I haven't lost anything," Knievel claimed. "I have had the gracious hand of God on me to let me live a dream of a life."

This idea soon would be put to a test. The final death throes of the Evel Knievel franchise came during his trip through jail. They of course were public, public, public. They of course were something to watch.

As a footnote, the Shah of Iran would fare no better. The first demonstrations against his autocratic rule already had begun in Tehran. Within a year and a half, he would be an exile without a country, the Iranian revolution complete.

28 Los Angeles, CA

He was scheduled to begin his six-month sentence on Monday, November 21, 1977, but the weirdness began three days earlier. On Friday, November 18, the newly convicted felon called a press conference to announce that he was going to have his spleen removed. And he was going to be dropped from the bomb bay of a World War II B-29 or B-50 aircraft at forty thousand feet. And he wouldn't be wearing a parachute. And he was going to land on one of thirteen haystacks.

Maybe.

"My name is Evel Knievel," he said as he appeared from behind a curtain in a function room at the Sheraton Universal. "I am a daredevil. I am the best at what I do."

He had lured maybe a hundred people, a group filled with many more friends and backslappers than press, to the room to announce his participation in "the most daring and spectacular feat in the history of man." (Steve Harvey of the *L.A. Times* pointed out that a first press release had referred to the event as "the most daring and spectacular fete known to man," causing many people to think that a lavish dinner was going to be announced.) He had a pointer, diagrams, facts printed on no-nonsense cardboard, plus a full set of his personal X-rays that he was glad to share.

This was it, he said, the end of his career, an end presumably not to be confused with any of those earlier retirements. He was done with motorcycle jumps, challenges, canyons, any and all long lines of cars, buses, or Pepsi Cola trucks, done with ass-over-teakettle crashes. He was done with the daredevil business . . . EXCEPT FOR THIS ONE LAST

COLOSSAL EXTRAVAGANZA, THIS ONE LAST MOMENT. What a moment it would be.

Thirteen haystacks would be laid out in the parking lot of some lucky casino in either Las Vegas or Atlantic City. A speck would appear in the sky at a distance, then take shape as it moved closer and closer. My God, it was that World War II bomber, the B-29 or B-50, piloted by an unnamed World War II hero who had flown over one hundred missions during the Big One and never missed a target! The payload would be a human being this time. Evel.

The game was to drop Our Hero through the bomb-bay doors from forty thousand feet as if he were another bit of bad news for the citizens of, say, Dusseldorf. The estimate was that he would be traveling as fast as 130 miles per hour in his descent. Because a man's spleen had proven to split open like an overripe grapefruit sometimes at downward speeds of over one hundred miles per hour, especially upon landing, the organ would be removed surgically from Our Hero a month or two before the Great Event by skilled physicians. While they were at it, the skilled physicians—or maybe a separate set of skilled physicians, no one ever specified—would implant a sophisticated "missile guidance device" in his chest.

His goal would be to land on one of the thirteen haystacks and not, of course, anywhere else. The "missile guidance device" would be keyed into transponders in the haystacks. Our Hero, not wearing a parachute, but with minimal protection in a pressurized suit and a special helmet, presumably would land with a *whomp* rather than a *splat*, hay flying into the air in celebration. The cheering would last well into the night.

"This will be my last and final act as a professional life-risker," Knievel said. "I will be forty years old in a year, and I would like to relax."

The live crowd would be enormous, spectacular, the television audience from around the world in the hundreds of millions. Life itself would stop for this one moment. There would be betting, probably an international lottery, people guessing which haystack would be the landing spot. The winners would take home fortunes. All bets would be off, of course, if Our Hero missed the haystacks altogether.

He said he had been thinking about this stunt for a long, long time, simply never had mentioned it. He figured that the up-front payment would be $20 million, and he would spend every cent before he jumped. Just in case. Ralph Andrews Productions would handle the television rights and productions. Casinos would bid against each other for the right to play host.

The date would be the Fourth of July 1978, eight months away, after he had finished this 180-day jail sentence, this nuisance. He would "soar like an eagle" on July 4, though before that happened he had to "go through garbage, like a dump or jail, like a seagull." He would do all of that. The old Evel Knievel, American daredevil, American icon, was going to be back, boys. One last time.

"Do you have a death wish?" a reporter asked.

"I do have a death wish," Knievel said in an attempt at his old iconic wit and charm. "I'd like to die in bed with a good-looking broad when I'm 103."

The joke sounded hollow and flat. The entire presentation sounded hollow and flat, desperate. This certainly was an attempt to rekindle the feeling, the excitement, of the weeks before Snake River, many of the same words and components dusted off and presented again, but now, well, everyone had seen Snake River. Everyone had seen a lot more of Knievel. Everyone pretty much had seen enough.

The absence of specifics for "Evel in a Haystack" was a giant indicator that the event would never happen. There was no deal with any casino on the books. There was no deal with any television network. There was no deal, period, for anything more than the rented room at the Sheraton, the chairs and tables, the buffet spread, and the words in the air.

Newspapers across the country mostly ran a little "People in the News" note the next day from the Associated Press or UPI or Reuters, mostly as another "hey look at this" bit of nonsense from Hollywood. The *Valley News*, a suburban Los Angeles daily, actually added some outside expertise to the story. A reporter called the L.A. County Medical Association and the State Board of Medical Quality Assurance to ask about the feasibility of removing someone's spleen so the someone could be dropped from a World War II bomber. The reply was that the operation would be "totally insane," "very improper," and a "highly questionable procedure."

The entire enterprise was highly questionable.

"I have earned millions of dollars through the years facing the greatest competitor in life—that is death," Knievel would write in response to a letter to the editor from James M. Perry, former commanding officer for the U.S. Army Golden Knights Parachute Team, who questioned all of the facets of the haystack jump in the *L.A. Times.* "I enjoy life. I love to live every day hoping it will never end. I will do my best to see that it does not. There are two things that have kept other men from doing what I am going to do; one is fear and the other is the sudden stop when you hit the ground."

He left out a third reason: no one cared. The announcement of the stunt was pretty much as far as the stunt went. The stuntman himself went to jail.

He showed up for that scheduled appointment on Monday, November 21, 1977, spleen still inside his body, at the county courthouse in Santa Monica to surrender to sheriff's deputies to begin his sentence. If there was any worry about what would happen next as he began serving the first true jail time in his life, he didn't show it. He acted as if he were a kid headed to summer camp in the mountains.

"Good morning, good morning, good morning," he said to gathered reporters as he arrived forty minutes early.

He was dressed in his usual Super Fly outfit, this one made of blue leather and cotton. The exaggerated collar on the jacket boasted the usual wingspan, same as a good-sized pterodactyl or medium-sized executive jet. He wore sunglasses to guard against the L.A. morning haze, any flashbulbs, and, of course, because he was who he was. He was accompanied by lawyer Caruso.

The major reason for his good nature was that he knew he wasn't going to be in jail very long. Caruso had wrangled a spot for his client in a work-release program that would allow him to leave every day between the hours of six-thirty in the morning and six-thirty at night to conduct normal business. Knievel would be allowed to wear his normal clothes, follow his normal routines, then return to prison denim and jail at night. This could start as soon as Wednesday. There was also a good chance his sentence would be shortened.

"With good behavior," Caruso told reporters, "he could be out in four and a half months."

Knievel surrendered in the courthouse to the deputies at 9:00 a.m., then boarded a bus with other prisoners for the trip to the Los Angeles County Jail. This was a famous place. Located on the top three floors of the massive Hall of Justice building in the city center of L.A. at the corner of North Broadway and West Temple Street, the county jail had, at different times, been home to characters like Bugsy Siegel, Charles Manson, and Sirhan Sirhan, the assassin of Robert F. Kennedy.

The major pieces of the L.A. judicial system—the sheriff's department, the district attorney's office, the coroner's office, eleven superior courts, and six municipal courts—were on the first eleven floors of the Hall of Justice. More than two thousand prisoners could be accommodated on the top three floors. The bars on the cell windows were obscured from the general public by long Roman columns, part of the building's beaux arts architecture.

Built in 1925, familiar to watchers of the television show *Dragnet*, the Hall of Justice was a one-stop monument to the American legal system, a layer cake of law and order.

The final leg on the trip to punishment in L.A. County most often was an elevator ride. Going up. When the ride ended, when the doors opened, a different life awaited.

"There were some serious convicts in that place," Lou Mack, one of the residents during Knievel's sentence, said years later. "Some hard-core criminals. Some guys serving life. There were stabbings and beatings. I had threats against my life. I got up on some guy's bunk one time, and he didn't like it, and the word went out that he was going to kill me. Just for that. I went an entire week without ever sleeping until it got resolved.

"The serious cons were supposed to be on another floor, but they'd get to move around. They'd come down to our floor at night to have sex with the gay guys. The guards were in their pocket."

Mack was a resident in the next cell when Knievel arrived at cell number 11. The moment brought a touch of excitement to bored lives. Everyone knew who Knievel was. A crowd gathered to watch the famous man, now wearing prison clothes, examine his new six-by-ten-foot living quarters, an area sometimes shared by as many as four prisoners at a time.

"I've got a yacht that's bigger than this," Knievel said.

And he did.

He was a different sort of prisoner from the start. After less than seventy-two hours inside the Hall of Justice, as scheduled, his participation in the work-release program began. He was outside again. Not only outside, but outside in style. His chauffeur appeared at 9:30 a.m. on Wednesday in the $129,500 white-and-gold vintage Stutz, and Knievel came out of the building in another Super Fly outfit and, *whoosh*, was off to his business day.

He had the office at Ralph Andrews Productions in Toluca Lake, the sign "Evel in a Haystack" on his door, but in a pattern that developed quickly, he spent most days at the bar of either the Sheraton Universal or the Polo Lounge at the Beverly Hills Hotel. The other work-release prisoners went mostly to menial jobs, traveling by bus back and forth to work in factories or to farms to pick vegetables, to wherever they could find any kind of employment. Knievel rode in the Stutz every day, off to the Polo Lounge.

"That was his place of business," publicist Rosenfeld said in mild defense. "That was what he did for his work. Talk with people."

At night, back in jail, he was the same celebrity he was on the outside. Bigger, in fact. The other prisoners admired his style. He brought back pictures of himself from the Toluca Lake office, signed autographs, answered questions. He had no trouble. His crime, whacking someone with a baseball bat, hey, the guy deserved it. The other prisoners recognized the approach.

Bunches of them gathered each night in his cell where he told stories about his jumps and surgeries, pitfalls and pratfalls. The crowd would extend into the hallways it was so large. He would turn serious sometimes, go back to the W. Clement Stone foundation, and dispense formulas for success, for changing your life in a positive way.

He could use his own success as a lesson in how to find a straight path, how to leave the criminal life and still fulfill dreams. If he could do it, hey, other people could do it, too.

"He was a real big boost and inspiration to me," Lou Mack said. "I was just some punk kid, a bad kid locked up in drugs and violence. He showed me how to look beyond my nose. To this day I say that him coming to jail probably was the best thing that ever happened to me."

"It amazed me that he could adjust to being in that cell after living his extravagant life," Victor Thomas, serving a sentence for burglary, said. "The guy was just like one of the boys. He showed us the scars all over his body from the bad, unlucky accidents he had while performing. All the plates, screws, and surgeries made him like the Six Million Dollar Man."

Knievel hired Thomas, known throughout the jail as a talented artist, to sketch a series of pictures detailing his stay behind bars. The pictures didn't necessarily have to show things he actually did in jail. Thomas captured him playing basketball (guarding an inmate with an enormous Afro), eating lunch, going through a strip search (rear view), sleeping on his bunk, signing autographs, signing in and signing out as part of the work-release program. Knievel said the pictures would be used in his future autobiography. There would be no cash payment, but Thomas would become famous when the world saw his art.

"Nothing ever came of it," Thomas said. "But I don't think he had any intention of coming through anyway."

The work-release program was nothing less than idyllic under the circumstances. Hang around the hotel bar during the day. Have a cocktail, perhaps more than one. Spend the night signing autographs and telling campfire stories to people who really wanted to listen. Never show remorse. Not once. Knievel was spotted one day playing golf. He was wearing yellow shoes that Doug Sanders had given him. This was *better* than summer camp in the mountains.

Rosenfeld, the publicist, was in the backseat of the Stutz one work-release morning with Knievel and some other people, moving through the Hollywood smog, when Knievel suddenly ordered the chauffeur to take a right at the next driveway. The driveway led to the front gate at 20th Century, the scene of the crime against Saltman. Guards came out of their little booth to bar the way this time when they saw Knievel. It was a good laugh. The work-release program was a laugh.

The *Los Angeles Times*, as often happened with newspapers and situations that are too good to be true, soon took notice. On December 15, 1977, less than a month into Knievel's sentence, a front-page story by veteran court reporter Bill Farr detailed a brewing storm about Knievel's work-release situation. The headline was "Knievel's Furlough Fuels Controversy." An accompanying photo by Art Rogers was stretched across five columns and showed Knievel leaving jail, the chauffeur waiting next to the elongated Stutz. It was not exactly a scene out of *The Birdman of Alcatraz*.

"If I couldn't be on this program, I'd end up having to file for bankruptcy, and that would not only hurt me and my family but a whole lot of other people I work with," Knievel said in explanation. "But I'll have to leave that to other people to say whether it's a fair thing."

The implication in the story was that his fame had given him a free pass. Ann Burnett, the deputy county probation officer, said again that Knievel was "a totally unsuitable candidate for work furlough." Deputy District Attorney Stanley Weisberg, the prosecutor, decried Knievel's continuing lack of remorse.

"My focus is on deterrence . . . ," Weisberg said. "As I have mentioned, he is a public figure. He claims a special relationship with the country's youth. This status carries with it special responsibilities. One is to set an example for those who may wish to follow him."

. . .

A story. On Christmas Eve, out on furlough, Knievel showed up for dinner at the Beverly Hills home of J. C. Agajanian, his old promoter. Agajanian had been through a rugged set of operations for lung cancer. Knievel wanted to cheer him up. A low public profile did not seem to be part of the plan. The daredevil arrived on a three-wheeled jet motorcycle that had been developed by Bob Truax for parades.

He wooshed down Sunset Boulevard, pulled into Agajanian's circular driveway in the Trousdale Estates with an entrance that involved noise, sparks, flames, the usual stuff associated with jet engines. Agajanian's family rushed outside to see what the commotion was.

"Evel drove the jet cycle around a little bit more, then we all went inside for dinner," Agajanian's son, J. C. Agajanian Jr., said. "He had to leave early to go back to jail, so we all went out to see him off. It was quite a sight, dark now, that thing roaring away with the flames coming out the back. Exciting."

The next morning, the first thing Agajanian Jr. heard was crying. He found his mother in tears on the front lawn. Every flower, every bush had been scorched by the flames. The entire garden was ruined.

"It was a real mess," he said. "That jet motorcycle put out a lot of heat."

On Wednesday, January 3, 1978, the work-release situation became a mess. Knievel, who said he had won a big bet to open the new year when the underdog University of Washington upset the University of Michigan, 27–20, in the Rose Bowl behind quarterback Warren Moon (apparently you also could make a bet while on work-release), used part of the winnings to order up a dozen Cadillac limousines to transport the other 117 members of the program back and forth to their jobs. He said this was his New Year's gift to his fellow residents in the jail. They would have the $17 per hour drivers, plus Cadillac limos, for the rest of the week, through Sunday.

"In order that this new year, 1978, may be started with a feeling of friendship, it is in personal gratitude that I offer the limousine and chauffeur service to my fellow inmates on a 24-hour a day basis . . . ," Knievel said in a press release. "Please accept this as an honest goodwill gesture for you and your families."

Rosenfeld, the publicist, part of the operation, was the man who had ordered the cars from Carey Limousines and put out the press release through the City News Service, telling reporters that the event would happen. He drove to the Hall of Justice to see how well everything worked. He found chaos.

"I said, 'How bad could it be?' " he said. "Then I got there. It was like the Oscars."

Limousines were everywhere. They created a morning rush-hour gridlock. Some drivers had parked in the spaces for workers at the Hall of Justice, including the spot reserved for Sheriff Peter Pitchess. Some had double-parked in the street. Knievel, who was met this day by his own driver in the customized Cadillac pickup truck, a customized motorcycle sitting in the back, finally was convinced by his probation officer to cancel the cars.

The probation officer, Dennis Caldwell, said that the prisoners would put their work-release status in jeopardy by accepting the rides. Only ten of the eligible workers had signed up because of this threat. The project—if that was the right word—was not viable. Knievel reluctantly agreed. He said that he was disappointed, that he had acted only out of friendship and concern for his fellow inmates, whom he saw struggling every day to travel to work.

The final words on the venture came from two of the $17 per hour chauffeurs.

"It seems kind of wrong to be driving criminals around in these big cars," one driver told Bill Farr of the *L.A. Times*. "But come to think of it, a lot of criminals drive around in Cadillacs anyway, so maybe it isn't such a mockery of justice after all."

"It's kind of unusual," the other driver said. "We usually take people around Beverly Hills."

Knievel, of course, was the one passenger bound for Beverly Hills. And he had his own luxury transportation.

On Friday, January 5, 1977, two nights after the limousine extravaganza, an all-points bulletin was issued to local law enforcement agencies notifying them that Knievel had escaped from work-release. He had not returned to custody by 9:30 p.m. after one of those Polo Lounge days. The rules gave him a three-hour grace period after the 6:30 p.m. check-in time, and after that he was considered a fugitive. His absence was classified as an escape.

He had called, told probation officer Caldwell that he was upset by certain world news reports on television and that he was leaving the country "until it straightens itself out." He didn't specify what the "it" was, but a spokesman for the sheriff's department said he understood that Knievel was referring to a tour of the Middle East by President Jimmy Carter. Or something like that. Someone suggested Knievel might be headed to Cuba.

Publicist Rosenfeld also received a call. Rosenfeld wasn't home, but his wife answered. Knievel told her in a rambling, roundabout monologue that he was upset with the breakdown in the moral fiber of the United States. Or something like that. She told him that he should go back to jail.

"She wound up talking to him for a long time," Rosenfeld said. "He kept saying that he wasn't going back. She kept saying that he had to go back, that he'd be in too much trouble if he didn't go. I think she's the one who finally convinced him."

He turned himself in at the Hall of Justice at two-forty in the morning on Saturday. He told watch commander Lieutenant George Corbett, "You wouldn't believe the troubles I'm having." These troubles were immediately extended as he was booked on a felony escape charge and transferred to a private cell, away from his new jailhouse friends and fans. His work-release privileges were rescinded.

His state of mind—his fractured state of mind—became part of the public record one week later. Fifty-three days after beginning to serve his sentence, seven days after his walkabout, he appeared before the three-member L.A. County Board of Parole Commissioners to appeal for his freedom. It was a memorable performance. His approach seemed to come straight from some 1940s black-and-white cinema vision of parole board drama.

He fought back tears. He pleaded. He begged. He gave a grand, over-the-top Evel Knievel performance.

"I need your help . . . ," he began in a shaky voice. "And you could parole me this minute if you believe in me."

The hearing was held in a room inside the central jail. He was seated at a single chair in front of the panel, dressed in his prison blues. He was as forceful in his contrition as he was in any of his pre-jump homilies. He mentioned family, God, and Christian pop singer Anita Bryant. He blamed the media for society's ills. He invoked the sadly departed image of Elvis. He admitted that he was pretty much broke, that he had squandered the millions that had come his way and now owed hundreds of thousands of dollars more. He lamented the loss of his daredevil youth. He praised Judge Rafeedie, "a fair man." He damned *Hustler* magazine for wanting to run a centerfold spread of Jimmy Carter's mother, Miss Lillian, naked. He missed only stray dogs, orphans, and spilt milk in his litany of sadness.

His trouble missing curfew . . . well, here, it started with Miss Rona Barrett saying on national television that he had been seen with "another woman" at a cocktail lounge while on work-release. That obviously wasn't true, of course not, but his wife had seen the report, and his son had called from Montana and said his mom was despondent, and, well, that would get to anyone.

"I felt society was against me, that the press had treated me wrong and I didn't care for this country . . . ," he said. "The press puts pressure on a lot of people, like a guy like Elvis Presley, who finally took his own life with drugs."

Look at *Hustler* and the things that it did, the mean words that it said about the God-loving (anti-gay) Miss Bryant, the proposal about Miss Lillian, the asshole award it had given to none other than Los Angeles police chief Edward M. Davis, a fine man. What was going on with this country? The world in general was a mess. The world of Evel Knievel in particular was a mess. It all was a mess.

"I'm not a poet or a singer or a dancer," he said. "I'm a professional risk-taker and at thirty-nine years old there is no future for me in this daredevil business. If you think like a young man at this age, you are dead."

Two friends had flown from Butte to help bolster his case. (They were met at the airport by the chauffeur and the customized Cadillac pickup truck of work-release fame. A buzz of curbside interest suddenly surrounded the two men as they stepped into the cab and were driven into town.) The first to testify was Gary Winston, the county attorney in Butte. He asked that Knievel be granted a transfer to Butte for post-jail probation.

"I promise you it won't be just a holiday for him," Winston said.

The second witness was Father Joseph Finnegan, who ran a boys' home at the old Hanson Packing Company. Father Finnegan detailed Knievel's trips to the home to speak to the boys, his generosity of spirit, his invitations to both the boys and their parents to visit him at his house on the golf course. It was one of the few looks at any charitable enterprise by the man.

"He'd encourage the boys to stop smoking," the father said. "He'd give them $50, $100 to stop. He was very good."

The board listened to all of the words, asked very few questions, then decided not to decide. A special hearing already was scheduled in five days in Santa Monica before Judge Rafeedie. The district attorney, John Van de Kamp, had decided in the end not to prosecute the felony escape charge, so the hearing was added to determine Knievel's immediate future in the California penal system. The parole board would await the decision of the court before making its own decision.

Judge Rafeedie was not amused by any of this.

"If a legitimate escape charge can be filed against Knievel, it should have been filed," he said in the *Times*. "I don't appreciate them throwing it back to me, but I will handle it."

The judge's crankiness had turned to base-level outrage by the time the hearing arrived. Looking down from his bench at a quiet, for once, Knievel, he said, flat out, "I don't want to hear about this case anymore." The judge then laid out the defendant with a gusto not seen since the many writers had gone to work on the daredevil three years earlier at Snake River Canyon.

Rafeedie characterized Knievel's beating of Shelly Saltman as "an act of extreme cowardice," not the "frontier justice" that Knievel seemed to think it was, not the "act of an heroic avenger." The frontier justice argument was nonsense. Someone else held Saltman while Knievel beat him with a baseball bat. This was not the act of some fearless and courageous character, some childhood idol. This was a coward at work.

To Rafeedie, Knievel's tumultuous and very public time in jail so far had indicated how little the man understood about the severity of his crime. The judge was fed up with all of it. He felt abused by Knievel's conduct.

"Some of the show business stunts and PR pipe dreams like lining up limousines in front of the jail served to inflame the public and to discredit a program in which thousands of men have served with dignity," the judge said. "You are not Evel Knievel, the daring daredevil, you are Robert C. Knievel, an inmate with a booking number. You ought to spend the rest of your time in jail in self-examination. Do your time in jail with some dignity."

The afternoons at the Polo Lounge were done for the duration of his sentence. Work-release privileges were permanently rescinded. Knievel would be shipped to the Wayside Honor Rancho in Castaic. This was a long way from San Quentin perhaps, a minimum-security, unlocked facility where seventy-two convicts worked as gardeners, growing plants for the rest of the prison system, but it also was a hundred miles from Beverly Hills. The fun was done.

The important news about Knievel during his work-release follies—it had been less than two months, remember, since he entered jail, less than four months since he attacked Saltman—had taken place further back in the papers than these many curious adventures on page 1, often not in the papers at all, quiet items about business decisions being made, about lawsuits filed and lawsuits decided, loans called in or rejected, properties seized. This was where the true punishment was being delivered.

A T-shirt company in Helena wanted money for shirts that had been made, shipped, and never paid for. Watcha McCollum's helicopter service still wanted the money for services rendered during the canyon jump. The town of Twin Falls wanted money for cleanup. The provider of portable toilets still wanted money for the toilets that were destroyed at the event. In Bal Harbour, Florida, the Transit Charter Company wanted $50,000 for the Dee Robinson renovations on its 116-foot Feadship, *Evel Eye 1*, that had not been authorized. The U.S. government wanted money from back taxes. The bill, with interest, now had crossed the $3 million mark. The state of Montana wanted money . . . the list did not seem to end. Oh, yes, a civil suit by Shelly Saltman for unspecified, but sure to be costly, damages already had begun its climb through the judicial process.

Our Hero's working capital had pretty much disappeared, simply because he had spent everything. His credit line now had also disappeared in a hurry. Unable to generate new interest in his career, no matter what he did, even offering his spleen to the daredevil gods, importing limos for convicts, crying and pleading before the parole board, his prospects had disappeared.

The biggest blow of all came from Ideal and the toys. Zeke Rose, the PR veteran of the Snake River tour, had delivered the company's blunt appraisal of the future for the Evel Knievel line on the day Knievel went to jail: the marketplace would decide. Christmas would be the test. The company was not happy with the events in Los Angeles.

"The company recognizes that it sells its products to children," Rose said, "and that it has a responsibility to the children and their parents."

Christmas had arrived and departed. Sales, which had begun to shrink before the attack, had disappeared from the charts. The Knievel toys had been responsible for 18 percent of Ideal's $137.6 million in sales during the previous fiscal year, ending on January 31, 1976. They had been the company's biggest seller for the past three years. Now, before the end of this fiscal year, they were discontinued.

Lionel Weintraub, the president of Ideal Toys, knew the news before Christmas. He sent the good-bye letter on December 14, 1977.

> Dear Evel—
>
> I would like to take this opportunity to clear any misunderstanding which may exist concerning Ideal and its relationship with you and the toys that bear your name.
>
> During the past five years, the sale of more than one hundred million dollars in Evel Knievel toys has been a revelation to the toy industry and testimony to your popularity and our ability to make quality products. It marked the first time that a successful toy was marketed bearing the name of a real person. Previously such successes were limited to dolls.
>
> Despite the quality and durability of the toys and your heroic exploits and public concern for the safety and welfare of children, the sales of Evel Knievel toys were destined to decline. This year, that decline was sharper than anticipated.
>
> I have always felt that our relationship was rewarding both personally and professionally, and trust you will emerge from your present difficulties to achieve whatever new goals you have set for yourself.
>
> May the new year bring you and your family Peace, Health and Happiness.
>
> Sincerely,
> Lionel Weintraub

"Based on what happened last fall, there's no reason to continue production," Zeke Rose said as the company made the official announcement on March 28, 1978, that it was taking the toys off the marketplace.

His estimate, same as Weintraub's, was that in their five-year run the figures and Skycycles and all the rest had earned Ideal over $100 million. He said Knievel had been paid between 2.5 and 10 percent of that figure. The toys always were Knievel's biggest source of revenue, a financial constant matched against the various schemes and appearances and get-rich-quick opportunities that came along.

Knievel still was a resident at the Wayside Honor Rancho when the Ideal announcement was made. His time there had been quiet, except for a three-day emergency trip to the University of Southern California Medical Center in February because one of the penal system's doctors had read his spinal X-rays and worried that paralysis might be imminent without an operation. (The doctors at USC did not agree.) The good behavior at Wayside did, in the end, win him parole, an early release on April 12, 1978.

A week before that release, he had Rosenfeld distribute a letter to the media detailing his new financial status. His point was that his time in jail, not his attack on Saltman, had knocked him low. He hadn't been able to work.

"Last year at this time I had 16 boats, three of them yachts, with a value of about $5 million," he wrote. "I've had to sell them all with the exception of three speedboats and one 80-foot yacht. My navy sure is decreasing in size."

He said he had two houses left, the one in Butte for the summer, Fort Lauderdale for the winter. (Which were all the houses he ever had.) He had sold all but the largest of his diamond rings. He estimated that through the years all of the Evel Knievel products—the toys, plus the bicycles, plus the pinball machines—had combined sales of over $180 million. He said his profits from that figure were what had financed his lifestyle.

"Things are tough," he said, "but I think I can make it."

Newspapers across the country had fun with the story ("Evel Down to His Last Yacht"), but the change in his situation, the speed with which it had happened, was staggering. Not much more than a year earlier he had been getting ready for the jump over the pool of sharks, ramping up the interest. The movie *Viva Knievel!* was going to hit in July. The toys were still selling, he'd signed a deal with ABC to do some commentary and a few jumps, he had a future.

Now he pretty much was broke. How could that be?

A few minutes after midnight in the first hour of April 12, 1978, Knievel was released from the county jail at the Hall of Justice in Los

Angeles. He had served four months and three weeks of his six-month sentence. He was on probation for the next three years. The Super Fly outfit was gray this time. The attitude still was unrepentant.

"I feel the majority of society understands the reasons for my actions," he said.

This was his continuing colossal misread of public opinion. Or maybe his simple stubbornness. Butte, Montana, was not America. Society didn't understand at all. He never would do another jump on network television. He never would be a rich man again, though he would try to keep that appearance. He never would be in demand.

On a Friday night, back at the Sheraton Universal, he threw himself a welcome home party. The honored guests were mostly convicts from the L.A. County Jail who had been released before he was, but also some guards and some friends. There was a lot of singing, prison songs. PR agent Rosenfeld was in attendance, one of his last acts working for Knievel. He had one enduring memory.

"Somewhere in the night, Evel was in a lot of pain," Rosenfeld said. "A doctor appeared from somewhere and gave him an injection, right there at the table, right into his hand. I'd never seen anyone get an injection into his hand."

29 Always, Forever Butte

There was a lot more to his story, of course, thirty more years until he died on November 30, 2007, at the age of sixty-nine, but at the same time there was no more. He was finished, done, broke, removed from the top shelf of American celebrity. The magic was gone. He was shuffled to that large warehouse in the back of the mind that is filled with retired athletes and disgraced politicians, faded ingenues and one-hit wonders, with entertainers who do not entertain anymore.

QUESTION: Evel Knievel?
ANSWER: Oh, yeah, I remember him.

The beating of Shelly Saltman took away any chance at a happy, controlled landing. There was a reason why toymakers always favored cartoon superheroes over real-life people: the cartoon characters never grew old, never lost their powers, never drank bourbon, never claimed to have slept with eight different women in a day, never whacked their former publicist with a baseball bat, never went to jail.

The fall of the famous daredevil was as breathtaking as any of his stunts ever had been. The hero became unheroic in an instant, viewed now as somewhere on a sliding scale between silly and flat-out despicable. The deals disappeared. The lifestyle pretty much went with them. There were no press conferences to announce any of this. Companies simply moved along to the next hot thing.

The affiliation with Harley-Davidson was an example. His contract with the company had expired, but nobody said a word about that fact. One Harley executive, Clyde Fessler, sent a memo to another executive, John Wilson, wondering why Knievel seemed to be representing the company without a signed contract. Wilson said basically that the company didn't want any adverse feedback or negative publicity. Fessler agreed with the approach.

"Let's let this die a natural death—hopefully in '79," he wrote in a later memo. "Do not push for a signature on a contract."

The pile of money, of course, had been shrinking for a while, but now there were only bits and pieces arriving to plug any holes. The famous daredevil liked to claim that he made $60 million in his run through the public consciousness, but that he spent $62 million. He sometimes said he made $35 million and spent $37 million. The numbers varied, depending on the interview, but the constant was that he spent $2 million more than he made. The specifics probably weren't important, except to the IRS, but the truth was that he made a lot of money and spent more than he made. The $2 million difference sounded quite reasonable.

His daredevil career sputtered to an end with a forgettable trip to Australia and another forgettable trip to Puerto Rico and a couple of other appearances in support of Robbie, who had taken over the family trade. Relations with Robbie, never good, would fall apart, get better for brief stretches, then fall apart again. Robbie went off to break his father's records, one by one, using lighter bikes, some basic technology, but never could capture the excitement, the charisma, his father brought to the game.

On May 14, 1979, Linda gave birth to Alicia, her fourth child with Bob Knievel. Alicia was sixteen years younger than Tracey, seventeen years younger than Robbie, nineteen years younger than Kelly. This was the first of his children's births that Knievel witnessed, and he told a reporter it was "something to see." Stop the presses.

He drank. He had meetings, chased deals. He went to Muhammad Ali's house in Brentwood, California, to pitch a shoeshine polish business. He told Ali they would make a commercial, do a jump. He would steer the motorcycle, Ali would sit on the back, and "we'd be the two most famous people in the world." Ali said, "Not me, boss," about the motorcycle. He said the same thing about the deal.

The dream house in Butte disappeared on August 21, 1980. Though Knievel had said the house and land were worth $900,000, they sold in foreclosure for $214,460, which was five dollars more than the minimum asking price. Stories said Knievel had not made one of his $4,008 monthly mortgage payments since October of 1979. He already had lost the boats, the planes, most of the cars, although he always seemed to drive an expensive car no matter what happened.

On December 22, 1981, a civil court awarded Shelly Saltman $12.75 million in damages from the attack that Santa Monica Superior Court judge Laurence Rittenband called "violent, brutal, vicious, unprovoked, and cowardly." Knievel represented himself in papers filed for the case, but never appeared in the courtroom. In later interviews, he declared that he had no remorse, that Saltman was the worst kind of bloodsucker and "never would receive a dime," but the judgment was another entanglement in his finances, another outstanding bill that would not leave.

In 1983 he began a career as an artist. His longtime Butte friend Jack Ferriter was a successful painter, and Knievel said he'd taken some lessons from Ferriter and done some paintings that he would sell. A licensing agreement with the Legend's Corporation of North Royalton, Ohio, was signed, and Knievel bought a big motor home and trailer to bring his artwork around the country. He would sell to galleries and to individuals, sign autographs and tell stories.

People in Butte noted that Knievel's artistic style looked almost exactly like Ferriter's style, hmmmmm, but Ferriter only said that he gave Knievel "tips" on what to do. A friend said he was in the studio when Ferriter delivered a tip. Knievel was adding a few brushstrokes and his signature to a work that Ferriter had done. Knievel seemed to be adding too many brushstrokes.

"Hey, don't fuck it up," the artist said.

Knievel made a documentary video to chronicle this time of his life called *The Last of the Gladiators: Evel Knievel*. He said in the video that he had given up alcohol and the nightlife and had found strength in God and family. That was his new life: God and family and art. He traveled in the motor home with Linda and Alicia, the older kids out in the world on their own, and this was a second chance.

"There's more to life than just wasting yourself on alcohol," he said in the video. "That's what drunks do. They're just soaking up alcohol. They're really hemorrhoids on the ass of progress."

The inevitable happened. The art business soon fell apart. Lawsuits were filed by Legend's Corporation. The family life fell apart. Linda and Alicia went back to Butte. Knievel went back to drinking, back to gambling, back to chasing all women. He spent a lot of time in Las Vegas. The hemorrhoids on the ass of progress won again.

When Robbie attempted to jump the fountains at Caesars Palace on April 14, 1989, to avenge the family honor on pay-per-view television, his father became a necessary part of the production. Disagreements had to be put on hold. After a week of dealing with Knievels, the televsion crew became more worried about the father's role on the day of the jump than the son's role. Father was supposed to ride out to the ramp on a motorcycle to talk with son and broadcasters before the big moment. This quietly became an exciting event. Father was inside the bar at Caesars until the very last moment.

"He was drunk," former ABC executive Jim Spence, producer of the event, said. "I was trying to figure out what we could do. We were worried that he was going to fall off the motorcycle. But out he came, rode right up there. Did it all."

The jump was perfect. Robbie had practiced for a week at a duplicate ramp set up at an airport. He knew exactly what to expect. The American public mostly didn't pay attention.

A story. One night, not so long after Knievel got out of jail for whacking Saltman, he went to a place called the Red Rooster on his round of Butte bars. He wound up gambling, played Texas Hold'em, caused a scene, one of those turn-over-the-table kind of scenes that shut down the game for the night. Knievel was mad at the dealer, a woman. He called her a long line of terrible names and made her cry before he finally left.

The game was backed by a large-sized guy named Jimmy Dick, who was not on the premises that night. The dealer was his girlfriend.

Dick, who did not know Knievel but certainly had heard about him forever, put retribution on a to-do list for further action. The time came soon enough. Knievel was back at the bar within weeks, noisy as usual, when Jimmy Dick and Terry Richards, another large-sized guy, arrived after an all-day rock concert. Terry Richards acted first.

"Hey, are you Evel Knievel?" he asked.

"Yes, I am," Knievel answered.

"Would you sign this cocktail napkin for me?"

Knievel signed with his usual autograph flourish. "Happy Landings, Evel Knievel." Terry Richards took the napkin, rolled it into a ball, put it into his mouth, and ate it. His eyes never left Knievel as he chewed.

Jimmy Dick then came into the picture. He planned to kick Knievel's ass.

"Hey, wait a minute, I know about you," Knievel said. "Jimmy Dick. I've heard of you."

A conversation followed. The result was vintage Knievel. He brought out the old Positive Mental Attitude, the W. Clement Stone PMA. Words followed more words, and Jimmy Dick not only was convinced not to inflict great bodily harm, but was now the newest employee of Evel Knievel. He was Evel Knievel's bodyguard. They were going to Australia.

The lure of Australia was that nobody knew much about Shelly Saltman in Australia. Promoters wanted Knievel's name to attach to a multi-act thrill show they would take across the country, forty-four cities in nine weeks. He didn't have to take big risks, mostly ride around and make way for a kid daredevil, Dale Buggins, sixteen years old, an Australian. Knievel didn't want to go, but did like the up-front money, the advance. He went to Australia.

The tour was the mishmash that could have been predicted. Knievel was drinking, impossible to handle. From the time he refused to talk at the opening press conference in Sydney to the time he decided the facility in the town of Griffith did not meet his standards and he refused to perform, to his eventual break with the show in Wagga Wagga after only eight of the forty-four dates, he made it clear that he didn't want to be there.

Jimmy Dick watched the entire scene. Knievel did not like being the second banana. Every night the Australian announcer would make the jumping sound like a competition between Knievel and the Australian kid, Dale Buggins. Every night Knievel would do a little jump. Every night the kid would be spectacular. It was part of the show, Australia beats the United States.

Dick would watch the show with Buggins's father. The kid did spectacular things, rode inside some kind of iron ball, leaped over fourteen cars, was routinely young and fearless. His father was excited. He kept asking for Jimmy Dick's opinion. How good was this kid? How good, really? The father obviously wanted Evel Knievel's friend to say that his son was better than Evel Knievel.

"Look, yes, your son can really ride a motorcycle," Jimmy Dick finally said. "He's great. That means he's got about 5 percent of this business covered."

No better explanation of Evel Knievel's success ever had been given.

• • •

Lou Mack, the resident of the next cell when Knievel checked into the Los Angeles County Jail, had taken the daredevil's inspirational advice, the Positive Mental Attitude speech, and made a new life when he was paroled. He became a showman himself, a dog trainer, the head of Cooldog Productions, on the road to amusement parks and state fairs with dogs that caught Frisbees, jumped through hoops, did spectacular feats. He was forever grateful for Knievel's encouragement, and whenever he ran into him was quick to say hello.

One of those meetings was in the lobby of the Stardust Hotel in Las Vegas. Mack asked Knievel what he was doing there.

"I'm a guest at the AVN Awards," he said.

Mack didn't know what the awards were. He saw a sign, "Adult Video News," when he was leaving. There was an abundance of pretty women in the lobby. Yes, of course. The women were all porn stars. The AVN Awards were the Oscars of the porn industry. Knievel was a guest at the porn Oscars.

That was where his life had landed. He made the headlines now and again: arrested in Kansas City for soliciting a prostitute; sued a man in Spokane for beating him up in a hotel room because he was sleeping with the man's girlfriend; arrested in Helena, Montana, on a concealed weapons charge. He did commercials for a bail bond firm in San Diego. He had assorted jams that did not make the news. He played golf, bet as much money as he could, then bet more. He hung out. He hung out a lot.

Writer Mike Edison, a self-described wildman, recounted a chance meeting and excursion with Knievel in Las Vegas in the book, *I Have Fun Everywhere I Go.* Knievel said he had sold his Skycycle to the newly opened Las Vegas edition of the Hard Rock Cafe for "a million dollars." He said he now had a check for $20,000, first payment, that no bars would cash. He alternately grumbled and boasted. Edison, who had been a fan of Knievel when he was young, was embarrassed for him now.

"After just a few drinks he was visibly drunk," Edison wrote.

He was still waving his check around, asking the bartender if he would cash it, and trying to pick up every cocktail waitress in the place. His basic technique was to holler, "Hey, do you wanna sleep with me tonight?" The girls failed to rally round for a Touch of Evel and it quickly became obvious that he had been hanging around the hotel for a while now, working the same material, and everyone was getting a little tired of his routine.

Gennifer Flowers, linked in scandal to Bill Clinton, said in a tell-all memoir that she had danced a slow dance with the famous daredevil. Jessica Hahn, the mistress of evangelist Jim Bakker, told Howard Stern that she had done likewise. Knievel explained to anyone who would listen his old idea that women were like buses. If one leaves, another will be along in five minutes.

At a charity golf tournament in Clearwater, Florida, in 1992, he met a twenty-two-year-old golfer from Florida State named Krystal Kennedy. He was fifty-three. They became an item. They became a live-in couple in Clearwater. They became golf hustlers, traveling around the country. Krystal was a secret weapon, supposed to play badly until the proper moment to win a big bet. They became a headline, Knievel arrested for suspicion of "inflicting harm over a coinhabitant" in an incident in a motel room in Sunnyvale, California, in October of 1994. Krystal refused to press charges. They stayed an item. They stayed a couple.

The long-frayed marriage to Linda officially ended in 1997. They had been married for thirty-eight years. Or at least she had. His concept of marriage always had been different from the normal concept. He had lived an entire famous life outside marriage. He probably never had been married.

"I ran into Linda on the street after the divorce," Jim Blankenship, Knievel's friend, said. "I asked her how she was doing and told her that she should have gotten the divorce years ago. I said—this was when O. J. Simpson was in the news—that the O.J. thing made me think about her and Evel. She said, 'Oh, yes, there was a lot of O.J. in Evel.' "

Knievel and Krystal Kennedy were married on November 19, 1999. The site was Caesars Palace, picked for reasons of both sentiment and economy. The altar was constructed on top of the fountains. Knievel drove up on a Harley. Krystal was escorted by a fake Caesar and a fake Cleopatra. She looked lovely. He looked ancient. The hair he had left was gray turning in a hurry to white. He wore red-tinted sunglasses. He was sixty-one years old, not so bad in the numbers, but sixty-one hard years old. She was thirty.

A renaissance had begun in the past few years for his career as a personality. In the court of public opinion, he apparently had served enough time in the corner. The kids who had watched him, who had played with the toys, who had hung his picture on their bedroom wall, were grown-ups now with their own kids. He was a certified blast from the past, a walking, talking irascible piece of nostalgia.

"He was a creation of network television," Bob Arum said, asked to figure out what had made Knievel popular in the first place. "We had three networks. People got used to watching three networks. On Saturday and Sunday afternoons, people watched the three networks. And ABC hooked onto Knievel because his jumping over buses and so forth attracted viewers and so forth, and they did a hell of a job promoting it.

"Everything is different now, of course it is, but how much different is that crazy reality television of today to that shit? It was the same thing! It was shit, it was shit, it was shit. It was shit that drove ratings at affordable prices . . . It was totally nonpurposeful shit, totally crap. That was what he was. That was what that was. There's always a market for that."

The shit of anyone's youth lives forever. The famous daredevil was now a slice of bubblegum rock from long ago heard on the radio. He was a pair of bell-bottoms and platform shoes found in an old box in the attic. He was a fuzzy video from when the grown-ups of today were young. He was shit perhaps, but their shit. A small demand arose. He appeared in commercials. Better commercials. His name became repeated again on late-night shows. He became a guest. His influence was recognized, his jumps seen as the start of all these extreme sports that had taken root. Skateboards. Snowboards. BMX. Motocross. The X Games. He was the godfather of all of this. He had not only lived on the edge, he had discovered it before anyone else knew it existed. He had made it his home.

What was Evel Knievel doing now? He was right there at Caesars Palace, married again to a pretty blond woman, the wily old son of a bitch. There were possibilities. All kinds of possibilities. He boasted that he was back to making $300,000 a year from signing autographs, doing endorsements, making deals.

Except his health was awful.

"Hell, I thought the first 40 years were Round 1," he told Jon Saraceno of *USA Today* on January 3, 2007. "I had 12 or 13 major open reduction surgeries, most of them major at least, and here since the Seventies I've gone through bleeding esophagus attacks and I had a liver transplant and I had a stroke. I had a stroke last September. And I have idiopathic pulmonary fibrosis where I can't breathe very easily and I just broke my ankle two years ago in Amarillo in a motorcycle parade. Damn motorcycle fell on me. I've had several things go wrong with me. This is Round 2. God never promised you a Rose Garden. That's just all there is to it."

He was a mess. The last ten years of his life were not pretty.

The clinks and clanks from all of that abuse to his skeleton, round 1, still were a problem. The seven different times he had broken his back left him with pain that he said, on a scale of one to ten, was a constant ten. It hurt so much on some days that he could barely talk. His broken hands, always bad, still were bad. He walked slowly with a stainless steel hip. The residual effects of all the surgeries, the plates and screws and rods, round 1, was an everyday ache.

"My back is really killing me," he said one day to Jimmy Dick.

Dick offered some sympathy.

"It's okay," Knievel said. "It's not like I was working in a library all my life, you know?"

Round 2 was a tougher pain to accept. This was the rebellion of his internal organs. This came from the rest of his life more than his daredevil life. This was from the dissipation, from the excesses, from the all-out ramble.

He was healthy enough when he first met Krystal, back in 1992. She remembered that the only pill he took every day was a Tylenol. Five years later, though, he was frail and tired. He thought he was going to die. His liver had broken down from the effects of hepatitis C, which he thought he had contracted from a bad blood transfusion during one of his surgeries, plus the effects of alcohol. All that alcohol. He now called Wild Turkey more dangerous than heroin.

He needed a liver transplant.

"I created the character called Evel Knievel, and he sort of got away from me," the famous daredevil told Bruce Lowitt of the *St. Petersburg Times* in June of 1998 while he waited for a liver. "When I was performing, I thought I'd get killed. But shit, I'm not ready to die today."

The liver arrived on January 28, 1999, a miracle right there, the operation performed at Tampa General Hospital, but he was left with a long recovery period, with the worry that his body would reject the new organ, with a shelf in his medicine cabinet full of pills to take every day. He still was recovering four months after the operation when he got married, still recovering more than a year later.

"This is a year and a few months after the transplant," he said. "Before I had it, my doctors told me that it would be the biggest thing I ever had to face, and believe me, when they take your liver out of you and put another one in, it's like replacing a football in your stomach."

He never really was healthy again. He was better sometimes, still alive, making jokes and pronouncements and steely-eyed deals, but never healthy. The drugs from the transplant, he said, gave him mood swings. The mood swings killed his marriage less than two years after it began. He still wanted to be married, left flowers and notes on Krystal's car, romantic stuff, then became angry when she refused to come back. Mood swings. She got an injunction against him two months after the divorce. He was angry on the steps of the courthouse.

"She's lucky I didn't hit her," he said. "I never want to see her again." Yes, he did.

He had the lung disease, the idiopathic pulmonary fibrosis, an advancing problem without a cure. He had diabetes. He had all of the other stuff. He had the mood swings. His mortality, which he had put on the line as a young man, challenged in the most direct ways, challenged and whipped, now looked back at him from the mirror every morning, winked and smirked. Round 2. The irony was that the man who had seemed destined to die in a flash, everyone wondering what he was all about, now took the long way home. He had time to explain before he walked out the door. He had time even to change.

An example. He made a public confession to his hometown. Speaking at the annual meeting of the Butte Press Club at the Knights of Columbus hall, usually a raucous gathering, a drinkfest for reporters, he apologized for the illegal acts he perpetrated as a young man. He was sorry he robbed Fran Johnson's sports shop. He was sorry he robbed Star Lanes. He was sorry he tried to rob the Prudential Bank, but was unsuccessful. He said he was not sorry he robbed the treasurer's office in the courthouse, because he didn't do that robbery. But he knew who did.

He said that he had tried, through the years, to pay back most of his debts from illegal acts. He read letters from various government agencies saying that he had paid certain bills. He said he thought he would finish paying off the last $60,000 adjusted payment for his debt to the IRS by the end of the year. He said if he had missed anyone, he was sorry, but he probably was drunk at the time and could not remember.

It was, on the whole, a public deathbed confession. Somber. He tried to pick up pieces he had knocked over in haste to get where he was going.

"I was a young man whose mind had not caught up with his body," he said.

Krystal came back as a friend and a companion, a caretaker, and that was good. They spent time in Las Vegas, spent time in Florida, spent time in Butte every summer, living in the motor home, spent more time in Florida as traveling became more difficult. He began to need oxygen every day for the lung problem. He had neuropathy, which made his feet and hands burn. He sucked on lollipops loaded with fentanyl, a pain-killer. He would take as many as fifty pills a day. He needed more and more rest.

"The price I have paid for notoriety and fame, it's just not worth it," he told the *Montana Standard* in 2004. "I would give anything for just one day of health. Anything."

He said he would wake up, feel great, walk fifty feet to the front door of his motor home, and be exhausted. He wanted to turn around, go back to bed.

"People think I've been through something in my life from what they've seen on national television, my accident at Caesars Palace, for instance," he told the Associated Press in 2006. "Look at what the hell I'm going through now. How much can the human body endure?"

The telephone became his best companion. He called everyone. He called without concern for clocks or time zones, called the way he always had. Three o'clock in the morning? Had to be that damned Knievel. He called with great regularity . . .

"He'd call me three times a week," Ray Gunn said. "Always at one o'clock in the morning. Which had to be four in the morning for him. He'd drive me crazy."

He called from out of the past, out of the long-ago blue . . .

"I was really surprised," Gary Frey from Moses Lake said. "We hadn't talked for a long time. I didn't know what it was about. Then I sort of figured it out. He was apologizing. He knew he was an asshole when I knew him. I think he was saying he was sorry in his own way."

He called, irascible as ever . . .

"He'd tell me he made love to all four of my ex-wives," Jim Blankenship, married five times, said. "I don't know. Maybe he had. We'd make bets. On football games mostly. He had everything figured out, the teams, the lines, everything. He made the football season a whole lot more exciting."

In the first months of 2007, in a motel room in Daytona Beach, the famous daredevil said he found Jesus. Respectful, if not religious, during the quieter times in his life, challenging God in his unquiet times, laughing at Linda's increased faith and involvement in church through the years, he now embraced the package of Christianity. He placed his bet on the Hereafter.

"I don't know what happened to me," he told the *Montana Standard*.

"I didn't see it on a TV show or see it in the newspaper or hear it on the phone or read it in the Bible. Something happened to me just so seriously that I just all of a sudden woke up."

Never afraid of sharing any thought about anything, Knievel called televangelist Rev. Robert Schuller and told him that he had "accepted Jesus Christ as his Lord and Savior." He asked to announce his feelings on *Hour of Power*, Schuller's long-running television show from the Crystal Cathedral in Garden Grove, California.

Schuller flew to Clearwater to assure himself that Knievel's feelings were real. Schuller came away more than convinced. He was ecstatic. The appearance was scheduled for April 1, 2007.

Shelly Saltman, still alive, still active at the age of seventy-six in the Los Angeles area, had a friend who knew Rev. Schuller very well. The friend heard about the upcoming show and had a suggestion: maybe Shelly could go to the baptism of Evel Knievel. It might be a nice moment of closure for everyone concerned.

"Sure," Saltman said, "I'd be happy to go to see him baptized . . ."

Pause.

"But only if I get to hold his head underwater."

Saltman did not go to the service.

Knievel looked weak when he stood at the altar, but he was his dynamic, forceful self as a speaker. There was more than one in the packed church and across America who thought that he would have been a very good evangelist if he hadn't taken other paths in life.

"I rose up in bed," he said about his conversion. "I was by myself. I said, 'Devil, Devil, get away from me, you bastard you. I cast you out of my life.' I went to the balcony of my hotel room, I said, 'I will take you, throw you on the beach. You will be gone, I don't want you around me anymore.' I did everything I could. I put my knees on the ground. I prayed that God would put his arms around me and never, ever let me go."

Less than eight months later Knievel would be dead.

A Story. Louie Markovich bought a plane ticket and went to Florida to see his friend one last time. The visit lasted for a week. There was little doubt about what would happen next as Knievel wore the oxygen tube all the time now and fought for each breath. He said the doctors told him there were no options left. Markovich felt an overwhelming sadness, didn't want to see what he saw. He wanted to leave, but he also never wanted to leave.

The two men had pulled stunts together that no one else would ever know about. Just teenagers, then a little older, they had been a two-man crime wave in Butte and surrounding towns. They robbed anyplace that could be robbed, fancied themselves as burglars, safecrackers, desperadoes. They worked on adrenaline as much as needed, cut through locks and walls and bullshit, tiptoed through the dark, watched for guard dogs and night watchmen, got in and got out, robbed for the money and the excitement of it all. They had secrets.

"There was no one else around like him," Markovich said about his friend. "He always wanted to do something. Hey, let's go. I was the same way. We went."

Knievel would come to his house on the bike, pick him up. His mother would start screaming, tell him not to go. He would jump on the back, Knievel would shift into gear, and they would disappear. He could hear his mother's opinion, even now, that they both were crazy, both were going to die. The night always awaited.

In the early days of the motorcycle jumping, Markovich was part of the original group of Hollywood Motorcycle Daredevils, and helped build the first heavy jump ramps in the parking lot behind the Ford dealership in Anaheim, California. Plywood and two-by-fours. Ramps that lasted for an entire career. When the problem arose in that second show in Barstow, when Jack Stroh was hurt and couldn't jump over the speeding motorcycle, Knievel offered the job to Markovich for an extra $50. Markovich said, "You've got to be kidding," so that was when Knievel did it himself and was injured for the first of many times.

"We had no money at all," Markovich said. "I won $2,000 one night, gambling in Reno, and that kept us going. When we went up to Yakima or someplace, we'd have to take the side roads all the way. We didn't have enough money to pay the fee at those weigh stations on the highway."

There was never any big announcement from Knievel that his career in burglary had stopped, it simply did. He didn't suggest projects anymore, and Markovich, whose career hadn't stopped, didn't suggest any in return. It was a conscious decision. He didn't want Knievel to get in trouble, screw up this possibility he had found.

Markovich eventually did get in trouble, went to prison, paid the price for his transgressions. When he came out, the friendship was still there.

He went to places with the famous daredevil, rode on the jets, the boats, argued with him, made deals, argued, got back together, a routine. The bonds were there for a lifetime.

So now the two men sat in Clearwater, Florida, and told the stories one more time. They talked about football and women and golf. They talked about safes and locks and the development of the electric eye, shooting laser beams across a dark room. They talked about characters and family and adventures, talked about everything.

Knievel told Markovich he had plans for him.

"I want you to be a pallbearer," the daredevil said.

Markovich declined. He said he hated funerals, maybe wouldn't even go. He couldn't be a pallbearer. Knievel said yes he could. The entire event was being planned. Right now it was being planned. Knievel went down a list of other potential pallbearers, debated each one. He went down a list of honorary pallbearers, debated each one. He laid out speakers, song selections, the entire program. He planned the funeral as if it were another jump over another obstacle. Which maybe it was.

"Here's the thing," Markovich said later. "Everyone he talked to, he told them he wanted them to be pallbearers. He must have given out the job a dozen times. It was perfect."

That was Bob Knievel. Cash the check as soon as you can. Because you never know when it is going to bounce.

He died on the afternoon of November 30, 2007, in Clearwater about a week after Louie Markovich left. There was no great crash, no explosion, no gasp from any crowd. He died. There were no last words. A hospice worker, a woman, had been there in the morning. He died in the afternoon. Krystal was there. He had trouble breathing, not an uncommon problem for him, but this time he quietly died.

His funeral was held on December 10, 2007, at the Butte Civic Center, the same place where the Butte Bombers took on the Czech Olympic team. Rev. Schuller presided. Robbie spoke, and Pat Williams spoke, and Matthew McConaughey, the actor, spoke, and other people spoke. Louie Markovich, yes, was a pallbearer. A recording of Sinatra singing "My Way" was played.

The famous daredevil was buried at Mountain View Cemetery right on Harrison Avenue, not a long way from the Butte Country Club and the house he once owned. A large headstone, larger than most of the other headstones in the cemetery, marked his grave.

An etching of Knievel on his motorcycle, heading left to right, occupied the top third of the stone. A fluttering American flag occupied the bottom third. The words were in the middle.

ROBERT CRAIG KNIEVEL
"EVEL"
Oct. 17, 1938–Nov. 30, 2007
Butte, Montana
WORDS TO LIVE FOR
"FAITH, HEALTH, EDUCATION, LOVE
WORK, HONORABILITY, DREAM"
BELIEVE IN JESUS CHRIST
AMEN

Wait. There was more. Walk 180 degrees, go to the other side of the headstone, and, yes, there was more writing. An etching of a rocketlike vehicle, the word "Knievel" along the chassis, three puffs of smoke coming from the back, occupied the top third of this surface. An etching of a fluttering American flag again occupied the bottom third. Again, the writing was in the middle.

ROBERT "EVEL" KNIEVEL
EXPLORER
Motorcyclist & Daredevil
A Mile-Long Leap Of The
Snake River Canyon
From This Point on Sept. 8, 1974
Employing A Unique "Sky Cycle"

A Man Can Fall Many Times In Life
But He's Never A Failure If He
Tries To Get Up.

The stone, of course, was the six-foot-tall, one-ton memorial donated by the Rock of Ages Corporation of Barre, Vermont, and shipped to Twin Falls, Idaho, in the midst of the frenzy thirty-three years earlier. It finally had a permanent home.

Acknowledgments

Robert Craig Knievel was a one-man tidal wave when he came through more ordinary lives. Thanks to anyone and everyone who talked to me about him. The stories were spectacular.

Thanks to Mike Byrnes and Joe Little for showing me the right places to go in Butte. Thanks to Pat Williams and Loretta Young for their insights into the famous daredevil's family. Thanks to George Hamilton for his insights into being the famous daredevil himself. Thanks to Bob Arum and Shelly Saltman for their tales from Snake River and beyond.

Thanks, of course, to Linda Finkle, to Leigh Alan Montville, to Robin and Doug Moleux, to the Garden Street Athletic Club, and to all of the usual suspects. (You know who you are.) Thanks to Esther Newberg, Jason Kaufman, and Rob Bloom.

Thanks again—great thanks—to anyone who helped.

A Note on Sources

In twenty minutes, it is said Evel Knievel can tell enough anecdotes
about his early life to keep a reporter busy for twenty years just
checking them out.

—Robert Boyle, *Sports Illustrated*

True. Any poor soul who tries to chronicle Robert Craig Knievel's
life—and no doubt there will be more poor souls to follow this one—is
doomed to follow one labyrinth after another, uncertain even at the end
if he has found the proper spot. The only course I found was to keep
whacking at the dense underbrush of exaggerations, strategic deceits,
and flat-out lies and see as much as I could see.

For a start, I was able to read three unpublished manuscripts that
contained personal observations by Don Branker, Bob Truax, and Brian
Cartmell. These were a great help. Thanks to Don, to Scott Truax, and
to Gary Cartmell for the privilege.

I seemed to refer often to *Evel Incarnate*, a fine book by Steve Mandich
that lays out the grid of the famous daredevil's life. Mandich also has a
website, SteveMandich.com, that contains all things Knievel. Highly recommended. I also found myself often on a site, CycleJumpers.com, which
has all kinds of fascinating information about people who jump over
things on motorcycles, sometimes with bad results.

The boilerplate of all biographies is found in the many newspaper stories written about or around the subject. No different here. The door that
is opened by a website like Newspapers.com is incredible, not to mention

the help from individual sites for other papers. YouTube is an obvious starting point for all video for a subject like this one. An assortment of websites provided an assortment of other basic facts, from the height of the fountains at Caesars Palace to the costars of *Viva Knievel!* There is even a website for Evel Knievel toys, EvelKnievelToyMusuem.com. Very good.

I talked with well over two hundred people during research for this book. I talked with a few who didn't want to talk, who had their own projects they want to pursue. Good luck to them. I read a bunch of books, watched a bunch of videos, went through some magazines like *Penthouse* and *Playboy* and *Oui* that normally aren't in the house. Went through some like *Sports Illustrated* and *Time* and *Newsweek* that are.

Any biography is a collage. All bits and pieces are more than appreciated.

Bibliography

Bailey, Beth, and David Farber. *America in the '70s.* Lawrence: University Press of Kansas Press, 2004.

Barker, Stuart. *Life of Evel Knievel.* London: Collins Willow, 2004.

Cardoso, Bill. *The Maltese Sangweech and Other Heroes.* New York: Atheneum, 1984.

Cavett, Dick, with Christopher Porterfield. *Eye on Cavett.* New York: Harcourt Brace Jovanovich, 1974.

Collins, Ace. *Evel Knievel: An American Hero.* New York: St. Martin's Griffin, 2000.

Conrad, Harold. *Dear Muffo.* New York: Stein and Day, 1982.

Cosell, Howard, with Mickey Herskowitz. *Cosell.* Chicago: Playboy Press, 1973.

———. *Like It Is.* Chicago: Playboy Press, 1974.

Edison, Mike. *I Have Fun Everywhere I Go.* New York: Faber and Faber, 2008.

Eszterhas, Joe. *American Rhapsody.* New York: Alfred A. Knopf, 2000.

———. *Hollywood Animal.* New York: Alfred A. Knopf, 2004.

Everett, George. *Butte Trivia: The Most Incredible, Unbelievable, Wild, Weird, Fun, Fascinating, and True Facts About Butte, Montana—The Richest Hill on Earth!* Helena, MT: Riverbend Publishing, 2007.

Flowers, Gennifer, with Jacquelyn Dapper. *Gennifer Flowers: Passion and Betrayal.* Del Mar, CA: Emery Dalton Books, 1995.

Gifford, Frank, with Harry Waters. *The Whole Ten Yards.* New York: Ballantine Books, 1994.

Gross, Michael. *My Generation: Fifty Years of Sex, Drugs, Rock, Revolution, Glamour, Greed, Valor, Faith, and Silicon Chips.* New York: Cliff Street Books, 2000.

Hamilton, George, with William Stadiem. *Don't Mind if I Do.* New York: Touchstone, 2008.

Hill, Napoleon. *Think and Grow Rich.* Chicago: Combined Registry Company, 1962.

Hill, Napoleon, and W. Clement Stone. *Success Through a Positive Mental Attitude.* New York: Pocket Books, 1960, 1977.

Hillen, Andreas. *1973 Nervous Breakdown: Watergate, Warhol, and the Birth of Post-Sixties America.* New York: Bloomsbury USA, 2006.

Howard, Joseph Kinsey. *Montana: High, Wide, and Handsome.* Lincoln: University of Nebraska Press, Bison Books, 1983.

Kearney, Pat. *Butte Voices: Mining, Neighborhoods, People.* Butte, MT: Skyhigh Communications, 1998.

Kisselburg, Orval. *Orval the Daredevil Clown.* Author, 2005.

Knievel, Evel. *Evel Ways: The Attitude of Evel Knievel.* Minneapolis: Graf/X Publishing, 1999.

Mandich, Steve. *Evil Incarnate: The Life and Legend of Evel Knievel.* London: Sidgwick & Jackson, 2000.

Murphy, Mary. *Mining Cultures: Men, Women, and Leisure in Butte, 1914–1941.* Urbana: University of Illinois Press, 1997.

Pirsig, Robert. *Zen and the Art of Motorcycle Maintenance: An Inquiry into Values.* New York: William Morrow, 1974.

Rickey, Les. *The Bad Boys of Butte.* Butte, MT: Old Butte Publishing, 2004.

Rowe, Chip, ed. *The Book of Zines: Readings from the Fringe.* New York: Henry Holt and Co., 1997.

Saltman, Shelly, with Maury Green. *Evel Knievel on Tour.* New York: Dell Publishing, 1977.

Saltman, Shelly, with Thomas Lyons. *Fear No Evel: An Insider's Look at Hollywood.* Rancho Mirage, CA: We Publish Books, 2007.

Scalzo, Joe. *Evel Knievel.* New York: Grosset & Dunlap, 1974.

Schulman, Bruce J. *The Seventies: The Great Shift in American Culture, Society, and Politics.* New York: Da Capo Press, 2002.

Smith, Giles. *Midnight in the Garden of Evel Knievel: Sport on Television.* London: Picador, 2000.

Spence, Jim, with Dave Diles. *Up Close and Personal: The Inside Story of Network Television Sports.* New York: Atheneum, 1990.

Spiegel, Marshall. *Evel Knievel: Cycle Jumper.* New York: Scholastic Book Services, 1978.

Tompkins, George. *The Truth About Butte . . . Through the Eyes of a Radical Unionist,* edited by Mike Byrnes. Butte, MT: Old Butte Publishing, 2003.

Walsh, Tim. *Timeless Toys: Classic Toys and the Playmakers Who Created Them.* Kansas City, MO: Andrews McNeel Publishing, 2005.

Writers Project of Montana. *Copper Camp: The Lusty Story of Butte, Montana, the Richest Hill on Earth.* Helena, MT: Riverbend Publishing, 1943, 2002.

Photograph Credits

Title page: PR shot, 1974
Insert:
page 1, top left: Courtesy of Loretta Young
page 1, top right: Courtesy of Loretta Young
page 1, bottom: PR shot, 1974
page 2, top: © Bettmann/Corbis
page 2, bottom left: Courtesy of Harry Ormesher
page 2, bottom right: Courtesy of Harry Ormesher
page 3, top: The Everett Collection
page 3, bottom: Heinz Kluetmeier/Sports Illustrated/Getty Images
page 4, top: Associated Press
page 4, middle left: Heinz Kluetmeier/Sports Illustrated/Getty Images
page 4, middle right: Associated Press
page 4, bottom: Associated Press
page 5, top: Express/Archive Photos/Getty Images
page 5, middle: Courtesy of Harry Ormesher
page 5, bottom: Associated Press
page 6, top left: PA Photos/Landov
page 6, top right: Express/Archive Photos/Getty Images
page 6, middle left: Bob Thomas/Getty Images
page 6, middle right: David Ashdown/Hulton Archive/Getty Images
page 6, bottom left: © Bettmann/Corbis
page 6, bottom right: PA Photos/Landov

About the Author

Three-time *New York Times* bestselling author Leigh Montville is a former columnist at the *Boston Globe* and former senior writer at *Sports Illustrated*. He is the author of *Ted Williams*, *The Big Bam: The Life and Times of Babe Ruth*, *The Mysterious Montague*, and *At the Altar of Speed: The Fast Life and Tragic Death of Dale Earnhardt*, among others. He lives in Boston.